Authentic Indians

A JOHN HOPE FRANKLIN CENTER BOOK

Authentic Indians

Episodes of Encounter from the Late-Nineteenth-Century Northwest Coast

PAIGE RAIBMON

Duke University Press *Durham and London* 2005

2nd printing, 2006

Printed on acid-free paper ♾
Designed by Amy Ruth Buchanan
Typeset in Dante by Tseng
Information Systems, Inc.
Library of Congress Cataloging-
in-Publication Data appear on the
last printed page of this book.

For my parents

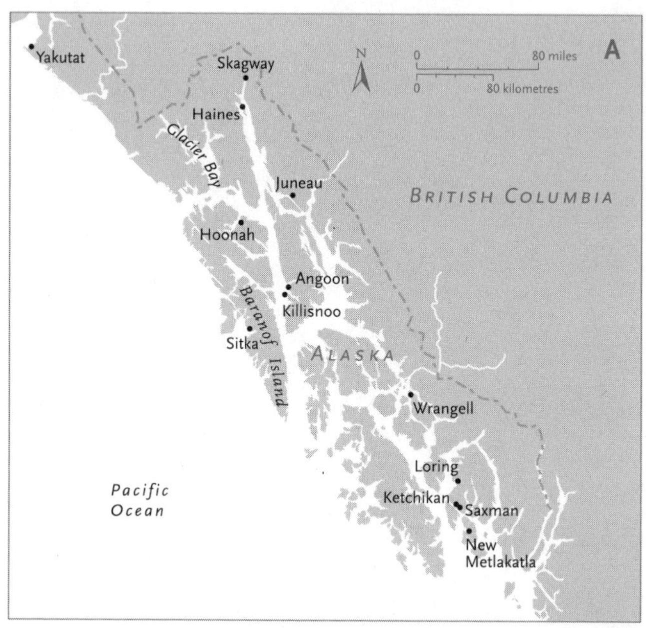
A
0
80 miles
0
80 kilometres
N
Yakutat
Skagway
Haines
Glacier Bay
Juneau
British Columbia
Hoonah
Angoon
Killisnoo
Baranof Island
Sitka
Alaska
Wrangell
Loring
Ketchikan
Saxman
New Metlakatla
Pacific Ocean

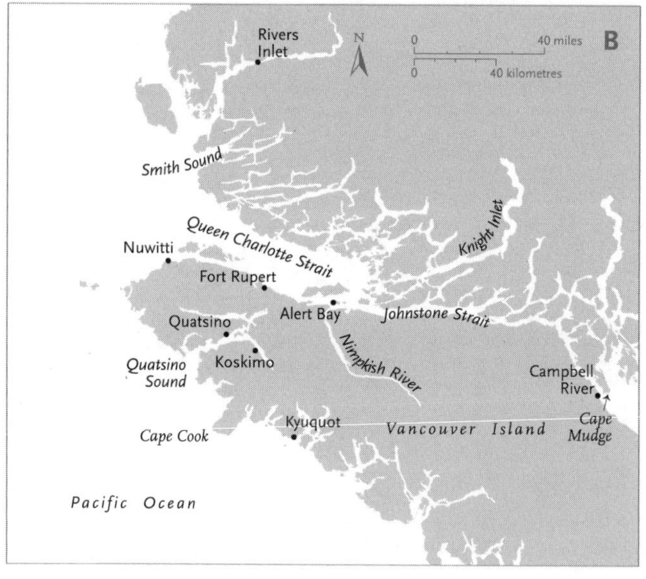
B
0
40 miles
0
40 kilometres
N
Rivers Inlet
Smith Sound
Queen Charlotte Strait
Knight Inlet
Nuwitti
Fort Rupert
Alert Bay
Johnstone Strait
Quatsino
Koskimo
Nimpkish River
Quatsino Sound
Campbell River
Cape Mudge
Kyuquot
Cape Cook
Vancouver Island
Pacific Ocean

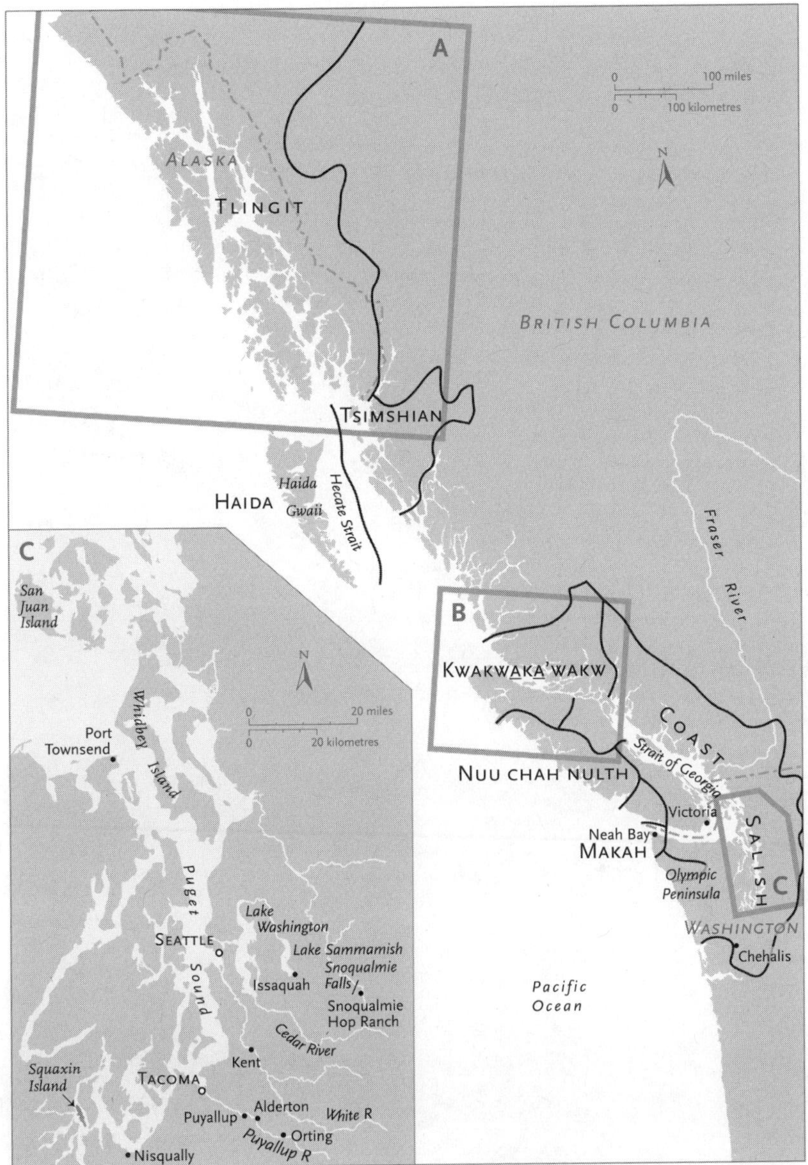

Map of the Northwest Coast showing Coast Salish, Makah, Nuu-chah-nulth, Kwakwa̲ka̲'wakw, Haida, Tsimshian, and Tlingit territories. Inset A shows the southeast Alaska region discussed in chapters 7–9. Inset B shows the northern Vancouver Island region discussed in chapters 1–3. And Inset C shows the Puget Sound region discussed in chapters 4–6. Maps by Eric Leinberger.

Contents

List of Illustrations

Acknowledgments

"We *are* what we remember," wrote the late Timothy Findley. This, it seems to me, is why history matters. And it is also why our relationships with other people are so precious. Just as societies create themselves through collective memory, so do individuals fashion a place in the world through personal connections. "Memory," Findley continued, "is other people—it is little of ourselves." It brings me pleasure to remember the many people who contributed something of themselves to this project. Over the years that this book has been in the making, I have benefited immeasurably from the kindness of strangers. That some of those strangers have since become dear friends is added blessing.

Research for this book took me across North America. Archivists and other staff frequently went beyond the call of duty to facilitate my research and I am ever grateful. In particular, I want to thank Dan Savard at the Royal British Columbia Museum; Kelly-Ann Nolin and Kathryn Bridge at the B.C. Archives; Victoria Cranner at Harvard's Peabody Museum; Mark Katzman and Tom Baione at the American Museum of Natural History; Andrea Goldstein at the Harvard University Archives; Greg Watson then at the Snoqualmie Valley Historical Society and Museum; Carolyn Marr at the Museum of History and Industry in Seattle; Nicolette Bromberg and the staff at the University of Washington Special Collections and Archives and Manuscripts divisions; Patricia Cosgrove and Tina Brewster Ray at the White River Valley Historical Society; Barbara Justice at the Issaquah Historical Society; Elaine Miller at the Washington State Historical Society; Steve Henrikson at the Alaska State Museum; Gladi Kulp and staff at the Alaska State Historical Library; staff at the Alaska State Archives; Nancy Ricketts, Evelyn Bonner, and staff at the Sheldon Jackson Stratton Library Archives; Chris Hanson at the Tongass Historical Society; Karen Meizner at the Sitka Historical Society; and Bruce Parham and Matt Mobley at the U.S. National Archives in Anchorage.

I completed all my research trips without spending a night in a hotel, a feat enabled by the hospitality of many people, including Susan and Steve Christianson, Steve Daskal, Betty Levinson and Elliott Wilk, Annie Lederberg, Brad Martin, Trevor Morrison, Mike Mullins, Mary Anne and Jack Navitsky, Bernice Tetpon, Joyce Walton Shales, Linda van Ballenberghe, and Cary Wright and Kama Ringwood.

I owe a special debt to the kindness and friendship of Rudolph Walton's granddaughters, Joyce Walton Shales and Mary Anne Navitsky. Joyce took me under her wing with her characteristic selflessness for which I will always be grateful. She provided assistance on issues that ranged from archives to accommodations. My work on this small piece of her grandfather's life would not have been possible without her help. Unforeseen circumstances have meant that Joyce's book on her grandfather, on which my work here relies, is as yet unpublished. When Joyce's book appears, it will give Rudolph Walton's remarkable life the full treatment in the form of a book-length biography that it deserves. My debt to the Walton family extends to Joyce's sister and brother-in-law, Mary Anne and Jack Navitsky. When I was in Sitka, Mary Anne and Jack fed me and housed me. As important, they offered me their warm company and their invaluable friendship.

Faculty at Duke University read versions of this text at various stages. They offered valuable insights with each reading. I owe thanks in this regard to Arif Dirlik, Larry Goodwyn, Malachi Hacohen, Irene Silverblatt, Wendy Wall, and Kären Wigen. Susan Thorne, Nancy Hewitt, Bill Reddy, Peter Wood, and John H. Thompson served as my dissertation committee. Always supportive yet discerning, their guidance greatly enhanced my work. I am fortunate to have worked with them all.

This book has also drawn on the expertise of many other generous individuals. Several scholars shared their insights, and thanks in this respect are due Judith Berman, David Buerge, David Cecelski, Bob DeArmond, Chris Friday, Bob Galois, Sasha Harmon, Elsbeth Heaman, Dan Marshall, Susan Neylan, Gwen Peroni, Coll Thrush, and Wendy Wickwire. Abner Thorne, Wes Modeste, and Mabel Modeste of the Cowichan First Nation shared their knowledge of hop fields and Shakers with me. Jason Camp, Hart Caplan, Elizabeth Fenn, George Koller, Kris Rothstein, and Megan and Jerry Smetzer assisted with a number of technical and other essential tasks. My time at the 2003 Lannan Summer Institute in American Indian History at the Newberry Library influenced many of my thoughts on this subject, and for this I thank Cari Carpenter, Ron Carpenter, Brenda Child, Tony Clark, Renee Cramer, Tony Fresquez, Jane Hafen, Fred Hoxie, Amelia Katanski, Matt Kreitzer, Katherine Osburn, Malea Powell, Erik Redix, Jeff Shepherd, and Michael Tsosie. Over the course of many years, Jean Barman,

Arthur Ray, and Dianne Newell provided intellectual and logistical support at every crucial juncture. Lawrin Armstrong, Tina Loo, Roxanne Panchasi, Mary Lynn Stewart, and other colleagues at Simon Fraser University likewise offered support and friendship for which I am deeply grateful.

Financial support for this project came in the form of several grants from the Social Sciences and Humanities Research Council of Canada and the Newberry Library. Comments by Nancy Shoemaker and other readers for Duke University Press improved the manuscript considerably, as did earlier comments by readers for the *Canadian Historical Review*. Thanks also go to Eric Leinberger for the maps; Hart Caplan for the diagram; and Marki Sellers and Andrea Gill for editorial assistance.

Friends and family provided tremendous patience, support, tolerance, and insight over the course of this project. Kelly Benhase, Julia Lawn, Renato Marena, Hae Chin Moon, Scott Priestman, Shirley and Richard Raibmon, Dan Levinson Wilk, Gwenn Miller, John Webber, and Suzanne Wolf each deserve a measure of credit for the completion of this book. Hart Caplan recognized the things that matter most from the very beginning and for this I offer my deep and ongoing gratitude. He has held fast to the promise of that initial recognition, and his faith buoys my own.

Introduction

Authenticity and Colonial Cosmology

> People are living in the middle of their cosmology, down in amongst it; they are energetically manipulating it, evading its implications in their own lives if they can, but using it for hitting each other and forcing one another to conform to something they have in mind.[1]

On 17 May 1999, the Makah Indians of Cape Flattery completed their first whale hunt in over seventy years. An 1855 treaty with Washington's territorial governor, Isaac Stevens, guaranteed the Makah the right to hunt whales, but with the near-extinction of the gray whale, they stopped whaling in the 1920s. By 1998, the gray whale was no longer on the endangered species list, and the Makah successfully applied to the International Whaling Commission for permission to reinstate their traditional and treaty rights. The Makah carried out the hunt using a combination of "traditional" and "modern" means. They harpooned the whale by hand from a canoe, then completed the kill with the use of speedboats and a 50-caliber high-powered rifle.

Public response was immediate, emotional, and violent. Within hours of the kill, the *Seattle Times* received almost 400 phone calls and e-mails; opinion was ten to one against the hunt. Schools on Indian reservations throughout Puget Sound received bomb threats; members of the Makah tribe received death threats. The slogan "Save a whale, harpoon a Makah" appeared on bumper stickers, an apparent call to return to the "Wild West" days of Indian killing.

Why did the whale hunt incite such outrage? According to the *Seattle Times*, "the most common reaction was disdain for a traditional hunt made with modern weaponry."[2] One man judged the hunt benign as long as all the Makah wanted was to "jump into leaky wooden canoes and row around, throwing sharpened sticks at passing whales." He changed his opinion when he learned of the technology the Makah planned to use: "If the Makahs intend to hunt whales in order to 'resurrect their cultural traditions and rebuild their community,' then they darn well better do it in the 'traditional' manner, sans elephant gun!"[3] Some held that the Makah would better honor the true spirit of their tradition through a whale-*watching* rather than a whale-*hunting* operation. This alternative seemed self-evident, since, as one man pointed out, "most tribes pride themselves on being close to nature."[4]

Opponents believed that the Makah forfeited their claim to traditional rights by using guns and motorboats. Critics dismissed Makah explanations of whaling's traditional spiritual importance as disingenuous and superficial. They condemned the Makah as greedy, opportunistic, and arbitrary in their use of selected elements of tradition and modernity. "How can they have it both ways?" asked one man. "They want to retain or regain their heritage and yet they want to use the conveniences of modern science too? . . . This was just a money-making publicity ploy on their part and I am disgusted with it."[5] A Seattle woman wrote: "if a people can pick and choose which old tradition to resume, does that mean descendants of white slave-holders should go out and capture themselves some slaves because they used to do that?"[6] She was not alone in comparing the resumption of ceremonial whaling with the justification of terrible cruelty. Others asked whether they now had license to return to days of unfettered cannibalism, human sacrifice, wife beating, and Indian-scalping.[7]

Opponents to the hunt believed the Makah whalers were anachronistic as well as disingenuous. Letters to the editor charged the Makah with "living in the past," being "stuck in the past," retaining "outdated and useless practices of the past," returning to "the Stone Age," and "refusing to join the modern world."[8] A Bremerton man asked: "How does any treaty written in the 19th century have any bearing in this day and age?"[9] For these people Indian tradition was of the past; motorboats and rifles were evidence of its irreconcilability with the present. One man's question summarized this perspective: "Why can't these people move into the 20th century like civilized folk?"[10]

For the Makah whalers, however, the hunt was part of the twentieth century rather than an escape from it. The whale hunt revived a traditional practice in a decidedly and self-consciously contemporary context. Fundamentally presentist community concerns, including anxiety about assimilation and a desire to remain culturally distinct from the surrounding non-Aboriginal population, made this a hunt for identity as well as for whales.[11] The significance of the hunt for the Makah cannot be disentangled from the outrage it provoked. The outrage was historically specific to the values of late-twentieth-century environmentalism, with its "save the whales" sloganeering. In this context, there was hardly a stronger assertion of difference from White society than whale hunting. This is not to say that the Makah were unanimous about asserting their difference in this fashion. Some embraced the self-presentation of Makah identity through the whale hunt, while others eschewed it.[12] The Makah engaged in their own struggle to define themselves. This struggle was poorly represented in the non-Aboriginal discussions of Indianness with which it only partially intersected.

As the Makah hunted for a twentieth-century identity, White opponents condemned them for trying to return to the nineteenth century. Both groups worked from assumptions whose roots lay buried in historically entrenched ideas about Indian authenticity. By the late twentieth century, these ideas had achieved a commonsense status that obscured their historical roots. This study excavates those roots by examining how Aboriginal and non-Aboriginal people on the Northwest Coast used late-nineteenth-century colonial ideas about authenticity. Throughout the chapters that follow, the word "authenticity" should be read as shorthand for these historically specific notions of authenticity. In this book, authenticity is not a stable yardstick against which to measure "the real thing." It is a powerful and shifting set of ideas that worked in a variety of ways toward a variety of ends.[13] The work that authenticity did is the subject of this book.

Whites imagined what the authentic Indian was, and Aboriginal people engaged and shaped those imaginings in return. They were collaborators—albeit unequally—in authenticity. Non-Aboriginal people employed definitions of Indian culture that limited Aboriginal claims to resources, land, and sovereignty, at the same time as Aboriginal people utilized those same definitions to access the social, political, and economic means necessary for survival under colonialism. The non-Aboriginal opposition to the Makah whale hunt is just one example in the long history of this dynamic. Notions of authenticity were key elements of a colonial cosmology. In the evocative terms of the anthropologist Mary Douglas, people lived down among them, manipulated them, avoided their implications, and hit each other with them.[14]

In the following chapters, I use three separate episodes to consider some of these implications in historical perspective. The first episode is the story of a group of Kwakwa̱ka̱'wakw from northern Vancouver Island who performed at the 1893 World's Columbian Exposition in Chicago. Clearly an example of cultural performance, their trip to the fair also stands as an example of modern wage labor and political protest. The Chicago World's Fair is an appropriate starting point because exhibits there galvanized the North American craze for Indian curios that plays a crucial role in subsequent episodes.[15] Aboriginal migrant workers who picked hops in the fields of Puget Sound in the late nineteenth century are the focus of the second episode. Though other studies have examined Aboriginal involvement in fishing and canning—industries with clear parallels to pre-contact economies—none have examined Aboriginal people in the hop industry. The story of hops is in some ways a mirror image of the World's Fair. At first glance, the Chicago trip looks like the simple performance of traditional cultural forms, but it proves also to be an instance of modern labor and political expression. The hop industry initially appears to be a straightforward example of modern capitalist wage labor, but it is actually also closely bound to an array of indigenous priorities. The third episode moves from performance and labor to the law. It revolves around a 1906 legal proceeding brought by the Tlingit artist Rudolph Walton in an attempt to have his mixed-race stepchildren admitted to the White public school in Sitka, Alaska. Walton's story epitomizes the complex blend of practices and values that Aboriginal people achieved in this period. At the same time, the court's attempt to determine whether his children were civilized enough to attend the school is sobering evidence of the very real limits that colonial definitions imposed on Aboriginal lives. Though ubiquitous, such limits were nowhere more apparent than in the courtroom.

In presenting these episodes together, I draw connections between some wide-ranging circumstances. Players in these episodes may not have shared the same page since 1893, when a speaker addressing the Women's Congress at the Chicago World's Fair discussed Tlingit hop pickers in the Puget Sound hop fields.[16] But if these episodes have not been told in the same breath before, the parallels revealed by so doing warrant such a telling. I use the commonalities of the episodes to challenge old generalizations, at the same time as I rely on their specificity to avoid the temptation to generalize anew. The people in these histories do not stand for "Aboriginal People of North America" or "Aboriginal People of the Northwest Coast," yet placed in a regional framework, their stories highlight broad strokes of common circumstance that can be obscured in traditional monographs and ethnographies.[17]

The convergence of a number of cultural and political developments makes the late-nineteenth-century Northwest Coast a particularly apt time and place to focus a study such as this. Washington, British Columbia, and Alaska were incorporated into the nation-states of Canada and the United States at a moment when public interest in authentic Indians and pride in successful Indian policy were important components of both countries' sense of nationalism. Western North America was not the only place where anthropological and nationalist interests were linked, but their co-emergence on the Northwest Coast draws the connection into sharp relief.[18]

Anthropology—the study of authentic Indians—was a freshly minted discipline in the latter half of the nineteenth century. Motivated to preserve what they believed were remnants of dying Indian cultures, salvage anthropologists attempted to document old ways uncontaminated by White influence. In so doing, they erased the historical specificity of their own day and of their informants' lives. They transformed the most traumatic and turbulent period in the history of western North American Aboriginal people into the benchmark of timeless Aboriginal culture.[19] Through fieldwork, publications, and museum displays, anthropologists filled the category of authenticity with attributes that still endure in popular understandings of Indianness. Anthropology's scientific status lent these concepts an aura of objectivity and legitimacy that was crucial to their persuasiveness.[20]

The Northwest Coast was the focus of attention for some of this era's most influential producers of anthropological knowledge. The region was the site of an international "scramble" for Indian artifacts.[21] It was where Edward S. Curtis, whose photographs became the visual epitome of vanishing Indian ideology, began his career. It was where Franz Boas, the foundational figure in professional anthropology in North America who made twelve trips between 1886 and 1930, conducted his fieldwork. And it was the destination of several prominent and well-funded scientific-ethnographic expeditions. The Jessup North Pacific Expedition, organized by Boas, ran from 1897 through 1903, and in 1899, the Harriman Expedition carried John Muir and Edward Curtis to Alaska. Such was the Northwest Coast's importance that one scholar has argued for its personification as an actor in the shaping of American anthropology.[22]

These individual and institutional attempts to capture vanishing Indianness resonated with contemporaneous cultural movements that highlighted concerns with authenticity. The so-called Great Divide between high (authentic) art and mass (inauthentic) culture gained prominence at the turn of the twentieth century. Emergent anthropology aligned itself with the former, and tourism did likewise with the latter.[23] These were also the early years of antimodernist sentiment in America. Antimodernists' quest for authentic experience fueled the growth of tourism and the Arts and Crafts movement. Both of these gave expression to the same sort of imperialist nostalgia that pervaded the myth of the vanishing Indian. Much like notions of authenticity, antimodernism reinvigorated elite dominance at the same time as it provided for expressions of alternative visions.[24]

Indians were not the only people in whom antimodernists would seek and find authenticity. Moving into the early decades of the twentieth century, antimodernists grew fascinated with rural populations in places as diverse as Nova Scotia and Appalachia, transforming them from hardworking fishers, miners, and farmers into "folk." Dual processes of romanticization and commodification characterized the creation of these White "folk" as much as it did the manufacture of Indian authenticity.[25] Yet there were differences too. For White rural poor, excluded from most of modernity's comforts, folk designations could be "wages of whiteness" that rendered them worthy of outside assistance and attention.[26] For Aboriginal people, discussions of authenticity had a different racial tenor, marking them as separate rather than similar, even when absent of explicit racial references like blood quantum, halfbreed, and full blood.

These cultural values affected a broad swath of colonial society. Anthropologists, government officials, missionaries, reformers, boosters, settlers, and tourists were diverse, their aims and goals often contradictory. Some bore aggressive assimilationist, even exterminationist, intent, and others acted with gestures of human empathy and cultural curiosity. Tourists and anthropologists encouraged and rewarded Aboriginal people who presented their authentic selves even as government officials and missionaries deplored such displays. Yet officials and missionaries were concerned about potential income for their Aboriginal charges and so could hardly overlook the tourist market. Anthropologists and tourists also had their differences, as they competed with one another over scarce artifacts. These "tensions of empire" produced heated political and ideological battles. They also opened spaces for Aboriginal action and expression.[27]

Whether they used definitions of Indianness in the context of policy,

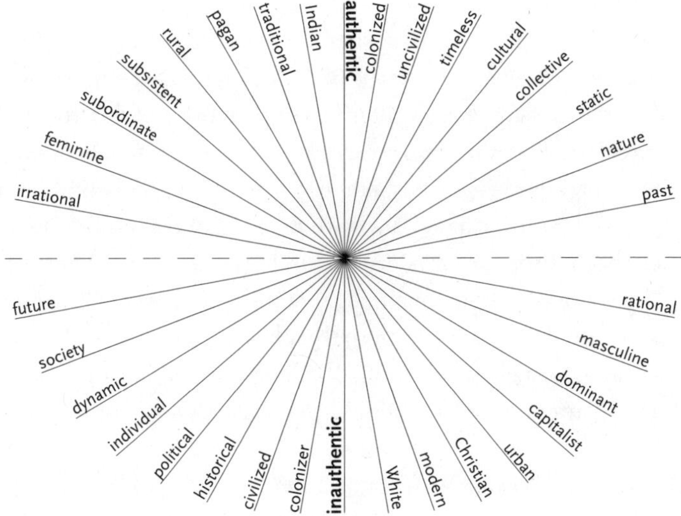

1. Binaries of Authenticity. In the late nineteenth century and the early twentieth, colonial society fashioned a powerful "either-or" notion of Indian authenticity that relied on a wide variety of associated binaries, a sampling of which are shown here.

religion, amusement, or science, colonizers shared an understanding of authenticity. They were collaborators in a binary framework that defined Indian authenticity in relation to its antithesis: inauthenticity. Parallel binaries followed. First among them was the distinction between Indian and White. Indians, by extension, were traditional, uncivilized, cultural, impoverished, feminine, static, part of nature and of the past. Whites, on the other hand, were modern, civilized, political, prosperous, masculine, dynamic, part of society and of the future.[28] Alignment between these oppositions was neither absolute nor without contradiction. Members of colonial society might value certain traits associated with Indians—like closeness to nature—positively or negatively. But non-Aboriginal people of all sorts set these traits in binary mortar, treating them as mutually exclusive and noninterchangeable. They agreed that real Indians could never be modern, and thus were (regrettably or thankfully, depending on the perspective) most certainly vanishing.[29]

Notions of immutable Indianness espoused by "Indian haters" in the eighteenth century became widely shared by Indian haters and sympathizers alike in the nineteenth.[30] The precise language of difference—race, culture, blood, or nation—was less constant than the certainty of difference itself.[31] Binary understandings of cultural markers could work in a manner akin to the "one-drop" racial rule, whereby Anglo-Americans deemed black any individual with even "one drop" of African blood. The non-Aboriginal outcry over the Makah whale hunt offers one example of this. If the Makah were *authentic* Indians, the argument went, they would eschew modernity's motorboats, high-powered rifles, and economic gains and embrace an exclusively spiritual hunt carried out with traditional equipment. Boats and rifles were both "drops" of modern technology and thus markers of inauthenticity. This binary logic concluded that the Makah were disingenuously posing to manipulate the situation to their best advantage. And the Makah were not the only ones. Self-identified Indians persisted throughout North America long after they gained English literacy, radios, guns, kettles, and casinos.

Although there has never been an official policy called "authenticity," shared assumptions have functioned as such in many respects. Official policies could not have developed as they did without widespread agreement on these assumptions. Only a handful of people worked as policy makers, but everyone who engaged in colonial interactions participated in the manufacture and popularization of notions of authenticity. Widespread agreement on the binary definition effectively served a number of contradictory interests, including, as the art historian Ruth Phillips notes, "those of the romantic primitivists seeking an escape from industrial modernity, and those of the economic developers seeking hegemony over Indian lands and resources."[32] This binary construction could also serve the interests of Aboriginal people who sought income in the face of receding economic opportunities under colonialism. Many Aboriginal people made good use of stereotypes; they "played Indian" for White audiences by performing dances and selling curios.[33]

This convergence of interests helps explain the aura of common sense that notions of authenticity quickly acquired. In the 1880s, Franz Boas complained of difficulty finding "real Indians," and German audiences charged a group of touring Nuxalk with being "false Indians," because they did not look the stereotypical part.[34] Through repeated enactment during literal and figurative performances, assumptions of authenticity became entrenched and increasingly invisible.[35] Ritual performance had long played a crucial role in Northwest Coast people's lives, but under colonialism, Aboriginal people could not always control when they went onstage. They felt the colonial gaze not only when they performed intentionally but also at home when Victorian tourists and ethnographers descended upon their villages and camps. Colonial viewers blurred the distinction between formally staged performances and the performance of everyday life. Whether at a world's fair, museum, curio-shop, or tourist destination, Aboriginal life was a spectacle for late-nineteenth-century North Americans.[36] Such interactions spawned assumptions that audiences could easily assimilate as natural truths. What could be more real, or more true, than something witnessed with one's own eyes?

Yet binary terms of authenticity constituted a powerful Catch-22 for Aboriginal people. The notion of a singular Aboriginal culture—a culture that could be preserved in the static representations of ethnographic texts, museum cases, or stylized performances—held Aboriginal people to impossible standards of ahistorical cultural purity. Aboriginal people inevitably deviated from their prescribed cultural set, because no culture conforms to an unchanging set of itemized traits, a fact that goes uncontested when the culture in question is the dominant one. But binary conceptions excluded those who adapted to non-Aboriginal culture from the narrow definition of traditional Indians. As Frank Ettawageshik of the Little Traverse Bay Band of Odawa Indians notes, policy makers consider "change in Indian culture as assimilation and 'assimilation as obliteration.'"[37] The Puyallup of Puget Sound were thus legally obliterated in the mid-twentieth century when, based in part on the testimony of anthropologists, a judge ruled the tribe extinct because he deemed tribal members assimilated.[38] British Columbia First Nations were stung by similar reasoning in 1989, when Crown Counsel subjected witnesses to the so-called pizza test, implying that supposedly modern foods and conveniences undermined the Gitksan-Wet'suwet'en land claim.[39] By this logic, modern Indians were not Indians at all, they were assimilated. Others were all too Indian; they belonged to a noble and tragic past but had no role in the future. Only the vanishing had legitimate claims to land and sovereignty; surviving modernity disqualified one from these claims. Either way, colonizers got the land. This double jeopardy resulted from dominant society's success at confining discussion of indigenous peoples to the parallel dichotomies of authentic versus inauthentic and traditional versus modern.[40]

On the late-nineteenth-century Pacific Coast, ideas about authentic Indianness underwrote the actions of colonial newcomers in multifarious ways. Assured that real Indians, by definition, could not survive into the future, settlers, tourists, and capitalist-developers could believe that the simultaneous processes of capitalist growth and indigenous displacement were natural and inevitable. From the Chicago World's Fair, through the Puget Sound hop fields, to the first cruise ships up the Inside Passage, images of authentic Indians advertised the availability of land and resources. Developers used picturesque images of Indians to attract tourists, investors, and settlers. In many instances, the weekday capitalist-industrialist and the weekend sightseer were one and the same. Indian occupancy of the land might have posed a deterrent, yet it did not. Viewed through the lens of authenticity, these Indians were vanishing—more pathetic than powerful—and clearly unable to make proper use of the region's natural riches. These Indians could, however, labor for the benefit of capitalist-industrialists. The most straightforward labor occurred in agricultural fields and fish canneries. But providing entertainment—performing dances and selling Indian art, for example—was labor too. Non-Aboriginal people used the images generated by this latter form of labor as publicity for the region. Non-Aboriginal people reaped a double yield from Aboriginal workers: directly from those who sold their labor, and indirectly from images of those who labored.

Aboriginal people on the Pacific Northwest Coast faced a situation familiar to colonized populations elsewhere. From India to China to western North America, colonial regimes achieved hegemony when elites—native and newcomer alike—came to agree on the terms of reference and the forms of discourse.[41] The nineteenth-century experiences of Northwest Coast Aboriginal people anticipated the situation of China's Miao minority a hundred years later. When they staked a claim to ethnic difference within modernity, they simultaneously helped preserve that difference in a cultural formaldehyde. As Louisa Schein writes, they thus reinforced the "hegemonic cultural system that stigmatized them."[42] This was the Catch-22 of colonialism that spanned the globe: engagement with colonial agents and categories—whether acquiescent, collaborative, or defiant—further entrenched colonial hegemony.[43]

Aboriginal engagement with colonial notions of authenticity, such as their performances at world's fairs and in Wild West shows, involved self-representations that used and reinforced the colonial categories that framed them as "other."[44] This begs the question why Aboriginal people participated in the commodification of their culture. In one sense, the answer is simple: they had no choice. As the political scientist James Scott notes, "for anything less than completely revolutionary ends the terrain of dominant discourse is the only plausible arena of struggle."[45] This is true of subaltern groups in general, be they peasants, slaves, or colonized subjects. None enjoy the power to determine the rules of engagement. For Aboriginal people on the late-nineteenth-century Northwest Coast, authenticity was a structure of power that enabled, even as it constrained, their interaction with the colonial world.[46]

Participating in the manufacture of authenticity could bring economic, cultural, and political gains. In many instances playing Indian provided much-needed income. Images that conformed to dominant society's expectations were images that sold.[47] Such financial considerations were critical. Ethnographic performance and art belong to Aboriginal labor history, itself an underdeveloped area of study.[48] The episodes I discuss in the following pages would misrepresent the historical reality of Aboriginal life were they not labor histories as well as cultural histories.

Through self-representations that conformed to colonial expectations, Aboriginal people also gained access to an international public forum, where they could make dynamic assertions of identity, culture, and politics to White audiences.[49] For indigenous people, the very act of entering this international public sphere contradicted the colonial cast of them as "backward cultural conservators" and challenged their exclusion from modernity.[50]

Aboriginal people were far less likely to gain access to this public sphere when they did not "play Indian." Contemporary Aboriginal people still find themselves subject to censure when they use nonindigenous forms to address political issues, or when, as with the Makah whale hunt, they play Indian in ways that offend the sensibilities of those who would believe in noble savages.[51] The same does not hold true for those who couch their politics in forms that audiences perceive as traditional. Of course, audience members' tolerance results, in part, from their blindness to the political meanings of indigenous expression. In the late nineteenth century, as in the late twentieth, Aboriginal manipulations of authenticity were living contradictions of the "either-or" dichotomy, but non-Aboriginal audiences rarely noticed. They saw images that reinforced their preconceptions. Only those with "local cultural knowledge" understood the deeper meaning.[52]

"Playing Indian" had complicated ramifications for the internal politics of Aboriginal communities.[53] Aboriginal people's engagements with authenticity were shaped by factors including status and ambition. Sometimes "playing Indian" brought elites the status or wealth necessary to perpetuate hereditary positions. As their ancestors a century earlier had done in the maritime fur trade, late-nineteenth-century elites seized innovative ways to earn status and wealth, capitalizing on anthropologists' and tourists' preference for products and performances by those they deemed authentic. Hereditary elites did so even as ascendant nouveaux riches also found ways to benefit from playing Indian. Engagement with authenticity could transform hereditary status as much as it could reinforce it. Chance, too, played a role. Sitka Tlingit, for example, had little choice but to collaborate in authenticity more frequently than their relations in villages that did not become tourist meccas. Aboriginal people created myriad combinations as they fused new notions of colonial authenticity with older notions of hereditary status.[54]

When the Aboriginal people I discuss in the following chapters engaged colonial categories, they invariably meant something different by them than did colonizers. Far from being smothered by a blanket of false consciousness, Aboriginal people twisted and transformed colonial concepts like authenticity in service of their own diverse and (for colonizers) unexpected ends.[55] It may thus be tempting to cast Aboriginal use of colonial categories as strategic essentialism. Yet, although significant strategic moments surely existed, reducing Aboriginal action to strategy alone misses some important truths. It overemphasizes the extent to which Aboriginal people lived in reaction to White society. It fails to account for the importance of notions of authenticity within Aboriginal communities. And it implies that Aboriginal engagements with authenticity were nothing more than fake simulation. Aboriginal people did not draw colonial authenticity around themselves like a curtain and continue on behind it with timeless "real" lives. There was no single, unified Aboriginal experience of true "authenticity." To suggest otherwise invokes an image of colonized populations so culture-bound by "the tyranny of custom" as to be devoid of human agency.[56] Aboriginal communities—like many others—crafted tradition and continuity through repeated and contested use. Emblems of cultural difference were broadly shared at the same time as they held varied meanings for different individuals.[57] Work, ritual, and personal relations are as much about politics as they are about culture.[58] Yet their political nature has often been obscured by the pathologizing of Aboriginal disagreements as "factionalism." Politics and diversity, after all, fall on the "White" side of authenticity's divide; the language of authenticity casts Indians as people of consensual culture rather than dissenting politics.[59] In fact, they were—and are—both. Aboriginal people were not subsumed by stereotypes, but nor did they entirely eschew them. If we oscillate between these two inadequate possibilities, it is because the roots of authenticity's false dichotomy are still so deeply embedded in our own mental terrain. Such choices are the stuff of colonialism's Catch-22. They are the stuff of outrage against Makah who hunt whales in motorboats. Moments of Aboriginal self-essentialization, strategic or otherwise, are less instances of fake "put-on" culture than they are examples of how cultural representation works. As Gayatri Spivak points out, "it is not possible, within discourse to escape essentializing somewhere."[60] Representations of culture inevitably distort what we experience more as feelings than as objects. Always difficult, cultural representation becomes even more so because colonialism raises the stakes, and as Nicholas Dirks points out, transforms representation into "one of the most contested commodities."[61] When representations become consumables, the value of an authentic stamp increases.

Aboriginal people on the late-nineteenth-century Northwest Coast confronted a dense thicket of options not of their own making. They pruned elements of "tradition" and "modernity" from this tangle and fashioned self-identities that were authentic on Aboriginal terms. This practice has not changed. Nor has the certainty of many non-Aboriginal people that these hybrid cuttings are inauthentic. Non-Aboriginal critics of the Makah whale hunt had no doubt that rifles and motorboats were aberrations of authentic Makah tradition. But, like Aboriginal people elsewhere, the Makah's tradition was one of change as well as continuity. The Makah who supported the hunt claimed legitimacy for their hybrid revival. They knew that, as twentieth-century Makah, they could use modern tools to honor their past and their ancestors without sacrificing their integrity or identity as Makah. This was itself a traditional act; countless generations of Makah had, in their own day, done likewise. The Makah created authentic meaning by reinventing old customs anew. As Dirks writes of another context, "the authenticity of the event was inscribed in its performance, not in some time- and custom-sanctioned version of the ritual."[62] This, as another scholar writes, is tradition's true lifeline: the "heart and passion the dead once gave but can no longer."[63] Tradition is not the unwavering reproduction of the past so often called for; instead static replication is tradition's grave marker.[64]

Today, the myth of the vanishing Indian is largely gone, as are government policies and public opinions that openly seek to eliminate Aboriginal people. But the binary mindset that legitimated such policy and opinion remains widespread, deep-seated, and largely invisible. This part of the past is very much a part of the present.[65] Those who set the terms of colonial engagement captured elements of Aboriginal "authenticity" and arrayed them like pinned butterfly specimens, physical evidence of the righteousness of colonial rule. Those markers of authenticity still remain pinned and encased. It is yet to be seen whether twenty-first-century society will breathe some life into these dead forms.

Chapter One

Local Politics and Colonial Relations: The Kwakwaka'wakw at Home on the Northwest Coast

Ten thousand spectators gathered on a hot August evening in 1893 at the Chicago World's Fair. Inside the stifling hall of the "Cavern of the Cliff," under the glare of electric lights, the audience watched Kwakwaka'wakw performers from Vancouver Island.[1] That night the troupe performed a dance adapted from their sacred winter ceremonial, the root of their spiritual and material order. When the two main performers stepped to the side of the stage and pulled off their shirts, the audience assumed the performance had ended. At that moment, however, the rest of the troupe surrounded the two young men and began singing and chanting to the beat of a drum. Horror-struck spectators watched as the troupe's leader, George Hunt, used a razor to slash four deep gashes across the back of each initiate. Neither man flinched as Hunt lifted the loose strips of flesh off their backs, slid ropes beneath them, and tied the ends together. As several performers yanked violently on the loops of rope, attempting to tear the flesh loose, the intensity of the singing increased. The initiates finally grabbed the ropes themselves, ripping flesh from their backs. The performance reached a fever pitch when George Hunt reappeared on stage and calmly offered his arm to one of the initiates. The young Kwakwaka'wakw man sank his teeth into Hunt's arm until he was dragged away, apparently having bitten off a piece of flesh as large as a silver dollar. The audience was immobilized with shock. No one understood that this was a theatrical performance prepared and orchestrated by the Kwakwaka'wakw.

The spectators in Chicago watched with a mixture of fascination and revulsion as their most lurid imaginings of wild and savage Indians played out before their eyes. Like colonial officials in British Columbia, they misinterpreted Kwakwaka'wakw behavior as attachment to superstition and tradition, in opposition to modernity and change. The Kwakwaka'wakw seemed to belong, as the *New York Times* asserted, to "an almost extinct race."[2] But even as the Kwakwaka'wakw enacted a drama that reinforced entrenched stereotypes about Indians, they simultaneously proclaimed their cultural survival and political defiance. Interaction with the colonial world was more than a defensive reaction aimed at preserving static tradition. At home on the Northwest Coast and on stage in Chicago, the Kwakwaka'wakw asserted their right to simultaneously engage modernity and tradition in distinctly indigenous—distinctly Kwakwaka'wakw—ways.

The Kwakwaka'wakw found themselves at the center of an ideological dispute within colonial society. On the one hand, anthropologists and tourists encouraged them to enact the most "traditional" elements of their culture, while on the other, missionaries and government officials pressured them to abandon "tradition" in favor of "civilization." The performers allied with the former groups when they traveled to Chicago. When they returned home, they used wages from the trip to further frustrate church and state officials, and in so doing continued a long pattern of using wage labor for their own devices. The Kwakwaka'wakw performers in Chicago played colonial viewpoints off one another in a manner that furthered their attempts to retain control over their lives. They rejected the dichotomies that animated colonial ideas at the same time as they used them.

The Kwakwaka'wakw had long engaged capitalism, Christianity, and civilization. The performers' trip to the Chicago World's Fair (also known as the World's Columbian Exposition) positioned this local conflict on a global stage in ways that unsettled Canadian authorities as much as it startled fairgoers. In Chicago, the agendas of the Kwakwaka'wakw performers, the Canadian government and Department of Indian Affairs (DIA), an Anglican missionary, and the anthropologists who organized the Kwakwaka'wakw exhibit clashed, generating multiple meanings around the seemingly discrete spectacle of the World's Fair. To understand these multiple agendas, we must consider the Kwakwaka'wakw "backstage," at home on the Northwest Coast of British Columbia. We must look as well to the ideology of late-nineteenth-century world's fairs that shaped exhibits at the World's Columbian Exposition. Placing the controversial performance within these two colonial contexts clarifies the meanings and implications of the performance for Kwakwaka'wakw performers and colonial authorities alike. It illuminates the creative responses of the Kwakwa̱ka̱'wakw as they engaged in internal and external power struggles.

Late-nineteenth-century missionaries in British Columbia viewed the Kwakwa̱ka̱'wakw as the most recalcitrant of Indians. When one missionary stated that four-fifths of the "heathen" in British Columbia were Kwakwa̱ka̱'wakw, he implied that they remained, as ever before, in a timeless state of uncivilized darkness.[3] But while much about the lives of late-nineteenth-century Kwakwa̱ka̱'wakw would have been familiar to previous generations, other conditions would have seemed strange and unfamiliar. Change and continuity coexisted.

Nineteenth-century Kwakwa̱ka̱'wakw communities occupied their traditional territory along the coast of northeastern Vancouver Island from Campbell River to Cape Cook and along the mainland fjords opposite Campbell River north to Smith Sound. They followed a seasonal round based on a solar year divided into winter and summer. The change in seasons was more than a change in weather; it was a transformation of the state of the world and a transformation of social roles. Winter villages were the sites for ceremonial and social activities. There, people met not only extended kin but spirit beings who visited human villages in the winter season. The grandparents and great-grandparents of the Chicago performers expected visitations by the warrior spirit Winalagəlis during their winter ceremonials. In the late nineteenth century, Kwakwa̱ka̱'wakw more commonly encountered Bax̱ʷbax̱ʷalanux̱ʷsiwiʔ, a spirit with an insatiable appetite for human flesh. Dances associated with this latter spirit would become the target of non-Aboriginal attack on Kwakwa̱ka̱'wakw spirituality and culture, an attack that set the context for the Chicago performance. Transition to the summer's intensive food-gathering period began with the oolichan and herring runs, which were followed by the halibut and salmon fisheries. Clams, berries, meat and cedar roots, bark and planks were other important resources.[4]

From the late eighteenth century, the Kwakwa̱ka̱'wakw augmented this cycle with income-earning opportunities that arrived on the coast with Europeans and Americans. They participated in the maritime fur trade, the advent of colonial capitalism on the coast, beginning in the 1790s. Kwakwa̱ka̱'wakw communities competed with other Aboriginal peoples for this new source of wealth, jockeying for positions as middlemen, and, when unable to obtain direct access to the trade, using war and pillage to gain the desired goods. In particular, the Lekwiltok, the southernmost Kwakwa̲ka̲'wakw, made warfare into a way of life, dramatically expanding their territorial reach by attacking Salish communities to the south.[5] Following the establishment of Fort Rupert by the Hudson's Bay Company (HBC) in 1849, the Kwakwa̲ka̲'wakw incorporated coal mining and the land-based fur trade into their economic round. If there was a measure of consent in the Kwakwa̲ka̲'wakw accommodation of the HBC presence, it was offset by a strong dose of coercion: in 1850, Company officers deployed British gunboats to destroy two Kwakwa̲ka̲'wakw villages on the northern tip of Vancouver Island.[6] In subsequent decades, Kwakwa̲ka̲'wakw communities lost access to valuable land and resources as the initial transitory newcomers made way for more settlement-minded ones. The recruiter of the Chicago troupe, George Hunt, was a child of this transitional era. His father, Robert Hunt, was an English fur trader at Fort Rupert, and his mother, Mary Ebbetts, was a Tlingit from Alaska.[7]

A generation after the establishment of Fort Rupert, opportunities in fur and coal had declined and others had emerged. Kwakwa̲ka̲'wakw migrated down the coast to Victoria where they found various types of employment. Some women worked as washerwomen and some as prostitutes. Others joined male relatives fishing and canning on the Fraser River or picking hops in Puget Sound. Traveling farther still to San Francisco, Hawaii, and Japan on whaling and sealing expeditions also became lucrative options.[8] Fort Rupert grew into a recruiting center for these jobs, which often took workers well beyond the bounds of their traditional territory. By 1893, many Kwakwa̲ka̲'wakw were accustomed to migrant labor.

Income from the colonial economy had implications for the Kwakwa̲ka̲'wakw system of social rank within which wealth had previously circulated among a confined group. Like many others on the Northwest Coast, Kwakwa̲ka̲'wakw organized their society into a hereditary hierarchy. For the Chicago performers, as for their grandparents, particular rights and obligations accompanied one's place in society, be it as noble, commoner, or slave. Members of each extended family unit, or *numaym*, meaning "those of one kind," shared a common supernatural ancestor. Each *numaym* contained a fixed number of positions or seats for which the nobility alone was eligible. Ranked seats bestowed access to material and symbolic property granted by the original ancestor. Material property included fishing, hunting, gathering, and other territorial rights; symbolic property included dances, songs, and masks of winter ceremonials that affirmed the relationship to the original ancestor. The winter ceremonials themselves were the source of the ecological world that sustained human life. Spiritual origins were inextricable from material existence.[9]

Slaves, along with resources and rituals, were part of privileged property owned by elite *numaym* members. The Kwakwa̱ka̱'wakw obtained most of their slaves through raiding and warfare. They viewed slaves as "wealth items" that enhanced the prestige of their high-status owners. They could be traded or given away. And they could be killed by their masters in ceremonial displays of wealth. While not the plantation system of the American South, this was no benign form of servitude.[10] The number of slaves held by Kwakwa̱ka̱'wakw masters swelled in the first half of the nineteenth century, as the range of the Lekwiltok raids reached Puget Sound, hundreds of kilometers away.[11] The indigenous slave trade declined at midcentury and may have been only a memory for the Chicago performers.

The Kwakwa̱ka̱'wakw validated hereditary rights and positions through public ceremonials, known in the colonial world as potlatches. Herein was the link between wealth and status. Display and distribution of property were fundamental elements of potlatches. One needed pedigree and wealth to sustain rank. Historically, the Kwakwa̱ka̱'wakw potlatched to mark community events, including marriages, coming-of-age ceremonies, apologies, debt repayment, and winter ceremonials. The dances and ceremonies performed at a given potlatch depended on the occasion and the ritual prerogatives of the host. George Hunt's son was entitled to the high-ranking *Hamat'sa* dance—from which the controversial performance was partly adapted—through his Kwakwa̱ka̱'wakw mother; but the legitimacy of this prestigious inheritance hinged on the presence of community witnesses at a potlatch hosted by his father. Potlatches enacted the symbiosis between the social, natural, and supernatural worlds. They linked resource rights, social hierarchy, and supernatural ancestry.[12]

The colonial economy affected the circulation of wealth by providing non-elite Kwakwa̱ka̱'wakw with access to the wealth necessary for potlatching. More significantly, it did so in the wake of a devastating demographic transformation. In the half-century from 1835 to 1885, the Kwakwa̱ka̱'wakw population declined 75 percent, from 8,000 to 2,000, producing emotional and material crises barely imaginable. The tragedy had particular implications for the social hierarchy, as *numayms* were left without enough high-ranking individuals to fill the ranked seats. Seats left unoccupied were vulnerable; their loss meant diminution of ritual status and dispossession from resources. In the early part of the century, most of the population were commoners, with a minority of families having the symbolic and material means necessary to be counted among the nobility. By century's end, there were more than enough seats to go around. The demographic collapse was accompanied by a democratization of wealth among those lucky enough to survive. It was a period of grim upward mobility.[13]

The hereditary nobility had little choice but to open the ranks of the ritual hierarchy. The creation of hereditary positions, known as Eagles, accommodated this inevitable social climbing.[14] The Eagle designation reflected both cultural innovation and elite ambivalence. It was a metaphor for "one who comes first, but not by his own rights." Eagles are scavengers who eat either carrion or food stolen from other birds. The metaphor suggested that individuals who took up Eagle positions similarly scavenged for privileges among the Kwakwa̱ka̱'wakw victims of epidemic disease.[15] Rooted in precolonial symbolic notions, this innovation grew as a result of the incursions of disease and capitalism. The Kwakwa̱ka̱'wakw responded to the disruptive forces of capitalism and disease by reinforcing the indigenous ceremonial economy as both nouveaux riches Eagles and traditionally ranked chiefs reinvested their wages into the potlatch system. When the Kwakwa̱ka̱'wakw seized hold of economic opportunities brought by White immigrants, they countered the social effects of epidemic disease by accommodating additional social change.

The Kwakwa̱ka̱'wakw had been interacting with Europeans since the 1790s, and large numbers of immigrants had been arriving in the colony of British Columbia since the 1857 gold rush. But few outsiders settled in Kwakwa̱ka̱'wakw territory before the final decades of the nineteenth century. Capitalist entrepreneurs—such as the marble quarry operator near Fort Rupert and S. A. Spencer, owner of the Alert Bay cannery—arrived in the 1870s. So too did missionaries and government officials. In 1878, the Reverend Alfred J. Hall of the Anglican Church Missionary Society (CMS) opened a mission among the Kwakwa̱ka̱'wakw; in 1879, federal government surveyors arrived; and in 1881, George Blenkinsop, the Indian agent representing the federal Department of Indian Affairs (DIA), opened an administrative and regulatory office in the newly established Kwawkewlth Agency. Examining the relationship between the Kwakwa̱ka̱'wakw and these colonial representatives sheds light on Kwakwa̱ka̱'wakw processes of cultural adaptation. It also shows that Hall and the Canadian government, rather than the thousands of Chicago fairgoers, were the most significant audience of the Chicago performance.

Missionary and government forces in British Columbia mounted a joint assault on Aboriginal life. Unwilling—or unable—to accept Aboriginal economic and cultural values structured around extended kinship and inherited resource rights, Christian missionaries and government officials attempted to instill a Western work ethic and a capitalist spirit. They strove to effect cultural as well as religious conversions. As early as 1881, nearly two-thirds of the province's Aboriginal population was nominally Christian; by 1904 the figure had grown to 90 percent.[16] The ensuing struggles between missionaries and Aboriginal people centered less on the issue of conversion than on questions of Aboriginal ideological and material self-definition.

Land acquisition was the bedrock of colonial policy. Two Kwagiulth communities at Fort Rupert signed land cession treaties with Governor Douglas in 1851, but the rest of Kwakwa̱ka̱'wakw traditional territory remained untreatied, as did most land in British Columbia. When British Columbia joined Confederation as a Canadian province in 1871, the federal government inherited responsibility for the province's roughly 26,000 Aboriginal people.[17] Unlike other Canadian provinces, British Columbia intervened in federal Indian policy and disputed the amount of land designated for Indian reserves. The federally appointed Indian Reserve Commission, a body created with the intention of resolving the dispute between the two levels of government, allotted reserves to the Kwakwa̱ka̱'wakw in a haphazard and confused manner. Commissioners allotted Kwakwa̱ka̱'wakw reserves in 1879 but did not confirm them until 1895. The Commission failed to consult residents and consequently misallotted land several times. The Kwakwa̱ka̱'wakw repeatedly registered their dissatisfaction with this process to the Indian agent and again in their testimony to the McKenna-McBride Royal Commission, set up in 1913 to investigate Indian affairs in British Columbia.[18]

The Kwakwa̱ka̱'wakw were similarly dissatisfied with the missionaries who came to work among them. In the early 1870s, a succession of a dozen or more Roman Catholic priests tried and failed to sustain a mission among

2. Village of Alert Bay, 1898. Alert Bay became the most populous Kwakwa̱ka̱'wakw settlement after a cannery opened in the early 1870s. Many Kwakwa̱ka̱'wakw moved to Alert Bay, and the missionary A. J. Hall and the Indian agent R. H. Pidcock followed. Photo by H. I. Smith, image 411790, American Museum of Natural History. Courtesy of Department of Library Services, American Museum of Natural History.

them.[19] Hall arrived following formal training in England, and informal—and unsuccessful—fieldwork on the north coast with his well-known CMS colleague, William Duncan.[20] Emulating Duncan, he hoped to establish a ministry free from what he saw as the corrupting influences of White settlers and traders. He thus judged Fort Rupert, the location of the HBC trading post, unsuitable for a permanent mission, and in 1880 he moved twenty-five miles south to Alert Bay on Cormorant Island, where he set up a school, as well as a lucrative and controversial sawmill. Unlike Duncan, however, Hall failed to persuade his congregation to move with him, and his missionary activities subsequently centered on the 'Na̱mgi̱s of Alert Bay, although he traveled regularly to preach in other villages.

Though longer lasting, Hall's mission was not much more successful than its Catholic predecessors. "The mission seems to have little influence here," observed Franz Boas upon visiting Alert Bay in 1886.[21] In 1894, the situation was unchanged, as the Indian agent Reginald H. Pidcock reported: "the Missionaries, Roman Catholic and Protestant have each in turn endeavored to do something with the Indians, but so far unsuccessfully."[22] Hall himself admitted in 1895 that "four out of every five heathen in British Columbia are in our district."[23] These numbers belie the reality that many Kwakwa̲ka̲'wakw were willing to incorporate Christianity into their lives. But for Hall—as for many Protestant missionaries of his time—conversion to Christianity involved a wholesale change in lifestyle including dress, economic activity, dwelling, family patterns, and language.[24] It involved conversion to "civilization." Hall offered Christianity as an either/or proposition. He insisted on conversion on *his* terms, and this the Kwakwa̲ka̲'wakw refused.

Throughout much of the province, the gift-exchange known as the potlatch was a focal point of the struggle between Aboriginal people and colonial society. This was particularly true for the Kwakwa̲ka̲'wakw. Hall was ready to combat the practice from the beginning. Arriving while a potlatch was underway in the spring of 1878, Hall immediately judged: "they are a bad set."[25] The Kwakwa̲ka̲'wakw returned the sentiment. Less than a year later, Hall noted that there was "some strong opposition to my work especially from the big Chief and a few elders."[26] George Blenkinsop too began his tenure as Indian agent prepared to fight the potlatch. His lack of sympathy would have been unsurprising to Kwakwa̲ka̲'wakw who remembered his key role in the violence at Nuwitti thirty years earlier. The Canadian government soon fortified the power of missionaries and Indian agents, outlawing the potlatch in an 1884 amendment to the Indian Act. For a variety of reasons, including public opinion and imprecise wording, the law proved unenforceable. Most DIA officials, from the Superintendent of Indian Affairs in Victoria to the Indian agents in the field, made little attempt to prosecute potlatchers. But the succession of Indian agents among the Kwakwa̲ka̲'wakw—first Blenkinsop and then Pidcock—were an exception to this laissez-faire rule. They attempted to enforce the law against the potlatch with a zeal unmatched elsewhere.[27]

Missionaries and Indian agents failed to appreciate Aboriginal meanings attached to the potlatch and were offended on at least two counts. First, potlatches often involved theatrical renditions of cannibalism and death that non-Aboriginals on the Northwest Coast found as horrifying as the Chicago spectators would in 1893. The most significant ritual at the end of the nineteenth century for the Kwakwa̲ka̲'wakw and for officious newcomers was the *Hamat'sa* complex. Many newcomers to the Northwest Coast misinterpreted these so-called cannibal dances as evidence of timeless savagery, when in fact the *Hamat'sa* was a historically specific ritual. The Kwakwa̱ka̱'wakw acquired the *Hamat'sa* complex in the 1820s through marriage and war with their northern neighbors. By century's end, the most prominent figures in the winter ceremonial were the flesh-eating spirit Bax̌ʷbax̌ʷalanux̌ʷsiwiʔ and the *Hamat'sa* dancers that it initiated. Young initiates were represented as salmon, the prey of human predators, who, in the ceremonial's "ecological convection," became predators of humans. After learning the appropriate songs and dances during a period of seclusion, initiates returned to the village possessed by a hunger for human flesh. Succeeding stages of the ceremony tamed the *Hamat'sa*'s desire for human flesh, restored his status as a human predator of salmon, and reintegrated him into the social community. This process secured the young man's inherited social rank and publicly acknowledged his entitlement to the accompanying material resources. More broadly, the *Hamat'sa* enacted principles of reversal and transformation fundamental to social order and ecological balance.[28] Thus, a rite which spoke to White society of chaos and depravity, spoke to the Kwakwa̱ka̱'wakw of balance between predators and prey, of relations between spirits and humans, and of the requirements for maintaining human society. This was difficult for even those with years of experience among the Kwakwa̱ka̱'wakw to grasp. Blenkinsop and Pidcock remained unsympathetic after decades on the Northwest Coast, and, in 1893, Hall's understanding of indigenous meanings behind the *Hamat'sa* was no better than when he arrived in 1878.

The second aspect of the potlatch that offended non-Aboriginal society had more to do with the ceremony's structure than its content. Potlatches drew Aboriginal people away from their homes and thus from the influence of missionaries and government officials. For months at a time, Aboriginal people did not earn wages but instead feasted and gave away large amounts of property. Potlatches clashed with Protestant values of progress, industry, thrift, and sobriety. This caused concern in government and mission offices alike. As early as 1876, Indian agents on Vancouver Island believed the potlatch was the cause of the Aboriginal poverty that necessitated government relief.[29] Hall agreed. Writing to a Victoria newspaper in 1896, Hall described two potlatches attended by 800 guests: "There they have been nearly three months and may remain five. This is the season to procure furs and oil. Have they (say 200 able men among them) earned or produced $2 per day, i.e. 1 cent per man during this stay? I believe not."[30] Such events seemed fundamentally opposed to the workings of capitalist markets.

Potlatches, or rather the mobility they required, also impeded the implementation of colonial policies. Potlatch gatherings frequently foiled agents' attempts to inspect their Aboriginal "charges." Agents made arduous canoe trips to villages, only to find the site deserted and the population dispersed. Typical was Pidcock's experience when he arrived at Nuwitti village in June 1888, only to find "that nearly all the Newitti's had gone the previous day to Kos-ki-mo."[31]

Hall faced similar difficulties when the absence of his would-be congregation confounded his evangelizing efforts. In 1879, he wrote from Fort Rupert, "although I have been here ten months the people have not spent more than four of these months at this camp. . . . For the third time since my stay here all the Indians have cleared out to visit other villages for the purpose of receiving blankets."[32] In 1880, he lamented that "the great part of the Fort Rupert Indians went to Zou-Witty River in June and did not return till November. They have again left to spend a month at Alert Bay. These migratory habits are a great hindrance to the work of the Mission—it especially checks our school work."[33] After he moved his mission to Alert Bay, Hall remained frustrated by Aboriginal mobility, even after he constructed a sawmill to "induce the young men to stay, instead of going to Victoria."[34]

Though Hall viewed the mobility of young men as improvident, he saw the mobility of women as immoral. He and Indian Agent Pidcock shared a sexualized image of Aboriginal women that led them wrongly to associate all women's mobility with prostitution. Hall, for example, cited the potlatch as "the reason the men send their wives and even daughters South [to Victoria] to make money by the prostitution of their own flesh and blood, which money is exchanged in Victoria for blankets." Insinuating that the depravity of women could be measured by the number of blankets with which they returned, he commented, "One woman has been known to bring back seven bales at one time."[35]

Hall's words resonated with an age-old colonial belief that Aboriginal women needed to be rescued from Aboriginal men.[36] Typical of White British Columbians of his day, Hall exaggerated the extent of Aboriginal prostitution at the same time as he underestimated women's agency.[37] Not all Aboriginal women worked as prostitutes in Victoria, but some did. And like Aboriginal men elsewhere in the province, Kwakwa̱ka̱'wakw men forged a tripartite alliance with missionaries and government officials in attempts to control Aboriginal women's sexuality.[38] In the late 1880s, Pidcock reported that young Kwakwaka'wakw men sought his assistance to prevent their female relatives from traveling to Victoria.[39] In 1895, thirty-three Kwakwaka'wakw chiefs complained that they could not control the movements of their wives and daughters who "are carried to Victoria for illegitimate purposes."[40] These requests to prevent Aboriginal women from traveling without written permission of the Indian Agent suggest that the women exercised their own will. Had coercive third parties been involved in "carrying" them to Victoria, the men would more likely have requested legal action against them. White men and Kwakwaka'wakw men collaborated to use the language of protection to articulate their attempts to control Kwakwaka'wakw women.

For some of these women, wages earned in Victoria, whether through the sex trade or through domestic service, may have been an avenue to increased prestige as potlatch hosts.[41] The wages may also have offered greater independence. Marriage was instrumental within the Kwakwaka'wakw system of ranked privileges, and women who sought an alternative may have posed a threat to elite Kwakwaka'wakw men. Parents typically arranged matches which might last only until the cycle of bride price and marriage debt was completed, at which point the marriage could be dissolved, and the father could remarry his daughter to a different man. Women accrued honor through each successive marriage, but perhaps some women sought honor independently of their fathers and husbands.[42]

The men's requests also had implications for women outside the circle of hereditary elites. Had it been passed, the legislation they requested would have curtailed the freedom of not only their wives and daughters but of all Aboriginal women, including those among the would-be nouveaux riches. Such women may have worked in Victoria in order to earn the wealth necessary to climb the rungs of the social ladder left vacant by epidemic disease.[43] Perhaps the chiefs' application was another sign of elite ambivalence about internal changes to Kwakwaka'wakw social order.

The request for legislation was the second notice sent to Indian Superintendent Vowell in less than a month that discussed the declining influence of hereditary chiefs among the Kwakwaka'wakw.[44] These thirty-three men struggled to maintain traditional authority in relation to their own communities as well as to colonial agents. In this notable instance, the chiefs — some of whom had been in Chicago — determined that the need for the former justified a measure of acceptance of the latter. The possibility exists that the

Chicago trip contributed to gendered dissent within the performing families. Regardless, the 1895 request reminds us that the trip occurred against the backdrop of the dual axes of internal and external power relations.

In one way or another, mobility was a central component of Kwakwa̱ka̱'wakw survival under colonialism. Contrary to colonial prescription, civilized wage labor had not created civilized wage laborers. Patterns of mobility proliferated with the growth of the capitalist wage economy. Instead of becoming sedentary when they entered the wage economy, many Kwakwa̱ka̱'wakw traveled farther and more frequently afield. The timing of the industrial wage labor cycle conveniently matched the cycle of older migrations for food and resource collection and usually did not interfere with the winter ceremonial season. More significantly, the opportunities presented by the new economy were too important to forgo. The wages were crucial for survival. The relative equalization of wealth *among* the Kwakwa̱ka̱'wakw during the nineteenth century should not obscure the colonial siphoning of wealth *away* from Aboriginal communities at large. As a group of Kwakwa̱ka̱'wakw complained in 1889, they had formerly "had plenty to support life with, now everything is being taken away."[45]

As important as the wages themselves was the freedom of choice they enabled. Outsiders could not control how the Kwakwa̱ka̱'wakw spent their money any more than they could control how they earned it. Although there were probably as many consumer strategies among the Kwakwa̱ka̱'wakw as there were wage earners, many reinvested their wages in the potlatch economy, and only a few contributed to the construction of a new church.[46] This tendency pleased storekeepers and traders as much as it frustrated the missionary. Wages made consumer goods more accessible, and potlatch exchanges consequently grew, rather than diminished. Thousands of manufactured items, particularly Hudson's Bay Company blankets, replaced the cedar blankets and carvings that the Kwakwa̱ka̱'wakw had previously exchanged. Instead of supplanting the potlatch economy, the wage economy stimulated it, even as the potlatch encouraged increasing Aboriginal involvement in wage labor, a supposedly modern activity.

Not all Kwakwa̱ka̱'wakw supported the potlatch economy. The anti-potlatch law had Aboriginal supporters—including many Christian converts—throughout the province. Jane Cook, a Kwakwa̱ka̱'wakw woman raised by the Halls, was among them. Some opponents may have rejected the political and social order that the potlatch embodied; others believed that this order could best survive colonial harassment if it was transposed into a Christian framework. Some used the colonial prohibition to escape reciprocal responsibilities incurred through previous potlatches; while those near the bottom of the social ladder may have deemed it unlikely that they would ever benefit from the traditional order, however transformed. Regardless, the ban set Aboriginal people against each other, as well as against Whites.[47]

Historically, mobility had been significant for drawing together kin from different villages. It now took on added resonance by providing an important measure of economic and cultural independence from the mounting assimilationist pressures of colonial agents. Even Kwakwa̲ka̲'wakw who opposed the potlatch did not clamor to donate their hard-earned wages to the Church. The ability to control their own movements and their own earnings allowed Kwakwa̲ka̲'wakw families to chart their own paths of change and continuity as personal circumstances and preferences dictated. Here was the reason why colonial officials—both secular and religious—found *all* absences from the villages problematic, be they summer labor sojourns or winter potlatch trips. Potlatches, prostitution, migratory wage labor, *and* trips to the Chicago World's Fair were dangerous because of their common characteristic: they entailed a measure of freedom from colonial authority.

The Kwakwa̲ka̲'wakw who resisted colonialism's prescriptive vision were not simply resisting change or modernity. They were asserting their right to a place *within* modernity. Unwilling to pay for a church, many Kwakwa̲ka̲'wakw willingly contributed to the construction of a school.[48] Many Kwakwa̲ka̲'wakw believed they had much to gain from a classroom education. They understood that in the increasingly "Westernized" environment of late-nineteenth-century British Columbia, their survival and independence hinged on literacy. Kwakwa̲ka̲'wakw communities often took the initiative themselves in requesting teachers.[49] Even Hall admitted that, despite consistent Kwakwa̲ka̲'wakw resistance to Christianity, "about the desire to learn and to read there can be no doubt."[50]

As the Kwakwa̲ka̲'wakw embraced education and wage labor, they also used some of the trappings of colonial government. In an attempt to curtail the potlatch, a local Indian agent, probably Blenkinsop, appointed a number of Kwakwa̲ka̲'wakw men anti-potlatch police officers and adorned them with symbols of colonial power: a uniform and a Union Jack. But as Franz Boas witnessed at a potlatch in 1886, the Kwakwa̲ka̲'wakw turned this plan on its head. Boas wrote, "In the lead was the chief, a man certainly over sixty. He had been given a uniform by the Indian agent so that he could serve as policeman and keep order, and especially, prevent the holding of large festivals. In order to carry out his duty he wore the uniform and carried the British flag, which he declared with the greatest pride had been given him by the king."[51] Rather than stopping the potlatch, the Kwakwa̱ka̱'wakw "police officer" participated in the ceremony, using his uniform to augment the authority and solemnity of the occasion. The Kwakwa̱ka̱'wakw had incorporated a symbol of colonial society into the very ceremony that colonial leaders most wanted to destroy.

To federal officials, such occurrences evidenced their failure to foster internal surveillance among the Kwakwa̱ka̱'wakw and motivated stricter mechanisms of law enforcement. When a dispute between the provincial and federal governments over Indian Act enforcement left federal Indian agents without access to provincial jails or courthouses, Pidcock collaborated with Hall and, in March 1888, the church began to double as a prison.[52] This spatial conflation of sin and salvation surely spoke volumes to the Kwakwa̱ka̱'wakw whom Hall tried to lure to Sunday services. Soon afterward, Ottawa and Victoria resolved the dispute when the province agreed to administer the Act in exchange for money collected in fines under its liquor clauses.[53] By December 1888, the provincial government had begun construction of a jail and stationed a White police officer in Alert Bay. The jail augmented the Indian agent's authority and also relieved the church of double duty as house of worship and incarceration.

Concurrent with the construction of the jail, Pidcock moved the offices for the Kwawkewlth Agency from Fort Rupert to a building in Alert Bay adjacent to the mission. The families of the agent and the missionary were already close friends: when the Pidcocks visited Alert Bay the two men spent hours playing checkers and drinking tea, and Pidcock family members frequently stayed at the mission.[54] Putting the agency next to the mission gave spatial expression to the solidarity between the sacred and secular colonial powers with whom the Kwakwa̱ka̱'wakw had direct contact. Hall hoped that this new arrangement would expedite the conversion of local Aboriginal people into "a goodly band of Christian Indians."[55] The new architectural arrangement would have sent a clear message to those who passed the dual structure or who heard tell of it at ceremonial, cannery, or hop field gatherings. In early 1889, Chief Lilakinis from a Mamalilikulla village could still hope that Hall might "show [his] love to them by urging the Government not to stop the 'potlatch.'"[56] News of the new structural alliance exposed the futility of such hope.

Not surprisingly, many Kwakwaka'wakw were apprehensive about the increasing intimacy between missionary and Indian agent. A group from Alert Bay expressed their disapproval to Pidcock while he was staying at the mission one evening in July 1888. Pidcock recorded the incident in his journal: "After dinner a lot of Indians came up and said they did not want me to build a house there, long Jim an independent fellow, being their spokesman. They also objected to a jail being built and in fact said they would leave if I came to live there."[57] Little did Pidcock or any of the protesters imagine that some would make it as far as Chicago.

Not long after the administrative changes of 1888, the Kwakwaka'wakw articulated their most direct challenge to Hall. In May 1890, a group of young chiefs wrote to the Church Missionary Society in London and requested a replacement. They asked for a missionary who would educate them in the skills they needed to survive in the changing colonial world. Turning the rhetoric of Christian charity to their own ends, the chiefs complained that Hall was more interested in making profits in his store than in providing them with educational and economic opportunities. They promised that they would attend neither church nor school until a "good man" was sent in Hall's place, adding that they and all their friends would attend both once the replacement arrived. The frustrated petitioners wrote,

> We the undersigned, natives of this place, wish to express ourselves to you so that you may know just how we are treated here, by the Revd Mr. Hall, who has charge of this mission. When he first came here to stop with us, we tried to treat him well, because he promised to be good to us, and to help us. He told us that a saw mill would be good for us, and that he would get some society to put up one for us if we would help him with our little mill. He told us if we had a saw mill, we would be all much benefited by it. We helped him all we could but he has not made his mill to be of any benefit to us, as we find out now. The Mill is cutting Lumber all the time, and as every person knows, there is a great waste in slabs and edgings, which cannot be sold for any price whatsoever. We have been to him to get slabs and edgings which are of no use to him in the mill, but he would not give us a single piece, after he has taken our money to help to build his mill. We feel angry at the treatment we get from Mr. Hall, and we do not like him, and we say that from now on, we agree to pledge ourselves, not to go to his church, or to his school, and not to let our friends go, if we can help

> it, just as long as he remains here. What we want is a good man, and one that will teach us some good and what is right, and also to keep his own word, but we found out that Mr. Hall does not do as he promises. We cannot respect him much because he is only a trader, and tries to make money in his store. He also does not attend much to doing good, but looks more after his store. We do not like him, and we would ask you to change him, and put some good man here in his place, for your society, and if you do so, we all promise to come to church and get all our friends to do so. We also say that we are not satisfied with Mrs. Hall's teachings because she attends more to her store than to her teachings, and that but few of the girls that have been brought up under her teachings have turned out to be good girls. And now we say that is why we want you to please to remove Mr. Hall from here and to send us a good man in his place.[58]

These Kwakwa̲ka̲'wakw did not ask for a return to some mythic past without Europeans, or even without missionaries. They asked for a missionary who would give them the resources, such as literacy, that they and their children needed to thrive, not one who would turn them into subservient dependents. They asked for a missionary who was sympathetic rather than hostile toward their culture. They wanted "White" skills, not so that they could become White but so that they could survive in a White world.

Aside from indicating the general dislike of Hall, the petition points to the personal animosity between Hall and George Hunt, the leader of the Chicago troupe. The petition requesting Hall's removal was penned by an employee of George Hunt's brother-in-law, Stephen A. Spencer. Spencer, a White trader, cannery owner, and professional photographer, was married to George Hunt's sister, Annie. The petition itself followed years of tension between the Hunt/Spencer families on the one hand and Hall on the other over the propriety of Hall's involvement with the sawmill and store. In the spring of 1888, Spencer complained about Hall to the CMS.[59] Hall believed Spencer was motivated by a fear of the growing friendship between Hall and Pidcock, as exemplified by the recent consolidation of Alert Bay's jail, mission, and Indian agent office.[60] Spencer was undoubtedly influenced both by his ties to the Kwakwa̲ka̲'wakw community and a self-interested desire to eliminate the competition that Hall's trading activities posed to his own livelihood. Despite the disapproval of Spencer, the Kwakwa̲ka̲'wakw, and eventually the CMS, Hall persisted in his secular, profit-making enterprises.[61]

Shortly after the Kwakwaka'wakw sent their petition to the CMS, George Hunt's increasingly difficult relationship with Hall erupted in public at the funeral of the Kwaguilth chief Suk-ur-ti. When Hall attempted to speak at the funeral, perhaps attempting to co-opt the situation for evangelical purposes, George and Eli Hunt intervened. A graveside scene ensued, and Indian agent Pidcock described the day as an "unpleasant one."[62]

The clash between Hall and Hunt was predictable. Though Hall called for strict adherence to the either-or terms of Christian civilization, Hunt's life was inherently hybrid. Among the Kwakwaka'wakw, the Hunt family had long been a prominent example of the possibilities for simultaneously embracing new and old ways. Hunt was the son of an English fur trader and a Tlingit woman. His parents were baptized, professed Christianity, and participated in potlatches. As a result of his parentage, George Hunt was an outsider and a "foreigner" among the Kwakwaka'wakw. Yet he grew up immersed in the upper echelons of Kwakwaka'wakw politics and tradition to an extent that was rare even among Kwakwaka'wakw youth. George Hunt eventually held potlatches to pass the prestigious *Hamat'sa* dance on to his son, an honor acquired through George's marriage to a Kwagiulth woman, Lucy Homiskanis.[63]

Others in the Kwakwaka'wakw community followed the Hunt family's example. When Hall urged the Kwakwaka'wakw to stop potlatching, they "invariably refer[red] to the action of this family and [said] the trader is a wise man and he would not allow his family to 'potlatch' if it were contrary to Christianity."[64] For many Kwakwaka'wakw it was reasonable "to hold Christianity with one hand and still retain their 'potlatching' by which they live."[65] For Hall it was incomprehensible.

Relations between Hall and George Hunt had not always been hostile. Hunt had long been an interpreter at Fort Rupert and had translated sermons and speeches in the early days of Hall's mission.[66] But ultimately Hunt found that his position as a cultural intermediary created greater affinity with salvage anthropologists such as Franz Boas.[67] Hunt became involved in collecting artifacts for ethnographers in the late 1870s and began working as interpreter and collector for Boas in 1888, activities that were sometimes a source of prestige and sometimes a source of controversy within Aboriginal communities. Hunt was instrumental in compiling the collection of Northwest Coast artifacts that accompanied the Kwakwaka'wakw performers to Chicago.[68] His sister, Annie, also worked as an ethnographic informant for Boas and others, an activity seemingly in contrast with the Victorian lifestyle she led as the wife of S. A. Spencer. Annie Hunt Spencer led a hybrid life too, although less visibly so than her brother George, who went on to become one of the most prominent Aboriginal players in the production of Kwakwaka'wakw authenticity.[69]

The disputes between Hall and the Kwakwaka'wakw community at Alert Bay were symptomatic of the less than congenial relations that prevailed at the time of the World's Fair in 1893. Moreover, the personal history of the Hunts reveals that George Hunt grew up as a skilled cultural broker who facilitated Aboriginal manipulations of colonial forms. Hunt was used to translating Kwakwaka'wakw culture—both literally and figuratively. As Judith Berman writes, "in a sense, Hunt's whole life was participant observation."[70] It was eminently appropriate that he assemble and lead a tour that epitomized this process.

Translation is a collaborative and creative act, and Hunt was not the only one skilled at it. Throughout the nineteenth century, Kwakwaka'wakw communities demonstrated creativity and strength in their conversations with colonial society. By the end of the century, many Kwakwaka'wakw were adept at turning the White economy back on itself. Facing challenges to the hereditary order on two fronts, elites simultaneously responded to internal dissent and external assault. They were prepared to embrace change, but not on just any terms. Historically, the *Hamat'sa* spoke to Kwakwaka'wakw people about the symbiotic relationship between the social, natural, and supernatural worlds. Given the readiness of colonizers to identify "cannibalism" in Kwakwaka'wakw ceremony, dances such as the *Hamat'sa* conveyed the additional message of resistance to colonial oppression. The Kwakwaka'wakw used opportunities derived from non-Aboriginal society to buttress themselves against threats posed by non-Aboriginal society. What postmodernity today casts as ironic, missionaries and government officials then found infuriating.[71] The Chicago performance was rooted in this contentious history of contact with non-Aboriginal people.

Chapter Two

"The March of the Aborigine to Civilization": Live Exhibits and the World's Columbian Exposition, 1893

Visitors to the Chicago World's Fair could expect to learn about Aboriginal culture not only by gazing at inanimate objects in glass cases but by viewing living, breathing Indians themselves. The Kwakwa̱ka̱'wakw traveled to Chicago to live on display for just this purpose. Formally scheduled dance and song performances were a small part of the larger tableau of what were known as live exhibits. These invariably featured a domestic scene set within a tepee, longhouse, or hogan containing implements that anthropologists deemed ethnographically appropriate. Millions of tourists filed by these re-created domestic settings during the course of the fair. Live exhibits of boarding-school students served as counterpoint to these scenes. Students appeared as the civilized ends that justified the means of government policy. These human exhibits were part of the powerful ideology of imperialism broadcast by world's fairs.

Late-nineteenth-century world's fairs were popular expressions of the interests of political and economic elites. Early examples of mass advertising, they helped generate public support for foreign and domestic policies.[1] The stories that fairs told gained credibility from their scientific and political underpinnings and gained force from their massive popularity. For young nations like Canada, international exhibitions were particularly important opportunities for self-promotion. They offered space for Canada to insert itself into larger narratives of progress and history—narratives that were highly gendered and highly racialized.[2] Colonized peoples—almost always of color and often feminized—were living evidence that countries such as Canada had graduated from colony to colonizer.

"Progress" was the theme of the 1893 World's Columbian Exposition, held to mark the quadricentennial of Columbus's arrival in America. The fair opened a year later than the actual anniversary, but organizers remained determined to demonstrate that the enterprise set in motion by Columbus had been fulfilled.[3] Replicas of Columbus's three caravels moored on Lake Michigan reminded visitors of this heady sense of destiny. The fair was situated on almost 700 acres of land in Jackson Park and consisted of some 400 buildings, as well as canals, lagoons, plazas, promenades, and a preserve of woods. The fairgrounds radiated symmetrically outward from the central neoclassical "Court of Honor."

Although the fair's nickname, "The White City," derived from the color of the buildings, the racial connotation is fitting. The White City illustrated a twofold notion of progress: evolutionary and industrial. Exhibits of human beings representing successive stages of race and civilization were a central aspect of this project. G. Brown Goode, the assistant secretary at the Smithsonian in charge of exhibit classification, envisioned the fair as "an illustrated encyclopedia of civilization" showing "the steps of progress of civilization and its arts in successive centuries, and in all lands up to the present time."[4] Aboriginal people were the yardstick against which to measure "the developments made during the past four centuries."[5] Goode believed that "to see is to know," and that these exhibits carried a straightforward message.[6] When visitors saw these live exhibits, they were supposed to know that their sense of White superiority was justified. Here was power inscribed and broadcast for all to see.

Goode was typical of his day's "culture of the eye," which brought people and things under increased public scrutiny. Set within their broader context, human exhibitions served a dual purpose: they demonstrated the state's power to impose conditions of performance upon the colonized; and, at the same time, incorporated viewers into a body politic that manifested its power through the ability to view.[7]

Though a similar philosophy had given rise to live exhibition of "exotic" peoples at the Paris Exposition in 1889, the World's Columbian Exposition was the first time human exhibits were part of a North American fair.[8] The live exhibits at European fairs tended to be from overseas colonies. Some of these peoples also appeared in Chicago on the "Midway Plaisance," an arcade housing people in conditions of simulated authenticity in a "Javanese Settlement," a "Moorish Palace," a "Turkish Village," an "Irish Village," a "Lapland Village," and a "Cairo Street."

The entertainment value of these Midway exhibits was high. But the political message behind the live exhibits in Chicago was different from those in Paris. The Midway housed Europe's, not America's, colonized peoples. For the North American audience, it was the internal colonization of Aboriginal people that required explanation during this the period of Aboriginal displacement through western expansion and development.[9] The Indian wars of the American Plains were recently ended, and a similar result had been achieved in the Canadian West through less militaristic—though equally coercive—means. Indian policy now contributed to the rhetoric of the vanishing Indian, not through violent death but through cultural transformation. Exhibit organizers intended the "savage" presence at the fair to be a living yardstick against which to measure the achievements of civilization. By representing an Aboriginal authenticity that was inseparable from savagery, the live exhibits served to illustrate the political and moral necessity of government policies such as removal, reservations, religious conversion, and assimilation through education.

Anthropologists were key players in this project. As one anthropologist notes, at the Chicago World's Fair the "fledgling discipline of anthropology flapped its wings to propel and popularize these dogmas."[10] Anthropology enjoyed a prominence in Chicago greater than at any previous or subsequent world's fair. In accord with the overriding theme of progress, exhibits of Aboriginal people fell into two opposing classifications: "savage" and "civilized." As one guidebook explained, here was "the red man as a savage wrapped in a blanket, and his child in the dress of civilization."[11] Taken together, the live exhibits spanned the primitive life of a previous age and the civilized life of modern-day uplift. Aboriginal dwellings stood "in amazing contrast to the white palaces stretching away to the north, that evidence[d] the skill and prosperity of their successors in this western domain."[12] Indians on exhibit were living proof of the static opposition between the traditional and the modern, an opposition visitors assumed was rooted in racial difference.

Contemporary accounts stressed the authenticity of the uncivilized exhibits by positioning performers in the past. A description of the Iroquois exhibit was typical: "If the visitor will turn aside into this curious village he will find . . . that he has dropped just 400 years out of the calendar of time, and is face to face with red men and women, dressed and accoutered exactly as their forefathers were when Columbus discovered the continent."[13] Navajo women similarly displayed industries, "which have existed among their people in the way of blanket-weaving, wool-dyeing and pottery-making long before Cortez's lieutenant Coronado, invaded New Mexico."[14] Newspaper headlines such as "The Man Columbus Found" reiterated this notion.[15]

These uncivilized, and thus authentic, Indians and artifacts appeared at the fair under a variety of banners. The Midway included two exhibits of Native Americans organized by private concessionaires. A group of Pottawatomie, Winnebago, and Sioux families lived in Midway exhibit 8a, the "American Indian Village." Next door, at exhibit 9a, was Sitting Bull's "original log cabin" from North Dakota, occupied by his niece, "Pretty Face," and the warrior "Rain-in-the-Face," a survivor of Custer's Last Stand.[16] An "Esquimau Village" of several dozen Labrador Inuit was also run by private concessionaires. Other Native Americans appeared in association with state exhibits. Wisconsin's exhibit included Winnebago, Chippewa, and Menominee families, and Minnesota sent some Chippewa and Sioux. New York State's exhibit included chiefs from the Six Nations Iroquois including Cornplanter's grandson. And Colorado displayed a Navajo family living in a hogan.[17] Beyond the boundaries of the fair, visitors could find an additional "live exhibit" at Buffalo Bill's Wild West show, where performers produced their own "savage" drama.[18]

The largest display of Aboriginal people was the anthropology exhibit organized by Frederic Ward Putnam, curator and professor at Harvard's Peabody Museum and head of the fair's ethnology department. Putnam incorporated several of the private and state-sponsored "live exhibits" into his larger ethnology display on the shore of the South Pond, where he erected a "great aboriginal encampment."[19] The encampment was bounded on one end (the "top") by a government schoolhouse typifying civilization. Next came the "Esquimau village, and, in order, Crees from Manitoba, Penobscots from Maine, Iroquois from New York, Quackuhls [Kwakwa̱ka̱'wakw], Chippewas from Minnesota, Winnebagos from Wisconsin, Sioux, Blackfeet, Nez Perces and other tribes from the far west." South American indigenous peoples followed: "Arrawacs and Savanah Indians from British Guinea and natives of Bolivia and other States." Ruins from the Yucatan provided the finale.[20]

The Kwakwa̱ka̱'wakw were part of the Northwest Coast component of Putnam's exhibit, organized by Franz Boas. Putnam envisioned the Kwakwa̱ka̱'wakw exhibit as a replicated space where the Kwakwa̱ka̱'wakw would "live under normal conditions in their natural habitations during the six months of the Exposition."[21] He positioned all the live exhibits in this manner. Newspapers reported that each of the assembled groups could be seen "under *ordinary* conditions and occupying a distinctive habitation."[22] In Chicago, this meant that the Kwakwa̲ka̲'wakw occupied Northwest Coast–style cedar plank houses imported from British Columbia. Cedar bark blankets and headrings and cedar canoes, masks, and totem poles were transported to Chicago as part of the organizers' attempt to mimic "normal" conditions. Only the most naive observer could have believed that performing for thousands of visitors a day and living under the gaze of more than 27,000,000 fairgoers were normal occurrences for anyone.[23] The impossibility of reproducing normal or ordinary conditions did not deter Putnam and other organizers, however, because what they were really attempting to create was not something normal in the sense of the everyday, as much as something they considered authentic. They omitted many everyday aspects of late-nineteenth-century Kwakwa̲ka̲'wakw life for the purposes of their "authentic" representation. Hudson's Bay Company wool blankets were one "normal" or everyday element that exhibit organizers excluded in favor of supposedly more "authentic" cedar bark ones. This was predictable. As one reporter put it, everybody knew that "the true Indian was ultra conservative in his beliefs and customs."[24]

Cultural refashioning that conflated Aboriginal authenticity with normality was typical of Putnam's approach. In his attempt to recruit a Navajo live exhibit, he was confounded by the realities of contemporary Navajo existence. He excluded kettles, tin pans, flannel, and beads from the display. He wanted the performers to wear pre-contact clothing, and he wanted a man to make stone arrowheads. Antonio Apache, Putnam's assistant in the Southwest, pointed out that nobody made "prehistoric" yucca fibre clothing anymore. The Navajo had used wool since the Spanish introduced sheep several hundred years earlier. Metal had a similarly long history in the Southwest and knowledge of flint arrowheads was obsolete.[25] Putnam's "timeless" authenticity required the obliteration of centuries-old elements of Navajo culture.

Putnam mandated these interventions in Navajo cultural representation even as he vetoed others. When Antonio Apache suggested that they acquire building materials for the hogan in Chicago, Putnam insisted that the hogan be built "in the Navajo country, and then taken down, carefully packed, and sent to Chicago by freight, that it may be reconstructed there. You will see that the Indians who come have all the fixings for the house. . . . We want everything as purely Indian as possible."[26] Authenticity further dictated that the Chicago hogan could not be heated. Putnam wrote, "The idea of placing a stove in their habitation was of course out of the question when we wished to represent their native mode of life."[27]

A different problem arose over the number of people Antonio Apache recruited. When 200 Navajo proved willing to come to Chicago, Putnam responded that he wanted only one family—clearly a nuclear family—of four or five individuals.[28] For Putnam the Navajo were specimens; the few could easily represent the many.

Putnam's notion of authenticity was not idiosyncratic. The private concessionaires who brought sixty-two Labrador Inuit imposed a similar notion of authenticity with an iron fist. The mock Labrador village included cabins, sealskin tents, a large pond, an exhibition shed, a church, a grave, a store, reindeer, and sled dogs.[29] The "Esquimau grave" was particularly disturbing evidence of the obsession with authenticity: organizers had brought the human remains as well as the grave marker. As one of the organizers explained, "there are only parts of its former occupant represented in the grave, though we tried to get all of him." He continued: "You see, we aimed to make everything as realistic as we could. So, of course, we needed a grave as you find them on the outskirts of every village. That pile of rocks there is a genuine imported grave." He had photographed the grave before disassembling it for shipment to Chicago. These photographs and advice from the Inuit were meant to ensure an exact replica of the original, "almost precisely as it was at home."[30]

Though the dead could not protest such treatment, the living could and did. As spring approached, the group became embroiled in a dispute with their employers over the terms of their "authentic" display. The managers' insistence that the Inuit wear sealskin clothing regardless of the heat exacerbated the village's already unhealthy conditions. As one performer explained, "They did not treat us right when they coaxed us from Labrador. They told us we would be well and only have to wear the skin clothes half the day, but when they got us here they made us wear them from 9 in the morning until 6 in the evening. No man can stand that."[31] The group also learned that their wages were far below those of other Aboriginal performers. On 16 February two of the Inuit "came out of their huts attired in blue jeans, leaving their furs behind them."[32] By breaching the terms of authenticity, they went on strike. Without authentic attire, there could be no display, and the Inuit paid the price. The employers locked them in their huts until they agreed to comply with orders.[33]

Peter Mesher, an Inuit who had fled the group the previous December, subsequently filed a suit against the employers for forcible confinement. In April, thirty others escaped in the dead of night.[34] Once free of the Esquimau Village, several of the Inuit worked as carpenters with contractors on the fair grounds. Others set up an "Esquimau village" of their own on nearby Stony Island Avenue, an area popular on Sundays when the fair was closed. Still another man found work with Buffalo Bill's show for $1.50 per day.[35] The roughly thirty Inuit who remained in the Esquimau Village suffered through the summer months in their fur clothing. Conditions grew dangerously unsanitary as people and animals alike grew sick. When measles broke out in the village in August, three Inuit died. Another boy drowned in the pond.[36] It is one of authenticity's ugly ironies that these conditions—exploited labor and infectious disease—were perhaps the most accurate elements of Aboriginal life in the display.

The Kwakwa̲ka̲'wakw were fortunately spared the poor treatment that the Inuit suffered. As independent participants in the ethnology exhibit, the Kwakwa̲ka̲'wakw worked directly for Putnam. They thus situated themselves in a different context from other Aboriginal people who were affiliated with state exhibits or private profiteers. This distinction proved highly significant to the Kwakwa̲ka̲'wakw, although it was unnoticed by most visitors. From the perspectives of spectators and organizers, all of the "authentic Indians," regardless of affiliation, were colorful contrast to the "other half" of the live exhibits, the "civilized" products of the Indian schools.

Exhibits of "civilized" Aboriginal people were the counterpoint to the authentic savagery of the "great aboriginal encampment." The governments and reformers who sponsored the "civilized" exhibits were often uneasy about the presence of "uncivilized" live exhibits, which they feared detracted from their own narratives of progress and civilization. But faced with its enormous popularity, exhibitors had little choice but to tolerate the spectacle of "savage" Indians and hope that visitors initially attracted by things "uncivilized" would be ultimately more impressed by displays of progress.[37]

The U.S. Bureau of Indian Affairs (BIA) exhibited a model Indian school filled with model Indian students. Over the course of the exhibition seven government schools sent rotations of students to demonstrate their civilized skills.[38] The model school was complete with workshops, classrooms, dormitories, kitchen, and dining room. Pictures of famous Indian chiefs and samples of Indian curios hung on the walls, while students studied, recited, and worked at various trades. The author and reformer Helen Hunt Jackson also brought a class of Indian girls from her Ramona Indian school in Santa Fe to the fair. Richard Henry Pratt, founder of the first U.S. boarding school for Indian children in Carlisle, Pennsylvania, likewise brought a contingent of students. Protesting the presence of "savage" Indians at the fair, he refused to allow his students to appear in the government exhibits. Organized into ten "platoons," the Carlisle students paraded in military formation and demonstrated their industrial and academic training.[39] They made no reference to their "uncivilized" pasts.

Canada's federal Department of Indian Affairs also mounted a "live exhibit." The DIA sent rotations of Aboriginal children from eight government residential schools, including the schools at Qu'Appelle, Battleford, Elkhorn, Regina, St. Boniface, and St. Paul.[40] Education exhibits had long been cornerstones of Canadian self-representation.[41] The Aboriginal children in Chicago were dressed as living examples of Canada's supposedly successful civilization and assimilation policies. As the DIA annual report stated, the exhibit was an opportunity to demonstrate "to the public the results of the policy of education which has been pursued among the Indians of the Dominion."[42] Officials took little account of the homesickness these children—already once removed from their families by residential school—must have experienced.[43] The children were displayed in a mock schoolroom where visitors watched them working at trades and skills they had learned at residential school. The exhibit's organizer boasted that "these children were born in tepees amid savage surroundings, and during the continuance of the Fair, day after day, they could be seen printing, making shoes, sewing, knitting, weaving and spinning."[44] The conspicuous absence of academic lessons from this schoolroom was consistent with Canadian residential schools' emphasis on industrial education. The products of the students' work were displayed and sold in the "Indian Tepee" in the Canadian Department of the Manufactures Building.

The boys operated a printing press on which they produced *The Canadian Indian*, a pamphlet likely authored by the Indian agent Charles de Cazes, the government representative in charge of the children. The pamphlet offered a blunt synopsis of the exhibit's intent: "to make known the steps by which the Canadian people have to a large extent succeeded in giving the aboriginal tribes their civilization with its advantages, in return for the lands they have received from them."[45] Exhibit organizers hoped this pamphlet would divest visitors of the notion that, as one guidebook to the fair suggested, the Canadian west was filled with only "the rude appliances of war and chase from tribes that still roam free by the Saskatchewan and Red River."[46] The exhibit suggested that, in western Canada, the transition from savage past to civilized present was a fait accompli that had occurred easily and without bloodshed.

Establishing its status as civilized was important to Canada, a new country in need of immigrants and investment capital. World's fairs, like smaller national-scale events, were obvious opportunities to promote the settlement of frontier lands.[47] Canadian officials thus strove to represent their country as a progressive society that had domesticated the land and the more than 50,000 Aboriginal people who had been "Confederated" along with the North-West Territories and British Columbia in 1870 and 1871, respectively.[48] Officials geared their message toward national as well as international audiences. On an international scale, they hoped to attract a much-needed influx of people and funds, while nationally they strove to convince current residents of their own prosperity.[49]

Canadian officials were worried, with good reason, about the Kwakwa̲ka̲'wakw presence at the fair. Indian dances evoked the primitive frontier that proponents of White settlement and development wanted to eliminate.[50] Although exhibits of residential school students derived much of their force from the opposition between savagery and civilization, Canadian officials shunned association with the primitive side of the equation. Canadians were more anxious than Americans in this regard. Their smaller and more dispersed numbers suggested they were still overpowered by "the forces of Nature," which many at the time assumed included Aboriginal peoples.[51]

The Canadian image at the fair relied on the display of "civilized" Indians in an additional sense too. Overall, Canada's presence at the fair paled next to that of the United States. Canada could not afford to compete with the United States in all areas and so focused instead on "strategic categories."[52] Federal Indian policy was the most strategic of these areas and was at the center of Canada's nationalist endeavor at the fair. Indian policy had long been one of the measuring sticks by which Canada asserted its moral superiority over the United States, claiming a method of civilizing Aboriginal peoples that was at once more humane and more successful.[53]

The exhibit of residential school students was typical of Canada's self-conscious impulse to compare itself to the United States. Hayter Reed, the Indian Commissioner for the North-West Territories, conceived of the Canadian exhibit of residential school students only upon learning of the BIA's similar proposal.[54] As a reporter for the *Ottawa Journal* expressed it, the Canadian exhibit would prove the superiority of "the mild methods of Canada" in comparison with those of the United States, which were marked by "scandals, cruelties, massacres, and wholesale thieving, on the one side, and desperation at ill treatment and violated pledges on the other." The exhibit would "afford an object lesson, the meaning of which no observant American can mistake of the possibilities of improving the nation's dusky wards."[55] Not a few American observers were convinced by this object lesson. After viewing the educational exhibits, a reporter for a Chicago newspaper stated, "in some particulars, the British method of managing North American Indians has been more successful than that pursued by white people south of the Great Lakes. . . . The Canadians have relied upon the education of the Indians to control them."[56] Displays of Aboriginal people reflected on Canada as a whole, so it was critical that "Canada's Indians" behave with appropriate civility.

Canada's agricultural exhibit complemented the message conveyed by the children. Bountiful yields of high-quality wheat and other grains demonstrated that the Canadian North-West Territories were not a primitive desert but a civilized garden. As one British Columbia reporter observed, visitors expected to see the products of a "barbarous country" when they came to the Canadian exhibit, and these expectations needed to be refuted. "The World's Fair is little more than a gigantic advertising scheme," he wrote, "and the result cannot be otherwise than the greatest national advertisement Canada has ever had."[57] The focus of Canada's agricultural exhibit was a pavilion eighteen feet square and thirty feet high woven from wheat, oats, barley, corn, peas, and beans and "surmounted by a graceful elk."[58] Although many states turned grass and grain into decorative art for the agricultural building, and Iowa even had a "Corn Palace," visitors were especially taken by the Canadian contribution. Comments in the exhibit's guest book indicate that visitors understood the message. Visitors were persuaded that the North-West Territories were the "future granary of the world" and the "future home of prosperous millions."[59] The exhibit was so convincing that it sparked debate over American annexation of the Canadian west. Visitors from both sides of the border fired comments back and forth in the exhibit's register:

— The Canadian Exhibit proves that Canada and the United States should be one Nation not two.
— Canada is the country of America.
— May we never have annexation.
— May we have annexation.
— Amen to the wish for annexation[60]

Annexation or no annexation, a visitor from Montreal best summed up the consensus: "I think that the North-West Territory exhibit will be extremely instrumental in the colonization of that vast country."[61]

The North-West Territories exhibit's offer of agricultural plenty appeared to have nothing to do with Aboriginal people. Yet this absence told a story. None of the visitors who signed the register linked the cultivation of the land to the displacement of Aboriginal people. The assumption that Aboriginal people were excluded from the future of "prosperous millions" was so deeply understood that it did not require articulation. This was another mark of the exhibit's success. Erasure of the connection between Aboriginal land and Aboriginal people was precisely what Canadian organizers hoped to achieve both in image and in practice.

The reality was not so simple. Canadian officials were well aware of the precarious nature of the image they had constructed for Chicago. Their exhibit's depiction of agricultural plenty and prosperous assimilation masked the dispossession, disease, and dependence of Aboriginal people on the Canadian prairies. In the year prior to the fair, the Indian Commissioner for the North-West Territories, Hayter Reed, divided his time between raising more money for the residential school exhibit and slashing food rations for reserve inhabitants. Those he deprived may well have been the families of children sent to Chicago.[62]

Conditions were no better off reserve. The residential school display proudly mounted by the DIA similarly masked the violence and deprivation that students suffered. Battleford Industrial Institute sent several children to Chicago, two of whom returned to Canada to work in residential schools themselves, one as a nurse and one as a seamstress.[63] But children who ran away from Battleford faced the school inspector's "reign of terror and despotism."[64] Battleford was likewise home to a "good deal of sickness" among the students that often proved fatal.[65] The boast of administrators that the cost per capita at the Qu'Appelle Industrial School had "been every year much lower than at any other industrial school in the Territories" almost assuredly indicated that the children there went hungry and cold.[66] And startling figures come from St. Boniface Industrial School, where twenty-one of fifty-seven student discharges between 1890 and 1893 resulted from the death or illness of either students or parents, or "dissatisfaction" with the school.[67] The story was much the same for residential schools throughout Canada.[68] Yet when students from these schools won prizes for work they displayed at the fair, they garnered international humanitarian accolades for Canada.

The "uncivilized" Kwakwaka'wakw, shrouded in Putnam's and Boas's carefully constructed image of authenticity, created highly visible, irreconcilable contradictions for Canadian image and policy makers. The counterimage that the Kwakwaka'wakw presented had the potential to undermine Canada's peaceful, civilized facade. Both Hall and Indian agent Pidcock had tried to dissuade the Kwakwaka'wakw from ever leaving Vancouver Island for Chicago.[69] By the time of the climactic cannibal performance, they would wish that they had tried harder.

Live exhibits were tools for asserting ruling-class authority. But this authority was neither monolithic nor absolute. The authority of dominant discourse consisted not only of government forces but of religious, economic, and educational ones as well. The fair's ideological umbrella was wide enough to encompass the agendas of strident assimilationists as well as sympathetic salvage anthropologists such as Franz Boas, who hosted a potlatch among the Kwakwaka'wakw the following year. All of these parties believed that the public would "know" when they "saw." But though Boas hoped the exhibit would foster greater public understanding of a noble, albeit vanishing, Aboriginal culture, government agents and missionaries hoped it would illustrate the need to control, civilize, and Christianize. Ultimately, these latter perspectives muted that of Boas. Indeed, Boas's experience as chief assistant of the anthropology exhibit dealt a blow to his belief in the ability of public anthropology to facilitate the entry "into the modes of thought of other nations," which he believed was the means to cross-cultural understanding.[70] The *Chicago Evening Post* voiced the perspective that so dismayed Boas: "Some people will call it an 'ethnographical study'—and welcome. But to the people it will be an out-of-door-circus, and you watch how the people will flock to it."[71] Reinforcement of dominant assimilationist assumptions and their attendant prejudices served the agendas of political and religious figures, but it conflicted with Boas's goals. Boas was the vanguard of a historical particularism and cultural relativism that were ultimately irreconcilable with the fair's evolutionist notion of progress.[72]

Two broad viewpoints were apparent: that of salvage anthropologists such as Boas, invested in the representation of Aboriginal people as traditional yet vanishing; and that of government officials and missionaries invested in the transformation of Aboriginal people into Americans and Canadians. Yet both views were animated by the same dichotomies of traditional/modern and Aboriginal/White. The notion of dynamic Aboriginal culture was beyond the imagination of those who controlled dominant images of Aboriginal people. The dichotomy between "traditional" and "modern" was ideologically entrenched, as the fair's popularity attests. It was also politically useful. The anthropological circumscription of authentic Aboriginal culture provided colonial governments and expansionists with scientifically based, and thus seemingly objective and respectable, rationalizations for the displacement and marginalization of Aboriginal peoples.

The fair's display of "savage Indians" did not go entirely uncontested. Groups of reformers and of Native Americans protested the display of "uncivilized" Indians, because, as they quite rightly argued, such exhibits served to justify national expansionism. Pratt's mini-defection was only one example.

The critic who garnered the most public notice was Emma Sickles. After working under Putnam as a collector for the anthropology exhibit, she went on to become his most virulent opponent. On behalf of her organization, the Universal Peace Union, she claimed that as a result of the controversial Kwakwa̲ka̲'wakw performance, "the worst feelings of both races are developed and their natural hostilities intensified by these revolting spectacles and the foundation laid for continuation of animosities and strife."[73] Allying herself with various groups of Native Americans, Sickles later claimed to have uncovered a "gigantic scheme" to manipulate the Cherokee bands and other "civilized tribes" by grabbing their land and excluding them from the Chicago Exposition. She charged that the fair's exhibits showed "savagery in its most repulsive form," and that the participants were drawn from "only the lowest specimens of the Indian race or by those noted for bloodthirsty deeds." Sickles understood that "these savages show the need of Government officials to civilize them, and furnish arguments to those who wish to drive them from their homes or plot to handle their money." For Sickles, the "civilized" Indians at the fair, the schoolchildren who exhibited their progress in the "Indian School," were no consolation. Rather, they only reinforced the false message that Indians needed government support because they were incapable of self-civilization or self-government.[74] Sickles and her allies understood that the opposition between the untamed "savages" and the civilized beneficiaries of White education and missionization worked toward complementary ends. The connection that Sickles drew between the representation of Aboriginal people at the fair and the displacement of Aboriginal people from their land was rarely so well articulated.

Though they did not garner the press coverage that Emma Sickles did, Native American leaders also expressed dissatisfaction with the misleading representations of "savage" Indians at the fair. More than two years before the fair opened, the Sioux leader Henry Standing Bear wrote to Indian Commissioner T. J. Morgan, after reading a newspaper account of the plan for live displays of Indians at the Chicago World's Fair. Standing Bear expressed mistrust of those charged with bringing Indians to the fair, including Emma Sickles, who worked for Putnam at the time. Standing Bear asked Morgan to arrange government funding for old chiefs who wanted to attend the fair. Standing Bear explained that his people would like to come to the fair, but they wanted "to come as men and not like cattles driving to a show." They wanted to present a positive image of themselves and of Indians in general to the public: "They do not wish Buffalo Bill or some government scout or any that party who will misrepresent our race." Standing Bear knew that world's fairs were promotional campaigns, and he wanted to mount his own advertisement. He understood that the fair would be an opportunity for "the Indian" to be "before the eyes of the public" and show himself "above these words uttered against him, these funny ideas of people in the Indian."[75] Standing Bear also suggested that the government use the fair to educate Aboriginal people: "Our tribe has fund in Washington which I consider belongs to all the tribes old Indians as well as the young ones, and that part of fund using for any suitable education of our people can be most properly spend in assisting chiefs to come to the Fair"[76] His suggestion was apt; organizers designed the fair with pedagogy in mind, though their target students were more often White than Aboriginal.

A year later, Standing Bear along with Honoré J. Jaxon, "Secretary of the Métis National Council," and Manuel S. Moldano, "South American Secretary of the Indian. Rec. Com.," addressed a similar letter to Putnam. Claiming to represent the "Nations of the Indian Territory; of the Dakotah Indian Nation; of the Six Nation Indians of New York; and of the Latin-Indian Nations of North and South," these men expressed their hope that Putnam would not support any form of "Wild West show at the expense of the dignity and interest of the Indian nations."[77]

Sixty-four leaders from the Brulé and Crow Creek Agencies also sought Aboriginal control of Aboriginal representations. They wanted to organize their own exhibit of Native American life and history since Columbus's arrival. In a petition addressed to the World's Columbian Commission and the President of the United States, they explained that their people were discouraged by the destruction of their herds and the failure of their agricultural attempts. And they pointed out the origin of their difficulties: "We are almost in despair," they wrote, "and it is inevitable that our people trace the cause of that despairing to the very event which, with such large expenditing of wealth you are about to celebrate." The group was anxious to demonstrate that their progress over the last four hundred years had been "much greater than is usually supposed." But at the same time, they insisted it was "not fitting nor wise that you so celebrate a great event, without considering what it meant and still means to a people once great in numbers, power and empire; and who still constitute a considerable part of the people of this most beautiful and for you, prosperous country."[78] The petition and the letter to the president went no farther than Putnam's files.

Such attempts to reshape the exhibits of Aboriginal people at the Chicago World's Fair are evidence of these people's ability to read the political implications of cultural displays. Their critique rings true today, and scholars studying Aboriginal performances level many of the same criticisms. The large and growing literature on world's fairs deals with important issues of power, representation, and colonialism, but it has left largely unaddressed the question of what "being exhibited" in self-congratulatory colonial spectacles meant for Aboriginal performers.[79]

To answer this question, we need to dismantle the presumed oppositions between savage and civilized, traditional and modern. These oppositions structured not only the exhibits of Aboriginal people but the critiques of the exhibits as well. Close examination of the Kwakwa̲ka̲'wakw and their experience at the fair demonstrates that the poles of these oppositions are not the only possibilities; indeed, they are not even the most likely ones. Ethnographic tours are vivid examples of the syncretic blends that Aboriginal people have fashioned for centuries out of supposed opposites: "modern" (non-Aboriginal) labor and "traditional" (Aboriginal) culture. The Kwakwa̲ka̲'wakw performance in Chicago was not simply a commercialized corruption of traditional practice. It was simultaneously traditional ritual *and* modern labor; it was a manifestation of colonial displacement *and* an assertion of Aboriginal mobility.

This dynamic reality of Kwakwa̲ka̲'wakw cultural life contrasted with the binary understanding of dominant society. Aboriginal people lived with this binary conceptualization as the given terms of their public self-expression. Problematic and limiting though these terms were, Aboriginal people could and did exploit them for meaningful gain. But the overall cost of such an endeavor was significant. The Kwakwa̲ka̲'wakw had very little control over the terms of the colonial discourse in which they were enmeshed. They worked with what they had. When they performed their controversial "cannibal" dance, the Kwakwa̲ka̲'wakw exploited popular assumptions about "savage" Indians in order to contest the colonial policies of missionaries and government officials at home.

Chapter Three

Theaters of Contact:

The Kwakwaka'wakw at the Fair

When George Hunt recruited performers for the Chicago World's Fair on behalf of Boas and Putnam, he offered more than a unique and exciting wage-earning possibility. He offered an opportunity to defy the Church and government's assimilationist program on an international stage. And he offered the chance to publicly assert the endurance of Kwakwaka'wakw cultural practice. These were possibilities that spoke to audiences both at home and in Chicago.

The idea of performing for a non-Aboriginal audience was not new to the Kwakwaka'wakw. Describing the sights at Alert Bay, a nineteenth-century travel guide noted that the local "Indians will give the old peace and festival dances in costume, if a sufficient purse is made up by their white visitors."[1] The Kwakwaka'wakw had also had a previous opportunity to perform abroad. In 1885, Norwegian collectors Adrian and Fillip Jacobsen unsuccessfully attempted to recruit eleven Kwakwaka'wakw for a European tour. Journalists attributed their refusal to a fear of Europe fostered by Hall, who told them that "they would be sold as slaves in Europe and never see the shores of their native land again."[2] This scare tactic, likely fabricated to induce the group to stay at home, resonated with the historical legacy of European kidnappings of Aboriginal people dating back to the sixteenth-century voyages of Martin Frobisher and Jacques Cartier. The Jacobsens, however, salvaged their expedition without recourse to coercion. They recruited nine willing Nuxalk from Bella Coola who toured Germany for over a year and returned to British Columbia in 1886.

Any number of factors may have influenced the decision of those who signed on for Hunt's proposed tour. Favorable reports about the experience of the Nuxalk who went to Germany may well have helped convince others to make the trip in 1893.[3] Other events between 1885 and 1893 must also be taken into account. In 1885 the anti-potlatch law had just been promulgated and in 1888 the first arrest and summary conviction against a Kwakwaka'wakw man named Hamasak occurred. Although he was later released on a habeas corpus defense, the arrest and harsh sentence of six months conveyed the message that the stakes had risen, that legal coercion had supplanted moral suasion. The involvement of George Hunt, an experienced cultural broker with a history of antagonism toward Hall, may also have helped persuade some people to participate.

The lucrative contract must have also been a significant factor in the decision. Troupe members were well paid at twenty dollars per month for seven and a half months, a term that included travel time. Though the performers' salaries were generous, they paled next to the ninety dollars a month Hunt received for a full eight months.[4] For his work as head of the fair's physical anthropology section, Boas received only fifty dollars per month, while other assistants in the anthropology department earned between twenty-five and forty-five dollars a month.[5] With such a salary at stake, Hunt had good reason to make sure he succeeded in his recruitment efforts and to convince Putnam and Boas that the value they placed on his services was well justified.

The Kwakwaka'wakw troupe consisted of nine men, five women (including two married couples), a five-year-old girl, and an eighteen-month-old boy. They sailed along with George Hunt and the Scottish trader and collector James Deans from Vancouver Island to Vancouver aboard the *St. Danube* on 29 March 1893.[6] They traveled across the continent on the Canadian Pacific and Chicago and Northwestern Railways, arriving in Chicago two weeks later on 11 April.[7] The Victoria *Daily Colonist* reassured its readers that the group would not embarrass their young province: "Constant contact with white men, beginning many years ago when the Hudson Bay Company first opened a trading post on Vancouver's Island, has civilized them more or less."[8]

Only two members of the Chicago troupe were 'Namgis from Alert Bay, where Hall lived and ran his school and mission. The rest came from surrounding villages and included Kwakiutl and Gwetela from Fort Rupert, Tlatlasikwala and Nakomgilisila from Nuwitti, and Quatsino from Quatsino Sound.[9]

This list of villages might indicate Hall's success at dissuading people from going to Chicago, but it more likely reflects the range of Hunt's contacts and the dispersion of rank and ritual privilege across Kwakwaka'wakw territory. Alert Ḇay had never been a traditional village site; by 1880 it was the center of interaction with the non-Aboriginal community.[10] Hunt had at least a twofold reason to draw performers from beyond Alert Bay. First, it would have pleased his bosses. Preoccupied with the simulation of authentic conditions, Boas and Putnam preferred "authentic" chiefs from traditional villages. Second, it would have pleased Kwakwa̱ka̱'wakw elites, whose cooperation Hunt needed in order to satisfy his bosses. New centers of wealth and status like Alert Bay undermined the historical hierarchy of Kwakwa̱ka̱'wakw tribes. In the 1890s, hereditary elites of traditional villages may have already felt the stirrings of Alert Bay's ascension at the expense of their own previously higher-ranking tribes.[11] A troupe drawn exclusively from Alert Bay might have furthered this trend, and chiefs must have weighed this possibility against whatever reluctance they felt about displaying sacred, often secret, hereditary privileges in public. Realizing perhaps that authenticity was being manufactured in Chicago, they may have preferred to see their own hand in the final product rather than someone else's.

Throughout their tour the group had an array of promoters and detractors that included Boas, Putnam, Hall, and DIA officials. Yet none identified the "live exhibits" by name. The identities of the troupe's members must be gathered piecemeal from scattered sources. Hunt, who acted both as manager and interpreter, was accompanied by several of his family members from Fort Rupert, including his eldest son David, his father-in-law MĖ'lid, and his brother William. Also from Fort Rupert was Chief Johnny Wanuk and his wife Dōqwăyis. According to Boas, Chief Wanuk was "head of the Chicago group," but it was his wife's performances that were featured in newspaper accounts, which variously misspelled her name as Taquasay, Toquaysa, Toquasa, and To-Cut-Iss. Dōqwăyis and Chief Wanuk brought their young son with them to Chicago and included him in the public performances. The child's name was variously listed in the newspapers as Kroskirass, Kow Sta, and Koh-Ste-Sah-Lass. The other child in the group was a five-year-old girl named Yah-Ko-Guah. The performers from Quatsino Sound on the west coast of Vancouver Island included a man named Hais[ε]haxēsaQEmē, and two women, Quany (or Kua Nah) and Whane, one of whom was married to William Hunt. From Nuwitti came John Drabble, who reappears in the historical record among those arrested in the wake of Dan Cranmer's 1922 potlatch. Rachel Drabble, or LaLahlewildzemkæ, who would live to be the last surviving member of the Chicago troupe, accompa-

3. Kwakwa̱ka̱'wakw performers at the Chicago World's Fair, 1893. Back row, left to right: LaLahlewildzemkæ (Rachel Drabble), Johnny Wanuk, MĖ'lid (standing), not identified, not identified, Qlū'LEas, King Tom, not identified. Front row, left to right: David Hunt, "Chicago Jim," HaisᵋhaxēsaQEmē. Photo N 29640, Peabody Museum, Harvard University.

nied her husband John to Chicago. An apparently well-known and respected man, identified by the Kwakwa̱ka̱'wakw artist Mungo Martin as "King Tom" and by Boas as "my old interpreter, Tom," also joined the group, as did Tom's brother Qlū'LElas. These brothers were members of the Tlatlasikwala tribe from Nuwitti. The trip to the fair made an indelible impact on the identity of at least one performer, who was known ever after as "Chicago Jim." The fifth woman in the group may have been an individual named Malete or Matele, although the source that cites this name fails to specify the individual's sex.[12]

Exhibit organizers viewed the Kwakwa̱ka̱'wakw as ethnographic objects rather than performers, which a dispute over their return train fare reveals. Putnam had agreed to pay the performers' way to Chicago, assuming that they would travel home free of charge as the chief agent of the railway had promised all "exhibits" would. Putnam insisted that the Kwakwa̱ka̱'wakw "were exhibits in every sense of the term," but the representative of the Canadian Pacific Railway was not so sure.[13] Eventually Putnam agreed to

4. Replicated Kwakwa̱ka̱'wakw village at the Chicago World's Fair, 1893. George Hunt poses in front. Photo by A. J. Rota, image 322807, American Museum of Natural History. Courtesy of Department of Library Services, American Museum of Natural History.

pay only the difference between the one-way fare he had already purchased and the return fare, rather than an additional one-way ticket. When the bill, which still exceeded five hundred dollars, arrived, Putnam dodged responsibility again and foisted the invoice on the Director General of the Exposition, George R. Davis. The Kwakwa̱ka̱'wakw returned home, but it is unclear if the bill was ever paid. It remained outstanding in August 1895.[14]

When the Kwakwa̱ka̱'wakw performers arrived in Chicago, they lived in the livestock pavilion and slept on mattresses on the floor. They shared three rooms, heated by two stoves that Putnam added as an afterthought.[15] They remained there over a month waiting for their house site to be completed.[16] The houses they were to live in for the duration of the fair were physical expressions of the authenticity that so obsessed Putnam and Boas. Rather than replicas, the Kwakwa̱ka̱'wakw dwellings were actual houses from the Northwest Coast that had been disassembled and shipped to Chicago. One of the houses came from the Kwakwa̱ka̱'wakw village of Nuwitti. The other house was not Kwakwa̱ka̱'wakw at all; it came from Haida Gwaii. The absence of Haida performers to give life to it was a regrettable slip in the authentic facade.[17] One of the first "performances" of the Kwakwa̱ka̱'wakw—

and here the line between performance and labor truly blurred—was to reconstruct the buildings. In the midst of the White City, where *everything* was new and modern, the need to *re*construct the buildings for the ethnological exhibition underscored the message that Aboriginal people were not of the present but of the past.

According to George Hunt's daughter, Mrs. Tom Johnson, it did not take the Kwakwa̲ka̲'wakw long to complete their houses.[18] They built their mock village facing the water, as was typical of Northwest Coast villages. The fairground's South Pond stood in for British Columbia's Johnstone, Queen Charlotte, and Hecate Straits. They raised totem poles and pulled canoes up on the sloping shore in front of the houses to add to the verisimilitude. The "crests of the [house's] owner," the thunderbird and the moon, were painted above and on either side of the front entrance, and the house posts were carved in the typical manner. The house belonged to a member of the Ne-ens-sha *numaym* of the Nakanigyilisala tribe from Nuwitti. Reports highlighted the house's authenticity by pointing out that it had actually been occupied by a Kwakwa̲ka̲'wakw family when it was selected for exhibition.[19] Perhaps John Drabble or one of the other troupe members from Nuwitti brought their house with them.

Once the building was physically ready, the Kwakwa̲ka̲'wakw prepared it spiritually. Combining custom with public performance, the group conducted the appropriate house-naming and dedication ceremonies. Newspapers reported two names for the house, "Qua-Qua-Kyum-Le-Las," "the house so large that you cannot see the people on the other side," and "Na Gagith," "house of the waves."[20] The house-naming performance approximated ceremonies conducted with increasing frequency during the late nineteenth century on the Northwest Coast as more Kwakwa̲ka̲'wakw moved from outlying villages to Fort Rupert and Alert Bay. A ceremony was necessary whenever such a change in geographical location took place. It helped spirits who identified with the local geography of the ancestral villages adjust to the new location.[21] The construction, decoration, and inauguration of houses and poles integrated new locales into the spiritual past of ancestral village sites.

Newspaper accounts referred to the house-opening performance as a "ghost dance," in which the chiefess Toquaysa, dressed in a blue shawl with scarlet edge and a beaten copper headdress trimmed with ermine, danced and then disappeared behind a curtain, supposedly captured by an evil spirit. Hawmissilatl then began a dance intended to appease the evil spirit that

5. Kwakwa̲ka̲'wakw performers at the Chicago World's Fair, 1893. George Hunt is on the left. This photo was misidentified as a group of "Alaskan Indians," in James and Daniel Shepp's promotional book, *Shepp's World's Fair Photographed* (1893). Image ICHi-25062, Chicago Historical Society.

had carried her away. A carving representing the angry ghost, "a hideous looking chap with red eyes and blue ears," then appeared from behind the curtain. "He talked angrily to the Indians at first, but they sassed him back, sang him a new song, and he finally lowered his tone until he got it down to a saw-filing cadenza and told them he would return their Queen to them," at which point Toquaysa reappeared and danced again.[22] The performance continued past midnight and was followed by an oolichan oil feast and gift distribution.

Besides the "ghost dance," the Kwakwa̲ka̲'wakw performed an array of other dances for Chicago audiences that included prominent visitors such as the Infanta Eulalia of Spain and Prince Roland Bonaparte of France.[23] Versions of the revered *Hamat'sa* dance were prominent in the Kwakwa̲ka̲'wakw repertoire. They also performed dances initiated by the winter spirit, *Winalagəlis*, "Warrior-of-the-World": the *Tux̌ʔid*, the *Mamaq'a*, and the

Hawinalal. All of these dances belonged to the most important components of the winter ceremonial, and all featured graphic theatrics of blood and violence. In the women's *Tux̌ʔid* dance, for example, the dancer called out for someone to "Cut my neck! Open my belly!" The other participants then appeared to drive a wedge through her head or to split her shoulder with a paddle. Strategically placed kelp bladders filled with blood burst at the appropriate moments, adding to the realism of the performance.[24]

The *Mamaq'a*, or thrower dance, was similarly graphic and elaborately theatrical. A reporter for the *New York Tribune* described its performance in Chicago:

> In the first dance the performer was assumed to be engaged in the exorcism of a spirit of disease. He danced around the fire, keeping it always to his left (this rule was not deviated from in a single one of the dances), and as he went he grasped at the spirit, supposed to be flying before him. Finally, he feigned to catch it and throw it from him. It was then supposed to enter a double-headed snake, which was jerked into the air from the floor, where it had been hidden. A master of ceremonies, concealed behind the blanket, pulled the string to which the wooden effigy was fastened. The spirit escaped from the snake (so it seemed to the novice in Kwakiutl shamanism), and the exorcist started in pursuit again. He caught it a second time, and this time swallowed it. Then two companions rushed forward to support him, while he went through most violent contortions, in imitation of retchings. Finally he was supposed to vomit blood, and with this came release from the malevolent spirit.[25]

The Kwakwa̲ka̲'wakw also performed the *Hawinalal* dance, which, according to some, involved real suffering by the performers, who had ropes passed through strips of flesh cut into their backs. The performers were sometimes suspended from the rafters of the house until the ropes tore loose.[26] Other accounts mention a raven mask dance, a "sunrise dance," a woman's "peace dance," a mosquito dance, and a "hop vine dance or harvest dance."[27]

The daily activities of the Kwakwa̲ka̲'wakw at the fair also included wood carving and basket weaving. Here the performance of everyday life produced items for sale. For Putnam, this simulated marketplace blended the exoticism of tourism with the authenticity of anthropology. "There is no doubt," he wrote, "that this sale of native manufactures by the natives themselves, dressed in native costume and living in their habitations and largely negotiating by sign language, will form a special attraction to visitors," who will purchase the goods, "in the same way that a traveler going to their respective countries would purchase a few articles from their wigwams or tepees." Putnam carefully set the terms of this authentic shopping experience, insisting that all sales be made "by the natives within or at the doors of their respective habitations and that nothing of the character of a booth or shop shall be allowed." Equally if not more important, Putnam forbade non-Aboriginal people from selling Indian arts or curios.[28] Proceeds went first toward the troupe's transportation and accommodation costs. Profits above this amount were divided three ways with George Hunt and the Ethnology Department each receiving one quarter, and the performers sharing the remaining half. These commissions augmented the considerable wages that the Kwakwa̱ka̱'wakw earned. In their transplanted home, the Kwakwa̱ka̱'wakw thus combined theater, workplace, marketplace, and residence under a single roof. As Mrs. Johnson remembers of the house, the performers "used to use it for everything."[29]

In addition to this busy schedule, there was ethnographic work to be done. The Kwakwa̱ka̱'wakw spent time with music ethnographers. George Hunt, Malete, and others recorded songs on gramophone cylinders for a project organized by Boas and the musicologist John C. Fillmore. During the fair, Boas gave Hunt instruction in writing Kwak'wala with phonetic script so that Hunt could send him ethnographic texts. It was an important moment in what would be an enduring collaboration between the two men.

At their site on the South Pond, the Kwakwa̱ka̱'wakw lived in close quarters with other residents of the "great aboriginal encampment." Given their spatial proximity and similar situations, contact between these groups was inevitable, although the extent of their communication is uncertain. Such contact was clearly meaningful for Kwakwa̱ka̱'wakw performers at the 1904 fair in St. Louis. In his autobiography, Charles Nowell, a chief from Fort Rupert, details his friendship there with "a little African pygmy."[30] And in her account of the late-twentieth-century potlatch, Gloria Cranmer Webster has described the performance of a *sudi* dance that the Kwakwa̱ka̱'wakw received from the Sioux at the St. Louis World's Fair in 1904.[31]

Questions of language and literacy would have shaped interactions between the Kwakwa̱ka̱'wakw and other fairgoers—both Aboriginal and non-Aboriginal. Perhaps some performers' inability to understand English protected them from the racism directed toward them.[32] But newspapers claimed that "the younger men and women understand English and some of them write it with ease."[33] This scenario is more than plausible given the value many Kwakwa̲ka̲'wakw placed upon literacy. Certainly Tom, whom Boas referred to in 1894 as "my old interpreter," knew English well, as did George Hunt.[34]

The Kwakwa̲ka̲'wakw failed on occasion to behave as Boas and Putnam would have liked. Some reports describe them drinking liquor and interacting with visitors outside formally scripted performances. When one dancer received a tip, he took it directly to the "Big Tree Pavilion," where he spent it on a beer. In another instance, the group procured alcohol from an audience member.[35] Hunt too was less cooperative than Boas would have liked. During a visit to British Columbia in 1894, Boas complained that Hunt "acts exactly as he did in Chicago. He is too lazy to think."[36] What Boas called "laziness" may have been a preference to explore the fair rather than exchange ethnographic knowledge and techniques. However stereotyped, these accounts of drinking and laziness indicate that the Kwakwa̲ka̲'wakw resisted Boas's and Putnam's attempts to control them. This resistance was never more apparent than during the graphic August performance.

The Kwakwa̲ka̲'wakw timed their drama carefully. They had previously created a public stir during Victoria Day celebrations in May when they projected just the sort of image of Canada that Canadian officials wanted to discourage. The reporter for the *New York Times* described the "boatload of braves of Quackuhl Indians who have been brought from their primitive home on Vancouver Island, British Columbia" as part of a "queer looking and almost extinct race of North American Indians" who "stood up and howled and danced to the jingle of the tambourine in the chief's hands." Canadian officials must have winced as they read on: "Several thousand visitors were quickly drawn to the scene. The throng of spectators could not understand why the British flag should be floating over such a fierce and savage looking lot."[37]

Whatever anxiety the Victoria Day performance generated among Canadian profiteers, politicians, and bureaucrats paled next to what the Kwakwa̲ka̲'wakw held in store for August. It was the eve of the fair's "Great Britain Day," and the eyes of the public and media alike were trained on representatives of the British Empire. Officials, desiring "to make the demonstration as imposing as possible," carefully planned the proceedings to include a grand parade, a martial display, and the singing of “patriotic songs.”[38] Canada excluded the Kwakwa̱ka̱'wakw from its contribution to these imperial displays. But the Kwakwa̱ka̱'wakw ensured that their place in the empire could not be overlooked.

The Kwakwa̱ka̱'wakw had a live audience of 10,000 people for their “brutal exhibition,” as one reporter dubbed the performance. They raised a public outcry and received major press coverage, including pieces in the *New York Times* and the London *Sunday Times*.[39] However exaggerated, these accounts had tremendous impact. Judging by the newspapers' inflated language, which incorrectly labeled it a “sun dance,” the performance was a cross between the *Hawinalal* and *Hamat'sa* dances. The account in the London paper was particularly graphic:

> [The performers] began a queer sort of monotonous chant, interrupted at times by a peculiar low wailing cry to the dull beat of an Indian music drum. George Hunt then produced a sharp knife and two pieces of rope. He cut four deep gashes in the back of [Two-Bites and Strong Back] just between the shoulder blades. Raising the flesh he passed the ropes beneath the loose strips and tied the ends firmly together. Two-Bites and Strong-Back standing motionless as statues during the operation. The low monotonous chant of the Indians, squatting in a great half circle, now became wilder and more vehement. Several Indians rushed to the center of the platform and seizing the ends of the ropes, pulled them violently, uttering loud cries. . . . During a pause Two-Bites and Strong Back attached stout ropes to the ends of the small ones passed through their backs, and throwing their weight upon them, tore them from their fleshy fastenings. By this time the expression of Two-Bites face was that of a famished wolf. His eyes gathered like those of a furious wild animal, and, kneeling on the platform, hc uttered hoarse cries. Two Indians sprang upon him and caught him by the shoulders. He turned on them, snapping and snarling like a mad dog, until George Hunt, the interpreter, walked over and extended to him his bare arm. Two-Bites gave a dismal howl, and fastened on it with his teeth, making them meet in the flesh. It was with difficulty, after being dragged half-away across the platform, that he could be induced to relinquish his hold, when it was discovered that a piece had been bitten out of Hunt's arm as large as a silver dollar; but the interpreter smiled and showed no signs of pain.[40]

Hall had witnessed a similar performance in Fort Rupert in 1878.[41] Now, in 1893, while on furlough in London, he picked up the Sunday paper and found this account of his would-be congregation members. He had previously been censured for his inability to control the mobility of the Kwakwa̱ka̱'wakw; this latest episode on the Chicago stage, the most public stage of the day, dramatically revealed his failure and reflected very poorly on him, indeed.[42]

Outraged and embarrassed, Hall demanded that Canadian officials halt the Kwakwa̱ka̱'wakw performances immediately. He complained that the U.S. government had exhibited signs of successful civilization programs in its industrial school exhibits, while the Kwakwa̱ka̱'wakw representatives from Canada "were chosen by Dr. Boaz because [they were] the most degraded he could find in the Dominion."[43] Hall overlooked the fact that the United States too had sent many "savage" Indians to the fair. His letter was above all a self-indictment, since these "most degraded" of Indians were his own flock of fifteen years. Although the fair's juxtaposition of savage and civilized Indians ultimately supported Hall's ends, the means to those ends had, in this case, dealt a blow to his reputation.

Canadian policy and image makers were also embarrassed, though more politically than personally. Apparent cannibal dances did not project the image that attracted settlers and investors. The Kwakwa̱ka̱'wakw were not the Indians policy makers wanted the world to see. The Victoria newspaper attempted an explanation by distinguishing between the everyday and the authentic, claiming that this performance had scientific value only as an example of the "barbaric rites practised by their ancestors centuries ago," and that such illegal acts had "not been enacted for years."[44] The British Columbia Indian Commissioner, A.W. Vowell, characterized the Chicago performers as "adept in the art of very cleverly conducted jugglery."[45] Putnam likewise portrayed the dance as pure fabrication.[46] But none of this lessened the visceral impact of the spectacle and its subsequent journalistic renditions on the non-Aboriginal public. As was often true of world's fairs and exhibitions, the popular reading was determinative.[47]

In the ensuing flurry of correspondence between Deputy Superintendent General of Indian Affairs Lawrence Vankoughnet, A. W. Vowell, and Indian agent Pidcock, each man attempted to absolve himself of responsibility, proclaiming his unconditional disapproval of such performances. Eventually, officials admitted that "the Department unfortunately cannot invoke the law to prevent or put a stop to the disgraceful scenes referred to, as the law of Canada which prohibits the celebration of such orgies in British Columbia is of course inoperative while the Indians are in the United States."[48] Since the Kwakwa̱ka̱'wakw were in Chicago not as part of the Canadian exhibit but under the auspices of the Hunt/Boas/Putnam anthropology team, the Canadian government was powerless to recall them. Yet Putnam was similarly unable to discipline the Kwakwa̱ka̱'wakw. As he asserted in self-defense to his superior, "The Indians from Vancouver Island . . . are entirely outside the jurisdiction of the United States."[49] Putnam was caught in the lines of authenticity he had helped spin and he struggled to explain that it had been his wish only "to have these Indians appear in a manner purely native."[50] Removed from a national context, the Kwakwa̱ka̱'wakw appropriated the Chicago stage and fashioned a response to government and Church attempts to destroy their way of life. In this instance the primitivist discourse that separated Aboriginal people from national histories worked to the Kwakwa̱ka̱'wakw's advantage.

For the Kwakwa̱ka̱'wakw performers, the Chicago dances were part of colonial politics. But the dances were simultaneously embedded in Aboriginal lives in ways that bore little relation to the supposed dichotomy of traditional versus modern or authentic versus inauthentic. Long before the Chicago fair, many Kwakwa̱ka̱'wakw used modern wage labor to reinforce the potlatch, supposedly the most anti-capitalist and most traditional of practices. The Chicago performers turned aspects of the potlatch itself into wage labor by commodifying their dances for the Chicago audience. The trip to Chicago was much like a trip to the Washington State hop fields or the Fraser River canneries. As was typical of Aboriginal migrant workers, several members of the group, including George Hunt, John Drabble, and Johnny Wanuk, spent their "modern" wages hosting large potlatches once they returned home. As Hunt later explained to Boas, "When we came back to Fort Rupert, Wāg'ides [Johnny Wanuk] went into his house, and he said at once that he would buy oil with the money that he had obtained, paid by you, Dr. Boas. Then he gave a grease feast to all the tribes."[51]

Accounts of other Aboriginal people who went on similar tours or worked with anthropologists demonstrate that Aboriginal people commonly compared ethnographic activities to other wage-earning opportunities. The Bella Coola who went to Germany in 1885 were on their way to Washington State when Jacobsen intercepted them and persuaded them to substitute cultural performance for hop picking. Charles Nowell, a Kwakwa̲ka̲'wakw chief who performed at the 1904 St. Louis fair, similarly preferred anthropological work to other forms of labor: "whenever Dr. Newcombe comes, I stop working in the sawmill and go around to other villages with him."[52] A group of Makah and Haida, on the other hand, declined Newcombe's invitation to St. Louis in 1904, unconvinced that they would earn as much selling crafts and art as they would fishing or picking hops.[53]

In many respects, the trip to Chicago was like canning salmon or picking hops, but it was not *just* like them. The most conspicuous difference was the direct commodification of Kwakwa̲ka̲'wakw cultural practice that the Chicago performance required. Dances historically performed by and for Aboriginal elites at potlatch ceremonies during the sacred winter season were presented during the secular summer season for a non-Aboriginal audience. This was not the first time the Kwakwa̲ka̲'wakw had made adjustments nor would it be the last. In the late nineteenth century, the effort to reconcile the capitalist and ritual gift economies was "a general problem" with which the Kwakwa̲ka̲'wakw grappled.[54] The long history of theatrical performance in Kwakwa̲ka̲'wakw culture facilitated the adaptation of sacred dances to the secular context in Chicago. The Kwakwa̲ka̲'wakw understood potlatch dancers as actors. And they were accustomed to the practice of "fictitious rivalry" or "play potlatch" in which performers lampooned the dignified pretensions of real potlatching.[55]

Their history of ceremonial theater did not mean that the Kwakwa̲ka̲'wakw adjusted sacred ceremony lightly or even unanimously. Detailed negotiations likely took place to plan the Chicago performances. The performers of the 1890s did not, as would Kwakwa̲ka̲'wakw dancers half a century later, decide to omit selections drawn from the winter ceremonial in favor of dances from the secular *Tlasula* repertoire.[56] They did, however, predominantly choose older dances inspired by *Winalagəlis*, rather than the chief spirit patron of the late nineteenth century, Bax̌bax̌alanux̌ʷsiwiʔ. They thus accommodated Boas's penchant for "old ways," at the same time as they avoided potential complications of presenting dances that were directly embedded in their own personal practice. Whatever compromises to the Kwakwa̲ka̲'wakw mythosocial order that Chicago's commodification of ceremony engendered, the winter ceremonial, the primary expression of that order, retained its sacred character.[57]

The processes of ceremonial transposition and transformation misled reporters then—just as it sometimes misleads observers now—to conclude that the commercial performances were a mark of cultural capitulation, that colonialism had reduced the Kwakwaka'wakw to mimicking their former cultural glory, and that the performers were thus no longer "authentic" Indians. As one reporter at the fair put it, "back of the [Kwakwaka'wakw performance] was some ancient superstition, some mythological occurrence, which is now forgotten, or but half-remembered."[58] This reporter's conclusion was rooted in the assumption that Aboriginal people must be either "traditional" or "modern," and that authentic Aboriginal identity hinged on upholding static "tradition."

Survival under colonialism required compromises, but these compromises were not necessarily symptoms of decline and could be signs of resiliency. Without a willingness to compromise, hereditary elites could not hope to sustain the hierarchy of rank and privilege. A chief from Quatsino Sound articulated his understanding of the link between tradition and change in a speech during the 1894 winter ceremonial. He acknowledged that "my grandfather's rules were strict, but those of my father were a little less rigid. Our rules of the winter ceremonial are much less strict than those of olden times." He then urged his audience to listen carefully and take notice of what he had learned from his great-grandfather, whose knowledge, in turn, originated with the Maker of Dances at the beginning of the world. The chief identified the man who would inherit the cedar bent-box containing important spiritual items, including the red cedar bark for the *Hamat'sa* ceremony.[59] For this chief, rituals changed, but the careful attention paid to oral narrative and family history did not. Alterations that made ritual practice "less strict" did not mean ceremonials were dying out. On the contrary, they ensured that markers of inherited tradition survived for coming generations. Here, as elsewhere, cultural authenticity was not the same thing as cultural purity.[60]

Despite the spatial, seasonal, and social recontextualization that marked the Chicago performances, significant elements of continuity linked the international stage with the local one. These elements, likely of great significance to the performers, were largely invisible and probably irrelevant to Chicago spectators. Aboriginal performances for non-Aboriginal audiences commonly include elements of significance to cultural insiders that are invisible to outsiders.[61] The consumption of oolichan oil and the exchange of gifts that followed the house-opening ceremony in Chicago were two examples of continuity. The ceremony itself was a third. The house originated in Nuwitti, and the Kwakwa̲ka̲'wakw performed a house opening specifically associated with the Nuwitti and Quatsino tribes.[62]

The identity of at least some of the performers was another continuity between the two settings. Historically, the right to perform certain dances was a hereditary honor publicly confirmed at a potlatch. Some of the troupe's members were high-ranking Kwakwa̲ka̲'wakw with knowledge, and, at least in the eyes of many, the authority to dance. The dances in Chicago, though far removed from home, do not seem to have been entirely displaced from their hereditary owners.

The elite status of the Chicago performers fits within a larger pattern of interaction between anthropologists and Aboriginal people. Anthropologists up and down the Northwest Coast commonly relied on a narrow group of high-ranking individuals as informants, suppliers, and performers, a generalization that holds especially true for world's fairs.[63] Such arrangements served the interests of authenticity-hunting anthropologists and status-conscious informants alike. Challenges to the hereditary political, economic, and social order originated with colonial forces such as disease and capitalism, as well as with internal dissent. In the face of these challenges, elites sought new ways, including the sale of artwork and ethnographic performance, to acquire the wealth necessary to potlatch and retain hereditary positions.[64] This was precisely the end to which many of the Chicago performers turned their wages.

For the performers, the Chicago trip can be seen as part of elite Kwakwa̲ka̲'wakw attempts to maintain the authority of ritual ownership and hierarchy, attempts that seem to have been successful. Well past the turn of the century, the requirements of ritual ownership survived to a degree that often frustrated Boas, who complained in 1923 that "everywhere on the coast everyone is afraid to tell something that does not belong to his family. That makes my work hard."[65] In late-twentieth-century Kwakwa̲ka̲'wakw performances, displaying evidence of appropriate rights remained essential.[66] In Alert Bay at the turn of the twenty-first century, young performers still explained how they inherited or obtained permission to perform each dance before they began.

Despite these important continuities, stories of the Chicago performers defy smooth narratives about the uncomplicated reproduction of timeless tradition. The shift from the local to the international stage created openings for performers to synthesize change with continuity. David Hunt was one of the performers who had a legitimate claim to the *Hamat'sa* dance, for example, although he had not yet been initiated when he performed at the fair. His initiation as *Hamat'sa* took place in Fort Rupert the following winter at the large potlatch that his father, George Hunt, hosted with his Chicago earnings. The event blended Tlingit prerogative with Kwakwa̲ka̲'wakw practice, simultaneously linking David to his mother and his paternal grandmother.[67] Thus David Hunt became *Hamat'sa* in the hybrid, but no less sacred, Kwakwa̲ka̲'wakw context only after he had performed secular, hybridized versions of the ceremony in Chicago. A speaker at the 1894 potlatch complimented George Hunt's generosity, saying, "This is the first time that such a thing is done. His property runs from him in streams, and if one of his rivals should stand in the way he would be drowned in it."[68] This unique potlatch became a key moment in the manufacture of Kwakwa̲ka̲'wakw authenticity on several levels. George Hunt used his high salary from Chicago to reinforce the position of himself and his son within Kwakwa̲ka̲'wakw society, positions otherwise derived from his wife, and in a twist of ethnographic fate, from Franz Boas, who crowned him resident expert on Kwakwa̲ka̲'wakw culture. Boas in turn related the grandeur of Hunt's potlatch in his *Kwakiutl Ethnography*, casting it there as a benchmark of ahistorical, authentic practice.

The circumstances of another family who traveled to Chicago similarly resist categorization as timeless tradition. Dōqwăyis was correctly identified in Chicago newspapers as a woman of high rank. Dōqwăyis traced her status, which reporters variously labeled "princess," "Queen," or "chiefess," to her position as daughter of the chief of the *numaym* DzEndzEnx'q·'ayo. George Hunt later described her as a "princess" or "queen." According to Hunt, Dōqwăyis was her "chief's name" inherited upon the death of her father, and ᵋmāxŭlayugwa was her "princess name."[69] Dōqwăyis was married to Chief Johnny Wanuk. Wanuk owed his title as chief not to a high-ranking family background (which he lacked) but to his marriage. According to George Hunt, this was "called by the Indians 'a-newly-made-chief.' "[70] His marriage and subsequent chiefly designation placed Wanuk within the pool of high-ranking anthropological informants and performers and thus probably facilitated his admittance into the Chicago group. As George Hunt wrote to Boas: "I only wish you to know that Wāg'ides [Johnny Wanuk] probably thought that you considered him a real chief."[71] Through his unconventional marriage, Wanuk had entered the ranks of the Kwakwa̲ka̲'wakw elite before his trip to Chicago. Upon returning from Chicago, he used his earnings to solidify that position. At the grease feast that Wanuk

6. Blankets piled up as part of the wealth to be distributed at the 1894 potlatch in Fort Rupert. Photo by F. Boas, image 33066, American Museum of Natural History. Courtesy of Department of Library Services, American Museum of Natural History.

hosted with his Chicago earnings, Dōqwăyis "gave him the marriage name Kwākŭx·âlas for the feast name of her husband."[72] The hereditary rights of his wife helped Wanuk strengthen his position as "newly-made-chief" through the "traditional" means of a grease feast, which he paid for with "modern" wages. Both George Hunt and Johnny Wanuk achieved social prestige by marrying into high-ranking Kwakwa̲ka̲'wakw families. This prestige would have remained precarious without the potlatches paid for with their Chicago earnings.

The history of the photographs that Franz Boas took of the Kwakwa̲ka̲'wakw performers at the fair likewise challenge simplistic oppositions between "traditional" and "modern," or "authentic" and "inauthentic." Boas used altered copies of the photos to illustrate his ethnography, *The Social Organization and the Secret Societies of the Kwakiutl Indians*.[73] By brushing out the background, Boas transformed them from images of staged performances situated in a particular time and place to timeless, decontextualized ethnographic specimens. As in his account of Hunt's potlatch, Boas decontextualized practices produced by Chicago in order to manufacture the authenticity he sought.

The Kwakwa̱ka̱'wakw attached different meanings to these photographs, meanings rooted in the very context that Boas painstakingly obliterated. In February 1894, Hunt wrote to Boas and asked him to send pictures of the performers in Chicago. When Boas came to Fort Rupert in November 1894, he hosted a feast at which he fulfilled Hunt's request. He made a speech addressing the people who had been in Chicago and presented them with pictures of themselves performing in their ceremonial regalia at the fair.[74] He distributed the Chicago photos along with apples and other gifts. The simulated ceremonials performed on the summer stage in Chicago thus came home, where the Kwakwa̱ka̱'wakw incorporated them into a Northwest Coast winter ceremonial.

Hunt also had a different sort of photograph of himself taken at the fair—a formal portrait in which he wore jacket, vest, and tie. He presented this photograph to Frederic Ward Putnam with the inscription "To Professor

7. David Hunt performing *Hamat'sa* dance at the Chicago World's Fair, 1893. When Franz Boas hosted a feast in Fort Rupert in 1894, he distributed photographs such as this to the Kwakwa̱ka̱'wakw performers. Boas later erased the background from these photographs, including this one, and reproduced them in *The Social Organization and the Secret Societies of the Kwakiutl Indians*. Photo N29641, Peabody Museum, Harvard University.

8. Chief speaking at feast hosted by Franz Boas, Fort Rupert, 1894. Image 355772, American Museum of Natural History. Courtesy of Department of Library Services, American Museum of Natural History.

Putnam—compliments of George Hunt."[75] Though he was charged with escorting supposedly "uncivilized" Indians, the image Hunt portrayed in this photograph was one of eminent civility. This was the same man who returned home from Chicago and potlatched "streams of property." He did so during the very winter ceremonial at which Boas distributed the images of the performers in their most "traditional," "uncivilized" and "authentic" stances.[76]

The civilized image Hunt presented in the photograph to Putnam can be seen as part of his struggle to be taken seriously by non-Aboriginal society. Hunt was frustrated that his responsible and high-paying position at the fair had not garnered him respect. On the return train journey from Chicago, for example, he was insulted by the treatment he received from James Deans, another of Putnam's employees. As Hunt wrote to Boas, "The time we left Chicago Mr. deans acted Bad he would not let me know what he was Doing or going to Do and would not let me see what he signed for and told Every Body that I was one of his Indians ."[77] Hunt's irritation at being cast as "one of [Deans'] Indians" seems rooted less in the designation "Indian"

9. Front and back of studio portrait of George Hunt at the Chicago World's Fair, 1893. Hunt gave this photograph to F.W. Putnam. A handwritten comment on the back of the photograph identifies Hunt as the "Halfbreed in charge of the Indians from British Columbia, 1892–3." Box 37, Frederic Ward Putnam Papers, Harvard University Archives. Courtesy of Harvard University Archives.

than in the derogatory implications of subservience. Deans conflated the identities of Indian and subservient, but Hunt believed in his right to be equal and Indian at the same time.

Just as Hunt refused to act the subservient role that Deans expected, so the Kwakwa̲ka̲'wakw refused to acquiesce to the authority of White society. By 1894—if not before—they had incorporated defiance of colonial authorities into potlatch performances. Through Boas, we have the following account of a man's address to the assembled guests: "I dreamt last night that I came into the winter ceremonial house and that I was speared." His words indicated his desire for someone to fulfill his dream by spearing him. The guests refused, saying, "That is not allowed by the police. We are afraid of the white people." At this point, the speaker's elder brother stepped forward and announced, "I am not afraid of the police. I will spear my brother."[78] Such exchanges—whether directed at Boas specifically, or White society more generally—evinced an audacity and fearlessness also apparent in the "brutal exhibition" of the *Hamat'sa/Hawinalal* performance in Chicago.

The advantage that the Kwakwa̱ka̱'wakw gained through their daring decision to perform the *Hamat'sa/Hawinalal* dance was nonetheless a limited one. Though the Kwakwa̱ka̱'wakw returned home to hold potlatches, they did so under threat of persecution and arrest. They returned home to a province where their political and cultural rights continued to be violated. They returned home to Hall and Pidcock. As leader of the group, Hunt bore the brunt of the blame. In 1894, he told Boas that he expected "trouble from the missionary here every day for he's trying to find out what I have been doing in the Fair," and that Hall "came to me and said that I show some Dance against the Law and that I will get myself into trouble."[79]

Pidcock alluded to the controversy in his 1893 annual report when he wrote that "with one exception, the conduct of the various tribes has been very good."[80] Pidcock had known from the start that Hunt was in charge of the Chicago group, but he later denied this.[81] In the fallout from the controversy, he stated that he "should not consider that [Hunt] was at all a fit and proper person to have charge of a party of Indians."[82] Pidcock took direct aim at Hunt in 1900 when he launched charges against him for allegedly participating in the mutilation of a corpse during a potlatch.[83]

Surprisingly, Pidcock was willing to consider another Kwakwa̱ka̱'wakw tour in 1895, when a group of fifteen 'Na̱mgi̱s requested permission to go on a performance tour of British Columbia. Pidcock did require their assurance that there would be "nothing objectionable in the exhibition" before he forwarded their request to Vowell.[84] Higher-ranking DIA officials were less forgiving, or at least less trusting, than Pidcock. In the years following the fair, DIA officials routinely denied requests by various promoters and anthropologists to take Canadian indigenous peoples on ethnographic or performance tours.[85] The 1895 amendment to the Indian Act, which the DIA hoped would make the anti-potlatch law enforceable, included precise definition of what did and did not constitute acceptable Aboriginal performance. It banned performances with the exception of presentations at agricultural shows or exhibitions, since agriculture was widely held to be the distinguishing mark of civilization.[86] When the DIA granted permission for the Stony from Alberta to perform at a Wild West show in Banff in 1915, it was on condition that "the Indians do not appear in aboriginal costume."[87] Canadian officials took seriously the lesson they learned from Chicago's public relations debacle.

The gains from Chicago were limited in an additional sense. The performers may have derived benefits from their bold act, but they were themselves a limited portion of Kwakwaka'wakw society. Not all Kwakwaka'wakw favored retaining the potlatch. The Kwakwaka'wakw performers mounted not a generalized Kwakwaka'wakw protest but a protest from the particular position of those with some degree of access to the upper echelons of Kwakwaka'wakw hierarchy. The larger discursive consequences were mitigated for these high-status families who stood to gain in the short term from their engagements with anthropologists and their participation in the production of authenticity. Other Aboriginal families who enjoyed no such mitigating influence were nonetheless tied to the same notions of authenticity co-spun by colonizers and Aboriginal elites.

For many decades before 1893, the Kwakwaka'wakw assimilated imported "modern" practices into "traditional" indigenous ones. They used tactics that non-Aboriginal people found an incomprehensible mixture of the "traditional" and the "modern." Yet, as the Kwakwaka'wakw tried to make clear to missionaries and Indian agents, and as the performers told the world when they appeared in Chicago, this dichotomy was false. The Kwakwaka'wakw struggled not against change itself but against colonial newcomers who attempted to dictate the terms of that change.

The Chicago fair was a new arena for a decades-old struggle between the Kwakwaka'wakw and White authorities in British Columbia. The Kwakwaka'wakw performance in Chicago added to the arsenal in the specific struggle to retain the potlatch and the more general struggle to retain autonomy over their culture, identity, and way of life. Whereas wage opportunities, such as commercial canning, fishing, or hop picking, provided for an image of a modernizing "Indian" and allowed Hall to claim some success for his mission of civilization, the graphic and controversial Kwakwaka'wakw performances forced Hall to confront his failure. Ironically, by performing versions of their rituals in Chicago that were far from "traditional," the Kwakwaka'wakw contributed to the dominant colonial image of traditional Aboriginal culture.[88] Whether the White audience perceived the Kwakwaka'wakw performers in a positive or negative light, the message the Kwakwaka'wakw conveyed through the performances was that they were not "White-man" but were still vibrantly (or savagely) Indians.

The results of this endeavor were double-edged. At the same time as the Kwakwaka'wakw ingeniously combined cultural affirmation and adaptation, they contributed to the identification of Kwakwaka'wakw culture as a static relic of the past. The *Hamat'sa/Hawinalal* performance in August 1893 was both traditional ritual and modern labor, but White audience members saw only its traditional aspect. Stripped of its larger context, the performance affirmed many of the audience's basest stereotypes about Aboriginal people and reinforced their belief in the opposition between "traditional" and "modern."[89]

In the process of negotiating a cultural identity that was simultaneously authentic and dynamic, Aboriginal people made choices and concessions, both conscious and unconscious, sometimes strategic, sometimes sentimental. Individuals and groups carefully considered which beliefs and practices could be adjusted in order to preserve what they deemed most important. The Kwakwa̱ka̱'wakw's use of wages was a widespread example of this process. At the World's Columbian Exposition, Kwakwa̱ka̱'wakw performers carried this process to a new level by transposing their demonstration of political defiance and cultural persistence onto the public world stage in front of an international audience. It was not just the Kwakwa̱ka̱'wakw who went "on tour"; their struggle with the Church and the DIA went on tour as well. Their performances in Chicago fused cultural tradition, modern labor, and political protest.

Chapter Four

Picking, Posing, and Performing: Puget Sound Hop Fields and Income for Aboriginal Workers

In June 1899, the story of Kwelth-Elite, a female Aboriginal slave, appeared in the California-based magazine the *Overland Monthly*.[1] The narrator began with a description of morning bustle on the Seattle waterfront, "at an hour when an excursion train was about pulling out for Snoqualmie Falls and the hop-fields." A sea of people confronted her: "The sidewalk for half a block in front of the station was occupied by a crowd of Northern Indians, who had come hundreds of miles for the hop-picking in their high-prowed canoes, like Egyptian galleys." Kwelth-Elite, or "Proud Slave," stood out among the crowd. She was accompanied by her owner, "a dreadful old woman who fiercely resented all the new fangled ways and notions of the younger generation." But the old woman needed "the Boston Man's money to buy the Boston Man's goods," and so had "brought her slave to earn it in the Boston Man's hop-fields." The presence of the White narrator was typical: "For in the days when a hop-field was a fortune, the Snoqualmie Hop Ranch was the largest single field in the world, and the people came from afar, on excursion tickets, to watch the hop-pickers." Kwelth-Elite's laborious life as a slave became intolerable when her owner's grandson threatened sexual assault. In desperation, Kwelth-Elite sought out the "magic doctor of the Upper Sound, who had come to the picking rendezvous, bringing all his familiar *Me-sahtch Tamahnahwis* (evil spirits) and *Tsi-at-cos* (nocturnal demons) along with him." This shaman was no hop picker. "He had not come to the hop-harvest to labor with his hands, but to gather in the shekels of the credulous, and was filling his coffers to bursting." According to the narrator, "not only did the red men from all sections consult him, but many of the white pickers and visitors willingly paid his somewhat high fees to satisfy their curiosity, if for no other motive." Kwelth-Elite paid the shaman's expensive fee not with hop-picking wages (which presumably went to her owner) but with another source of income available to hop pickers. She used "the one treasure she had acquired in her lifetime—a silver dollar given her the week before by a kodak fiend to induce her to pose for him." In exchange for the dollar, the shaman told Kwelth-Elite that she could do away with her enemy by crossing his heart three times with a charred stick. Kwelth-Elite carried out this task, struggled with her tormentor on a granite abutment above Snoqualmie Falls, and sent him over the edge to his death, much as Chief Seattle was said to have done to a Yakima war party.[2]

By this time, the hop harvest was finished, and "the hop-pickers from the north returned to Seattle and camped on the beach a short distance from the town." They "went to and fro in their canoes, trading and junketing for a while before returning to their far country." Kwelth-Elite's owner meanwhile lay dying, suspicious that the slave had killed her grandson. From her deathbed, the old woman commanded that Kwelth-Elite be buried alive beside her corpse.[3] The narrator happened upon the scene and rescued Kwelth-Elite just as she lay in the grave next to her dead mistress. Kwelth-Elite proceeded to "serve with ardent devotion for some years in the family of one of her deliverers, until she married a prosperous half-breed rancher on the Puyallup reservation."

Even in condensed form, this fictionalized account of the annual Aboriginal hop migration to western Washington rings with the romanticized language of the vanishing Indian. But it would be a mistake to dismiss this story as wistful fabrication. It contains a remarkable degree of historical accuracy: the profitability of the hop industry and its importance for Aboriginal elites, the large numbers of pickers from afar, the sightseers on excursion tickets, the shaman's presence, the income earned from a sight-seeing "kodak fiend," and perhaps even the role of slave labor. Each of these details was a feature of late-nineteenth-century hop harvests in Puget Sound. The story is representative in another sense too. The contradictory relationship between its form and content—it uses the tragic trope of the vanishing Indian to recount the participation of Aboriginal people in modern wage labor—mimics the attitude of non-Aboriginal colonial society, which saw signs of imminent extinction in every aspect of Aboriginal life.

The Puget Sound hop fields are fertile ground for studying Northwest Coast Aboriginal economy and culture in the late nineteenth century. Trade goods, smuggled liquor, and fugitives from the law were all passengers in the canoes that converged in Puget Sound for the hop harvest after the close of the major salmon canning season. Wages, of course, were a key motivation for going to the fields. But at the same time, hop picking fit within larger indigenous agendas. The journey to Puget Sound afforded an array of opportunities to earn money trading, selling goods, gambling, and providing services not unlike the shaman's in the Kwelth-Elite story. Just as important, Aboriginal people traveled south for reasons unrelated to the White economy. They gathered with friends and relatives and exchanged goods and information. These gatherings were embedded in local Aboriginal politics and culture. When migrant workers traveled, they brought their practices and priorities with them.

Although hops have medicinal purposes, their primary use has long been as a preservative and flavoring in beer. The hop industry came to western Washington in the 1860s, when pioneer agriculturalists planted hops in the Puyallup and White River valleys and on the Snoqualmie Prairie above Snoqualmie Falls in King County. Hops quickly became a hallmark of Washington's agricultural promise and a promotional tool for investors and developers. When the Northern Pacific Railroad created its exhibit for the Chicago World's Fair in 1893, it included Washington hops in its display. Railroad officials chose wisely; the hops won an international agricultural award.[4]

Hop farming was capital- and labor-intensive. Farmers planted runners from the roots of established plants in the spring. Growing vines needed to be trained and tied to tall poles, eight to sixteen feet high. By August, the vines hung heavy with the sticky yellow cones to be harvested. Harvested hops needed to be dried as soon as possible in a hop kiln, or their quality diminished. By 1888 there were 2,000 acres of hops in the Puyallup Valley; 60 acres was considered a large farm.[5] A different pattern developed in King County, where the Snoqualmie Hop Growers' Association planted 350 acres of hops on what was reputed to be the largest hop farm in the world and was certainly the largest in Washington.[6] Even a few acres of hops could prove lucrative for farmers.[7] But it was a risky enterprise, and the hop market was highly speculative. Wherever commercial production took root, the same pattern recurred: economic fortunes for some and economic ruin for others.[8] On the world export market, where demand was inelastic and the price out of growers' control, prices fluctuated wildly—even within the same season—from 18 cents to $1.08 per pound.[9] This boom-bust pattern led to apt comparisons with the gold rushes of the nineteenth century.

10. Family of Aboriginal hop pickers in Puget Sound, ca. 1890–93. Negative NA 4189, Special Collections, University of Washington Libraries.

By 1910, an aphid (*phorodon humuli*) infestation had destroyed the hop industry in western Washington for good. The expense of effective pest control rendered the Puget Sound industry untenable. Hop fields subsequently expanded in the Yakima area of eastern Washington where the drier climate offered protection from the louse. Hop migrations remained an important part of life for many Aboriginal people who shifted their destination to the hop fields of eastern Washington. Others continued their annual migrations to western Washington to work instead in commercial berry fields.

Some White and Chinese workers picked hops in Puget Sound, but the overwhelming majority of pickers were Aboriginal people from Washington, British Columbia, and Alaska. Extended families converged on the hop fields every August. Elderly men and women worked alongside young children, but the bulk of the labor force consisted of women. It was this majority, at least in some cases, that decided whether and where a family would

11. Aboriginal hop pickers in Puget Sound, ca. 1900. Children worked in the fields alongside their parents and grandparents. Image 90.45.11, Museum of History and Industry, Seattle.

pick.[10] When they did not pick hops, Aboriginal men worked elsewhere on the farm or hunted and fished in the vicinity.[11]

In 1885, an Indian agent, W. H. Lomas, reported that 6,000 Aboriginal people from British Columbia were away in the hop fields of Washington Territory.[12] If his estimate was close to accurate, an astonishing one quarter of the Aboriginal population of British Columbia took part in the migration.[13] From the hop industry's early days, Washington growers explicitly recruited thousands of pickers from British Columbia, often looking to cannery workers at the end of the salmon season.[14] The journey was familiar to many Aboriginal people from British Columbia and Alaska who had traveled to Puget Sound annually to work in sawmills and at other wage work since the 1850s. They came south by canoe or steamer, which pleased growers who otherwise bore the cost to bring workers from Oregon on the Northern Pacific Railroad.[15]

Growers expressed a racial as well as an economic preference for Aboriginal pickers. Anti-Chinese public opinion excluded Chinese workers from the industry and sometimes garnered Aboriginal workers higher wages.[16] In Tacoma's anti-Asian riots of 1885, White residents evicted Chinese residents and destroyed their property. This racial violence endangered Indians too. In 1886, Indian hop pickers along the White River fled anti-Chinese violence with the assistance of a local farmer.[17] Anti-Chinese sentiment also took root in the fields themselves. After a farmer in Issaquah hired Chinese pickers in 1885, a group of Whites accompanied by several Indians ordered the farmer to send the Chinese pickers back to Seattle. The farmer refused, and the vigilantes shot into the tents where thirty-seven Chinese workers slept, killing three men and wounding three others. A jury later acquitted the gunmen.[18] Snoqualmie tribal accounts relate that the Indian men who took part in this episode "were fighting to protect their families' income from foreigners."[19] Faced with a shortage of Aboriginal pickers in 1888, and fearing a repetition of the events of 1885, the territorial government offered transportation subsidies to White pickers in an attempt to prevent farmers from turning to Chinese labor.[20] Despite this, Aboriginal workers continued to dominate the labor force.

Pickers were paid a dollar for each box—usually fifteen bushels—they filled. Hop picking was hard work and filling a single box kept an experienced picker in the fields from sunup to sundown. Families could fill two or three boxes a day if they worked collectively. Inexperienced pickers struggled to fill one box in a day, especially before they learned to pick into

12. Aboriginal hop pickers in Puget Sound, ca. 1900. Pickers commonly earned one dollar for each wooden box that they filled with hops. Negative NA 865, Special Collections, University of Washington Libraries.

smaller baskets or containers until they had enough to fill the box. It was otherwise impossible to fill the big boxes as the weight of hops piled on top compressed those lower down.

While most Aboriginal people who came to the fields worked as pickers, the segmented labor force offered select positions to some Aboriginal men. "Hop bosses" played a crucial role in the industry. When Skagit man John Fornsby worked as a hop boss, he supervised the pickers and took responsibility when workers misbehaved.[21] Unlike pickers, hop bosses were paid on a seasonal or daily basis. In 1904, Thomas Leadman, a Canadian-born immigrant to the United States who ran two hop farms in the White River Valley, paid "Indian boss" Chester Wanderhard three dollars per day for sixteen and a quarter days, for a total of forty-nine dollars.[22] If Wanderhard's salary was typical, work as a hop boss was lucrative.

The pole puller was another important position in the fields. Described by one writer as the "aristocrats of the company," pole pullers also earned more than pickers. On the Leadman farm, their wage was $1.75 a day.[23]

These men uprooted the towering vertical poles of hop vines and laid them horizontally so pickers could reach the hops. When pickers finished a vine they yelled "pole man!," and he would come lay down another pole. Pullers thus partially controlled pickers' productivity by affecting both the rate of progress and the allocation of vines. Their discretionary power made them subject to accusations of favoritism. According to Arthur Wellington Clah, a, Tsimshian, Haida men monopolized this position at the Snoqualmie hop farm. Clah complained that Haida pole pullers allocated the most plentiful, and thus most profitable, vines to Haida pickers and left lower-yield vines for Tsimshian and other pickers. In this instance, the Haida advantage might have derived from familial connections: the sister-in-law of one of the farm's owners was Haida.[24]

Hop bosses and pole pullers occupied the top of a labor hierarchy; slaves may have occupied the bottom. Although evidence is slight, the possibility exists that Aboriginal masters put slaves to work in the hop fields. Such use of slave labor was not unprecedented, and one scholar of Northwest Coast slavery believes that Whites employed Aboriginal slaves more than they realized. Accounts exist of Aboriginal slaves being hired out to pack furs, paddle canoes, and sell sex.[25] One account describes a Twana man who charged White men five dollars for sex with his female slaves; another, dated to the 1860s, tells of a Skokomish man who put his slave to work in a sawmill for him.[26] Slaves typically accompanied their masters on long journeys, so the travel required was no deterrent to using slave labor in the hop fields. The story of Kwelth-Elite captured many aspects of the hop harvest extraordinarily well: the slave laboring in the hop fields for her owner may be another of its truths.

Living conditions at hop camps were an important consideration when potential pickers decided where to work. Some farmers built houses for laborers. The Snoqualmie Hop Ranch had a dozen houses for Aboriginal families who worked on the premises year round.[27] On farms in the Puyallup Valley, some pickers lived in tiny temporary huts. More commonly, pickers erected tents or makeshift structures themselves. They brought rolls of canvas sheeting or woven mats and located wood for the frames once they arrived at the fields. Some Aboriginal people found the living arrangements substandard—even uncivilized. When government officials proposed removing the Twana to the Puyallup reservation, the former Twana sub-chief Big John visited Puyallup, "partly to pick hops, and partly to see how the Indians there were getting along." Big John found these

13. Aboriginal hop pickers and a "pole-puller" in the White River Valley. Pole pullers earned more than pickers and held positions of power in the fields. Negative A. Curtis 00438, Special Collections, University of Washington Libraries.

14. Camp of Aboriginal migrant hop pickers in the White River Valley. Negative A. Curtis 00442, Special Collections, University of Washington Libraries.

people living in "small huts, not like our houses, or even barns, but more like chicken coops, while we have houses and are civilized."[28]

Pickers also had to consider the availability of provisions. When Clah and his family arrived to pick hops on the Cedar River, they found the situation lacking: "Place looks like empty no potatoese turnips cabbages [c]arrot onions all nothing to our use." There were only hops, and these they could not eat: "Only 20 acres hops. no good to eated." The family decided they could do better: "So we keep think to moving were the place for food." Clah sent "the boys" to the White River Valley to procure food and look for other work. After a few weeks at Cedar River, Clah and his group paid three dollars for a ten-mile wagon trip to the White River Valley, where they began work on a hop farm owned by P. C. Hayes.[29]

Careful evaluation of living conditions at the hop fields was more than a matter of assessing comfort. Disease was a constant threat. Some seasons, people stayed away altogether for fear of infection.[30] Health problems were inherent in the structure of the camps. Even the best-intentioned growers had difficulty maintaining a sanitary environment for thousands of workers concentrated in a small space for a month's time.[31] Infant mortality under such conditions was high. The son of a Cowichan man, Charlie Meshel, born just six weeks earlier in the hop camp, died in October 1889. Meshel wrote to Lomas from Kent, Washington, and asked him to tell his relatives that the "baby is dead the baby is 6 weeks old and has been sick ever since he was born he died on Wednesday evening at 4.o clock." Meshel's wife was also "very sick" and "very [sad] since she lost here baby."[32]

There could have been any number of causes for the child's death. Measles was a likely one. In 1887 and 1888, measles afflicted thousands of pickers from Vancouver Island and the north coast and took an especially high toll among children. Some pickers were too sick to travel home; others died on the way. Those who made it back to their respective winter villages spread the epidemic throughout their communities.[33]

Indian agents attempted to vaccinate Aboriginal people before they commenced their annual summer travel, but many still left home unprotected.[34] This left them vulnerable not only to disease but to quarantine restrictions. To avoid quarantine, homeward-bound pickers asked growers or Indian agents for letters confirming their good health. In other years, Cowichan pickers worried that quarantine restrictions would prevent them from reaching the hop fields.[35]

Hop picking carried health risks aside from epidemic disease. Some pickers developed painful rashes on their hands and faces in reaction to the hops.[36] Damp, rainy days spent in the fields caused other problems. Pickers from Kuper Island arrived home in November 1888 with colds and rheumatism, and in 1891, several young Cowichan men "died from the effects of severe colds contracted by exposure at the Canneries and Hop Fields."[37] Their deaths are grim reminders that it did not take an epidemic to bring death to late-nineteenth-century communities.

Given the prevalence of disease, the presence of Aboriginal medicine men, healers, and shamans in the hop camps is not surprising. At the hop camps, healers found patients in need with the resources to pay. Andy Wold, who grew up on his father's hop farm in Issaquah, remembered visiting the cabin of an Aboriginal worker who was reportedly dying. When they entered the room, "Dr. Bill," a medicine man from Lake Sammamish, was at work. The sick man lay in the middle of the floor surrounded by a group of Indians pounding short pieces of wood together. Dr. Bill knelt at the man's side, sucked blood from his left breast, and spat it out on the floor. The following week, Andy Wold recalled, "the dying man we saw that night was up and working."[38]

From his days as hop boss at Puyallup, John Fornsby tells a similar story about a Nuu-chah-nulth healer. When a man named Johnnie Joe got a salmon bone lodged in his throat, Fornsby gave him ten dollars and told him: "You had better go get that West Coast fellow. He will cure you." The man

> sang a curing power song. Ladies came and helped him. That man worked with his mouth. He sang. He sucked that thing out on the outside of the throat. He didn't work hard. He pulled the bone outside. He got the bone out and showed Johnnie Joe it was a salmon bone. He asked him, "You all right?"

Johnnie Joe answered in the affirmative and paid the fee. Ten dollars was a lot of money—the equivalent of ten days' picking wages. As Fornsby put it, "Gosh, he made money fast."[39] This may have been doubly true if, as the story of Kwelth-Elite suggests, not only Aboriginal pickers "but many of the white pickers and visitors willingly paid his somewhat high fees to satisfy their curiosity."[40]

Growers had reason to pay attention to their workers' health. Vines ripened in late August or early September and had to be picked within three or four weeks to prevent mildew, frost, or over-ripening. This required a substantial labor force and every grower needed workers at the same time. Finding enough workers was always a problem. Farmers could not hope to draw the required number of pickers from local residents alone.[41] Between 2,500 and 4,000 pickers were required in the Puyallup Valley and an equal number on the Snoqualmie Hop Ranch.[42] Local periodicals expressed farmers' anxiety: "The question of questions with the hop growers is, Will enough come? If so, will they arrive in time? From a supposed short supply of help timid growers become scared and begin to bid up and run after fresh arrivals."[43] The famous naturalist John Muir believed that labor was the primary factor limiting the growth of the hop industry in western Washington.[44]

Hop growers had a variety of methods for attracting Aboriginal laborers. Sometimes they used Indian agents as conduits into Aboriginal communities. C. O. Bean of Puyallup wrote to Indian agent Lomas in July 1889, and promised favorable conditions for the nearly one hundred pickers he needed: "The hop yards are within one mile of the Puyallup R.R. Station. My hops will be heavy but clean. Some of them will be early and other late giving employment from first to last. A good camp ground is easily had with good spring water and plenty of wood."[45] Many growers, such as William Lane of Alderton, hoped to attract the same pickers year after year. In 1888, Lane wrote to Lomas asking George and Mary Siltamult to come pick hops at the end of August.[46] Three years later, Lane asked Lomas to relay another message to George and Mary:

> I wish you would see George & young indians and ask them if they are coming with there indians to pick hops for me this year tell George that I sent a leter to him some time ago telling him that I want to comense the first of September . . . say to him to tell the woman with the half-breed children to come . . . and the felow that got the plow to come and bring all his foalks.

Lane lured returning pickers with two dollars additional "booty" and eventually offered to pay Lomas a commission if he persuaded George and Mary to come earlier than usual.[47]

On occasion, Aboriginal pickers from British Columbia wrote home from Washington telling relatives where to find them and how many people to bring. In 1884, Cowichan man William Roberts sent a letter to "Brother Charley" telling him to start for Washington as soon as he received the letter: "I want you to bring 55 pickers with you fifty five. I am going to work for Mr. Beckett at Orting where we picked hops last year. you will find me at Tacoma where I was last year."[48]

Growers also made formal arrangements with labor agents or hop bosses, some White, others Aboriginal. The agents traveled to Seattle, Tacoma, and on occasion farther afield to recruit the necessary labor. Recruiting could be as easy as showing up at the right place at the right time. When would-be pickers traveled long distances from home to Puget Sound, as Clah did in 1891 and 1899, they could expect to be met by labor agents recruiting arrivals off the steamers from the north.[49] As enticement, recruitment agents arranged and paid for workers' transportation to the fields, which could be both expensive and complicated.[50] The trip to the Snoqualmie Hop Ranch, for example, entailed either a stagecoach ride on rough roads or a combined water-land journey crossing Lake Sammamish, poling through Squak Slough, and crossing Lake Washington.[51] Hop bosses sometimes assembled teams that moved from farm to farm during the season. "When we got picking hops in Puyallup, they moved us up to Nisqually and then to Chehalis. We kept on going," recalled John Fornsby. Hop bosses also recruited for more than one farmer at a time. Fornsby remembered that he "had a pretty good boss, Quarry, from Puyallup," and that "Jimmy Pinkums was another man who wanted me to get pickers."[52]

For most growers, Aboriginal men like John Fornsby with extensive kin and community connections were critical links to the Aboriginal labor pool. Fornsby's hereditary ties with Coast Salish communities on both sides of the border enhanced his ability to find workers. Not only did these ties give him a pool from which to draw, they actually drew potential workers to him. One elderly woman brought her grown sons to Fornsby at Chehalis, because "they had found out that I got pickers." The woman shook hands with Fornsby and identified her lineage: "'I am one of the tribe of kwaskedib, Snatlem. My mother was Snatlem's sister.'" Realizing that the woman "had found from my name that I belonged to her relatives," Fornsby replied, "I heard about your mother, that Squakson Indians married her. I knew it."[53]

The largest hop farm, the Snoqualmie Hop Ranch required the largest pool of laborers. One of the ranch's owners, Henry Emmanuel Levy, did much of the recruiting himself, paying annual visits to his former home of Victoria, British Columbia, where he hired between twelve and fifteen hundred pickers.[54] It may seem surprising that the largest recruitment effort did not use Aboriginal hop bosses as other fields did. But Levy had an extended Aboriginal kin network of his own on which to draw. His brother's wife, Emma Levy, was Haida. Without this connection, Henry Levy would undoubtedly have had difficulty recruiting so many pickers.

Aboriginal laborers were well aware of growers' dependence on them. They enjoyed a seller's market in which growers scrambled to hire enough pickers.[55] Under these conditions work stoppages were an effective method of labor protest. Halfway through the 1877 season, for example, pickers struck to demand higher pay.[56] In 1903, pickers on the Overlock farm in Kent went on strike when the boxes appeared larger than the usual size.[57] Work stoppages during the peak of the harvest put the growers' entire crop in jeopardy. The year after the 1877 strike, local residents organized a militia to keep order among the crowd of Aboriginal workers assembled for the harvest, though there is no indication that the militia was deployed.[58] Growers could not afford to be too heavy-handed, as they had few alternate sources of labor, especially once the harvest began. Strikers on the Overlock farm were back at work the following day, presumably at an increased rate per box or with smaller boxes.[59] Some strike efforts may have suffered from division among workers rather than crackdowns by farmers. An attempted strike on the Snoqualmie Hop Ranch failed, for example, when pickers refused to follow the leadership of a Haida instigator.[60]

Lucrative wages were only one reason to come to the hop fields. The thousands of Aboriginal people who responded to farmers' needs for a flexible migrant labor force found that they also satisfied the desires of White audiences in search of Indian spectacles. A thriving tourist industry accompanied the Puget Sound hop harvest from its inception in the 1870s through the turn of the century. As early as 1874, a Puyallup newspaper remarked that "the Valley has been exceedingly lively during the season of picking, occupying the past two weeks, and has been visited by very many from town."[61] When John Muir visited the Snoqualmie Hop Ranch in the late nineteenth century, he listed the hop fields as among the premier tourist attractions in the Puget Sound area.[62]

When the hop pickers traveled to the fields, sightseers followed close behind, providing Aboriginal people with additional opportunities for income. The fictional narrator who watched Kwelth-Elite board the train for the hop fields was typical of many non-Aboriginal people of the day for whom Indian hop pickers were a spectacle, not of a modern wage labor force that fueled production of a world-export crop but of a disappearing traditional way of life. Many agreed that the hop pickers presented "a most picturesque sight, and one long to be remembered."[63]

Hundreds of tourists a day converged on rural towns like Puyallup and the surrounding hop fields, traveling from Seattle or Tacoma in carriages and on the frequent interurban passenger trains.[64] The interurban electric cars between Tacoma and Puyallup ran daily from 10 a.m. to 8 p.m. and charged twenty-five cents for a round trip. The Northern Pacific also ran eighteen passenger trains per day for the fifteen-minute ride between Tacoma and Puyallup.[65] These trips to the country were typical tourist excursions of the period. The relatively cheap fares on the interurban trains and electric streetcars meant that the experience crossed class boundaries. As one historian aptly put it, the electric car was "the poor man's carriage."[66]

Day-trippers turned vacationers when hotels opened at or near the hop farms. A tourist hotel was built in Puyallup in 1891.[67] From there, guests

15. Meadowbook Inn, Snoqualmie, ca. 1895. The inn attracted boosters, photographers, and sightseers alike to the Snoqualmie Hop Ranch. Negative 13164, Special Collections, University of Washington Libraries.

drove out in carriages to the surrounding farms to see the fields and pickers. The less accessible Snoqualmie Hop Ranch opened a hotel even earlier. The hotel was part of developers' attempts to increase the ranch's accessibility by attracting a railway line. In 1886, they built a three-story, twenty-two-room hotel facing the river. Surrounded by an orchard, lawn, and flower beds, the hotel became a popular destination for visiting businessmen and summer vacationers. Investors representing the Seattle, Lake Shore and Eastern Railway stayed at the hotel in 1888 and were suitably impressed. Snoqualmie Valley not only got its railway line but, reportedly, one of the state's nicest railway depots too.[68] The railway facilitated the growth of a summer resort, but more important for growers, it replaced the cumbersome journey by road and water formerly necessary to carry pickers to work and hops to market.

Aboriginal hop pickers were at the center of this convergence of urban tourists.[69] Muir found they made "a lively and merry picture in the field, arrayed in bright, showy calicoes, lowering the rustling vine-pillars with incessant song-singing and fun. Still more striking are their queer camps on

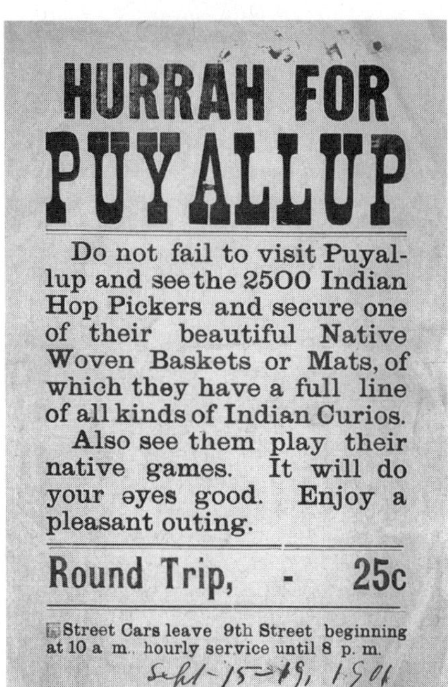
HURRAH FOR PUYALLUP

Do not fail to visit Puyallup and see the 2500 Indian Hop Pickers and secure one of their beautiful Native Woven Baskets or Mats, of which they have a full line of all kinds of Indian Curios.

Also see them play their native games. It will do your eyes good. Enjoy a pleasant outing.

Round Trip, - 25c

Street Cars leave 9th Street beginning at 10 a. m., hourly service until 8 p. m.

16. Flyer, 1901. Negative 1903.1.60, Washington State Historical Society, Tacoma.

the edges of the fields."[70] Contemporary accounts praised the hop fields as colorful spectacles and ethnographic opportunities. The laborers' camps were "always worth a visit and study," for they housed representatives of "many tribes and several ethnological families . . . the Siwashes of the Washington coast, the Chimsyans and Haidas of British Columbia, and the Thlinkets of Southeastern Alaska."[71] An encampment of almost 400 Cowichan from southern Vancouver Island on the Klaber hop farm was the "chief source of attraction to both visitors and residents" in the Puyallup Valley in 1903. According to the local newspaper, "people go there in groups and curiously watch the mode of life and habits of these fish-eating aborigines from Vancouver island."[72] The situation of these hop pickers bears surprising resemblance to the Kwakwa̱ka̱'wakw who lived in Chicago's "great aboriginal encampment."

Contrary to the narrator's claim that Kwelth-Elite "did not know that she was part of a wonderful picture,"[73] Aboriginal hop pickers were well aware of their audience. And though the tourists' gaze must have been an annoyance, it was also an opportunity. Many Aboriginal men who came to the hop camps worked not as pickers but as hunting and fishing guides for tourists. Other Aboriginal migrants used the hop harvest to reach what they knew would be a ready market of basket buyers and carving collectors. Printed flyers, likely issued by promoters and boosters of trains and hotels, gave free advertising to these hop pickers cum merchants. "Hurrah for Puyallup," proclaimed a 1901 flyer: "Do not fail to visit Puyallup and see the 2500 Indian Hop Pickers and secure one of their beautiful Woven Baskets or Mats, of which they have a full line of all kinds of Indian Curios. Also see them play their native games. It will do your eyes good. Enjoy a pleasant outing."[74]

The sale of handmade items provided important income for the Aboriginal pickers. Recognized by local papers as "experts in the art of weaving blankets and mats," Cowichan hop pickers sold split rush baskets for prices ranging from twenty-five cents "for the common ones . . . to $2.50 . . . for those made of more intricate workmanship."[75] Other baskets sold for as much as three dollars.[76] Basket making was skilled, time-consuming work, and three dollars was the equivalent of three dawn-to-dusk days in the fields.

Photographs were another favorite tourist souvenir that provided income for pickers. Professional photographers often paid pickers for permission to take their photo, as did some of the amateur photographers who abounded after the invention of the Kodak camera in the 1880s. For Aboriginal people, posing became a source of income in its own right.[77] Kwelth-Elite's story is again instructive: she paid the shaman's "rather high fee" with "a silver dollar given her the week before by a kodak fiend to induce her to pose for him."[78]

The vast number of photographs that survive of Aboriginal hop pickers indicate that the appearance of photographers in the hop fields was a regular occurrence. Edward S. Curtis began his career as a photographer in Seattle, and some of his first Aboriginal subjects were hop pickers. His younger brother, Asahel Curtis, was also a photographer who took his craft to the hop fields (see figures 13 and 14). Other late-nineteenth-century photographers, Frank laRoche and Thomas Prosch, were guests at the Snoqualmie Hotel.[79] These photographers used the hop season as an opportunity to capture images that met the public demand for photographs of Indians. Their photographs were commodities which they sold as cabinet cards, stereographs, and postcards. Postcards of hard-working pickers were mailed east by Washington residents who invited their New England kin to come west. Stereographs bearing likenesses of Quillayute hop pickers and even of Arthur Wellington Clah joined scenes of exotic locales like the

Egyptian pyramids in the baskets of stereograph sets that furnished Victorian parlors.[80] Later, scholars would use these photographs to illustrate general works about Aboriginal people of the Pacific Northwest.[81]

Photographs could bring added income to Aboriginal pickers even when the subjects were not paid. Images of hop pickers advertised an "authentic" Indian spectacle. Some of the non-Aboriginal people who saw these images in photographs or on postcards would eventually want to see the spectacle for themselves. Photography fed the fire of sightseers, just as sightseers fueled commercial photography.

In many ways, life at the hop camps was a de facto performance for Aboriginal pickers, who found themselves in front of an audience without setting foot on an actual stage. But pickers also catered to spectators by organizing formal performances. One day in 1891 when rain shut down picking on the Snoqualmie Hop farm, Haida workers staged a public dance performance motivated perhaps by a desire to make up the day's earnings. They drew one hundred spectators, each of whom paid a twenty-five-cent entrance fee.[82] Even if split among several performers, the twenty-five dollars earned would have exceeded a day's wages. Such dance performances may have been common. Farms with White pickers often held "hops" or dances in the evenings, and Aboriginal dancers may have provided added entertainment. By 1893, Aboriginal dances at the hop fields were common enough to

17. Postcard of Aboriginal hop pickers, ca. 1903. Negative 1970, Special Collections, University of Washington Libraries.

18. Stereograph of Quillayute hop pickers, 1904. This image was sold as number 16055 in an untitled series of "views" published by James M. Davis, in New York City and St. Louis. Image 19061, Museum of History and Industry, Seattle.

lend their name to the "hop-vine" dance performed by the Kwakwa̲ka̲'wakw at the Chicago Fair.[83]

While many hop pickers sold culture to tourists, others sold sex. Free and enslaved Aboriginal women from British Columbia had worked in the Puget Sound sex trade since the 1850s.[84] Frank and Henry Allen, Twana informants working for the anthropologist William Elmendorf in the 1940s, recounted that Nuu-chah-nulth men prostituted their wives to White men at the Puget Sound hop fields around the end of the nineteenth century.[85] Indian agent Pidcock believed that many Kwakwa̲ka̲'wakw women headed for the hop fields worked in the sex trade while in Puget Sound.[86] Some of these women likely returned home to host prestigious potlatches with their earnings.[87] Given the scarcity of such accounts, however, it is impossible to know whether prostitution was a regular feature of the hop field economy. The amount of control the women exercised or lacked likewise remains unclear.

As the rural spectacle of the hop fields indicates, late-nineteenth-century Puget Sound residents and tourists were inclined to see Aboriginal people as a romantic show. This proved as true within the city limits as beyond them. The tourist industry spawned by Aboriginal pickers in the hop fields had a thriving urban counterpart. Recall that the opening scene of Kwelth-Elite's story occurred as the narrator stood among a crowd on the Seattle waterfront watching the pickers headed for the Snoqualmie hop fields. In the late nineteenth century, Aboriginal encampments dotted the Seattle and Tacoma waterfronts—visible reminders of the porousness of reservation boundaries.[88] These shoreline encampments attracted photographers and pedestrian onlookers who sought colorful subject matter.[89] Aboriginal hop pickers were considered a sight to behold, whether in the fields or on their way there.

One early Seattle resident, Robert F. Farran, remembered hop-pickers-turned-vendors as a mainstay of the Seattle streetscape after the big fire of 1889.[90] And newspapers hailed the annual arrival of the hop pickers as a picturesque addition to the city scene. Headlines charted the cyclical migration of Aboriginal laborers: "Siwashes Again Seek the Street—Summer Weather Once More Brings Them Out of Hibernation and Makes Them City Features," "Great Influx of Indians—More Coming Up to Pick Hops than for Many Years Past," and "Indians Returning from Hop Fields."[91]

Aboriginal and non-Aboriginal people alike recognized specific urban sites where these sojourning migrants could be found. These coastal urban Indian villages contained a shifting composite of Aboriginal residents—some transient, others permanent—from the length of the Northwest Coast. In Tacoma, sightseers visited the tide flats to purchase baskets and curios.[92] In Seattle, the center of Aboriginal activity was the area known as "Ballast Island," located on the waterfront between the city's two busiest piers, Yesler's Wharf and the Oregon Improvement Company's King Street coal bunkers. This manmade peninsula was made of ballast dumped by ships arriving to pick up coal or lumber. It was where *Harper's Weekly* directed readers who wanted to see Indian hop pickers.[93] Aboriginal people first fashioned camps atop this pile of rocks and rubble in the 1870s, where they became a locally recognized exception to the 1865 ordinance that banned Indians from residing within Seattle's city limits. In 1891, waterfront companies, worried about the effect that the "clam-selling, garbage-raking remnants of a great people" might have on their public image, evicted Aboriginal people from the site.[94] General consensus held that Indians were disappearing, but for some people they were not disappearing quickly enough.

19. White spectators watching the camp of Aboriginal migrant workers on Ballast Island, Seattle, ca. 1892. The migrants fashioned tents, and a measure of privacy, out of their canoes. Negative NA 1508, Special Collections, University of Washington Libraries.

Despite the 1891 eviction, Indians continued to camp at Ballast Island through the mid-1890s, when they moved their camps south, farther away from the downtown core. Indian watchers and curio-hunters followed. The *Seattle Post-Intelligencer* informed its readers that this was now the place to glimpse Indians returning from the hop fields and to purchase samples of the "baskets, toys and trinkets" that Indian women made.[95] During the late 1890s, some hop pickers also camped north of Ballast Island on the Seattle waterfront.[96] The foot of Washington Street was another waterfront site for curio or clam selling, canoe racing, and Indian watching.[97] Perhaps desiring to escape the intrusive gaze of Indian watchers, other hop pickers, including some Nuu-chah-nulth from the west coast of Vancouver Island, stayed in rough cabins across the bay near the West Seattle grain elevators.[98] In exchange for greater privacy, these people endured the inconvenience of a longer commute to the urban tourist market.

Conditions at these encampments varied. Sometimes, there were basic cabins, as in West Seattle. On the Tacoma tide flats, Aboriginal people lived in "wooden houses, built after the style of the white man."[99] These were long-term structures, occupied perhaps by those who remained on the urban periphery through much of the year. For those who were more transitory, tentlike structures were common. As at the hop fields, tents were made of a variety of materials, ranging from cedar bark or rush mats to canvas sheeting. Some people erected their shelters on the ground; others used their canoes as the foundation over which they hung canvas or mats.[100]

Daring sightseers could venture into the waterfront camps themselves. But Aboriginal people did not simply wait to be watched. On the contrary, they set out in the mornings with wares from wherever they were camped. Those at the elevator site had to cross the bay either in their own canoes or on the Seattle ferry. By nine or ten in the morning, Aboriginal merchants occupied the busy downtown street corners along First and Second Avenues. They unpacked their wares from baskets and colored handkerchiefs: miniature carved canoes and paddles, woven mats and baskets, seal, elk and bear meat, animal pelts and skins, and freshly dug clams. One observer recalled that Aboriginal women brought "some of the finest needlework and beadwork, blankets and baskets one ever saw."[101] Women also took their wares door to door during their hop season visit to Puget Sound, trading baskets directly for food and clothing.[102]

Many writers attempted to represent these Aboriginal merchants as passive relics. They claimed that the "squaws [who] have small trinkets for sale . . . conduct their trade without spieling. The passer-by may take the goods or let them alone, according to inclination."[103] Such claims belie what we know about the experience and astuteness of Aboriginal people in trade. Indeed, such claims are typically embedded in the most heavily stereotyped descriptions dominated by the trope of inferior Indians giving way before a superior civilization. Writers whose work was less shaped by this trope, such as the one who identified Nuu-chah-nulth migrants and accurately described their style and technique of basketry, present more believable accounts of Aboriginal sellers. This writer described adroit merchants who could "quickly size up the situation" by distinguishing an Easterner from a Westerner and who would not hesitate to take greater advantage of the Easterner.[104] Sometimes young, English-speaking Aboriginal people bartered with buyers for the best price on behalf of the elderly carvers and weavers.[105] Robert Farran witnessed a different sort of incident between Aboriginal vendors and a group of customers. The tourists admired, handled, and priced many items but ultimately made no purchases. At this point, "a big buck Indian let out a grunt and said, 'Hyas Wa Wa; haylo chickamun,' which means, heap big talk, no money."[106] These experienced sellers had little patience with casual browsers.

Trips to the Puget Sound hop harvest provided Aboriginal people with a variety of economic opportunities. Wages from hop picking were only the most obvious. It was the non-Aboriginal inclination to view Aboriginal people as spectacles that provided the more wide-ranging, and possibly more profitable, income opportunities. This inclination was strong enough to mute the contradiction of supposedly authentic, primitive people harvesting a crop for distribution on the world market of a modern capitalist economy. It created a market for souvenirs of "vanishing," "authentic" Aboriginal culture. Such souvenirs took a variety of forms, from photographs and postcards to Indian curios, the memory of an Indian dance or a visit to a medicine man. Unlike the Kwakwa̲ka̲'wakw who went to Chicago, most hop pickers did not consciously choose to perform. Despite this, they often had an audience. The hop pickers were adept at making the most of these stylized interactions with non-Aboriginal society and at performing their culture in ways that non-Aboriginal observers expected. Whether in rural fields or on urban waterfronts, they turned opportunities for picking, posing, and performing to their best advantage. Vendors' impatience with Indian watchers who looked but did not buy is easy to understand. The income was badly needed, but the loss of privacy that resulted from constantly being cast "on stage" must have grated. Aboriginal people probably needed to vent this frustration as much as they needed the money. Sarcastic remarks that went over the head of potential customers could provide just this sort of outlet.[107]

Chapter Five

Harvest Gatherings: Aboriginal Agendas, Economy, and Culture

Indian watchers saw a romantic spectacle when they looked at Indian hop pickers, but spectacle encompassed only a fraction of these workers' lives. Migration to the hop fields was part of a larger indigenous network of economy, politics, and society that ensured Aboriginal survival. This network had little to do with the work of playing Indian for White spectators. Out of both necessity and preference, Aboriginal people wove their own agendas into their harvest journeys. One indication of these agendas is the extended time they spent on migration. The hop harvest lasted only three to four weeks, but Aboriginal hop pickers stayed away much longer. Pickers routinely spent a month or more on their way to the fields.[1] Postharvest travels could be similarly drawn out. In December 1890, for example, three months after the completed harvest, a Cowichan man named Nicholas was still living at the Snoqualmie Hop Ranch.[2] As the Kwelth-Elite story noted, pickers "camped on the beach a short distance from the town . . . trading and junketing for a while before returning to their far country."[3]

Most Aboriginal people lacked a single source of income upon which they could rely. They consequently spun themselves an economic safety net by moving between seasonal occupations.[4] This strategy characterized Aboriginal subsistence and trade long before White settlement, and Aboriginal people put it to work under the economic uncertainty of colonial capitalism. Though potentially high, income from the hop harvest fluctuated wildly from year to year. A bad year for growers meant a bad year for pickers. When wages at the hop fields fell, Aboriginal people sought other sources of income. When wages were high, workers used them to compensate for the shortfalls of poor fishing, canning, or sealing seasons. In relatively prosperous years, Aboriginal people probably traveled less.[5]

Given the economic uncertainty, competition for work could be intense. This was particularly true at the end of the harvest when the demand for labor fell off, creating a glut. A group of Haida faced this situation in October 1886, when they stopped to look for work in Port Townsend on their way home from the hop fields. They telegraphed a farmer on Whidbey Island and offered to dig potatoes for him. Owing to this "clever bit of enterprise," the Haida not only "secured the job ahead of their rivals" but also surprised a contemporary observer with their "appreciation of the telegraph"—presumably because the observer considered the telegraph modern technology unsuited to primitive Indians.[6] In this instance, the money earned digging potatoes likely supplemented the Haida's harvest income. A year earlier, when the hop harvest had failed, this sort of work might have been the only thing between these families and a hungry winter.

Difficulties suffered by the Kyuquot from the west coast of Vancouver Island were typical. Some who had left for the hop fields in July 1885 returned in August with the bad news that farmers were paying only seventy-five cents per box, rather than the standard dollar.[7] The price of hops fell so low that growers left most of the crop unpicked.[8] By early October, Kyuquot who had remained in Washington faced starvation. They averted disaster only by finding a "big seam" of clams in the Sound, which they sold in Seattle. They returned home in January 1886, with enough wealth to host a potlatch at which they distributed 180 blankets, five canoes, ten iron pots, eight guns, twelve trunks, and five dollars cash. These Kyuquot more than compensated for the loss of hop picking wages. Others were less fortunate. Throughout the winter, groups of three or four canoes continued to return home to the west coast of Vancouver Island with little or nothing to show for their time in Puget Sound.[9]

Similar situations prevailed when other mainstays of Aboriginal wage earning fell short. Stó:lō people on the Lower Fraser struggled when the fishery failed, the Kwakwa̱ka̱'wakw suffered the decline of the fur trade, and the Nuu-chah-nulth endured the vicissitudes of the sealskin market. All turned to hop picking.[10] And, if hops too failed, groups might spend the winter in Puget Sound selling goods or digging clams.[11] Success in this economy required skill at piecing together diverse economic activities. Most years, this meant Aboriginal workers could rely on one source of income if others failed.

When Aboriginal people found themselves in dire straits, it was because multiple sources of income failed in a single year. Although some Indian agents implied that the Kyuquot were at fault for naively relying on a single and inherently unstable source of income, this was not the case. The 1885 fall in hop wages brought Kyuquot hop pickers to the brink of starvation because by the time they arrived in western Washington their other sources of income in British Columbia—sealing, procuring dogfish oil, and salmon canning—had each, one after another, already failed. The Kyuquot had taken a united stand against the drop in the value of fur seals in February 1885. After being offered $2.50 for each large fur skin, they decided not to go sealing at all. At the winter feasts, speakers instructed guests not to accept less than five dollars per skin. Some sealers broke solidarity when the price rose to four dollars per skin, but most focused instead on harvesting herring roe and rendering dogfish oil.[12] But the price of dogfish oil was down too. Even with skins at four dollars each, the Kyuquot earned only half of what they received from the same sources in the previous year.[13] Their difficulties were compounded by the fact that there was less work and lower wages at the canneries than usual.[14] In such a year, the hop fields were the last resort, and low wages there spelled disaster.[15]

Such difficulties were the inevitable accompaniment of integration into the boom-and-bust resource economy, and Aboriginal people had little choice but to weather them. This was particularly true for those in British Columbia, where the provincial government implemented land policy with the explicit design of propelling Aboriginal people into the marketplace.[16] But federal Indian agents in British Columbia invoked the volatility of wages in their efforts to convert Aboriginal people into farmers. They believed that migratory labor encouraged improvidence, and that agriculture was preferable to the "precarious help which may or may not be obtained from outside sources," such as hop fields or canneries. They failed to appreciate the work ethic of those who planted grain in the spring before leaving for the canneries and returned home to harvest it in the brief interval before hop season on the Sound.[17] Moreover, farming was itself precarious. Picking and canning wages saved many Aboriginal farmers from destitution after floods destroyed crops in the Fraser Valley in 1894.[18] Recovery was more difficult three years later when an early frost that destroyed the Fraser Valley potato crop coincided with a poor hop crop.[19]

Aboriginal people's seasonal movements were not always driven by need. In years when people were healthy and the "back-up" system worked well, the hop harvest and its adjunct enterprises were lucrative. Combined with fishing/canning income earned earlier in the summer, a profitable hop harvest could leave some workers with several thousand dollars at the end of September.[20] After a tiring summer's labor, many were in no hurry to return home until they had spent some of their hard-earned cash. They would often draw out their homeward journey, shopping for goods or gathering winter provisions along the way. Hannah Jensen, who lived on San Juan Island in the late nineteenth century, remembered Indians on their way home from hop picking who stopped to gather wild salal berries and pick apples from her family's orchards at Garrison Bay. Migrants also gathered reeds for basket making—perhaps with next year's hop-field tourists in mind.[21]

The apparent ease with which Aboriginal people traveled from British Columbia to the Puget Sound hop fields makes it easy to forget that they crossed an international border in the process. These crossings presented opportunities as well as problems. Some opportunities were economic, as Aboriginal people—or "intelligent Northern Indians" as the *Washington Standard* called them—incorporated unsanctioned international commercial trade—"smuggling"—into their travels.[22] One of the principal items "smuggled" across the line during this period was dogfish oil, an important commercial product and source of income for the Coast Salish and Nuu-chah-nulth since the 1850s. Demand for the oil came from coastal sawmills that used large quantities to lubricate their machinery.[23] Aboriginal fishers caught hundreds of fish at a time using single lines set with hundreds of herring-baited hooks. Nearly all the products of this industry were destined for sale in the United States at fifty cents a gallon.[24] Desire to stem this illicit trade prompted the placement of a customs inspector at Neah Bay in 1878.[25]

Liquor was another commodity that flowed illegally across the international boundary. Popular nationalist belief on each side of the border blamed the liquor trade on the lax morals of Indians across the line.[26] In fact, Aboriginal people carried alcohol in both directions. In 1878, an Aboriginal man from British Columbia brought a keg of liquor to the Clallam community at Elwha, while John Fornsby recounts that the Skagit "learned to drink whiskey" in Victoria from the Songhees. A Skagit man, in turn, was fined for possession of alcohol in a Cowichan village in 1887, and, in 1894, other Indians from Washington traded whiskey to the Hesquiat on the west coast of Vancouver Island. Kwakwaka'wakw migrants regularly imported whiskey and gin home from Puget Sound.[27]

Trading liquor was one thing; consuming it was another. Indian agent Lomas believed that Aboriginal migrants seldom spent their money on liquor.[28] Other accounts suggest that excessive drinking did occur during the harvest. A Twana subchief named Tatum told Myron Eells that he was "afraid of that which is covered overflowing with rum, for I have truly seen that there is plenty of whiskey there, and that is why I will not go to Puyallup at hop picking time again."[29] In 1885, a Nuu-chah-nulth man named Hayoutk reportedly died as a result of drunkenness in the Washington hop fields.[30]

When Aboriginal people were charged with alcohol-related or other offenses, the border crossing offered more than economic gain—it offered asylum. In 1884, for example, a number of Kyuquot escaped across the border to the hop fields after, as Indian agent Guillod reported, "some sixty of the tribe made forcible entry into [the priest's] house and three of them held him while the others released the boys," whom the priest had confined for failing to attend school.[31] A similar tactic worked for a group of Cowichan, wanted for exercising a murderous "reign of terror" on Saturna and Pender Islands in the Strait of Georgia, who evaded provincial prosecution by escaping to the U.S. islands.[32]

Though the border was an opportunity for some Aboriginal migrants, it was a hindrance for others. Customs was a common problem for hop pickers returning from the United States with newly purchased goods. In Victoria, on his way to the hop fields in August 1899, Arthur Clah noticed "custom house men opening every bodys bundle to found anything new come from USA."[33] He would have been right to take this as an omen of what awaited him on his own return journey, when customs officers confiscated goods unless the owners paid duty.[34] On at least one occasion, the Indian agent Lomas found himself in the contradictory position of explaining to two Cowichan men, Tair-Kertum and Workkomilt, why the harnesses they had brought from Washington were seized by customs. One of the men had purchased the harness with his hop wages; the other had received it in payment from the grower. The men presumably intended to use the harnesses to work their agricultural land, the very occupation Lomas incessantly stressed. Lomas intervened on the men's behalf and succeeded in having their harnesses returned to them, but only after they paid the duty.[35]

These examples aside, most Aboriginal people managed to transport goods without paying duty.[36]

Economic considerations were just one set of factors that influenced a family's decision to join the extended hop migrations. Families on the move wove political and cultural imperatives into their travel itineraries. The migratory cycles created large gatherings of Aboriginal people at centralized locations. In autumn 1891, for example, over 500 Aboriginal people from the North Coast and the Skeena River converged in Victoria on their way home.[37] Such bottlenecks offered opportunities to link labor travels with visits to extended kin and attendance at Aboriginal gatherings. Workers must have welcomed the days of festive enjoyment that punctuated the arduous cycle of migratory labor. The gatherings also served more specific —and sometimes contradictory—ends, both facilitating and undermining hereditary systems of status and rank.

Opportunities for gatherings were particularly significant in the context of colonial rule. During the late nineteenth century, colonial interventions made it more difficult to host and attend Aboriginal gatherings such as potlatches. Colonial boundaries were one reason. Colonialism had drawn lines dividing Aboriginal people from one another, an international line divided them into "Canadian" Indians and "American" Indians, while intranational lines divided them into "reservation" and "non-reservation" Indians. These lines hindered movement, curtailing not only personal freedom but cultural practice.

Government and missionary attempts to suppress the potlatch in Canada and the United Stated posed additional impediments. Migration was one way to evade colonial interference. In British Columbia and Washington alike, off-reserve mobility functioned as an "escape valve" that sometimes proved permanent.[38] The Squamish chief Simon Baker remembered the turn of the century as a time when "the church, you might as well say, ran the reserve. . . . Those who didn't want to accept that environment left the community. A lot of them moved to the States."[39] Hop-field migrations and the Kwakwa̱ka̱'wakw trip to Chicago could act as short-term escape valves. The mobility inherent in hop picking helped ensure that though colonial obstacles hindered, they failed to halt Aboriginal gatherings.

Chief Squiquoi, or Billy Barlow, devised an ingenious combination of labor and potlatch to circumvent the will of colonial officials. When Barlow wanted to host a potlatch in April 1904 on Whidbey Island, Indian agents prevented Indians from leaving their reservations unless they could produce proof of employment. Barlow solved the problem by giving "jobs" as potlatch gifts. Guests were paid "wages" for attending and taking part.[40] Four hundred people attended the potlatch in this way, some likely from across the border. Barlow was a cousin of Charlie Wilson, a Penelekut from Kuper Island in the Strait of Georgia.[41]

Ironically, the same migrant wage economy that helped Aboriginal people evade colonial control posed a third order of threat to Aboriginal gatherings. In the new industrial economy, salmon ran and hops ripened without regard to hereditary obligations. As wage labor became a necessity for more and more families, forgoing canning or picking wages became less likely. This could lead to difficulties, as it did on Vancouver Island in the mid-1880s, when a Nuu-cha-nulth chief struggled to find guests willing to attend his daughter's puberty potlatch. Puberty potlatches were among the most important of family events, and the presence of guests as witnesses was essential to maintain status in the community.[42] Chief Sayach'apis' had been preparing for years and had constructed a large post-and-beam house for the occasion. But when he and his emissaries delivered invitations at the Steveston canneries, the Songhees, Saanich, and Cowichan declined. "You are too late," they told him, "we are going to the hop fields."[43] Women traveling in a party of ten canoes gave a like reply on behalf of their group: "We might be late for the hops."[44]

These refusals were a serious slight. Chief Shonhin, who accepted the invitation, decried the others for shirking their responsibility to their ancestors and extended kin. "Fie on the tribes," he said, "I wonder if hops are their grandparents. . . . The tribes apparently have no sense for that which you are doing is important." Shonhin helped save Sayach'apis' from insult by distributing invitation sticks to his neighbors. He secured enough guests and Sayach'apis's "heart rejoiced" when he learned that "all the people were willing."[45]

Sayach'apis' was most certainly not the only chief to encounter difficulty when the wage economy conflicted with the hereditary order. Incorporating gatherings into the round of migrant labor addressed this problem. It turned the potential threat of the wage economy into an asset, while simultaneously fending off colonial interference. Hop picking was a reason to cross colonial lines while pursuing a goal acceptable to colonial officials:

wage labor. It created spaces away from the prying eyes of missionaries and government officials. It brought potential guests together in one place. And it put the wealth necessary for such gatherings into the pockets of potential hosts.

It is not surprising then to find that Aboriginal laborers commonly combined economic, political, and cultural activities. On Clah's way through Victoria to pick hops in August 1899, he made a point to "see all friends." On the return journey, he met not only other homeward-bound hop pickers but Aboriginal sealers returning from Japan.[46] Maybelle Cultee Thomas, a Quinault woman born in 1910, believed that for many people, including the large numbers who came to Alderton from Canada, one attraction of the hop fields was the chance to meet with others.[47] This social prerogative was sometimes reason enough to travel to the hop fields, even in seasons when pickers knew wages would be low.[48]

Clah's diaries describe the integrated pattern of labor and gathering. In 1899, he worked at a cannery in Rivers Inlet from the end of June until early August. During his time at the cannery, groups of Aboriginal workers came and went from social gatherings and weddings, often traveling by steamer with canoes in tow.[49] Clah traveled from the cannery to the hop fields, where he recorded a "flathead" (Salish) feast held on the Hayes hop farm attended by about 100 people. This may have been a mortuary feast, as Clah noted the death of a young man in the same diary entry.[50] Alternatively, there may have been no connection, and the host may have chosen the site to take advantage of the presence of extended kin or to evade interference by authorities. Perhaps the "hop vine dance" that the Kwakwa̱ka̱'wakw performed in Chicago derived from this sort of situation rather than from fieldside tourist performances.

Such explicit references to Aboriginal feasts at the hop camps are rare. But innumerable accounts exist of pickers importing elements of potlatches to the fields. Gambling, horse racing, canoe racing, and trading were all typically present at potlatch gatherings and hop harvests alike. Although the ethnographic record on potlatches focuses on displays of hereditary privilege and property distribution, contemporary descriptions of nineteenth-century potlatches sound, as the anthropologist Wayne Suttles notes, like "a grand extended picnic."[51] This is exactly how Dora Williams Solomon, a Lummi born in the 1890s, described the annual gathering at Gooseberry Point: "The Lummi Tribe a long time ago, they had a picnic and they called it potlatch."[52]

Gatherings and gambling had long gone together on the Pacific Northwest Coast.[53] Aboriginal hop pickers carried gambling games from their historic locations to the hop fields and back again. Aboriginal gambling games and non-Aboriginal card games were common evening diversions at the hop camps. For men who did not work in the hop fields, the chance of a windfall may have been the primary economic draw of the hop fields. For men and women who spent their days picking, these activities were entertainment that filled their evenings and days off.[54] Sometimes the hop fields reunited opponents who had begun matches at the Fraser River canneries earlier in the summer.[55] Migrants used their hop-picking wages to gamble once they returned home too.[56]

The central and southern Coast Salish played three main gambling games: one with round disks, one with bones, and one with dice made of beaver or muskrat teeth.[57] The disk and bone games were men's games, and the dice game was a women's activity. The disk game was the most popular and ritually significant game prior to White settlement, a fact underscored by its frequent appearance in oral narratives.[58] At intertribal hop field gatherings, the bone game, or slahal, in which one player guessed which of his opponent's hands held a marked game piece or bone, eclipsed the disk game in popularity and importance. Whether or not they came from Coast Salish villages, hop pickers were familiar with the bone game. Slahal was a local name and variant of "hand-games" played by Aboriginal peoples throughout the Northwest coast.[59]

The Coast Salish considered gambling a manifestation of relations with supernatural powers and believed supernatural intervention was essential for victory. Some took gambling as their profession. Shamans—who had obvious spirit power—were often successful gamblers.[60] Some players brought their own "personal gambling paraphernalia," which they treated as they did other ceremonial objects.[61] As Henry Allen, a Twana man, told W. W. Elmendorf: "You have to get a special vision for slaha'l. The gambler may see the slaha'l bones in his vision." Allen went on to describe how his cousin acquired slahal powers on his way home from hop picking at Puyallup. "He had no luck in the gambling at the hop picking. He lost everything and had to walk home. On the way he lay down by the road to sleep, and he got a slaha'l song from a hazel bush there."[62] The use of spirit power in gambling games was likely familiar to non-Coast Salish players too, as many Aboriginal peoples have long linked gambling to rituals, spirits, and oral histories.[63]

Onlookers played an important role. A "ritual audience" that could number in the hundreds sang songs invoking spirits to help their team leader. Every game had a spirit song, the singing of which was led by the individual who had received the song in a dream or vision.[64] Bets made by spectators augmented the spirit power from the songs.[65] At the hop fields, White sightseers often participated in these important sideline bets.[66]

The stakes could be high, particularly at intervillage matches, such as those at the hop fields. A list of commonly wagered items resembles a list of potlatch gifts. Players even bet their hop tickets, the stubs they received for filled boxes and handed in at the end of the week to receive their pay.[67] As Indian constable Jerry Meeker remarked, people "bet fishing tackle and anything thats loose."[68] The high stakes sometimes led to disputes. In one instance, Meeker intervened when a British Columbia chief won a large amount of money at cards from a Puyallup man at Orting. "I got all the money back for the Puyallup," remembered Meeker.[69] The highest stakes imaginable—human slaves—were sometimes exchanged too.[70]

Horse racing was another activity that generated excitement during the hop harvest. It had been popular among the Southern Coast Salish since they obtained horses in the late eighteenth century. By the end of the nineteenth century, most Puget Sound groups had their own race track.[71] As with gambling, the longstanding practice of pitting different tribes against one another continued at hop field horse races. In 1891, for example, Clah recorded the victory of the Klickitat over the Snohomish.[72] The presence of Clah, a Tsimpshian, further illustrates the contact that the hop camps created between geographically and culturally distant groups.

The horse races common at the Snoqualmie and Puyallup hop fields were a spectacle for White observers as well as for Aboriginal observers and participants. Horse races attracted large crowds every Sunday during the harvest and typically marked the finale of the picking season.[73] Aboriginal men rode and Aboriginal women reportedly dressed in their finest clothes to watch.[74] Sometimes Aboriginal women rode too, scandalizing Victorian observers by riding astride "Amazon" style and fulfilling Victorian expectations of savage Indians.[75]

Gambling and racing were popular among many Aboriginal and non-Aboriginal people, but reform-minded individuals saw them as evidence of moral decline. For critics, horse racing, gambling, and drinking were a triumvirate of vice that sprouted from the hop fields. The Reverend Myron Eells dubbed the popular racetrack near Puyallup "The Devil's Playground."[76] Some singled out the evils of Indian, rather than White, gambling as the problem.[77] Others drew judgment from the dual wellspring of race and class, condemning non-Aboriginal gamblers, whiskey traders, and "trashy whites generally."[78]

Canoe races were another activity that Aboriginal people incorporated into the labor cycle. Robert Farran of King County remembered postharvest canoe races in the late 1880s and early 1890s. Homeward-bound workers "held a 'potlatch,' going to some selected spot, where they prepared a great feast. This was indulged in by many tribes, having different kinds of sports and dancing and then the great canoe races—and such races having 12 to 14 men in a canoe and all paddling—a great sight."[79] As Farran's reminiscence suggests, canoe races were spectacles for White audiences. They were likewise chances to earn money. At one Fourth of July race in Washington, the prizes ranged from fifty-five dollars for first prize in the war canoe category to five dollars for third place in the women's and double-paddle canoe races.[80]

Spectacle aside, canoe races were also public affirmations of Aboriginal identity and community. During this period, canoe racing took on an importance independent of functions explicitly known as potlatches. While the colonial economy interfered with many Aboriginal cultural practices, it facilitated others, including canoe races. The greater degree of approval Whites granted this activity made canoe races easier to hold. Over the twentieth century, races became powerful reinforcements of social connections between participants.[81]

As with gambling, contestants divided themselves into American and Canadian Indians. This was especially true on national holidays. Aboriginal people from both sides of the border participated in canoe races at Victoria Day celebrations in British Columbia.[82] Washington Indians apparently won only rarely. In 1891, a forty-foot racing canoe christened "Greyhound" became the first Puget Sound canoe to beat British Columbia teams on Victoria Day.[83] Just as American Indians traveled north for Victoria Day, Canadian ones went south for the Fourth of July.[84]

Intra-Aboriginal trade also occurred at both hop fields and potlatches. This was an activity imbued with cultural as well as economic significance. Like gambling, trade was an integral part of potlatches.[85] Aboriginal networks extended from eastern Washington, west through Puget Sound and the Olympic Peninsula, up the coast of British Columbia through Haida

Gwaii and the Stikine River Valley, to southeastern Alaska. The array of indigenous goods traded included dishes made from mountain sheep horns, pipes, buffalo robes, baskets, dentalia, rattles, masks, and canoes.[86] The trade that had characterized early-nineteenth-century potlatches was augmented and, to some extent, replaced by trade at the hop fields.[87] Aboriginal people claimed this new trading space at the same time as colonial policies and capitalist markets disrupted long-standing patterns of Aboriginal interaction, potlatching, and trade.

By bringing gambling, racing, and trading to their temporary hop camps, Aboriginal pickers generated multiple points of continuity between their historical gatherings and capitalist wage-earning ones. The gathering itself was perhaps as important as the activities. By bringing together large numbers of Aboriginal people from afar, the hop camps perpetuated links between extended families. Indeed, to a certain extent the hop industry depended on the vitality of these links. Growers and labor recruiters relied upon them when they sought workers.

The varied connections between work and potlatch were especially significant for high-status Coast Salish. As elsewhere on the coast, Coast Salish potlatches were expressions of wealth and status that could last days or weeks. But among the Coast Salish, validation of status required an audience drawn from the extended kinship network of the intervillage community. Intervillage marriage and potlatch relations fostered connections between geographically separated kin rather than physically close but unrelated neighbors. The "upper class" was an intertribal community.[88] Thus travel had *always* been a prerequisite for maintaining Coast Salish status. When the Canada-U.S. boundary sliced intervillage communities in two, many of the required journeys became border crossings. Coast Salish, who traveled from British Columbia to Washington, reentered a familiar orbit of extended kin more than they entered a foreign country. High-status Coast Salish had especially good reason to participate in the hop-season migrations. They stood to lose their positions if they did not validate them before intervillage audiences.

The survival of intervillage ties among the Coast Salish can be read partly through genealogy. Family ties and marriages continued to cross reservation and international boundaries.[89] The pattern that Squamish man Alec Julian described for women in the 1950s who went to pick hops and berries in Washington was not new: "Quite a few girls go to the States, get married, never come back."[90] In the twentieth century, physically distant Coast Salish kin were drawn closer by modern technologies such as cars and telephones.[91] Hop picking was an earlier but no less "modern" means that facilitated the maintenance of intervillage ties.

The cultural practices that Aboriginal people enacted at the hop fields were about more than continuity. The hop fields were places of change, where new forms of intervillage community coalesced. Here again, John Fornsby's experience as a labor recruiter is illustrative. Although Fornsby drew pickers from his extended kin, he also recruited workers from "those people back of Seattle [who] talked a different language." Fornsby had no previous contact with these groups: "All I saw of those people was when I went hop-picking." This was likewise true of Aboriginal people from the west coast of Vancouver Island and the "islands off Vancouver." Fornsby recalled: "they came down in the early days when they first raised hops down at Puyallup. They never came before. I never saw them when I was a kid. They just came down when they raised hops. They are just the same kind of people as us, only they speak a different language."[92] Fornsby's comment reveals a kernel of common identity sprouting from collective experience. In his identification with others who "are just the same kind of people as us, only they speak a different language," Fornsby suggests how interaction at the hop fields might have engendered broader forms of Indian identity. Other suggestions of shifting identity are apparent in the varied alignments of gambling and canoe-racing teams, as participants lined up under the banners of nation-states or according to older local or intervillage ties. The emergence of slahal songs in the late nineteenth century that set lyrics in British Columbia Aboriginal languages to Puget Sound melodies is further evidence of the creative transformations that grew from interactions between Aboriginal people from both sides of the border.[93] Pan-Indian identities are commonly seen as having taken root only later in the twentieth century, often as products of boarding and residential schools. But identities were dynamic long before the twentieth century. The beginnings of pan-Indianism certainly date to at least the late-nineteenth-century collective experiences in hop fields, canneries, and even the "great aboriginal encampments" at places like the Chicago World's Fair.[94]

Settlers and colonial officials worried when they saw evidence of the sense of common cause expressed by Fornsby. White concerns about collective Aboriginal resistance were easily fanned. Gatherings were occasions when not only identities might be molded but political information might be exchanged and political action initiated. Increased interaction between groups of people facilitated the flow of information and ideas. Colonial officials worried about what Aboriginal people discussed when they gathered. Indian agent Lomas knew that in 1885 political issues such as "the Metlakatla Land troubles and . . . the Northwest Rebellion have been talked over at all their little feasts and not often with credit to the white man."[95] He worried that the circulation of such information among Aboriginal people was dangerous in a province where Aboriginal title was unacknowledged and Aboriginal rights were increasingly disregarded: "Although tribal feuds and jealousies have for long kept distant bands from uniting the present labor fields throw the different bands together, and they hear each others grievances."[96] Even in the absence of an uprising on the land question, Lomas believed such discussions fueled attacks on miners and settlers.[97] U.S. Indian agents similarly feared Indian assemblies. In 1898, Indian agent Goven on the Tulalip Reservation worried that Shaker healing ceremonies would encourage "a spirit antagonistic to order and government." With troops away in the Spanish-American War, Goven felt that the threat of an "Indian uprising" was heightened.[98] To some degree, Lomas and Goven expressed stereotypical paranoia about "Indian war parties." At the same time, the Indian agents recognized that Aboriginal people were cognizant of their political environment and, given the opportunity, would exchange information and take action.

The Shaker gatherings that concerned Indian agent Goven exemplify the complicated and shifting identities that swirled around labor camps. The Shaker religion generated new institutional identities among its followers at the same time as it perpetuated intervillage ties among the Coast Salish. The Musqueam learned of Shakers through their friends and relatives from Washington and Vancouver Island, whom they met at labor camps, potlatches, and winter dances.[99] A Nuu-chah-nulth man named Tom likewise converted to the Shaker church after a trip to Washington. And when one hundred Shakers met at Neah Bay, seventy reportedly came from British Columbia.[100] The doctrine of the Shaker church is an additional example of information—this time religious, rather than political—exchanged at the hop fields.

The Indian Shaker religion, not to be confused with that of the New England Shakers, originated in 1882, when John Slocum, a Sahawamish speaker from Squaxin Island in southern Puget Sound, died and was resurrected. Slocum had received a revelation, and he promised salvation and healing for those who repudiated gambling, drinking, and Aboriginal medicine. Slocum's followers built him a church at the site of his resurrection. A year later, Slocum was again near death when he was healed, not by the attending shaman but by his wife after she was overcome with shaking during prayer. Following this incident, Aboriginal people from around Puget Sound came to the church Slocum's relatives had built, and the Indian Shaker church was born.[101]

More isolated than some other Puget Sound groups, the Squaxin community would have found the hop-field gatherings particularly useful opportunities for disseminating Shaker beliefs to Aboriginal people from Puget Sound, eastern Washington, British Columbia, and Alaska.[102] As sites of gambling and horse racing, the fields would have drawn Shaker proselytizers. More significantly, Shakerism is a healing religion, and a majority of conversions have been linked to experiences with curing ceremonies. When Shakers traveled to help the sick, they won converts.[103] The hop fields were a location where Shakers could be sure their services were needed and where migrants could see Shaker healers at work. As one missionary-ethnographer commented, perhaps more aptly than he realized, the Shaker religion "seemed to be as catching, to use the expression of the Indians, as the measles."[104]

Some scholars who argue that Shakers built upon or "reformed" shamanism characterize relations between Shaker healers and shamans as relatively benign.[105] Certainly the aims and techniques of the two were similar, and the experience of Susie Sampson Peter, a Skagit woman with spirit power and training to be a medicine woman, supports this interpretation. Peter transferred her healing powers to the Shaker church after attending a meeting at the Chilliwack hop fields in 1916.[106] Other scholars have argued, however, that Shakers condemned and abhorred shamans. During the last decades of the nineteenth century, shamans acquired a reputation for using their powers for ill and for exploiting others, in part through the high fees they sometimes charged.[107] Shakers, on the other hand, did not charge for their healing services, nor did they restrict their services to the converted.[108] Moreover, Shakers offered to rid people of the bad spirits that proliferated as shamans increasingly abused their powers.[109] The hop fields were a site where Shakers could confront shamanistic practices and offer their own healing alternative.

In the 1890s, the Shaker religion traveled a trajectory remarkably similar to the seasonal economic cycles of Aboriginal people. It crossed the Cascade Mountains to the east into Yakima, where hops were an expanding industry, and it crossed the international boundary to the north into Songhee and Cowichan territory on Vancouver Island, into Musqueam territory on the mainland. An example from the hop fields in Yakima gives some idea of Shakerism's path. Yakima man Enoch Abraham first heard the Shaker word from Mud Bay Louis, one of the most influential early converts and proselytizers at the Yakima hop fields in the summer of 1899. He returned to the coast with Louis, where the two men spent the winter digging oysters on Puget Sound.[110] Like the gamblers they opposed, Washington Shakers appeared in the Fraser River canneries before moving south again to the hop fields accompanied by Aboriginal people from British Columbia. In 1898, Shakers arrived at the canneries during an outbreak of measles.[111] They found a receptive audience in at least two Cowichan families: "Tooshalie, his wife and his son Timothy, also Jimmy Somenos and his wife." This conversion divided the Cowichan community, causing Cowichan man Comeakin Joe to complain to the Indian agent Lomas,

> We have asked them not to do so, as it is against the wishes of the whole of us; but the [Shaker] meetings are still being held and our wishes ignored—this state of affairs as you will understand is bringing discredit upon us, & holding us up to ridicule in the eyes of all the other Indians, who laugh at us and say, all the Cowichans are "shakers."[112]

Comeakin Joe asked Lomas if he would intervene and ask Devlin, the New Westminster agent, to ban the meetings.[113] Devlin, however, apparently had a more relaxed attitude than Lomas, who previously ran a Shaker contingent out of Victoria with two hours notice.[114] Or perhaps Devlin was occupied with the threat of the measles epidemic and welcomed whatever help he could get dealing with the crisis. Cowichan Indian constables were left to discourage the Shaker gatherings.[115]

The Shaker religion remains important in many Pacific Northwest Aboriginal communities. Wayne Suttles has identified the Shaker church as one of three systems through which Coast Salish communities continued to sustain "organized systems of intervillage relations" into the twentieth century.[116] These intervillage relations were encouraged and sustained in the nineteenth century partly through hop-field migrations. The Shaker religion has thus carried on the function of the hop-field gatherings to which it may owe its own initial growth.

Seasonal migrations to the hop fields in Puget Sound were an important part of economic, political, and cultural life for thousands of late-nineteenth-century Aboriginal people. By traveling to the hop fields, Aboriginal people participated in the burgeoning capitalist economy. They incorporated the hop-field migrations into a diverse itinerary that included labor as fishermen, cannery workers, sealers, and farmers. None of these occupations alone could provide a stable income for Aboriginal people. But taken together, their separate threads sustained a flexible weave that served, in most years, as an economic safety net. Hop pickers from British Columbia also found some advantage in the international border crossings they made when going to and from the hop fields. Although the international boundary imposed restrictions, it also created opportunities.

Aboriginal mobility was about politics and culture as well as economics. Aboriginal people brought to the hop fields activities that were historically entrenched aspects of Aboriginal gatherings. They took advantage of the migrations to visit friends and kin, attend potlatches and other significant gatherings, hold gambling matches, horse and canoe races, and provision themselves for winter. Hop-field migrations provided important occasions to sustain the intervillage links bisected by the international boundary. And at the same time, the migrations fostered new senses of identity and the sharing of new political and religious information.

Aboriginal migrants embedded the logic of political processes in their hop-field migrations. But the dynamics of colonial capitalism were uneven. Hop migrations buoyed the hereditary status of Coast Salish chiefs who sought the means to sustain intervillage ties; yet those same migrations threatened the position of the Nuu-chah-nulth chief, Sayach'apis'. Moreover, transformations of a different kind may have occurred if individuals historically excluded from hereditary rights attempted to use the hop fields as social spring boards. Just as several members of the Kwakwa̱ka̱'wakw troupe used their wages from Chicago to ease their way into hereditary hierarchies at home, so too might hop pickers have used their wages to enter the potlatch economy. Might nascent hop camp communities have provided new configurations of witnesses to validate recently acquired status? Regardless of whether they fostered the ascent of nouveaux riches, hop migrations could simultaneously support and undermine historically and genealogically entrenched political configurations.[117] Hop-field gatherings became occasions for adjudicating change and continuity at a time when colonialism undermined many previously existing patterns of existence. The annual migrations of Aboriginal people to the hop fields were part of a complex strategy for dealing with the challenges presented by colonialism and for exploiting its opportunities.

Chapter Six

Indian Watchers: Colonial Imagination and Colonial Reality

Aboriginal survival strategies were tenacious and often ingenious, but they did not crack the thick crust of colonial assumptions. The multiple attractions of the hop fields for Aboriginal people were invisible to most non-Aboriginal observers. Tourists saw vanishing Indians; missionaries and government agents saw shiftless wanderers. They were unable to imagine the complex web that Aboriginal people wove to sustain the fabric of modern Aboriginal existence. In order to understand why this was so, we need to turn from the importance of the hop harvest for Aboriginal pickers to its significance for members of non-Aboriginal society including growers, merchants, and tourists.

Like the Aboriginal migrants, non-Aboriginal people benefited from the harvest in economic, political, and cultural ways. Many of these benefits grew from the colonial positioning of Aboriginal life as performance or spectacle. Investigating what non-Aboriginal people stood to gain through the creation of Indian spectacle reveals the double-edged nature of that spectacle for Aboriginal people. The immediate economic benefits Aboriginal people derived from marketing their culture by selling baskets and carvings, posing for photographs, and performing dances reinforced larger assumptions about authenticity that situated Indians in opposition to modern, civilized life. These were the same assumptions that legitimated colonial assertions of superiority and control. This was the dark side of the ideology of authenticity.

Non-Aboriginal people reaped significant economic benefits from hop-related businesses. Local merchants and hoteliers welcomed the hop season for one because they benefited from the business of recently paid Aboriginal pickers. During the harvest "shrewd tradesmen" earned large profits at temporary stores set up to cater to the needs of the pickers, and fruit and vegetable vendors visited the farms daily with produce for sale.[1] Then, at the season's close, crowds of pickers descended on local shops, creating a summer's-end "Christmas shopping season."[2] Pickers came to town with earnings from growers and tourists in hand, where they were said to "plant the profits of the picking season as generously as princes of the realm."[3] In a good year, they ended the season with significant amounts to spend. One season, pickers from Snoqualmie spent almost $17,000 in Snohomish City before heading home.[4] This led some observers to label homeward-bound pickers spendthrifts who did "not scruple to spend it for anything which may attract their attention in the store windows, and [whose] canoes start homeward laden with purchases."[5] Officials in British Columbia likewise commented on the consumer goods that workers brought home from the hop fields. I. W. Powell, the Indian Superintendent of British Columbia, wrote in 1884 that work in Washington hop fields enabled Aboriginal people to "purchase clothing and quite a number of luxuries not usually within their reach."[6] As with the initial decision about whether or not to go to the hop fields, Aboriginal women exercised a significant measure of control over these purchases, since, at least according to Lomas, among the Cowichan "the wife's purse is generally entirely separate from the husband's," and the money earned by female pickers was their own.[7] These so-called luxuries included furniture, stoves, and sewing machines. Fancy ribbon-trimmed hats and dresses were also popular.[8]

Tourists drawn to the spectacle of Aboriginal hop pickers further benefited White boosters and businessmen. The presence of Indian pickers so increased the appeal of urban centers like Seattle and Tacoma that it gained special attention in national publications. According to Mamie Upton, who wrote for the California-based *Overland Monthly*, "These Indians with their boats and rush tents, their baskets and babies, their cards and gambling, and all the hoo-doo and tamanamus, or midnight dances, make the autumn in the Sound country a time of panoramic interest."[9] *Harper's Weekly* agreed: "The city of Seattle, picturesque at all times, acquires an additional feature of interest when it is invaded by the Indians who come hither by thousands to do the picking on the big hop ranches of Washington."[10] The most prominent writer to discuss the Indian hop pickers was John Muir, who gave a glowing description of the Snoqualmie Hop Farm in an essay entitled "People and Towns of Puget Sound."[11]

20. Puyallup hop ranch, 1888. This composite image of hop fields, a hop barn, and Aboriginal migrant workers and their camp ran as a featured illustration in *Harper's Weekly* on 20 October 1888. The accompanying article attempted to lure hop farmers to the Puyallup Valley by promising great wealth, picturesque scenery, and Indian labor that "melts away" at season's end, not unlike the snow on Mount Tacoma (Rainier) in the background. Negative NA 4015, Special Collections, University of Washington Libraries.

Visitors who came to see the hop pickers made the city streets of Puyallup bustle with as much activity as the fields. "Yesterday was a great day for Puyallup," boasted the *Washington Standard* on 24 September 1886. "There never were so many people in this town before . . . the surging throng which fairly packed the streets, crowded into the stores buying goods, swarmed around peanut stands, traded and sold horses, sat together in groups conversing, and rode horseback and in carriages up and down the streets." Aboriginal migrants and local Snoqualmie Indians mingled with Whites, presenting a view in the street of "white and red mixed in about equal quantities." And at the horse track a mile from Puyallup, "some sheds were found in which restaurants and booths were doing a good business."[12]

These activities flourished through the turn of the century, even after the hop louse diminished the crop's profitability. In 1904, the *Puyallup Valley Tribune* reported that "the streets of Puyallup present an animated scene and for some weeks yet will be the Mecca of busy crowds, as well as many interested sight-seers from Tacoma and Seattle. As a result, business of all kinds is flourishing and local merchants report a satisfactory trade."[13] Thus, while many Whites probably did not want Indians as their next-door neighbors—hence the City of Seattle's relegation of Aboriginal residents to Ballast Island—they were glad, indeed, eager to have them as customers in their store and to reap collateral benefits from the tourist influx they precipitated.

The importance of economic gain to White residents could also work against Aboriginal migrants. The depressed economic conditions of 1892 resulted in an uncharacteristic surge of anti-Indian labor sentiment.[14] The U.S. Immigration Department enacted an alien labor law that prohibited Aboriginal people from British Columbia from crossing the border to pick hops. In contrast to most other accounts of hop pickers' spending habits, the Port Townsend *Leader* complained that

> while these Indians spend a portion of their money before they return, still they take out of the State between $7000 and $10,000 every year. The Indians thus usurp the rightful employment of resident whites, who would be glad of an opportunity to do the work; especially would such employment this year be a timely Godsend to a great many people. . . . Under the department's ruling thousands of white people in this state will obtain employment, which they sorely need, and which is their rightful inheritance.[15]

This newspaper piece contrasts with the more commonly expressed contemporary opinion that there were not enough White pickers to bring in the harvest, and that Aboriginal pickers were preferable to Chinese workers, the only other option. With the economic depression of the early 1890s, racialized nationalism produced an upsurge of sentiment against Aboriginal workers. In subsequent years, however, Aboriginal pickers continued to cross the border from British Columbia.

In one of authenticity's ironic twists, the spectacle of Aboriginal hop pickers may actually have helped growers recruit more White workers. Watching hop pickers was already firmly entrenched as a middle- and upper-class holiday excursion. Why couldn't hop picking be a parallel holiday excursion for the working class? The threat of labor scarcity loomed over every season. Faced with a potential shortage of Aboriginal pickers and with vehement public opposition to the employment of Chinese pickers, growers urged the White population to join the picking force. The governor's report for 1888 stated that certain kinds of work, including hop picking, had been racially stigmatized and were thus "eschewed by white people . . . without investigating its merits."[16]

Growers and hop-industry promoters tried to mitigate this stigma by demonstrating that the work was clean, respectable, and fun. Newspapers abetted these interests by running stories that opened with sentences like "Let us one and all shift the cares and responsibilities of life to other shoulders for a month and go forth to gather the festive hop."[17] According to the *Overland Monthly*, "the hop-picking season is the joyous season of labor. People for whom work is a necessity welcome the chance to escape from the irksomeness of their daily duties by going to the hop-fields. It is as pleasant a change as a sojourn by the sea is for the wealthy idler."[18] Another reporter claimed suggestively, " 'The fun that's in it' leads many of the boys and girls to the hop field; but it is not to be found there, but at night, after the day's work is accomplished."[19] Dances, walks on country roads, and their inevitable offshoot, young love, were the stuff of the hop harvest. "The possibilities of the hop field are multifarious," promised *The Seattle Mail and Herald*. "Not least among these is the possibility of coming back, wearing a fierce, sunkissed blush and some young fellow's engagement ring—for they say the hop field do be next to the sea side as a pleasure resort and it is said that under the mistletoe is nowhere compared to a moonlit night and a good healthy cluster of Washington hops."[20] By 1905, newspapers reported that for White and Aboriginal pickers alike " 'hop picking time' has come to have in Washington a peculiar meaning of its own, being a time when industrious persons desiring a summer vacation with change of work as well as of mode of life, go by hundreds to the hop fields where they make a holiday of helping to harvest the crop."[21]

Not only was hop picking *fun*, it was also *healthy*—or so contemporary articles claimed. Asserted one writer, "In addition to its scenic beauties and pleasant surroundings, a hop field is a sanitarium for the invalid, and a resting place for the weary and overworked. . . . There is not a rural panacea or health resort from Southern California to Vancouver Island that will afford a tithe of the good solid enjoyment with the revivifying influence so beneficial to the constitutions or shattered nerves."[22] Or, as another promised, "Pale seamstresses and nervous housewives grow strong and rugged in the outdoor air and life."[23] The abundant verdure of the prolific vines was good for the soul, while "inhaling the aroma from the hop kilns is said to have very beneficial results on invalids."[24]

Given the reality of disease and other health risks associated with the hop fields, such claims were imaginative fabrications. But claims to healthfulness had great rhetorical power. They linked the Puget Sound hop industry to other hop-growing regions, such as California and New York, where popular belief held that picking was good for one's health. As one writer queried, "Are you nervous, miserable or dyspeptic? . . . Whatever your suffering or regret, why go hopping, up hill and down dale, and be cured."[25] The claim that hop picking improved one's health also helped position the activity within the realm of the nineteenth-century holiday destination. Throughout North America, health concerns were a driving force behind late-nineteenth-century tourism. In many Western industrial societies in this period "the wilderness holiday" became an antidote to fears of mental and physical degeneration.[26]

The romantic, vanishing Indians, who were such an integral aspect of the day-tripper's hop-field experience, were an implicit aspect of the campaign to recruit White workers. In their attempt to downplay any racial stigmatization of hop picking as "Indian-work," writers rarely mentioned Indians in literature aimed at potential White pickers. Nevertheless, the association of Indians with the hop harvest was too strongly entrenched in late-nineteenth-century Washington for it to pass unnoticed, even if it was sometimes left unsaid. Because Aboriginal people were believed to be part of a vanishing race, White citizens did not treat them as the same sort of racial threat as Asians.[27] It was not unknown for Aboriginal and White pickers to work side by side on hop farms.[28] The flyer that claimed watching Indians pick hops "will do your eyes good" spoke to the potential White picker as much as to the White spectator. For participant and observer alike, the hop season was touted as an opportunity for a healthy holiday.

Merchants and growers had clear economic reasons to promote hop pickers and harvest as spectacles. Despite this, public opinion was fickle in its attitude toward Aboriginal pickers. Widespread as the appeal of the hop-picking spectacle was, non-Aboriginal urban residents were ambivalent about the status to be accorded to mobile populations of Aboriginal pickers. This ambivalence found physical expression in the circumstances of the Ballast Island encampment. Although citizens of Seattle had ejected Aboriginal people from the city streets, they allowed them to camp close to the commercial heart of the city, still near enough at hand to offer regular entertainment for Indian watchers. But even this compromise did not go uncontested, and Ballast Island inhabitants were plagued by regular rounds of eviction notices.

A poem by J. A. Costello about the encampment of hop pickers on Ballast Island captures the contradictory sentiments common among Indian watchers attracted by romantic notions of vanishing Indians and repelled by the perceived cultural and racial differences between Indians and themselves.

There's dusky maids
In pinks and plaids,
Maids from the forest free;
  In bright attire,
  Aglow, afire,
On Ballast island by the sea.

There's the chief of his clan
With his ugly Klootchman;
The gay young dude and his bride,
  With bows and quiver,
  And dog fish liver,
And the ictas of his curious tribe.

Camped below,
in the beauteous glow,
Such a "gypsy" crew so novel and bold;
  In their long canoes,
  And moccasin shoes,
From the land of the Totem pole.

Dotted all over,
Like pigs in clover,
The wickyups cover Ballast isle;
  Brown flitched salmon,
  Pappooses agammon
Pots and kettles in curious pile.

When picking's o'er
We'll have no more
The smell that comes from Ballast isle;
  Glad then my eyes
  My spirits rise,
For they've gone back to their paradise.[29]

Simultaneously fascinated and repulsed, Costello telescoped his general ambivalence into characterizations of Aboriginal women, domesticity, and sexuality. His representation of the scene was both derogatory and romanticized. In all this, it was typical. Strong negative images were not the inevitable accompaniment to romanticizations of Aboriginal people, but they were frequent undercurrents. Indian watchers commonly viewed Aboriginal people as "pathetic as well as picturesque."[30] The romanticization of Aboriginal life rendered Aboriginal people unequivocally foreign and absolutely other, a process that prepared fertile ground for racist outgrowths like Costello's.

The romanticized ambivalence Costello expressed was basic stock for the myth of the vanishing Indian. It is here that we can address the question of why Indian hop pickers were so appealing in the first place. The familiar story of the vanishing Indian fits within a larger pattern. For late-nineteenth-century Americans, the frontier, the place "where civilization disintegrated and merged into the untamed," was fast disappearing. Echoing the pronouncement made by Frederick Jackson Turner a decade earlier at the Chicago World's Fair, one writer declared in 1902, "the Frontier is gone, an idiosyncrasy that has been with us for thousands of years, the one peculiar picturesqueness of our life is no more." Untamed wilderness and untamed people alike appeared to be vanishing. "We may keep alive for many years yet the idea of a Wild West," he wrote, "but the hired cowboys and paid rough riders of Mr. William Cody are more like 'the real thing' than can be found today in Arizona, New Mexico or Idaho." In becoming "conscious of itself" the frontier had become inauthentic. "It acts the part for the Eastern visitor; and this self-consciousness is a sign, surer than all others, of the decadence of a type, the passing of an epoch."[31]

It was at this historical moment, as political and economic conditions seemed to ensure the disappearance of Aboriginal people and culture, that non-Aboriginal fascination with romantic images of vanishing Indians flourished. By the 1890s, the population of Washington consisted not primarily of pioneer settlers with long histories of interaction with Aboriginal people, but of recent arrivals, whose unfamiliarity with Aboriginal people inclined them to see Indians as exotic curiosities.[32] The sight of Kwelth-Elite did not evoke images of Aboriginal people adapting traditional practices to the modern capitalist economy but instead, in the narrator's words, "conjured up confused visions . . . of a Prehistoric World and a Vanished Race, whose ragged remnants cling like burrs to the fringes of a new-born civilization on a new-born continent."[33] With the military defeat of Aboriginal peoples in the American West firmly behind them, White residents of Washington could safely mourn the disappearance of Indians and express nostalgia for things sacrificed in the name of progress.[34] By the late 1880s, William Lane, who had been shot in the leg during the Indian War of 1855–56, employed Aboriginal laborers on his hop farm.[35] Whites now took aim with cameras instead of guns. The Indian transformation from hostile threat to acquiescent "derelicts of destiny," as the author of "Kwelth-Elite" put it, appeared complete.[36]

This transformation coincided with the development of tourism in the Pacific Northwest. In contrast to the eastern United States, most tourists in the Pacific Northwest were attracted by "natural wonders" rather than historical sites.[37] Nineteenth-century notions of history were defined by the Euro-American belief that only White people had history.[38] This belief excluded Aboriginal people from history and appointed them instead to the realm of nature. To nineteenth-century tourists, Aboriginal people, including hop pickers, were part of the "natural wonders" that spurred the boom in late-nineteenth-century western tourism.

Non-Aboriginal writers of the time commonly drew parallels between Aboriginal people and nature. They saw Aboriginal vendors who lined the streets and waterfronts of Seattle and Tacoma as residual elements of a natural world otherwise superseded by the urban environment. Describing a group of homeward-bound hop pickers in 1906, a writer for the *Seattle Post-Intelligencer* commented that these Aboriginal women with their array of baskets and canoes had long lent "a touch of nature to many an important corner."[39] Later that year, the Seattle *Mail and Herald* described an Aboriginal family on the corner of Second Avenue and Cherry Street in similar terms: "the group though unkempt made a striking and pleasant bit of color, as their scarlet and yellow kerchiefs gleamed through the mists of gray. . . . So God leaves no etching unfinished on Nature's canvas."[40]

The annual appearance of Aboriginal hop pickers on city streets reminded urban citizens that "everything has its season."[41] One writer's formulation was typical: "the going and coming of the Washington hop pickers is as regular as the annual migration of water fowl or the rotation of the seasons."[42] Another writer likened the pickers to creatures coming out of hibernation.[43] For many observers, the migrations of Northwest Coast Aboriginal people brought to mind the region's geographical diversity. A glimpse of Coast Salish pickers from Washington evoked "the pine clad shores of

Puget Sound," while the presence of Tsimpsheans and Haidas suggested "the frowning headlands and deep bays of the Straits, from the outlying masses of Vancouver and the Queen Charlotte Islands," and the sight of Tlingits elicited "the fiords of Alaska."[44] For city dwellers who did not venture as far as the hop fields, the Aboriginal people of the urban streetscape were remnants of this natural environment, set off by the contrasting surroundings of the built environment. For those who did undertake a weekend escape from the city to the country, the association between Aboriginal people and idyllic nature only intensified once they left the city limits behind.[45]

Ideas about the "primitive," the "pastoral," and the "past," already linked in many nineteenth-century minds, converged in the hop fields. Disappearing Indians stood alongside "nature's aristocrat, the farmer."[46] Here, both were found in their natural setting. The rural landscape of the fields was reminiscent of a bucolic ideal that was increasingly alien to the daily lives of American city dwellers. Popular late-nineteenth-century American opinion held that the rise of the city entailed the inevitable decline of the countryside. Ambivalence toward civilization peaked with the development of the "Nature Movement" in the decades following the Civil War. Leisure mended the urban-generated rift between people and nature.[47] At the hop fields, White sightseers—as well as White pickers—found themselves surrounded by a landscape in decline, a landscape that featured Indians they believed were in similar decline. When Indian watchers wondered whether these "children of the wild . . . were . . . not better as a class in primitive days?," they admitted that neither Aboriginal people nor nature seemed likely to survive civilized urban life.[48] Were Aboriginal people not as different from the civilized city dwellers as natural arcadia was from the civilized city? Modern Indians were degraded; their cultural glory lay irretrievably in the past.

Here, the observation of the anthropologist Johannes Fabian that "the posited authenticity of a past (savage, tribal, peasant) serves to denounce an inauthentic present (the uprooted, *évolués*, acculturated)" has relevance beyond his specific reference to the workings of his discipline.[49] Cultural views conflated the rural peasant and the Indian savage. Both represented the past of an authentic other. All things savage, tribal, and peasant were categorically excluded from the transition into the modern present. If they attempted to make that transition, they became something else entirely; as Fabian puts it, they became "the uprooted, *évolués*, acculturated" and forfeited their claims to cultural integrity, legitimacy, and authenticity. As the frontier receded into the past, sightseers' journeys to its vestiges rendered them time travelers. By driving out to the countryside, sightseers viewed what they believed were peoples and landscapes of bygone days.[50] Their holiday was a window onto an authentic past juxtaposed against their everyday present.

"Rural" and "untamed" were not the same thing, but this discrepancy passed, for the most part, unnoticed. Both were forms of arcadia, one bucolic and the other primitive, jointly born of the urban imagination, more mutually sustaining than opposing. Pastoral scenes embodied the virtues of wilderness and excised its vices.[51] Sightseers certainly understood that hop fields were not natural occurrences but the products of human labor. What mattered, however, was that hop fields were distinct from towns and cities and were physically closer to nature. One tourist account "doubted if the earth produces a more beautiful sight in the form of an annual crop of vegetation than that afforded by a hop-field . . . when in full bloom."[52] Even John Muir, one of the era's most discerning seekers of pristine wilderness, associated the Snoqualmie Hop Ranch with great, untamed beauty: "Here the dense forest opens, allowing fine free views of the adjacent mountains from a long stretch of ground which is half meadow, half prairie, level and fertile, and beautifully diversified with outstanding groves of spruces and alders and rich flowery fringes of spiraea and wild roses, the river meandering deep and tranquil through the midst of it." Far from diminishing the scenic beauty, the rows of cultivated hops augmented it. "They are a beautiful crop, these vines of the north, pillars of verdure in regular rows, seven feet apart and eight or ten feet in height; the long, vigorous shoots sweeping round in fine, wild freedom, and the light, leafy cones hanging in loose, handsome clusters."[53]

Muir expounded not only on the beauty of the hop fields but on the opportunity for trout fishing and bear hunting that a visit to the fields afforded. Such outings were doubly interesting, as, more often than not, an Indian guide could be hired to accompany the party. This phenomenon was not limited to Indians. In the post-Victorian novels of E. M. Forster, it was Italian carriage drivers who communicated Italy's authenticity to English travelers in the Tuscan countryside.[54] In both instances, the native guide allowed tourists to commune simultaneously with vanishing landscapes and their premodern inhabitants. Sightseers were afforded a rare glimpse of nature and natives as they retreated together before modernity's onslaught.

At the same time as popular associations between Indians and nature flourished, significant aspects of Aboriginal relationships to the landscape went unnoticed by non-Aboriginal observers. Newcomers believed that the land on which the Snoqualmie Hop Ranch stood was a "natural prairie."[55] White observers failed to realize that Aboriginal people had carved this prairie out of dense forest through long-term fire-ecology management. Even John Muir's ecological knowledge and curiosity took him no further than the observation that the "gravelly plain" on which the Snoqualmie Ranch stood had been "deforested by fire many years ago."[56] Muir assumed that the fire was either accidental or natural. His assumption was typical of colonial notions of landscape that deterritorialized Aboriginal people.[57] Before it became a hop ranch, the Snoqualmie Prairie was *Sdoqualbixw Baxeb*, the site of Aboriginal camas bulb cultivation.[58] The double irony in this is that the land-management techniques that White settlers overlooked were the same ones that rendered the indigenous landscape of the Snoqualmie Prairie so appealing to them and that drew the enormous hop farm into the heart of Snoqualmie Indian territory. The hop growers, who naturally attempted to select the portions of land that could be "most easily cleared," found the open prairie ideal.[59]

Non-Aboriginal ignorance of fire-management practices—an ignorance that persisted even among scientists well into the twentieth century—shows that rhetoric linking Aboriginal people and nature did not necessarily generate awareness of the real relationship between the two. But the rhetorical conflation of Indians, nature, and the past had significant material consequences for Aboriginal people. The most obvious of these was the tourist industry that took shape around the hop fields. There were other consequences of naturalizing Indians, as well.

Western conceptions of nature shifted significantly in the mid-nineteenth century. According to the Marxist literary critic Raymond Williams, it was at this time "that nature [was] decisively seen as separate from men," rather than bound up with human nature. This shift occurred among "the improvers"—industrial capitalists—at just the moment when their exploitation of nature and its resources accelerated to previously unheard-of levels. The idea of nature as something apart and outside, untouched and unspoilt, underwrote the self-serving urban view of city life as distinct from and unrelated to nature. Referring to industrial capitalist investors, Williams writes: "established at powerful points in the very process which is creating the disorder, they change their clothes at week-ends, or when they can get down to the country; join appeals and campaigns to keep one last bit of England green and unspoilt; and then go back, spiritually refreshed, to invest in the smoke and the spoil."[60] Williams's critique pinpoints the unintended and often hypocritical implications of unselfconscious leisure values that embrace certain manifestations of nature (the countryside) and deny the authenticity of others (the city). Such implications are common among "back to nature" and other antimodernist movements. The private struggles that drew many people to such movements often had unforeseen public consequences. They cemented values that inspired widespread allegiance to the status quo and ultimately reinforced the position of the dominant classes.[61]

For all Williams's skill at defining historical shifts in ideas of nature, he misses a critical aspect, one that admittedly seemed less pressing for the nineteenth-century English than for nineteenth-century Americans. The ideological purging of "man" from ideas of nature did not dislodge Aboriginal people from their natural perch. Many nineteenth-century Americans and Canadians understood Aboriginal people to be a part of, rather than separate from, nature. Even as notions of pristine, empty wilderness came to mandate the removal of Aboriginal residents from the newly constructed confines of national parks, Aboriginal people became tourist attractions at Glacier and Yosemite National Parks. Aboriginal people could and did remain within park boundaries so long as they conformed to the images of authentic Indians that tourists wanted.[62] The late-nineteenth-century wilderness ideal could not admit the presence of independent, self-sufficient, Aboriginal communities, but it tolerated and even drew strength from the presence of supposedly traditional and apparently vanishing Indians.

What, then, were the implications for Aboriginal people of being situated within a definition of nature that was widely believed to exclude people? Williams's weekend environmentalists who spent their weekdays investing in the "smoke and spoil" had their counterparts in the weekend Indian watchers who worked during the week as railroad, mining, timber, banking, and political magnates. The urban tourists who watched Aboriginal hop pickers when they passed through the city and who ventured into the countryside to observe these vanishing "children of nature" in action were the same individuals whose lifestyles and business investments accelerated the vanishing process.

The register at the Meadowbrook Hotel on the Snoqualmie Hop Ranch was replete with the names of such guests.[63] Seattle's founder, Arthur A.

Denny, stayed at the ranch when he was interested in the iron mines near the summit of Snoqualmie Pass.[64] Arthur Denny's son, David T. Denny, a prominent banking and railroad investor, also visited.[65] Henry L. Yesler, owner of Seattle's first sawmill and "easily the most active agent in Seattle's growth,"[66] was a guest, as was steel manufacturer Peter Kirk.[67] Charles C. Terry, known for his "insatiable hunger for land," visited.[68] So too did Dexter Horton, "one of the foremost bankers and financiers on the Pacific Coast," founder of the first private bank in Washington Territory and an original investor in the Seattle and Walla Walla Railroad and Transportation Company.[69] The hotel was also the retreat of many Seattle, Lakeshore and Eastern Railway investors.[70] The first state governor, Elisha P. Ferry, who also held positions as territorial surveyor-general, territorial governor, and vice president of the Puget Sound National Bank, also stayed.[71] So too did Samuel le Roy Crawford and Charles T. Conover, proprietors of Seattle's largest real estate firm, known for having sold "at least seventy-five per cent of the best real estate in Seattle" and for successfully attracting settlement and investment to Washington from across the country.[72] The vast investments of these men and others like them spawned the urban and industrial infrastructure of Washington. Having reshaped the land and displaced Aboriginal people in the process, they could romanticize both as part of a wild and pristine past. Samuel Crawford was typical in this regard. He supplied American flags to be placed on Chief Seattle's grave for more than twenty years and was known as a "staunch friend" of Chief Seattle's daughter, Princess Angeline.[73] The dual romanticization of nature and Aboriginal people ultimately masked the culpability of those who were materially responsible for the degradation of the environment and the dispossession of Aboriginal people.

Tourism and investment dovetailed particularly well on the Snoqualmie Hop Ranch. There, Aboriginal people earned much-needed wages from the hop harvest at the same time as they inadvertently attracted investment in the railroads that would undermine their sovereignty. Railroads had long been a prime marker of the "advance" of the frontier, and they were critical to the development of tourism in the Pacific Northwest.[74] The connections linking Aboriginal people, hops, and the railroad at Snoqualmie were manifest in the Seattle, Lake Shore and Eastern Railway's 1889 promotional publication, *A Report on Washington Territory*. This illustrated volume detailed prospects for development and settlement, particularly along the proposed railway line, which terminated at Seattle. It contained a plate of Aboriginal hop pickers, with the caption "Indians Gathering hops, Washington Territory, on line of Seattle, Lake Shore and Eastern Railway."[75] The Seattle, Lake Shore and Eastern Railway promoted itself with images of Indians in much the same way the Canadian government did at the Chicago World's Fair. In Puget Sound, hop pickers helped promote the railway; in Chicago, residential school children advertised the availability of agricultural land in the Canadian West. In both instances, Whites used images of Aboriginal people to promote the process of their own dispossession.[76]

Sometimes the weekend role of the weekday investor extended beyond amateur Indian watcher to ethnographer/anthropologist. The Puyallup Valley land speculator and ethnographic writer Judge James Wickersham was a prominent citizen of Tacoma who had opened a law practice in 1883 together with the pioneer hop grower, Ezra Meeker. Wickersham was instrumental in acquiring land for the Northern Pacific Railway, which ran through the Puyallup Valley.[77] A recognized authority on Aboriginal culture of the Puget Sound region, he published several learned articles on Aboriginal people, including one on Nisqually mythology that appeared in the *Overland Monthly*.[78] He also corresponded with well-known ethnographers and archaeologists, including Frederic Ward Putnam, organizer of the anthropology exhibit at the Chicago World's Fair.[79] Although Wickersham earned a reputation as a defender of Indian rights, his interest in Aboriginal culture was closely linked to his activities in land and railway development. Wickersham's writings presented Aboriginal people as ethnographic objects, as authentic others. They were interesting spectacles who had no use for the land they occupied. Not coincidentally, this was the same land Wickersham and other developers coveted for the growing town of Puyallup and the railway right of way. In an 1892 letter Wickersham bluntly stated his position: "the Indian doesn't care [about retaining reservation land]—clams, a split cedar shanty on the beach, a few mats and kettles, leisure and a bottle of rum once in a while are all he wants—anybody can have the land that wants it. Really why should our govt go to such enormous expense in trying to make a white man out of an Indian?"[80] Wickersham's self-serving view was based on the notion, propagated through his own ethnographic publications, that Aboriginal people were passing relics with no possibility of success in a modern era. The sad, though not unpredictable, result for the Puyallup was that they lost all but a few acres of their originally allocated reservation. The historian George Castile argues that Wickersham's interest in "authentic" Aboriginal culture was an opportunistic attempt to justify

21. Illustration of Aboriginal hop pickers taken from promotional material for the Seattle, Lake Shore and Eastern Railway, 1889. This image helped draw funding for the proposed railway. It placed Aboriginal people among the region's attractions on at least two counts: they were picturesque sights, and they were willing labor. Ruffner, *A Report on Washington Territory*, plate facing p. 74.

22. Aboriginal hop pickers, originally captioned "Faith, Hope, Charity." Another version of this photograph bore the title "The Three Graces." Images like this depicted Aboriginal people as objects of pity who quietly acquiesced to their inevitable demise. Negative NA 661, Special Collections, University of Washington Libraries.

23. Postcard of elderly Aboriginal hop pickers, originally captioned "Siwash and Klootchman." The workers on the right are Friday Consauk and his wife Mary Patense. Pictured here as too elderly and frail to pose a threat, these Aboriginal workers are depicted as benign features on the landscape of opportunity awaiting pioneer farmers. Negative NA 4093, Special Collections, University of Washington Libraries.

the land grab.[81] He comes close to suggesting that Wickersham consciously began ethnographic work on Aboriginal people because he knew it could further his railroad and land speculation interests. Whether Wickersham operated with this degree of calculation is less significant than the end result: the dovetailing of his views of Aboriginal people—popularly viewed as sympathetic—and his business interests, which aimed to dispossess Aboriginal people of their land and rights.

Aboriginal hop pickers reaped important economic benefits from both the harvest and from the accompanying tourist industry. But ultimately they paid out much more than they earned. The romantic images they presented were a cornerstone of the colonialist paradigm that defined Aboriginal people as equally raw and undeveloped as the forests, mountains, and waterways of the Pacific Northwest. Fittingly, it was the regional booster and commercial photographer Asahel Curtis who chose hop pickers as his photographic subjects more frequently than did his salvage ethnographer brother, Edward.[82] Non-Aboriginal people's enthusiasm for development did not impede their sympathetic admiration for what they imagined Aboriginal people once had been, but neither did their sympathy mitigate the sense of necessity and righteousness that drove development projects—be they logging operations or reservation schools. On the one hand, posing for photographs and selling baskets helped Aboriginal people make a living. On the other, their roles as photographic subjects and curio vendors fed the ideological underpinnings of political and economic systems that threatened their ability to remain self-supporting. The "Indian Hop Picker" became a poster child for the industrial development of the region. She attracted the sources of her own disenfranchisement.

Supposedly contradictory elements coexisted in the hop fields: tradition and modernity, Aboriginal opportunity and Aboriginal dispossession, vibrant Indians and vanishing Indians. Here again, the story of Kwelth-Elite is instructive. The characters were wage laborers in a modern industry. But the author rhetorically froze them in the past by using the language of the vanishing Indian and comparing them with inhabitants of ancient Greece and other lost civilizations. The story reproduced in miniature the larger picture of late-nineteenth-century Aboriginal hop pickers and of late-nineteenth-century Aboriginal people more generally. Regardless of adaptations they made to new ways of life around them, non-Aboriginal people continued to view them as "derelicts of destiny."

Chapter Seven

The Inside Passage to Authenticity:

Sitka Tourism and the Tlingit

On 26 January 1906, Rudolph Walton received a letter from the clerk of the local school board, Mrs. George Stowell. Stowell informed Walton that his stepdaughters, Dora and Tillie Davis, were no longer permitted to attend the public school in Sitka as they had been doing for the previous few weeks. "Dear Sir," the letter read, "The School board has decided that your children cannot attend the White school while living in the Indian Ranche."[1] Rudolph Walton was Tlingit, a member of the *Kiks.'adi* clan. He worked as a jeweler and owned a store in Sitka. The children were his wife Mary's, from her marriage to then-deceased Fred Davis. In a certain sense, the expulsion of Tlingit children from a White public school in 1906 is unsurprising. It had been a decade since *Plessy v. Ferguson* legally acknowledged the principle of racially segregated "separate but equal" facilities in the United States. De facto segregation had existed in Alaska schools since the late 1880s, and the federal Nelson Act of 1905 entrenched this segregated education system in law.[2]

But segregation, especially of mixed-race children, was no simple task. Policies assumed that racial classification—like cultural authenticity—could be defined in binary terms, and they treated mixed-race children in an either-or fashion. For officials, mixed-race children embodied the impossible; their existence brought the fictitious nature of colonial dichotomies into sharp relief.[3] Inevitably, officials encountered difficulty interpreting and implementing the 1905 law which distinguished between "Eskimos and Indians of Alaska," on the one hand, and "white children and children of mixed blood who lead a civilized life," on the other. The former were to continue in schools under the direction of the federal government; the latter would attend schools controlled by locally established school boards. This distinction left many, including Rudolph Walton's family, in an ambiguous position.

As respected members of the Tlingit community, the Waltons' children could have attended the Indian school, as Dora and Tillie had done for a time. But when the Indian school year ended abruptly in January 1906 after only a few months of instruction, Walton decided to exercise Dora and Tillie's right to attend the White public school. The law viewed Dora and Tillie as "children of mixed blood," because their mother was known, in the terminology of the day, as a "half-breed."[4] Rudolph and Mary Walton were both graduates of the Sitka Training School, and Rudolph was a well-known local storekeeper, an accomplished jeweler, and an active member of the Presbyterian Church. Surely none who knew the Waltons could question their civilized qualifications. But this is exactly what the school board, many of Sitka's non-Tlingit residents, and finally the district court judge *did* question. A judicial hearing was held to determine whether the Waltons and several other families could be said to lead a "civilized" life.

At the turn of the century, Tlingit in southeastern Alaska faced many of the same colonial conditions as Aboriginal people in British Columbia and Washington. In response, they, too, collapsed the poles of authenticity's supposed dichotomies. Sitka Tlingit wove lives that defied binary categorization as "traditional" or "modern," authentic or inauthentic, in order to survive in a changing and often hostile world. Rudolph Walton knew about the difficulties of surviving and thriving in a colonial world; his life in many ways epitomized this process. From an early age, Walton confronted non-Tlingit ideas about civilization and authenticity. As Joyce Walton Shales, his granddaughter and biographer, notes, he navigated the "stormy seas" of Tlingit life under American colonization with skill and success but not without difficulty.[5]

The Davis case offers a stark manifestation of the contradiction between the rhetoric and reality of colonialism. It illuminates the contours—and more particularly, the limits—of Aboriginal people's power to manipulate foreign notions of authenticity and civilization. But before we can make sense of the testimony and decision in the Davis case, an understanding of life in turn-of-the-century Sitka, of the tenor of relations between Tlingit and non-Tlingit, and of non-Aboriginal society's assumptions about "Indians," civilization, and authenticity is necessary. A look at the growth of tourism in Sitka reveals connections to industrialists and developers not unlike those that characterized Puget Sound. Missions also had great influence on

24. Rudolph Walton, 1901. Photograph courtesy Ketchikan Museums, image 71.7.14.10, Tongass Historical Society Collection.

life in Sitka and on Rudolph Walton, in particular. The success of missions—like that of capitalist development—was tied to tourism. The triangulation of capitalism, missions, and tourism provides the context for in-depth analysis of the court transcripts. The testimony tells us a great deal about White assumptions about civilization and authenticity. Earlier episodes explored how Aboriginal people wrung some benefit from these assumptions. The Davis case demonstrates the stark limitations these assumptions imposed on Aboriginal lives—particularly in legal contexts.

The traditional territory of the coastal Tlingit, where Rudolph Walton grew up, covers the islands and fjord-ridden coastline of what is today known as the southeastern Alaskan panhandle. His social world was divided into two moieties, Raven and Eagle (also called Crow and Wolf respectively), and further subdivided into clans, and then house groups of ten to forty members. Clan and moiety were matrilineally determined, so Walton belonged to the same moiety, Raven, and clan, *Kiks.'adi*, as his mother. These designations anchored his social position, responsibilities, and privileges. They likewise determined who was an eligible marriage partner, a rule that Walton would live by. While moiety and clan influenced the general social conditions of Tlingit life, house groups structured the material conditions of everyday living. Walton belonged to the *Tin.aa Hit* or "Copper Shield House." Regardless of moiety, clan, or house group, Tlingit residents of a given location were collectively known as *k̲wáan*. Walton, like his neighbors, thus belonged to the *Sheet'kak̲wáan*, or inhabitants of Sitka.[6] As was true of other Aboriginal peoples as far south as the Kwakwa̱ka̱'wakw, Walton's world was one in which the crucial role of social rank was partly regulated by the ability of clan members to host *k̲ooéex'*, ceremonial feasts and give-aways, dubbed potlatches by non-Tlingit.[7]

As among the Kwakwa̱ka̱'wakw, ceremonial and ritual activities were tied to the economics of the seasonal round. Walton's ancestors included fishing, sealing, gathering herring roe, berrying, and hunting in their economic cycle. They traded these products to other indigenous peoples along the coast, and, beginning in the mid-eighteenth century, to Russian, Spanish, and English explorers and fur traders. In exchange, the Tlingit received not only European-manufactured goods but, all too often, epidemic disease. With the reestablishment of a Russian fort at Sitka in 1804—the Tlingit destroyed the initial fort built in 1799—Sitka Tlingit found added economic opportunity in supplying food to the dependent Russians. In return, they gained access to Russian goods and religion, and many converted to the Russian Orthodox Church.

The Tlingit encountered another wave of new arrivals in the wake of the American purchase of Alaska in 1867, the year Rudolph Walton was born. The early years of the American regime in Sitka were marked by a strong military presence, interracial hostility, and economic depression. But by the late 1870s a great many changes were under way including American—primarily Presbyterian—missionary activity, wage labor in the growing capitalist economy, and the explosion of a tourist industry.

The first of these developments, the missionary activity, was spearheaded by the Superintendent of Presbyterian Missions in Alaska and U.S. General Agent for Education in Alaska, Sheldon Jackson. Presbyterians opened a day school in Sitka in 1878 under a missionary, John G. Brady, who later became a leading businessman and Alaska's governor. The day school became a boarding school—the Sitka Training School—in 1881, when several boys, including Rudolph Walton, reportedly requested permission to live in the school.

The 1870s and 1880s also saw the increasing integration of Alaska into the

American economy. In many respects, Sitka stood apart from these developments. Mining, for example, flourished in Juneau, on Douglas Island, and in the interior. Loring was the center of a major canning operation, and Killisnoo the location of the Alaska Fish and Guano Company. By contrast, sawmill ventures around Sitka on Baranof Island proved disappointing.[8] Where Alaska's growing industrial economy offered employment opportunities to the Tlingit, it did so in places other than Sitka. This did not mean Sitka Tlingit failed to benefit from the new economy. They incorporated commercial labor into their annual migratory cycle by fishing for or working in canneries, mining, logging, sealing, and even hop picking in Washington.[9]

But Sitka itself needed another solution if it was to survive as an American town. The military presence provided one of the few viable occupations for Whites, but this was diminishing by the 1880s.[10] Tourism grew in the context of this dilemma. Although the local paper proposed that some combination of fishing and mining might yet "make our town a place of some importance," tourism seemed the only sure promise for the future. "Fishing and mining are not to be relied upon with any confidence as a support for our people, but Sitka will always be an attraction to visitors and through their agency mainly it must rise, if it rise at all, above the common place."[11] This editorialist proved correct. Sitka would rise on tourism, but not without protests from would-be industrialists. Throughout the district, popular opinion juxtaposed the interests of Aboriginal people and commercial developers. Aboriginal people were seen as Alaska's vanishing, albeit authentic, past. Tourism encouraged the preservation of this past and generated the impression among visitors—and worse yet, in Congress—that Alaska was an antiquated backwater rather than a progressive economic region. Such was not the road to statehood. Critics held that if the district government devoted as much energy to the promotion of capitalism as it did to the well-being of Aboriginal people, Alaska would already be knocking on statehood's door.[12]

Tourism was not, in fact, situated in such direct opposition to political and economic development. It did become a primary industry throughout much of Alaska, but not at the expense of other forms of commercial and industrial development. As in Puget Sound, local boosters and promoters found that tourism could further their own goals. In practice, tourism and development were closely intertwined.

Rudolph Walton's life was profoundly influenced by the successive waves of missionaries, capitalists, and tourists that washed up on his shore. One of the first students to attend the Sitka Training School, he remained a Presbyterian throughout his life. He was familiar with both the commercial-industrial and tourist economies. He worked as a miner in Juneau before becoming an artist, jeweller, and storekeeper in Sitka, a homecoming made possible by the growth of the steamer-based tourist industry.

But missionaries, industrialists, and tourists were bound together by more than their common influence on lives like that of Rudolph Walton. They were joined in ways that lent material and rhetorical strength to colonialism and that sustained ideas about authenticity much like the ones with which Aboriginal people further south contended.

Sitka's tourist industry was a larger and more elite version than the one in Puget Sound's hop fields and city streets.[13] By the time the hop industry began to boom in Washington Territory, summer steamboats already carried a steady stream of tourists up the Inside Passage to Alaska. The journey began at an American port, most often in Puget Sound.[14] The trip took in the coast of British Columbia with occasional stops in Victoria or Nanaimo. When steamers took on coal in Nanaimo, tourists toured the mines: like Aboriginal hop pickers, White coal miners could be spectacles too.[15]

Steamship companies initially sold tourist excursion tickets in the early 1880s to augment income from the transportation of gold, fish, timber, mining equipment, and supplies. In 1884, the Pacific Coast Steamship Company (PCSC) initiated tourist-specific voyages.[16] Owners of the PCSC further expanded their passenger business when they arranged for their tickets to be handled by Canadian and American transcontinental railroad lines. Promotional literature marketed the Inside Passage as an extension of the natural wonders of the American West. The culmination of the wide-eyed easterner's tour had once been Yellowstone; now it was Alaska.[17] John Muir's 1879 letters from Alaska, in which he enthused about his "discovery" of Glacier Bay, appeared in newspapers across the country. Tourists soon began to arrive, well in advance of U.S. government surveyors and mapmakers. By 1899, the glacier sported boardwalks that accommodated over 5,000 annual tourists.[18]

Travel writing proliferated as accounts published by adventurers like Muir attracted more visitors, some of whom published their own travel accounts. Many came to see America's newest and largest acquisition. And as in the Pacific Northwest, "natural wonders," of which Glacier Bay was among the most spectacular, were major draws. Writers described vistas of emerald-green islands, glaciers calving off into the ocean, and vertical mountains rising from the sea. During his 1879 voyage John Muir wrote that it was a "true fairyland . . . never before this had I been embosomed in scenery so hopelessly beyond description."[19] Although more prone to hyperbole than many, Muir's description of Alaskan scenery was typical.

But Muir was atypical in his relative inattention to the Aboriginal inhabitants. Other writers treated Alaska Natives and the curios they produced—like the hop pickers of Puget Sound—as part of the region's natural wonders. Indians attracted tourists just as surely as forests, glaciers, and mountains.[20] By 1903, the PCSC's letterhead bore an image, not of mountains or sea but of Aboriginal women. The company dubbed its Inside Passage voyages "The Totem Pole route," a designation that remained for well over a decade.[21] The Alaska Steamship Company offered itineraries that took travelers to Indian villages in more remote locales than the regular ports. Such routes catered to those who wanted "to see Indians in their home and get baskets and curios first hand."[22]

Sitka was unusual among western tourist destinations because it had "historical" as well as "natural" attractions.[23] Much of western North America lacked the long-term occupation by Europeans or their descendants that Whites commonly believed qualified as "history." Sitka was an exception. As the former capital of Russian America, the town had significant historical appeal and was a highlight of almost every Alaskan tour. The old Russian Orthodox Cathedral of St. Michael's and the castle ruins were material remnants of the picturesque Russian past that had been superseded by the American present. Americans commonly viewed Alaskans of Russian heritage as less than fully civilized, though more civilized than the Tlingit. At Sitka, visitors could celebrate American superiority over Russians and Tlingit alike. Sitka was the site of a twofold colonial victory.[24]

When the steamer pulled in, the excitement of tourists on disembarking was rivaled by the excitement of town residents. The arrival of the steamboat was an important local event. When Francis Sessions arrived in Sitka in the summer of 1890, she said that it "seemed like a gala day, with its inhabitants all out of doors," as a crowd of Whites and Tlingits thronged to the wharf.[25]

Sitka residents had reason to be excited by the steamer's arrival. It meant the return of family or friends. It meant the arrival of mail, which came sporadically outside the tourist season.[26] And it meant the delivery of imported food and goods on which non-Tlingits relied. As one writer, identified as

25. Steamer *City of Seattle* at dock in Sitka, ca. 1897. Many residents of Sitka relied on steamers for mail, groceries, supplies, and economic opportunity in the form of tourists. Negative La Roche 409, Special Collections, University of Washington Libraries.

"Hickey," wrote, "Well, we can't be blamed for our steamboat-arrival maniacism. Give us more steamers or so arrange it that those which do visit us may come with some sort of regularity; and then we will look upon the arrival of a steamboat with a nerve of a California highwayman. Three weeks without a word from the outside world, without being able to replenish our stocks of eatables, most of which we are obliged to import."[27] In Alaska, the development of basic infrastructure, such as shipping and postal services, rode in the wake of tourist steamers.

Like many others, Hickey hoped the tourist industry would facilitate even larger leaps and gains for Alaska. He contrasted the neglect Alaska received from Congress with the praise it earned from "globetrotters": "Their unanimous verdict is that the scenery through the inland seas of Alaska borders on that of enchantment and is beyond the power of the pen to describe; that the old curious customs of the natives is a study in itself." He maintained that "given the widely-acknowledged value and importance of Alaska, tourists wonder why Alaska should not have attained a higher place in the eyes of Congress and the commercial world and wonder why this rich country has been so neglected." Although Alaskans had voiced their desires, "the fact is that Congress pays no more attention to the demands of the people of Alaska than a harsh father does to the cries of a two-year old child wanting a stick of candy."[28] Hickey clearly hoped that tourists' interest in Alaska would encourage, or at least embarrass, Congress into extending political rights to White Alaskans.

Hickey's preoccupation with attracting federal attention was typical of many Alaskans' frustration during this post–Civil War period, when that attention was focused on Reconstruction and the unity of the contiguous United States. Americans who had moved to Alaska following its purchase by the United States in 1867 expected that Alaska would be incorporated first as a territory and eventually as a state, replicating the experience of earlier American frontiers. They were disappointed. Alaska remained a customs district under ad hoc military rule, without civil government or law until 1884. The 1884 Organic Act finally established Alaska as a civil and judicial district, but it still denied Alaskan Americans all but the most minimal elements of self-government. Under the act, Alaska gained a governor and a cadre of government officials, but these positions were federally appointed. Perhaps even more troubling to industrialist developers and fortune seekers, there was no provision for extending U.S. land laws to Alaska. The authority of settlers to preempt land for settlement or economic development, such as mining, remained uncertain until homestead laws were extended to Alaska in 1898 in the wake of the Klondike gold rush. When the elements of locally controlled civil government were finally created at the turn of the century, one writer commented that Alaska's pioneers had "worked as long and earnestly for the yoke of civil law as any oppressed people ever fought for liberty and release from odious government."[29] During this long campaign for political rights, Alaska developers and boosters like Hickey used tourist interest as a bargaining chip.

The tourist industry also brought more immediate gains. Tourists arrived with dollars to spend. The report on the 1890 census estimated that average Alaskan tourists spent between fifty and one hundred dollars during their trip, a significant portion of which they spent in Sitka.[30] The tourist market promised a significant return for those who tapped it. When an editorial in *The Alaskan* charged the PCSC with indifferent service, one reader rose to the company's defense, urging fellow Sitkans to keep in mind: "What line of steamers brings the tourists to us?" The author reminded readers that tourists benefited Sitka even more than the rest of southeast Alaska: "visitors purchase curios to a very large amount from our natives and whither does the purchase money go? Into the coffers of our merchants."[31] Tlingit and White merchants competed for the tourists' business, but White merchants stood to gain either way. The money tourists spent with Tlingit vendors came back to the White store owners when Tlingit, in turn, bought food and goods from them. White Sitka merchants reaped the same collateral benefits from the Aboriginal tourist industry as Puget Sound merchants did from the hop-field spectacle.

Above all, visitors to Sitka spent their money on Aboriginal curios or art. Late-Victorian taste held that "every well-appointed house might appropriately arrange an Indian corner."[32] Tourists on the Inside Passage, like those at the Chicago World's Fair or in the Puget Sound hop fields, sought Indian souvenirs or curios as much as they sought views of the local land- and humanscapes. In 1887, John G. Brady wrote that clerks in his store were "wrestling with tourists in the curiosity room."[33] Vendors of Aboriginal wares enjoyed a market where demand always seemed to exceed supply. According to *The Alaskan*, tourists rushed from the steamers and began "buying greedily from the Siwash squaws squatting in rows along the streets, with their gaudy baskets, spoons of horn and wood, bracelets, rings, and Indian relics." As soon as "the store doors . . . opened for the expected throng," the article continued, "skins, fur, photographs and curios are snapped up with an avidity of competition that is sometimes as laughable as it is frequent."[34] When Emily Carr traveled with her sister to Alaska, she recorded their purchases in her journal along with a sketch:

> As the day of our departure from Sitka drew near, we betook ourselves to the Indian village, and procured a curio or two as mementoes of our happy trip and offerings for our freinds; sister purchased a bird of melancholy mein so resembling herself she had difficulty in restraining her emotions, a sad faced seal-dish, and othe trifles. While an Indian tom-tom, a browstrap of bears claws, a deer-hide, and eagles leg rendered me joyously hilarious; my cheifest delight being a hollow bears tooth, through which I could whistle tunes, secular when surrounded by ordinary mortals, sacred when in the presence of "St. Juno."[35]

It seemed one could hardly travel to Alaska and *not* bring back a picturesque and authentic specimen from America's newest acquisition. As a 1906 brochure for the Alaska Steamship Company declared, "No home is complete now-a-days without a neat and artistically arranged Indian basket corner."[36]

Aboriginal craftspeople capitalized on this romanticization of their products. For Tlingit women "steamer day [was] salesday in Sitka."[37] When the steamer arrived—regardless of the weather or the hour—they immediately gathered up their baskets and other wares and headed to the waterfront.[38]

26. Sketch from Emily Carr's "Alaska Journal." In this sketch, Carr (pictured on the right) poked fun at herself and her sister as she satirized the behavior of tourists who competed for the best souvenirs in Sitka. I-67766, British Columbia Archives.

Tlingit vendors extended from the wharf along the walk into town; they lined waterfront and boardwalk alike.[39] Certain locations—such as the customs house porch—were particularly popular, and there was some jostling for the best positions. At the same time, the women took care not to undercut one another with regard to price. As one tourist commented, there "must be a Trades Union here, for the uniformity of prices was remarkable, and there was a positive firmness in the market."[40]

By selling goods on the wharf and on the street, Tlingit vendors intercepted tourists before they reached the stores owned by White merchants. W. P. Mills, Edward DeGroff, and John Brady all stocked large quantities of native "curiosities," "manufactures," and ethnographic photographs in their general merchandise stores. By specializing in these items they attempted to capture the tourist dollars that circulated in search of authentic souvenirs.[41] These were the same dollars that Tlingit vendors sought.

Just as tourists wanted postcards of the scenic vistas they saw, so too they wanted photos of the Indians they saw. And, like hop pickers in Puget

27. Sitka, ca. 1900. This shot, which includes Tlingit women selling goods on the sidewalk, was reproduced on postcards of the day. Negative INA 2577, Special Collections, University of Washington Libraries.

Sound, many Tlingit insisted on payment for being photographed. "If not paid," reported Eliza Scidmore, "the family seem ready to tear the camera fiend to pieces."[42] Other basket vendors simply hid their faces in silent protest against intrusive photographers.[43] Photographs of Tlingit vendors, like images of hop pickers, were sold as snapshots of a disappearing primitive past, despite the fact that they showed Tlingit women engaged in calculated, competitive business transactions.

Of the goods for sale, baskets were probably most popular. Weaving had always been an important skill for Tlingit women, and with the growth of the tourist industry, basketry's importance increased. Many Tlingit excelled at basketry, but the ethnologist George T. Emmons claimed that the Sitka people "spurred by the tourist trade, took the most prominent place."[44] Tlingit women wove baskets for an array of indigenous uses from berry gathering to baby carrying and produced astonishingly water-tight drinking and cooking vessels. Different shapes and designs appeared in items designed for the "curio corners" featured in travel literature. Baskets shaped

28. Postcard of Tlingit women weaving baskets for the tourist trade, Sitka, ca. 1897. Tourists purchased baskets as well as postcards of the weavers as souvenirs. Image 19061, Museum of History and Industry, Seattle.

like teapots, stew pots, bottles, and canes sat for sale beside older utilitarian designs. Women also commonly wove basketry mats and hats for sale.[45]

The wide price range of baskets helps explain their popularity. Regardless of how much or little travelers had to spend, they could afford a basket. Prices for basketry work depended on the quality and type of basket, as well as the buyer's gullibility and the seller's shrewdness. Some baskets sold for as much as forty dollars, but others were readily available for a dollar or less.[46]

Basketry was also popular because of its perceived link to nature and a vanishing past. As one poet wrote, "Fair token, deftly wrought by savage art / The craft of dusky fingers trained to twine / The supple willow, shaped in patterned line / Enweaving strand by strand the dearest part / Of storied lore wild nature can impart."[47] Or, as another had it, baskets were "the embalmed mummies of the mentality of ages that are past."[48] Baskets embodied the affiliation between Aboriginal people, nature, and the past that so many tourists expected to find in Alaska. They were the perfect souvenir.

Silverwork, the art chosen by Rudolph Walton, was also extremely popular.[49] Aboriginal and non-Aboriginal customers alike bought bracelets. Tourists also brought souvenir teaspoons home to their sideboard drawers as testimonials of travel to remote places.[50] Silver spoons became so characteristic of Tlingit work that they were displayed in the Alaskan exhibit at the Chicago World's Fair.[51] Aside from spoons and bracelets, silversmiths made rings and a wide array of other objects, including sardine forks, paper cutters, pickle forks, napkin rings, olive forks, gravy ladles, butter knives, sugar tongs, and stickpins.[52]

In the early 1890s, Rudolph Walton began making the silver spoons sought by tourists. Silverwork was already established in Sitka, and two other Tlingit silversmiths, Jack and Kooska, had difficulty keeping stock on hand.[53] The Sitka Training School newspaper, *The North Star*, described Walton's decision to turn from carpentry, which he had been forced to supplement with employment in the Juneau mines. "He did not like to leave his home here," reported *The North Star*, "and when he found so many tourists visiting Alaska, and all so eager to purchase curios of various kinds as mementoes of their visit, the thought came to him that perhaps here was an opening whereby he might stay at home and support his family. He concluded to make silver spoons of various shapes and patterns." Walton soon achieved the success of other silversmiths in Sitka. In the summer of 1891, the demand for pieces, which sold for between $2.50 and five dollars, "was so great that Rudolph could not supply it though he worked night and day."[54] In April 1900, Walton wrote in his diary, "I have been working on a silver bracelets for sale to the peoples on a steamers. Very good sale."[55] Walton expanded his area of expertise until he offered a variety of items besides bracelets, including gold work, ivory carvings, silver totem poles, miniature paddles and canoes, "Indian dishes," as well as repair services for watches and jewelry.[56]

Walton made his tools from various found objects. He fashioned an engraver out of a razor set into a lead handle, made molds for the spoon bowls out of a piece of ship's tackle, turned axe handles into different sized punches, and employed an iron ladle to hold the melting silver.[57] He used files and sandpaper to smooth and finish the items. Like other nineteenth-century Aboriginal silver artists on the coast, Walton used silver coins—dollars, half-dollars, quarters, and ten-cent pieces—as raw material.[58] He fashioned the shape of the spoon or bracelet by melting and pouring silver into molds, or hammering, stretching, and bending pieces of silver.[59] He then began the etching, typically a Tlingit design of a bear, wolf, raven, eagle, or salmon. Perhaps with Victorian sideboards, curio corners, and bric-a-brac displays in mind, he sometimes combined these patterns with scenic designs, as he did on one spoon with Mount Edgecombe in the bowl and a totem on the handle. On occasion, he added "Sitka" and the year as well.[60]

Walton likely made souvenir spoons exclusively for the tourist market, but the same was not true of his other items. High-status Tlingit women commonly wore multiple silver bracelets, wider than those made for and purchased by tourists. A wealthy local tradeswoman known as "Princess Thom" reportedly wore nine silver bracelets on each arm.[61] Rudolph Walton took special orders for silver and gold bracelets, rings, and earrings from some Tlingit customers, and he presumably sold ready-made items to others.[62]

Still, tourists constituted the majority of Walton's business. He had an important advantage over White store owners, as contemporary rhetoric lauded the superior authenticity of goods purchased directly from Aboriginal people. As one writer typically insisted of silverwork, it was "the charm of having purchased such souvenirs on the spot which forms half their value."[63] The Alaska Steamship Company elaborated on this notion and enticed travelers with the opportunity to use sign language or perhaps a few words of the Chinook trade jargon while they purchased items. "You can buy Indian baskets in Seattle, and nearly any Eastern city," admitted the company's brochure, "but baskets thus obtained lack the value of those bought from the old Indian woman, in the far-off wilds of Alaska." Buying from an Aboriginal vendor included the unforgettable experiences of the Indian village, "with its totem poles and dried fish; its smoky huts and dirty children; its stolid 'citizens' and numerous dogs; and the terrible time you had reaching an understanding with the Indian sales lady, and your unsuccessful effort to get a basket or mat at less than the marked price." A basket bought in an Alaskan Indian village, promised the brochure, "outvalues a dozen store baskets."[64]

Walton played on this sentiment. In his 1895 advertisements in *The North Star* he asked, "What Can an Indian do?" and then answered his own question: "Visit the workshop of Rudolph Walton, silver and goldsmith and see."[65] Walton's later advertisements likewise suggested that "tourists should call and see Indian working on curios."[66] Walton's advertisements often appeared adjacent to those of Edward de Groff's "Curios, Attu Baskets, Photographic Views, Furs, etc."[67] To compete with merchants like de

Groff, Rudolph Walton—like the women who sold basketry on the wharf—relied on tourists' desire to have an authentic purchasing experience as well as an authentic purchase.

Maintaining the authentic cachet of one's work became more important, as charges of degraded authenticity increased in conjunction with the growing popularity of tourist arts. Writers commonly derided innovation in design as mimicry. Eliza Scidmore complained that a popular silversmith in Wrangell "copies the civilized spread eagle from the half-dollar, and one can only shake his head sadly to see Stikine art so corrupted and debased."[68] The southeast Alaska silver market also faced charges of outright counterfeit. Other newspapers doubted *The Alaskan*'s claim that "Persons perchasing [*sic*] jewelry from the Indians may rest assured that they are getting INDIAN manufacture." In 1885 the *Oregonian* suggested that Alaskan Indians sold goods made in San Francisco to unsuspecting curio hunters.[69] One way to avoid falling victim to such schemes was to buy directly from Indian artists.

Though not accused of such direct frauds, Tlingit weavers met similar charges of declining authenticity. In 1892, Mrs. Brady complained that she could not "get as good work as formerly" but was still "obliged usually to pay quite high prices."[70] Complaints about rising prices were common. Procuring goods inexpensively was often an implicit dimension of authenticity. Tourists viewed Aboriginal people who charged high prices as corrupted by commercialization and stripped of authentic innocence. Racialized as inauthentic, Tlingit business acumen could even lead to assertions that Alaskan Natives were not Indians at all.[71]

Writers also critiqued weavers for using coarser weaves and synthetic, rather than natural, dyes. Scientifically minded observers blamed tourists for this decline: "The articles and utensils are made more gaudy and grotesque each year to catch the tourist's eye; as ethnological specimens they are no longer of the slightest value."[72] Another writer mourned the decline of the once "chaste designs and symbols," which were "gradually yielding, before the coarse taste of traders and tourist, to the more modern and conventional designs."[73]

Such choice of words likened the decline of authenticity to the loss of virginal innocence. The decline of the artifact mirrored that of the artist. Alaskan baskets displayed at the Chicago World's Fair were likewise presented as reflections of their makers. As one observer wrote from the fair, "The case of basketry marks two periods in the life of the people; the subdued dull colors in shapes to suit the needs of the makers contrast with the more gaudy aniline dyes of to-day to the great disadvantage of the latter, although the average tourist would disdain the former."[74] These examples suggest the ease with which viewers likened Aboriginal people to the objects they made.

These examples also reflect the elitist belief that tourists lacked the judgment to distinguish between authentic and inauthentic objects. Amateur and professional collectors competed early on. By the mid-1880s, professional collectors complained that tourists had driven up prices by two to three hundred percent, and Alaskan curators feared that eastern tourists would create a scarcity of artifacts in Alaskan collections.[75] In part, professional collectors had themselves to blame: the exhibits of Indian arts they assembled for public museums and world's fairs helped spark the tourist craze they disdained. From their perspective, the poor taste of tourists degraded quality and inflated prices. But for tourists, the perception that authenticity was declining—regardless of the cause—was reason to buy as many specimens as possible before it was too late.

The distinction between dilettante tourists and professional collectors was often aligned with binary characterizations of emotional women and rational men. Women were cast as tasteless hobbyists, indiscriminate consumers of mass culture's curios who drove up prices for more serious, professional male collectors of authentic high art and artifacts. Marketing techniques reinforced this assumption; newspaper articles about popular Indian arts invariably appeared on the daily woman's page.[76] But, of course, men also collected for hobby as well as for science. U.S. army and navy officers, who often purchased Indian-manufactured items and whose presence in Alaska preceded the tourist steamers by over a decade, were Alaska's first American "tourist collectors."[77] This reality was not reflected in tourism's gendered rhetoric.

High-minded disparagement of tourist arts reflected very little Aboriginal perspective. For Tlingit vendors and artists, tourists were a less discerning and far larger market than professional collectors, who preferred old pieces manufactured for Aboriginal use rather than for sale to Whites.[78] Given the uncertainty of the economic enterprises open to Aboriginal people during the late nineteenth century, artists and vendors had good reason to appreciate the tourists' steady demand for newly made items.

The missionary Livingston Jones was one of the few writers to express an understanding of the curio market that deviated from the authentic/

inauthentic, male/female, scientist/tourist binaries. "There are baskets, and baskets," he wrote. "That is, there are some coarse and worthless and some fine and valuable." For Jones, the value derived from the skill of the artist rather than arbitrary categorizations of authenticity. Jones also commented on the rise in prices, but unlike others he realized that even the several hundred percent increase did not adequately compensate weavers for the labor required to weave a truly fine basket. Jones understood the process required before weaving itself could even begin. Spruce roots had to be dug, roasted, peeled, and split; grasses had to be gathered and trimmed; and dyes had to be prepared.[79] This time-consuming labor was invisible to tourists.

Consumers who attempted to barter for ever-lower prices did not recognize or value the hours of Aboriginal women's labor that went into each piece. One wealthy woman from California reportedly spent an hour haggling over the price of a basket that had taken three days to complete. The artist asked twenty-five cents, but the tourist would pay no more than twenty: "It seemed to the lookers-on that her hopes for this world and the next depended upon her beating the dealer down five cents from the price asked." Insulted by this attitude, the artist eventually refused to sell the basket to the woman at all.[80] The obsession with authenticity that required authentic goods to be old, rare, *and* inexpensive did not speak to the Aboriginal need to make a living. On the contrary, it undermined that need just when Aboriginal people faced increasing economic uncertainty under colonial capitalism.

In their eagerness for authenticity, tourists often moved from the wharf and streetside stalls into the Tlingit village and even directly into Tlingit homes. According to one excursionist, "the first thing that most of our passengers did was to visit the Indian village."[81] In addition to material pieces of Tlingit life they could purchase and carry away, visitors sought eyewitness experiences of it. Sitka boosters boasted of the Tlingit village, or "Ranche," as a local attraction: "We have our Indian Ranch with its interesting but singular people with their frequent dances, potlatches, and festivals, ceremonial visits from neighboring tribes, coming from afar in their decorated canoes, crowded with men and women, young and old, robed in brilliant blankets and gay head adornments."[82] *The Alaskan* further suggested that visitors find a Tlingit guide for such an endeavor. "If possible get some one who knows the village to conduct you through, as many places of interest will be otherwise overlooked. Don't confine your attention to the front

29. Tlingit village at Sitka, 1906. Non-Tlingit dubbed this part of town the "Ranche," rhetorically likening themselves to colonizers elsewhere who used the term "Rancherie" for Indian villages in British Columbia and California among other places. Negative NA 2716, Special Collections,University of Washington Libraries.

row only, go in among the houses and see those on the back street."[83] Here would be found new sights as well as new shopping opportunities. "Generally the natives do not object to visitors entering their houses and often bring out curios (Khlinget, ichtas) for sale."[84] The Sitka Ranche attracted artists as well as curio hunters. Professional and amateur photographers captured Ranche life on film, and the British Columbia artist Emily Carr captured it on canvas.[85]

For these excursionists, the *people* as much as their *products* were the focus of attention. "There are quaintly carved totem poles and the quainter people who carved them," stated a brochure for the Alaska Steamship Company.[86] The interest in visiting the Tlingit Ranche and the popularity of photographs, postcards, and other mass-produced images of the Tlingit people are but two indications of this widespread sentiment. The example of the Sitka trader known alternately as Princess or Mrs. Thom is another. This high-ranking *Kaagwaantaan*, originally from Yakutat, became as much a

30. Interior of Tlingit home in the Sitka Ranche, 1887. Tourists trespassed upon Tlingit homes in search of souvenirs and their own flawed vision of authenticity. Negative NA 2547, Special Collections, University of Washington Libraries.

fixed item on the tourist itinerary as the wonders of Glacier Bay or Sitka's Russian Orthodox Church. She was widely known throughout the archipelago as a trader in furs and curios to Americans and in foodstuffs and blankets to the Tlingit and Haida. She originally made her rounds in a Haida canoe and later in her trading schooner *Active*. When Eliza Scidmore visited Sitka in 1885, she and her party had "heard of Mrs. Thom long before [they] reached Sitka."[87] By 1889, other travel accounts routinely referred to both Scidmore's work and Princess Thom, assuming the reader's familiarity with both.[88] Working to make the most of the attraction she presented, Mrs. Thom helped visitors find her house by erecting a signboard above her door on which she displayed the name given her by tourists, "Princess Thom," and the one given her by the missionaries, "Emeline Baker."[89] Other prominent members of the Sitka Tlingit community did the same.[90] No aspect of Mrs. Thom's life was unworthy of comment—her dress (notoriously gaudy), the state of her home (remarkably tidy and comfortable), and her marital situation (two husbands, one of whom was much younger than she and had formerly been her slave) were all favorite topics. Above all, writers commented on her wealth, estimated to be in the tens of thousands of dollars, and reportedly kept entirely in silver dollars, except for the amount represented by the dozens of silver bracelets and rings she wore. Mrs. Thom shrewdly turned her popularity into profit. The tourists who came to see the "sight" of Mrs. Thom also purchased baskets, carvings, furs, and occasionally even one of the famed silver bracelets right off her arm.[91]

Tourists who roamed the Sitka Ranche were much like visitors to the Chicago World's Fair and to the Puget Sound hop fields. Sightseers sought what they believed were everyday aspects of Aboriginal life and transformed them into spectacle. In so doing, they confirmed their belief that the characteristics they assumed to be authentic were also normal, or everyday, aspects of Aboriginal life. The tourist invasion of Sitka was more intrusive than the gaze of Chicago fairgoers or Puget Sound Indian watchers. In Chicago, the Kwakwa̱ka̱'wakw willingly placed themselves onstage, and in

31. "Princess Thom and Mrs. Mausbauer," ca. 1896. Tourists who visited Sitka treated the woman on the left as one of the town's attractions. When this image was published in F. Knapp's and R. L. Childe's *The Thlinkets of Southeastern Alaska* (1896), it became part of the tourist literature that helped turn "Princess Thom," as she was known, into somewhat of a legend. PN-1533, Royal British Columbia Museum.

Puget Sound, tourists entered temporary Aboriginal living spaces. In Sitka, visitors penetrated the inner sanctum of permanent Tlingit homes. Sitka Tlingit tolerated this intrusion, and like Aboriginal people elsewhere in the Pacific Northwest, derived some benefits from it. At the same time, White residents of Sitka reaped substantial gain from the Indian-watching tourists. The tourists brought economic prosperity and international attention to Sitka, which local boosters and developers hoped would translate into Congressional favor and eventual statehood.

Chapter Eight

"The Trend Is Upward": Mission and Cottage Life

In Alaska, as elsewhere in North America, shipping routes and other infrastructure grew up hand in hand with tourism. But in Alaska, tourism was also intimately tied to the missionary enterprise. The marriage of tourism and missions was not an obvious one, nor was it always harmonious. Missionaries worried, as did industrialists, that tourism would impede "progress." Definitions of progress differed—developers focused on capitalist growth and missionaries on Alaska Natives' progress toward civilization—but the belief that the authentic image demanded by tourists pointed to the past and not the future was the same. As one missionary sympathizer commented on Tlingit customs, "looked at from the tourist's point of view, all these and other similar features of Indian life are very interesting and amusing. But they seem very sad and disheartening to those to whom is deputed authority and the care for the welfare, spiritual and material of these people, who are still to an extent children of nature."[1]

However sad and disheartening they found old customs, missionaries depended on displays of "authentic Indians" to elicit much-needed financial contributions from sympathetic Christians. Seizing the opportunity presented by tourism, missionaries attempted to show the flip side of the image that tourists saw on the wharf and in the Ranche. They put mission life on display. In their attempt to capitalize on this supposed dichotomy between civilized and uncivilized, missionaries at the Sitka Training School engaged in an enterprise much like the one Canadian officials undertook in the mock Indian schoolhouses at the Chicago World's Fair. This enterprise brought them attention and prosperity, but it betrayed the rhetoric of equality they promised their students.

An article from the Sitka Training School newspaper illustrated the dichotomy upon which the mission relied. It contrasted a photograph of Tlingit women selling salmonberries in front of the old Russian trading post with the photographs of students that it usually published. As the writer explained, "In this issue we give you a view of some of the older women from the native village who have never been in school. This picture was made several years ago and shows the women as they were ready to sell berries on a day when a tourist steamer was at the wharf."[2] The students "were of the younger generation—a generation reaching out for new things: a written language, practical means of working, greater pleasures, added cares, new hopes, new faith, a new life. The trend is upward." The photo of the berry vendors, on the other hand, "shows a passing people. They represent the old life. They too have reached out for the new and have touched a bit of it; but it has been, as it were, reaching with one hand while with the other they have kept fast hold on the old . . . They represent a declining age."[3] These old ways were said to be disintegrating as surely as the logs of the old Russian structure in the background were crumbling. The article portrayed an absolute opposition between the authentic but uncivilized life of the Ranche and the civilized life of the mission. It denied the possibility of

32. Tlingit women selling salmonberries in Sitka. Tlingit vendors were part of the everyday street scene in Sitka, but when the Sitka Training School newspaper featured this photograph in 1910, it characterized the women as remnants of quickly fading old ways. Photo by E.W. Merrill, PCA 57-169, E. W. Merrill Collection, Alaska State Library.

33. Tlingit mission students pose with Sheldon Jackson, 1887. For Presbyterian missionaries, students such as these represented the civilized future that defined the mission's purpose. Negative NA 2552, Special Collections, University of Washington Libraries.

a middle ground. This was the message the mission hoped tourists would take away.

As with many supposed dichotomies, the opposition between mission and Ranche was at best exaggerated and at worst false. Mission and village residents continued to interact; their ways of life continued to overlap. Missionaries excused many of these continuities, arguing that they were outweighed by the material evidence of modern, civilized life among their graduates. Members of Sitka's White frontier society, many of whom did not share the Presbyterian certainty that the Tlingit were "civilizable," were less forgiving. They held out for a stricter dichotomy between savage and civilized than even the most successful missionaries could hope to achieve.[4]

When Presbyterian missionaries set out to turn the Sitka Training School and its students into tourist attractions, they met with remarkable success. Teachers and administrators of the school started the newspaper *The North Star* in 1886 with this end in mind, gearing it explicitly toward philanthropic tourists.[5] The mission became a must-see sight in Sitka, and visitors invariably left impressed by the success of the missionary project.[6]

Missionaries featured student accomplishments in a variety of ways. They led tourists through the school departments and invited them to watch the children perform music, songs, and recitations.[7] These performances entertained at the same time as they demonstrated students' proficiency in English. Tourists were also invited to inspect the civilized life of the mission cottages which housed graduates, including Rudolph Walton for a time.[8]

All of this was intended to contrast with the "uncivilized" Tlingit in the Ranche. But in some respects, the line between these supposedly "civilized" and "uncivilized" Indians was blurred. Like the women who sold their wares on the wharf and in streetside displays, the students of the Training School made carvings and baskets for sale to tourists.[9] Some student work was displayed at international expositions, such as the 1884–85 Cotton States and International Exposition in Atlanta, and some was sold to museums.[10] There was a circularity to the market for students' work. The sale of students' pieces to museums augmented the mission's income from tourist purchases. And displays of Aboriginal art at exhibitions and museums fueled public interest in Alaska Natives and ultimately helped increase the tourist traffic.

The museum that Sheldon Jackson founded on the school grounds in 1887 was an additional tourist attraction. As he instructed the curator: "Whenever you hear the gun notifying you that a steamer has arrived, you will go home and dress up for the reception of tourists at the museum."[11] Jackson's instructions meant that the museum sometimes opened at very odd hours, as steamers could arrive at any time of the day or night.[12] The museum was an ethnographic resource, a showcase for students' work, and a tourist attraction. Today it houses some extraordinarily fine pieces by Rudolph Walton.

The ultimate purpose of attracting tourists to the mission grounds and museum was to solicit donations in cash and kind. The Presbyterian mission relied upon donations from supportive visitors for many aspects of the school's operation. The practice of soliciting donations from tourists dated to the early days of tourist steamer service. Ministers conducted religious services on board and took collections for the Alaskan missions. In 1887, the Reverend Charles Baldwin of Washington, D.C., collected fifty dollars for the mission school in this manner.[13] The dependence of missionary activity on tourist donations was sometimes acute. The story of Frederick Moore, a Tlingit who graduated from the Training School and then became a missionary, is a case in point. Jackson and fellow missionary Alonzo E. Austin were forced to abandon their plan to send Moore to Oregon for mission work when the tourists of 1891 proved ungenerous. Austin reported to

Jackson, "Did not raise any money here last summer from the tourists for [Moore]. They were not a giving crowd for some reason."[14] Other projects were more successful. In 1905, Jackson raised money on board the S.S. *Queen* to fund construction of a new Aboriginal village at Saxman modeled after William Duncan's closely controlled Christian community at New Metlakatla on Annette Island.[15]

As mouthpiece for the Sitka Training School, *The North Star* was an important vehicle for soliciting donations. Writers often used examples of young girls to evoke sympathy and money from Christian readers and/or visitors. Much like the Reverend A. J. Hall in Alert Bay, missionaries in Alaska equated the lives of Aboriginal women with sexual exploitation and wantonness. They believed that Tlingit girls who remained in their villages would be forced into child marriages or prostitution. They also worried that girls were vulnerable to charges of witchcraft. A sample from 1888 is typical: "To take a girl from a heathen home, where she is liable to be sold as a slave—rented out to a life of sin—or tortured to death as a witch; to take an immortal being from such surroundings and train her to become clean and pure and gentle and industrious—to lead such a one unto Jesus is a work which angels might envy." All that was required to perform such a service was to fund a scholarship in the Sitka Training School.[16]

Donors also had the "privilege of re-naming" the children they sponsored—that is, of giving each an English name.[17] Rudolph Walton received his English name in just this fashion. Shortly after Walton entered the Training School, the Presbyterian congregation in Bryn Mawr, Pennsylvania, decided to support him and renamed him Rudolph Walton to honor the superintendent of their own church school.[18]

Sometimes school administrators solicited specific items from donors. When the school band instruments grew old the superintendent requested new ones: "I am exceedingly anxious that the band shall be ready for this summer's tourist season . . . if some friend to this work could give us a lift in this matter, it would be an immense aid next summer." A piccolo, clarinets, cornets, and "bellfronts" were needed.[19] The instruments were important, because the band was a highlight for tourists, and it often played at the wharf as the steamers pulled in and out.[20] Thus, even before tourists disembarked, they had an overview of the "savage" and "civilized" arrayed on the wharf.

Some tourists donated on their own initiative. One group of "influential Christian tourists" was so impressed by the school that the men purchased ten tool sets and benches for the new carpenter shop, and the women provided materials for the kindergarten class and sewing machines for the sewing room. One particularly generous couple also made "handsome individual contributions." That same summer, Mr. and Mrs. William S. Ladd from Portland, Oregon, made it possible for the school to replace its "tin plates, iron cups and rusty knives" with "crockery plates, cups and saucers, good substantial knives and forks."[21]

Pedagogically minded mission staff believed the benefits of such donations extended beyond the material realm. The new crockery, for example, reportedly resulted in the "general improvement in the behavior of the pupils at the table."[22] The presence of the tourists themselves was likewise assumed beneficial. According to *The North Star*, "the presence of so many Americans of the better class has given the natives a greater respect for the American people, and a higher conception of the power of the Gospel, which they think has made the difference between the good people they have seen and themselves in their ignorance and poverty."[23] Missionaries and teachers saw exposure to this "better class of Americans" as an antidote to interactions students had with miners, saloonkeepers, and other frontierspeople, who presumably constituted the "worst class of Americans."[24] This attitude matched the disdain of reform-minded individuals in Puget Sound toward the "trashy whites" who frequented Aboriginal horse races.

Tourist visits, however, created serious disruptions in classroom routines. The steamers unloaded between fifty and two hundred tourists at a time for visits that often lasted an entire day. It is doubtful that much schoolwork was accomplished during the months when the tourist season overlapped with the school year.[25]

Along with the school and museum, the cottages that housed graduates of the Training School completed the mission's triumvirate of attractions. The first three cottages were built during the fall of 1887, and by 1905 there were fifteen. Each cottage was fitted with a small brown and gold sign naming the cottage in honor of the individual, congregation, or society that had donated the money. The predominantly Northeastern origins of contributors was clear from the cottage names: Bryn Mawr, Cobble, Jamaica Plains, New York, Jarvis, Wellesley, and Northfield.[26] Rudolph Walton lived in Miller cottage, named for Reverend W. H. Miller of Bryn Mawr, Pennsylvania.

To obtain a cottage, young couples promised to observe the Sabbath, send their children to school, abstain from tobacco, liquor, and gambling, and renounce "heathen" customs. Cottage residents received their homes through something comparable to a no-money-down, interest-free mortgage. Over time, they were expected to pay back the cost of the cottage—between $350 and $500—to the mission, which would in turn reuse the money to build another cottage.[27] The system was meant to be self-sustaining, with the initial donations functioning as endowments. Confusion arose when some residents, including Rudolph Walton, were led to believe the cottages were gifts.[28] The variable costs for the different cottages also created problems, because some residents had to pay more than others. Eventually Sheldon Jackson equalized the amount that residents were required to pay.[29]

The origin of the funds for Rudolph Walton's cottage is suggestive of the relationship between eastern Christian philanthropists and the Sitka mission. Congregation members in Bryn Mawr maintained their support of Walton for years after they renamed him. Their relationship to him resembles relationships fostered by child-sponsorship programs of today. When fund raising for the cottage began, the congregation knew it was to be Rudolph Walton's home. They raised the money piecemeal from a variety of sources: the Sunday School, church collections, individual donations, and a "little Fair" organized by two young girls.[30]

The donors at Bryn Mawr expected a good deal of control over the specifics of the home they financed. Every detail mattered. Walton was pleased when the cottage was completed and sent the donors a drawing of the house. The donors, however, were disappointed, and wanted to know why the cottage looked smaller and less impressive than the five hundred dollars' worth they had contributed.[31] Jackson defended the cottage by providing a precise description of its layout and insisting that Walton now had "one of the best dwelling houses in the place . . . a better and more comfortable house than [was] possessed by any native or Russian and by 9/10ths of the Americans in Sitka."[32]

Rudolph Walton's cottage soon became a mission showpiece. Sitka Presbyterians often invoked Walton as living proof of their mission's success. In his description of "The Model Cottages" that appeared in both *The North Star* and *The Alaskan* in August 1895, Dr. Wilbur focused on the Miller cottage. Lauding the cottages "as perpetual arguments in favor of Christianity and education," Wilbur detailed the Waltons' domestic scene. Mrs. Walton entertained Dr. Wilbur while Rudolph Walton was in his workshop. Mrs. Walton's reluctance to speak English did not detract from the evidence of civilized life presented by the material surroundings. Approaching the cot-

34. Cottages built at the Presbyterian mission, Sitka. Rudolph Walton's home, the Miller cottage, is in front. PH3838, photograph collections, Sitka Historical Society.

tage, Wilbur noticed "the neat board walk and gravel walks around the side." He was then shown into "the room which is a parlor and sitting room, about twelve feet square—carpeted, sofa at one side, rocking chairs, table and book case, as we should find in any comfortable home. In a small room adjoining this sitting room we find a cabinet with some pretty china and a few odd trinkets treasured by the family. The dining room and kitchen in the rear though less pretentious are neat, while upstairs the two bedrooms are furnished with bedsteads and the usual furniture."[33] The material circumstances of the cottages were critical markers of Christian civility. White visitors typically focused on the bourgeois furnishings. For Dazie Stromstadt, a local schoolteacher, phonographs, pianos, and sewing machines were evidence that these were "the Indians who [were] living a 'civilized life.' "[34]

Indian curios were also part of this civilized scene. The fact that cottage residents offered beadwork and basketry for inspection and sale somehow augmented rather than diminished the cottage's civilized charm.[35] Cottage residents could expect visits from tourists at least as often as Ranche residents, and they took advantage. Perhaps this was what Rudolph Walton was busy with in his workshop when Dr. Wilbur visited: carving items for sale to tourists. In the case of the Sitka mission, the material surroundings of the manufacture and sale of curios seem to have made all the difference in how non-Aboriginal observers judged the vendors.

The critical eye visitors leveled at Walton's cottage suggests that the donors' concern about the house's physical appearance was well founded. It was important to Jackson and the donors at Bryn Mawr that the cottage be an unequivocal material marker of civility. A similar faith in the materiality of civilized traits gave rise to the belief that ceramic dishes improved students' behavior. Nineteenth-century Protestants commonly believed that outward conditions mirrored the less visible condition of an individual's inner self. As *The North Star* expounded, "how important the home influence; who in the world does not breathe into society the breath of the spirit imbibed at home. . . . Nowhere can Christianity prosper so much as in the homes."[36] A civilized house was presumed to mean a civilized heart. Rudolph Walton was instructed in this belief during his time at the Sitka Training School. He likely also believed that the contents of his heart would be recognized even if he left the mission cottage to live in the Ranche.

But from the perspective of mission administrators, supporters, and visitors, cottage life—separate from Ranche or village life—was the destination of a one-way journey toward civilization that took students from Ranche to mission to cottage.[37] The cottages embodied the kind of follow-through that Protestant reformers believed was necessary for the values and lifestyle imbued at the mission school to triumph over the lure of "old ways." They initiated the cottage program to "shield" young Aboriginal Christians from "the contaminating influences of the Ranch."[38] Missionaries hoped the cottage program would make graduates "strong enough to withstand the temptations of old friends and associates," something deemed "impossible if they resided in the Indian Village."[39] Missionaries had no doubt that a return to the Ranche meant a reversion to heathenism.

Skeptics of the missionary project often asked, "What will the children do when they leave the mission?" and "What shall be done with the Indian when he has become civilized and educated?"[40] Answering these questions could be tricky—and the cottage program provided the delicate compromise required. Many non-Aboriginal people already believed that devoting resources to Aboriginal people impeded Alaska's economic and political progress. They presumed Indians and development to be antithetical. While serving as governor, John G. Brady earned the pejorative nickname "Siwash Brady" for his perceived favoritism of the former over the latter.[41] Although many Whites wanted graduates to lead a "civilized" life, they did not want civilized Aboriginal people to interfere with the privileged economic enterprises of non-Aboriginal people. They did not want Aboriginal people to compete too successfully in the marketplace. Promoting the settlement of mission graduates in cottages—separated from "uncivilized" Indian neighborhoods and respectable White neighborhoods alike—was missionaries' way out of this bind.

For many Whites, the production of tourist arts was an ideal occupation for Aboriginal people, as it did not put mission graduates in economic competition with Whites. This was, in part, why *The North Star* held up Rudolph Walton's silversmithing as the "Providential answer" to the question of how graduates would make a living.[42] Walton's talent was undeniable. At the same time, generalized assertions of the inherently artistic nature of Tlingit and other Aboriginal people must be read in light of the prejudicial economic context of the day.[43] Objections to Aboriginal competition were on the rise.[44] Given the already limited economic options open to Aboriginal people, missionaries could hardly deny their followers access to the lucrative tourist and collector's markets even if it meant tolerating—and promoting—the persistence of some "old ways."

The success story that the cottages told was predicated on the juxtaposition of the mission settlement and the Indian Ranche. The cottages, editorialized *The North Star*, "with their neat and inviting appearance are an object lesson which strongly contrasts with the filth and squalor of the Indian huts in other parts of the town."[45] Moreover, with the Sheldon Jackson museum next to the cottages, tourists did not even have to walk across town in order to view contrasting evidence of "old ways." Even Dr. Wilbur, who was more sympathetic toward Tlingit life than most, could not help but see the cottages in stark opposition to the Ranche. For him, as for most non-Aboriginal residents and visitors to Sitka, the cottages were "models for the generally wretched and dirty houses in the Indian village."[46] Sympathetic as Wilbur, Brady, and Jackson were to Walton and other mission students, they never questioned the assumption that cottage and Ranche life were irreconcilably opposed. It was hardly in their self-interest to do so. Yet this assumption limited their vision and crippled their attempts to defend mission students against hostile White Alaskans. The Ranche and cottage opposition was just one of the dichotomies that carved out the exclusionary rhetorical space of authenticity.

This notion of absolute opposition between Ranche and cottage life served the needs of missionaries and tourists, but it bore little relation to the reality of residents' lives. As Walton's granddaughter, Joyce Walton Shales, has written, "most of the residents and students [in the model cottages] had one foot in each world; they had strong relationships with their family and kin in the Tlingit community and they were trying to meet the demands of the Presbyterian missionaries who felt that the Tlingit needed a complete makeover."[47] Rudolph Walton's work as an artist and Mrs. Walton's curio sales are two examples of continuity between cottage and Ranche life. There are many others.

Amid the glowing accounts of Rudolph Walton's Victorian domestic arrangements, it is almost possible to overlook the detail that Walton's cottage housed not a nuclear family unit of husband, wife, and children but an extended family that included Walton's mother and grandmother. The Waltons made the Miller cottage into a smaller version of the Tlingit "community house" that historically sheltered related family members. Widowed mothers were commonly included, and Rudolph Walton's mother had been widowed in 1891.[48] This extended family was also a bilingual one. Rudolph Walton's mother and grandmother both spoke Tlingit to his children and, for all we know, he and his wife did too sometimes. From this bilingual environment, Walton reportedly said that his children "get mixed."[49] The Tlingit language would have been an essential link to family and friends who lived in the Ranche, where Tlingit remained the vernacular. In 1914, the teacher at the Tlingit village school reported that the students still went by their Tlingit names and would not learn their English ones.[50]

Rudolph Walton's seasonal work patterns also contradicted the supposed dichotomy between Indian life in the Ranche and "civilized" life in the cottages. Long after he moved into the cottage and chose the silversmith's profession—reportedly because "he did not like to leave his home"—Walton continued to participate in commercial and subsistence activities that took him away from Sitka on a seasonal basis.[51] Into his work as an artist and storekeeper, Walton incorporated salmon fishing, herring roe gathering, berry picking, carpentry, boat building, lumbering, and hunting and trapping deer, mink, otter, and seals. Seasonal migrations brought Walton together with family and friends from the Ranche and the cottages alike. He went annually to the sealing camp on Biorka Island, where he had been born. As *The North Star*'s successor, *The Thlinget*, reported, "the native people are out at Biorka island in full force. . . . Both the native village and the Cottages are almost deserted."[52] These activities linked Walton to historical subsistence practices and kinship networks. The rhetoric of authenticity labeled such migratory activities authentic, and thus uncivilized. If a civilized life meant material dependency on colonial consumer goods, these activities did signal the incomplete nature of Rudolph Walton's incorporation into civilization. But for Walton, these activities were not opposed to his "civilized" cottage life as storekeeper and artist; rather, his various occupations complemented each other. Walton regularly carved while away at camp, for example.[53] In this, Walton was like hop pickers who stopped on their way home to gather basketry materials, and like many other Tlingit who folded the production of trade goods into their mobile economic routines.[54]

A large part of the attraction of these seasonal occupations was the income. A single seal pelt, for example, could bring as much as thirty dollars.[55] But as with the hop fields, it is unlikely that economics, however significant, was the sole consideration. The enjoyment gained from days or weeks in camp with family and friends had value. Rudolph Walton allowed the pleasure of such activities to shine through his otherwise dispassionate diary entries. The entries for February 1900, while Walton was away trapping mink and otter and hunting for deer, are replete with lines such as "We have very good time," "We have a very good time again," and "We have a very good time in camping."[56] Though understated on their own, set in the context of Walton's other entries, his descriptions of his many stays in fishing, hunting, and trapping camps reveal the deep satisfaction and happiness he derived from these occasions.

The Thanksgiving holiday meal was another manifestation of the ongoing relationship between Ranche and cottage residents. On 28 November 1902, Rudolph Walton recorded in his diary, "We give a big dinner to all Ranch peoples Thanks give [*sic*]."[57] By 1908, Thanksgiving dinner, which was served in the "Cottage Hall," had long been an occasion when several hundred people from the cottages and the Ranche came together for blessings, games, speeches, and, of course, the meal. Russian Orthodox Tlingit who lived in the Ranche came, as did Presbyterians from the cottages and the Ranche. Cottage residents organized and paid for the meal during the early years of the event, and Ranche residents shared these responsibilities after 1907.[58] In his work on the Tlingit Russian Church in Sitka, Sergei Kan emphasizes the distinction between "traditionalist" Tlingit who joined the Russian Church, and "Americanized" Tlingit who became Presbyterians.[59] But the Thanksgiving dinners are one indication of considerable social interaction between the two communities. Moreover, such occasions were moments when Tlingit practices could have been enacted alongside or within Christian custom.[60] This interdenominational cooperation became political when it characterized the founding of the Alaska Native Brotherhood in 1912.[61]

The population moved not just from Ranche to cottage, as on Thanksgiving, but from cottage to Ranche as well. Rudolph Walton frequently attended prayer meetings in the Ranche, as well as other meetings at the houses of Fred Davis or his brother-in law James Jackson.[62] Some cottagers made these moves permanent. In 1891, Willie Wells, another original cottage resident, built a home in the Ranche.[63] Rudolph Walton followed Wells's path back to the Ranche sometime in the 1890s.

These examples of contact and continuity between Ranche and cottage households challenge the oppositional framework of authenticity. Tlingit lives did not conform to the colonial discourse of authenticity, but neither did they lack a discourse of their own in which authenticity and authority were tightly imbricated. Authenticity was manufactured and contested from *within*, as well as from without. An example comes from a conflict in the 1890s between the *Kiks.'adi* and the *L'uknax.'adi* clans over the ownership of the frog as a clan emblem. Both clans located their proprietary rights to the frog within oral tradition. Open conflict erupted when members of the *L'uknax.'adi* clan erected a frog house in Sitka, provoking the powerful Sitka *Kiks.'adi*. Rudolph Walton played a key role in an attempt to broker peace in 1903. The dispute seems never to have been fully resolved, however. Fifty years after the initial trouble, the *L'uknax.'adi* told the *Kiks.'adi*, "You are our enemy. We don't forget the Frog House."[64] Here was a pitched battle for authenticity staged well outside the terrain of colonial categories.

The dispute dated to at least February 1899, when the Tlingit were "having rather serious trouble about their totems, crests etc."[65] Looking to Tlingit protocol, the Tlingit held a potlatch in an attempt to resolve the dispute. Describing the event to Sheldon Jackson, a Training School teacher, Olga Hilton, reported that the whole Tlingit population was "having a pow wow over a frog emblem. Two clans are quarreling over it and we are waiting to see how the trouble will end. The dancing and feasting takes up most of their time. More natives are expected to arrive and in their honor a home was erected." Significantly, she added, "even the cottage people take part."[66] Although his name was not mentioned, Rudolph Walton was quite possibly one of the cottage residents involved at this early stage. Even the Tlingit missionary Fred Moore was involved, having "come over for that purpose . . . very interested in the 'frog trouble.' "[67]

The resolution reached in 1899 did not last, and another attempt was made the following year. According to *The Alaskan*, "after a great pow wow, and many speeches by the leading men of the different clans, [they] finally decided to bury the hatchet and hereafter live in peace and enjoy life under the American flag."[68] Those present reportedly "decided to do away with the Frog, Eagle, Crow and other emblems over which there has been a great deal of discussion and much trouble, and allow each person or family to put up as many emblems in front or on top of their house as they desire, but it was thought that it would be best to put up the American flag, obey their countries laws and do away with clans, natives chiefs and the old customs."[69] Chaos rather than peace ensued, however. These "emblems" could not simply be "done away with." On 5 and 6 February 1901, Rudolph Walton wrote in his diary: "The Indians cut up the Frog totem on the fron[t] of the house," and "The Kicks-sat-ta cut up the frog totem on the house which Tom house [*sic*]."[70] This aggressive act led to a reported "riot" in Sitka. X'u-xʷAtc, the *Kiks.'adi* man who brought down the frog, subsequently commissioned a pole with *L'uknax.'adi* crests on it. He held the pole until the time of his death, when he expressed his desire for peace and sold the pole back to *L'uknax.'adi* man, Charley Kitka.[71]

Following the so-called riot, charges were laid for disturbing the peace. According to *The Alaskan*, the ultimate result of the court proceeding was "a true bill to the charge of injury to property but not to riot," and "five of the offenders pled guilty and were sentenced to three months in the District jail." Rudolph Walton's relatives James Jackson and Augustus Bean testified as witnesses.[72]

But judicial intervention did not resolve the issue. On 16 January 1903, Rudolph Walton met with Governor Brady to discuss the problem and perhaps to seek his sanction for the Tlingit peace ceremony to come.[73] It was not uncommon for Tlingit disputes to be solved along the dual axes of American and Tlingit law. Criminal cases involving Tlingit plaintiffs or defendants who appeared before the United States District Court at Sitka were frequently also handled according to Tlingit law through the distribution of blankets or other property.[74] This seems to be what happened in the frog dispute. According to the missionary George Beck, "Some of the [Tlingit] people said, We have tried the law, but it did not help us. We tried the Church—meaning the missionaries—and we are still enemies. Now, the only way is to make peace as our fathers did, by paying blankets and dancing."[75] Beck may have had some insight into the process. Two visits that he paid to Rudolph Walton immediately following the conclusion of the peace ceremony raise the possibility that Walton was an informant for Beck's published account of the dispute.[76]

This prolonged and emotional dispute must be understood within the context of Tlingit notions of property. The frog's significance for clan members is inadequately conveyed by the English word "emblem." For the Tlingit, the frog was *at.óow*.[77] *At.óow*—literally an owned or purchased thing or object—located an individual's status and position within a particular object. Land, a geographical feature, a spirit, a name, a story, an artistic design, all of these could be *at.óow*. Objects or articles of clothing that bore representations of *at.óow* became *at.óow* themselves. Tlingit elder Austin Hammond articulated the centrality of this concept to Tlingit society. When asked, "Where is your history?," Hammond referred to *at.óow*, the robes, tunics, blankets, and other regalia worn during Tlingit ceremonials, and said "We wear our history."[78] As we have seen, White Protestants believed they could discern an individual's civilized status through a semiotics of crockery, furniture, and sewing machines. *At.óow* were similarly markers of status for the Tlingit. Perhaps the Protestant connection between material possessions and identity was not entirely unfamiliar to Rudolph Walton and other Tlingit.[79] We know that Rudolph Walton accepted many ornaments of Western civilization. But his involvement in the peace ceremony indicates that he never relinquished the value he placed on *at.óow*. It remained important enough to him to warrant risking censure from the Presbyterian Church.

The peace ceremony Walton recorded in his diary matches that described by the anthropologist Frederica de Laguna in her later work on the Yakutat Tlingit.[80] Each side in the dispute took a hostage or *G̲uwakaan*, meaning "deer," so-called because of the deer's harmless nature.[81] According to Tlingit elder Charlie Joseph, Senior, the *G̲uwakaan* was a calm, gentle man without anger or violence. In this instance, the *G̲uwakaan* was Rudolph Walton. In de Laguna's description, the "deer" were "held for a period of 8 days, with dances every night. On the 9th night the hostages were taken home, where they and their captors were feasted, and on the 10th night, they all met together in one big house for a final feast and dance, when the hostages were freed."[82] The details of the process described by Walton differ slightly from de Laguna's description, but there is no doubt that the ceremony is the same. Walton's ceremony spanned more than ten days and had only six nights of dancing. Participants suspended the dancing on Sundays, and in contrast to anthropologists' assertions that deer were not permitted to see their spouses, Walton visited his wife during the proceedings.[83]

Walton's connection with the frog dispute offers a glimpse of Tlingit notions of authenticity. It demonstrates that strong respect and attachment existed between groups that scholars have tended to divide into "conservative" and "modern." It suggests that the Tlingit sorted themselves using categories different from those used by colonizers. Accounts that attribute Christian Tlingit involvement in the dispute to the "traditionalist" nature of the Russian Orthodox Church congregation overlook the fact that prominent members of the Presbyterian Church such as Rudolph Walton were intimately involved too.[84] Although Walton had not been personally involved in the desecration of the frog emblem, he was implicated as a member of the *Kiks.'adi* clan, and he took the action expected of him as a high-ranking *Kiks.'adi*. It was an honor to be selected *G̱uwakaan*.[85] In the eyes of the Tlingit community, neither Walton's membership in the Presbyterian Church, in which he was an elder by this time, nor his bourgeois house furnishings undermined his eligibility, or responsibility, to play this important role.

Presbyterian Church officials saw things differently. They believed Walton's "civilized" traits should have alienated him from the Tlingit community and prevented his association with Tlingit events. Walton chose not to appear before the presbytery when it met to discuss his involvement in the "Frog trouble," and he narrowly avoided suspension from Church eldership.[86] Church officials likely saw Walton's participation in the ceremony as an example of the backsliding they so feared in their graduates. But for Walton, participation in the peace ceremony did not mean renunciation of his "civilized" Christian life and principles any more than his seasonal hunting and fishing migrations meant turning his back on his "civilized" occupation as shopkeeper. His was a very different view of Tlingit authenticity.[87]

Several years after the peace ceremony, Rudolph Walton again acted on his belief that allegiance to the Tlingit community and customs was compatible with the life he had led in the cottage settlement. This time, Church officials were less forgiving. In 1904, his wife Daisy died, and in August 1905 he married Mary Dick Davis, a clan relative of his deceased wife, a prominent *Kaagwaantan*, and widow of Fred Davis. Walton faced serious censure from the Church for this marriage, which had been performed "according to heathen custom," that is, according to Tlingit social custom. Moreover, the couple lived together for several days before they were legally married. As Shales writes, by marrying Mary Davis in this fashion, Rudolph Walton "indicate[d] his respect for this particular aspect of Tlingit culture." As a result, he was suspended indefinitely from Church eldership.[88]

Shales offers another example of how her grandfather simultaneously lived in what colonial society told him were two mutually exclusive worlds. Recounting one of her family's important stories, Shales writes,

> Rudolph's second wife, my grandmother, was angry at Rudolph's insistence that the children go away to mission schools. She felt he was being too hard on them. . . . According to family lore, our grandmother, Mary, left home due to this disagreement. And according to Tlingit tradition [in] order to get her to come back home, Rudolph had to compose a love song, which he did.[89]

There could have been any number of reasons for Mary Walton's objection to the mission schools, ranging from conflicting cultures and values to the health of the children. As Shales points out, "going away to school at that time didn't just mean that children were gone from home for a while, but that many children were thrown into unhealthy situations, became ill, and died at school. Our grandmother knew of these situations, and was concerned for the well-being of the children, a concern that led her to leave home in protest."[90] Mary Walton's fears were not unfounded: Rudolph and Daisy's oldest son, Thomas, died in 1911, at the age of twenty-four, while at school in Washington. He had been away from home since he was sixteen.[91]

Rudolph Walton's love song is a poignant example of how Walton wove together different values. He clearly valued education.[92] When this brought him into conflict with his wife Mary, he was willing to see her leave home over the disagreement. But education and all it represented were not the only values he held dear. Walton's love song reminds us of the maze of choices faced by Aboriginal people on the Northwest Coast at the turn of the century. In order to mend the familial rift created by his adamant belief in "modern" education, Walton turned to a longstanding Tlingit way of making amends to a loved one. The historical use of these love songs was also linked to peacemaking ceremonies.[93] These ceremonies of peace and reconciliation, and by extension the Tlingit sense of balance and reciprocity, were important to Rudolph Walton. They were values he refused to relinquish, values he reconciled with his life as a model mission graduate. Walton's love song also sheds light on the context of the Davis case. Joyce Walton Shales does not relate at what point in her grandparents' relationship this dispute took place. But Mary Walton's vehement opposition to mission schools may help account for the extraordinary length to which Rudolph Walton went in order to enroll the Davis children in the public school in Sitka.

Chapter Nine

Civilization on Trial: The Davis Case

> Civilization, though, of course, the term must be considered relative, includes, I apprehend, more than a prosperous business, a trade, a house, white man's clothes, and membership in a church.[1]

> I don't see what this has to do with the school.[2]

It is hard to know whether Rudolph and Mary Walton expected difficulty when they decided to send Dora and Tillie to public school in Sitka. Given Rudolph's personal history with the mission school, he may have wanted to send them there were it not for Mary's opposition. At the same time, memory of Church censure over the peace ceremony and his marriage was probably fresh and painful. Unwilling to compromise his commitment to the children's education, he may have hoped to spare them some of the conflict—both public and inner—that he had endured. The Waltons also may have feared that after their controversial marriage the children would be unwelcome at the mission school.

Regardless, the Walton family ended up at the center of a legal procedure that proved personally wrenching at the time and that remains historically illuminating today. The testimony treated Sitka Tlingit according to the same binary terms of authenticity that were familiar to the Kwakwa̲ka̲'wakw in Chicago and the hop pickers in Puget Sound. Many Aboriginal people wrung benefits from this binary discourse. But the courtroom's legal arena brought the limited nature of authenticity's rules of engagement into sharp relief. Images of authentic Indians were the stuff of lucrative tourist attractions, but they were also the stuff of social exclusion and inequality. Legal counsel easily extrapolated a "one-drop" theory of civilization from the binary discourse of authenticity. The Waltons and other involved families faced a no-win situation.

The year 1905 had been tumultuous for Alaskan educators, parents, and students. The Nelson Act, enacted by Congress on 27 January 1905, restructured the disposition of Alaska's public revenue derived from license fees. The new law had particularly deleterious effects on unincorporated towns such as Sitka, halving their educational funds.[3] The law also provided for the establishment of local school boards to administer the now-reduced funds to "white children and children of mixed blood who lead a civilized life."[4] A Sitka School District was established in March 1905, and the school board elected shortly thereafter.[5]

Prior to this, education in Alaska was explicitly provided without reference to race.[6] Education of White and Alaska Native children alike was under the federally appointed General Agent for Education in Alaska, a position held by Sheldon Jackson from its inception in 1885 until 1907. Under the Nelson Act, education of Alaska Native children remained a federal responsibility. But the new law also meant that where schools for Alaska Native children had previously been funded along with the White schools through local monies, they now relied solely on federal appropriations.[7] The inadequate amount at Jackson's disposal, slashed by two-thirds to $50,000 for the 1905–6 school year, had to provide for the vast majority of students in Alaska.[8] As a result, the Sitka Tlingit School closed indefinitely for want of funds in early 1906.[9] In 1907, the federal appropriation was doubled to $100,000.[10] This alleviated the schooling crisis for Alaska Natives but not in time to avert the school conflict in Sitka, which put the definition of civilization on trial.

When Rudolph Walton received notice from the school board that his children were not permitted to attend the school, he turned to Governor Brady for help. Citing Section 7 of the Nelson Act, which referred to "children of mixed blood who lead a civilized life," Walton claimed the right of attendance for the girls. Brady wrote to the school board, but to little effect.[11] W. P. Mills, treasurer, and Mrs. George Stowell, clerk, refused to alter their position. The board's director, W. A. Kelly, resigned, claiming he could not work with Stowell and Mills without sacrificing his self-respect.[12] Kelly would represent Walton in the hearing. Mills and Stowell meanwhile asserted the board's right to decide who would attend the school and claimed that their interpretation of the law was backed by the U.S. Attorney of the District Court.[13]

Certainly Section 7 of the Nelson Act was open to interpretation. The

Nelson Act presumed a clear-cut boundary between Alaska Natives and "mixed-bloods" and between civilized and uncivilized that simply did not exist. By the turn of the century, the Russian presence in Alaska dated back over a century, and many believed that a large proportion of Alaska natives had some White or mixed ancestry.[14] Confusion over racial heritage was linked, in turn, to fears that mixed-race students would swamp public schools.[15] A reporter for the *Seattle Post-Intelligencer* captured the mood: "If half-breeds are admitted in the Sitka school on the score of their being mixed blood, it will mean that there will be little call for schools conducted from Washington by the Bureau of Education, as a vast majority of the so-called natives in Alaska have white blood in their veins, and so would come under the provision in the law 'mixed blood.' "[16] This, in turn, raised the issue of finances: school boards were unwilling and in most cases probably unable to fund schools for all local children. Numerous students of "mixed blood" already attended the public school in Sitka. White Sitkans feared acknowledgment of this situation would lead to its official sanction.[17]

Orthodox Russians and Creoles had different reason to be wary of Section 7. Their position had grown increasingly tenuous since Alaska's transfer in 1867.[18] In Sitka, Creoles generally enjoyed higher social status than the Tlingit, but less than that of the Americans. Resentful of this fact, many Creoles attempted to maintain distance between themselves and the Tlingit. In the 1890s, the Tlingit Orthodox population grew to outnumber the Russian and Creole population by three to one, and Creoles feared that the Tlingit would be granted equal status in the Orthodox Church.[19] Creole children had long been accepted as students in the White public school. Just as it seemed the Tlingit had swamped their church, it now seemed they might swamp their school. For the Creole population, the Davis case was about holding ground.

Once it was clear that the school board was going to stand *its* ground, Kelly filed a motion on Rudolph Walton's behalf to request a writ of mandamus. The writ, if granted by the court, would compel the school board to admit the Davis children and several other mixed-race children as part of its statutory duty. The Sitka school board was named as the defendant, and Rudolph Walton was appointed guardian to litigate on behalf of several plaintiffs. Dora Davis, Tillie Davis, John Littlefield, Lottie Littlefield, Lizzie Allard, and Peter Allard were all children who had attended the Tlingit and/or the White school.[20]

Sitka residents quickly coalesced into opposing sides. Undercurrents of race and class ran together, mixing with local histories of personal relations. Sitka was a small town—the White community numbered no more than 500—where most people knew everybody else. The two local newspapers quickly became embroiled. *The Alaskan* and the *Sitka Cablegram* were run by individuals who agitated for and against Walton, respectively.

The Alaskan was owned by Governor Brady's sister-in-law, Cassia Patton, who had taught for many years at the Tlingit and White schools in Sitka, as had Brady's wife.[21] The derogatory nickname "Siwash Brady" summed up Brady's reputation for promoting the interests of Alaska Native communities over those of the White population.[22] A Skagway paper believed that Brady's pro-Indian policies held the territory back from statehood and saw Brady's orchestration of the ethnographic exhibit at the St. Louis World's Fair as evidence of this favoritism: "What assistance could the miners of Alaska receive from the financial world by an exhibition of Indian curios, such as totem poles, toboggans, beaded moccasins, etc.?"[23] Sitka readers knew that any paper associated with the Brady family was pro-Indian.

The Brady and the Stowell families had a long history. Mrs. Stowell's husband previously handled *The Alaskan's* editorial page but had "severed" this connection several years earlier.[24] Both Mr. and Mrs. Stowell remained influential members of the Presbyterian Church, where they came into frequent contact with the Bradys.[25] The couple had been part of the Bradys' social circle, and the families' children attended school together.[26] Her apparent hostility toward mixed-race children aside, Mrs. Stowell exhibited a serious hobbyist's interest in Tlingit culture. An active member of the Sitka Ethnological Society—to which Cassia Patton also belonged—she had presented several papers on topics such as Tlingit food and Chilkat blankets.[27] Mrs. Stowell's refusal to admit the children to the school left Brady feeling betrayed by someone he had "supposed to be friendly to the natives."[28]

The other member of the board who took a stance against Walton and the Davis children, W. P. Mills, was estranged from the Bradys even before the Davis incident. Mills had brought a suit over water rights against Brady in 1902.[29] According to Brady, "the whole Mills outfit are enemies of the Bradys."[30] Mills and Rudolph Walton had their own history. Mills was one of the town's largest traders in indigenous manufactures.[31] Although Walton had on occasion sold items to Mills's business, the men were competitors.[32] Mills was no doubt unhappy about Walton's competition, especially since it bore a stamp of "authenticity" that Mills, as a White American, could not match. These negative feelings were no doubt exacerbated, when, following the Davis children's expulsion, Ranche residents called for a boycott on purchasing goods from Mills and on selling furs and baskets to him.[33]

The Sitka Cablegram spoke for individuals, such as Mills, who opposed the Bradys and the Waltons. The *Cablegram* began publication in 1905 as an explicitly "anti-Brady" paper.[34] Concurrent with the Davis controversy, Mr. Robinson, who ran the *Cablegram*, allegedly attempted to blackmail Brady over a business deal with the Reynolds Alaska Development Company.[35] Robinson's marriage to a "Creole" woman of mixed Russian and Alaska Native—probably Koniag or Aleut—descent further distanced him from Brady's interests.[36]

Before the hearing began on 11 May 1906, most residents had already rendered their verdict. As early as February, the *Seattle Post-Intelligencer* summed up Sitka's mood when it reported that "the town has taken sides, with the majority siding with the board."[37] The school board election on 3 May tested public opinion on the incumbents' actions. The results were clear: unconditional support. A hundred and forty White residents cast votes—over twice the number who voted in the previous election. Tlingit residents were ineligible to vote. Mills was reelected in a landslide. Mrs. Stowell did not run again, but the *Cablegram*'s other candidates won huge majorities. The results were a vindication of Mills and Stowell and a denunciation of Kelly.[38]

The U.S. Commissioner Edward DeGroff presided over the hearing. DeGroff had lived in Sitka for twenty-five years and had long been a public figure. He owned a store dealing in dry goods, groceries, "curiosities," photographs, and "Alaska souvenir totem spoons," and was thus a business competitor of both Mills and Walton.[39] He was Alaska's Commissioner to the 1893 World's Columbian Exposition in Chicago, had served on the Sitka School Committee, a precedent of the school board, and since 1900 had been U.S. Commissioner, a position that combined the responsibilities of justice of the peace, coroner, probate judge, and recorder.[40] During the Davis hearing, DeGroff acted solely as "referee." As he explained, "The testimony taken here is all to be sifted at Juneau and its relevancy or irrelevancy passed upon, and I would understand that all questions are to be admitted on either side."[41] DeGroff forwarded the transcribed testimony to District Judge Gunnison in Juneau, who rendered the decision.

DeGroff's passivity created a highly prejudicial environment. As Joyce Walton Shales points out, "the obvious lack of respect for the Tlingit witnesses and the type of questions they were asked say much more about the cultural and racial climate in Sitka than anything else the white community could have done."[42] DeGroff sat by as counsel for the defense bullied and mocked Tlingit and mixed-race witnesses. Nor did he intervene when White witnesses refused to answer direct questions. Counsel for both sides (Kelly for the plaintiffs, and Mills and Robinson for the defendants, on the first and second days respectively) asked leading questions that put words in witnesses' mouths, and still DeGroff remained silent.

The prejudicial atmosphere of the court was apparent in the list of witnesses. Most witnesses were White residents of Sitka—teachers, professionals, bureaucrats. Only three Tlingit witnesses appeared, including Rudolph Walton. This imbalance reflected contemporary belief in Alaska that indigenous people were untrustworthy witnesses in a court of law.[43] Of the Tlingit witnesses, only one was a woman. None of the children's mothers had the opportunity to testify. Nor were the mothers named in the legal documents. With the exception of Lizzie Allard's grandmother, Aboriginal women were entirely absent from this American legal debate over civilization.

White fathers of the children testified, but their working-class status and their intimate associations with Tlingit women diminished the value of their testimony and cast their civility—and their Whiteness—into doubt. William, or "Wasca," Allard, was thirty-one years old and was born in Sitka, to an American father and a Russian mother. He had long lived in the Ranche with a Tlingit woman, to whom, by 1906, he was legally married in the eyes of the Church. In his own words, he made his living "at anything I can." This included handling coal and other goods on the wharf and working for various employers, including both Mills and DeGroff.[44] Sixty-five-year-old George Allard was William Allard's father. Born in New England, he was a White man who had fought in the Union Army and served in the U.S. Marines. He married the Tlingit woman who was the mother of Lizzie Allard in January 1889 in the Russian Church. Allard made his living working "off and on" at the Lucky Chance Mine. When "off," he earned money cutting wood. His wife was deceased, and his daughter Lizzie lived with her grandmother in the Ranche. He paid only occasional support toward his daughter's care.[45] John Littlefield Sr. worked as a "machinist or engineer." He and his family divided their time between a "company house" in Killisnoo and a house in the Sitka Ranche.[46]

Judging by the "material" requirements of civilization, Walton was the superior of these men. In the eyes of the court, they were the liquor-drinking, fortune-seeking frontiersmen from whom missionaries wanted to shield their Tlingit converts. As a machinist, Littlefield worked at a skilled trade, but the judge ignored this gradation within the working class, and in his decision referred to Littlefield simply as a "laborer."[47] As elsewhere, colonial authorities conflated laboring classes and racialized subjects.[48] The civilized status of these fathers went on trial alongside Walton's. In light of Walton's accomplishments, their refusal to conform to bourgeois domesticity was deplorable to colonial reformers and it destabilized their efforts to draw a simple equation between Whiteness and civilization.[49] Perhaps the school board feared admitting these men's children even more than it did Walton's. In the Davis case, dramas of race and class were almost indistinguishable.

The issue at the center of the Davis case involved the interpretation of what it meant to "lead a civilized life." Brady had no doubt that Rudolph Walton's family qualified as civilized: "there is hardly a citizen in the town who has more reason to be treated with . . . respect than he has."[50] Brady enumerated the qualities which, from the colonial perspective of the day, were usually associated with "civilized" people. Rudolph Walton was

> educated at the mission here, reads and writes, owns his own property, conducts a store, pays a license to the government for conducting the same, has hired a white man to work out his road tax and has a receipt for the same, has his house supplied with water by the town water works. While he is a storekeeper, he is an ivory carver and silver engraver and also repairs watches and clocks with suitable tools for the same. The children who are denied the privileges of the school are his stepchildren by his wife, a half blood, whom he recently married. She is well respected. The children have always been well kept, tidy and clean.[51]

As *The Alaskan* remarked, "that seems to take in about everything classed 'back East' as 'civilized,' including several counts overlooked by the average city flat dweller."[52] Each of these points would be investigated at length in the hearing to come.

Both sides concentrated on material ornaments of civilization. This focus on outwardly visible characteristics of civilization had long characterized the Presbyterian mission effort. It was the wellspring of the belief that crockery plates and metal cutlery improved students' behavior, and it underlay the Bryn Mawr congregation's insistence that Rudolph Walton's cottage *look* like a $500 cottage. Students who had passed through the Sitka Training School had been taught that these characteristics were the building blocks of a civilized life. No friends of the missionary camp, the defendants nonetheless relied upon the same categories of material civilization that the Presbyterian mission school had inculcated in its students for more than a generation. The use of butter rather than seal oil was measured against the use of Tlingit language; dinner at the governor's house was weighed against attendance at a potlatch. Such lines of questioning revealed the assumption—shared by both sides—that relative weights could be assigned to discrete pieces of evidence, which, once accumulated, would produce the absolute sum of each plaintiff's civilization.

Ornaments of civilization was only one of the testimony's themes. The defendants also addressed questions of association and friendship. Their argument was akin to "guilt by association," which in this instance could be more accurately characterized as "uncivilized by association." The defense implied that the plaintiffs' civilized attributes were mere window dressing on uncivilized interiors.

As long as the court conceived civilization in all-or-nothing terms, the defense's argument was effective. Either-or logic held that even a single lapse was enough to disqualify. That an educated, Christian, skilled businessman like Rudolph Walton went sealing on Biorka Island and participated in Tlingit peace ceremonies did not challenge this conception of civilization. Instead, it implied that a wolf of savagery lurked beneath the sheep's clothing of Western habits. Witness by witness, the defense suggested that even those who appeared as civilized as Walton still engaged in uncivilized activities, and thus remained uncivilized.[53] Colonialism's either-or logic had Walton trapped. By this same reasoning, if Walton had instead pressed his Aboriginal right to land or resources, for example, he would likely not have seemed uncivilized enough. In a different context, Walton might have seemed all too authentic an Indian.

Surprisingly for a hearing focused on the status of mixed-*blood* children, there was almost no explicit mention of race. But implicitly at least, the discussion about factors that shaped the character of "mixed-blood" children was always about race, about Indianness and Whiteness. The either-or conception of a civilized life that emerged was not entirely divorced from racial discourse. It paralleled the Anglo-American rule that any individual with even "one drop" of African blood was black. Transmuting the one-drop theory of race into a cultural one-drop theory of civilization created a powerful tool for policing the social body. It could cut both ways, simultaneously doing the work of class as well as race. It could facilitate the exclusion of men like Rudolph Walton and of the White fathers too. In this instance, a one-drop theory of civilization proved capable of maintaining boundaries with greater certainty than the rhetoric of blood quantum. Elsewhere the reverse could prove true: Whites could use a single drop of White blood to classify Indians as civilized regardless of lifestyle.[54] In this context, the exclusion of the Davis children was overdetermined.

Although many of the missionaries and their supporters—including Brady—held sympathetic views of the Tlingit and mixed-race population, they engaged with and promoted this absolute, either-or definition of civilization. The missionaries saw categories and definitions they had spent decades enforcing used to discredit their mission work. Presbyterian missionaries, more than Russian Orthodox ones, had insisted on conformity to principles of civilization and modernity.[55] They disparaged notions of compromise between authentic and inauthentic, civilized and uncivilized, primitive and modern. This is what doomed their arguments on behalf of Walton and the other mixed-race families. They had generated a standard impossible for even their model student to live up to.

When questioning began, familiar assumptions about markers of civilization quickly emerged. Witnesses consistently avoided answering "yes" or "no" to what might have seemed a simple question: Do the plaintiffs lead a civilized life? When asked whether his daughter and her grandmother lived "the life of white people," Lizzie Allard's absentee father replied with an apparent non sequitur: "They have butter."[56] Other witnesses similarly answered this question by enumerating "customs of civilization" including the fact that the grandmother, Mary Susie, did not live with extended family, did not attend potlatches, washed clothes to earn money, and owned and used a sewing machine.[57] Mary Susie, whose Tlingit name the stenographer approximated as "Kashdacash," but the 1910 census recorded as Ahn-doot-ya, got the chance to speak for herself, albeit through a translator. She took the opportunity to cite additional household items: "indian provisions and white provisions . . . shoes, clothes, nice things."[58] She may not have understood English, but she understood the colonial language of civilization.

William Allard testified that he and his Tlingit wife, Mary—whose name we know only from the U.S. Census—"live(d) like other white people" as well as they could. Mrs. Brady concurred that she could "not see anything but signs of civilization" in their home, where "their beds are clean and nice" and "their cooking utensils are hung up and as far as they can have such things curtained off."[59]

The level of inquiry into the Walton and Davis families' lives exceeded that of the other families, and here again, witnesses and counsel treated civilization as visually apparent. Several witnesses testified to the fact that Fred Davis and his wife (now Mrs. Walton) led a civilized life together before Fred Davis's death. Mrs. Brady testified that the Davises "had the appearance of being well to do civilized people."[60] Others were more specific, stating that the Davises had a working "graphaphone," a "nice carpet," a "nice home," a Chinese servant, and that they wore "citizens clothes." John Brady's sister-in-law, Cassia Patton, was most explicit when she confirmed that she "consider[ed] people who had carpets and curtains as being civilized." Unsure whether the Davises ate butter or seal oil, Patton conceded that they probably ate fish eggs, a transgression she attempted to qualify by admitting that she ate them too.[61]

When it came to Rudolph Walton's life, no detail escaped scrutiny. Mrs. Brady volunteered "many signs of civilization" on behalf of the Waltons. She saw Mr. Walton "dressed in civilized clothing . . . and at work working in a civilized manner." She found everything "around his place of business in nice shape," he furnished his mail orders quickly using the registered post, paid his road taxes, repaired watches and eyeglasses for her family, and sold goods to them too. Rudolph Walton verified these signs of civilization. He stated that he and his first wife were educated at the Sitka Training School and that while he now lived at the "end of the Native town," he still owned his mission cottage. He stated he was a silversmith, owned a store with a cash register, paid license tax and road tax, had piped water in his home, rented a lockbox in the post office, obeyed American laws, and was married in the Presbyterian Church.[62]

The defense attempted to diminish this list of civilized attributes, insinuating that Walton's store barely qualified as such because Walton did not employ clerks or keep adequate stock. Under Mills's badgering, Walton insisted that his store had "fine things" among its two thousand dollars worth of stock and a cash register worth $385. Mills then mocked the cash register, in which Walton obviously took some pride: "You think you need a cash register of that kind when you have no clerk."[63] Here Mills reflected a long tradition of belittling Aboriginal use of money. Tourist writers similarly made fun of Princess Thom's "gaudy" silk dresses and scorned the colors and styles purchased by homeward-bound hop pickers.[64]

The defense also cast aspersion on Walton's involvement in the production and marketing of Tlingit art. When asked whether he made totem poles, Walton admitted that he had received $130 for carving house posts for James Jackson. But he resisted incrimination, however, stating that the posts were "for ornament" and indicated "nothing except they belonged to the tribe." He stressed that he carved them as a business transaction, just like the "little totem pole" he had for sale in his store.[65] Walton seemed to draw a distinction here between carving for business and carving for culture. His assumption that the former would pass as civilized while the latter would not was consistent with his education at the Presbyterian mission and his experience in the tourist trade.

There is no question that Rudolph Walton saw his education, business, and church membership as examples of "white ways." In a poignant exchange, Kelly asked him, "You have always tried to live like the white people." Walton replied, "Yes, since the white people came here I have been trying."[66] Yet Walton lived by Tlingit ways too. For Walton, "trying to live like the white people" did not imply relinquishing all things Tlingit. These continuities and continued associations with Tlingit community and culture formed the hearing's other central theme.

Counsel for the defense incorporated evidence of the plaintiffs' personal associations into their case. They trumped specific citations of material civilization with information about the families' circle of friends. Under questioning by Mills and Robinson, witnesses testified that the children and their parents maintained Tlingit associates, and thus remained enmeshed in "tribal relations."

The proof given that Martha Littlefield was an irredeemable "halfbreed indian squaw" was not her blood quantum but the fact that she "adhere[d] to tribal relations."[67] Sitka's deputy marshall testified that Ranche residents were "very much connected with their tribal relations," that Mary Susie lived "among the natives," and Lizzie Allard associated with "nobody but

35. One of two house posts carved by Rudolph Walton for James Jackson for the potlatch held in 1904. In 1905, Governor Brady borrowed the posts and sent them to Portland to be displayed at the Lewis and Clark Centennial Exposition, an event designed to lure capital and developers west. When Walton went to court to have his stepchildren admitted to the Sitka public school, counsel for the school board implied that the practice of carving such objects was uncivilized. Thirty-five years later, Walton kept this photograph pasted in the back of his diary. PH1036, photograph collections, Sitka Historical Society.

natives."[68] Another witness similarly submitted that although Marie Susie lived in a single-family house, "all of her associates are natives, she lives in the natives village and comes in town once in a while."[69] House, butter, and sewing machine aside, the implication was that these people led uncivilized lives.

Wasca and Mary Allard's family received a similar verdict. Witnesses for the defense agreed that they lived "with the natives wholly," and that Allard was "recognized as a white man" who lived "over in the Indian Village . . . in a house of his own" with his Indian wife.[70] Allard himself testified that the only people who visited his wife were "some indian people" who called "once in a while." The question of Allard's personal choice was key: "Do you live in the Ranch from preference?" asked Robinson. When Allard attempted to avoid answering, Robinson pressed on, "You don't understand. Do you prefer to live in some other part of town?"[71] Allard's decision to live in the Ranche earned him the derogatory epithet "Squaw Man."[72] The term applied in the definition of the day "to white renegades who are living outside the bounds of matrimony with indian women."[73] The term cast judgment on men who spurned the virtues of civilization into which they had been born; it attempted to revoke their inheritance of racial privilege.

Rudolph Walton's preferred choice of residence was similarly suspect—although for different reasons. He had inhabited, and still owned, a cottage on the mission grounds, yet he now lived in the Ranche. Witnesses confirmed that Walton "lives at the indian village, all his associates are natives."[74] This choice of association offset the visible manifestations of "white ways" in Walton's life. In his final decision, the judge commented on the issue of preferred associations: "Those who from choice make their homes among an uncivilized or semicivilized people and find there their sole social enjoyments and personal pleasure and associations cannot, in my opinion, be classed with those who live a civilized life."[75] This generalization held true for both Whites and Indians. White men such as William Allard forfeited their racially advantaged claim to civilized status when they chose to live with Tlingit wives among Tlingit communities. But unlike men such as Allard, the Tlingit had no initial leg-up in their claims to civilized life. In order to receive credit for the "white ways" he adopted, Rudolph Walton had to swim upstream against dominant assumptions about "uncivilized" Indians.

Parents' guilt by association tainted their children, as well. Allard's and Walton's choice of residence meant that their children played with Tlingit children. Walton's insistence that these were "very good children" did little to mitigate the impression that these parents bequeathed their questionable preferences to their offspring.[76] The defense cast further aspersion on the children's playmates, insinuating that too much playing in Lizzie Allard's life, particularly inappropriate play with boys, indicated that she was being raised in a less than civilized manner.[77]

As best he could, Kelly—who represented the plaintiffs—attempted to counter evidence of Tlingit association with proof that the plaintiffs also had ties to the civilized upper crust of Sitka society, particularly the family of Governor Brady. Mrs. Brady testified that she had known Fred Davis since he was a boy, and that he and his wife lived "separately and apart from tribal relations." Mrs. Brady had entertained the former Mrs. Davis and had found her "being of very nice appearance and manner and very much of a lady."[78] The Bradys had likewise hosted the Waltons and the Littlefields on a number of occasions.[79] But dinner at the Bradys did little to change general or judicial perceptions of Rudolph Walton and the other families. The judge stated in his decision,

> Savages, ere this, have been entertained by white men of culture and refinement; but that cannot be considered as a criterion of civilization. To me it is an evidence of the kindliness and of the interest and effort of the hosts in behalf of a people for whom they have labored long and assiduously, not an evidence of the civilization of the guests.[80]

It was far easier to fall from civilized grace than to obtain it. An individual's associations with "uncivilized" people were accepted as evidence that he or she too was uncivilized. But the reverse did not hold. Promotion to "civilized" ranks required more than an invitation to dinner. It was far more difficult for associations with Whites to lift the Waltons up than it was for associations with Indians to bring them down.

Defense counsel illustrated the result of maintaining "tribal relations" by citing examples of seasonal migration. Like the Kwakwa̱ka̱'wakw and the hop pickers, the Tlingit refused to relinquish longstanding patterns of mobility. And like colonial powers further down the coast, White residents of Sitka equated that mobility with itinerant, irregular, and uncivilized habits.[81]

For Lizzie Allard, it was berry-picking excursions with her grandmother that cast doubt on her lifestyle.[82] For Fred Davis, it was sealing.[83] Well-meaning Cassia Patton probably did more harm than good when she attempted to defend Davis by pointing out that "all the natives . . . usually go [sealing]."[84] Berrying and sealing were important activities that, for part of every year, took much of the Tlingit population away from Sitka to communal camps. Both activities were ones that Rudolph Walton did throughout his life. The fact that the Russian school closed during the sealing season likely heightened the sense that the Russians were less civilized than the Americans and negated Kelly's attempt to score "civilized" points for Lizzie Allard by pointing out her past association with the Russian Church school and choir.[85]

Assumptions about sedentary residence were clearest in the examination of the Littlefields' lives. Mills argued that the Littlefields actually resided in Killisnoo, rather than Sitka. As with definitions of civilization, residency was assumed to be an either-or issue. The exchange between Mills and Mrs. Brady was typical of this either-or perspective:

> Q In regard to the Littlefields residing in Killisnoo for the last three or four years.
> A The Littlefields live in Killisnoo part of the time and part of the time here; his family are here more than he is.
> Q His family have visited here.
> A I don't call it visiting.
> Q Did you say they had a home in Killisnoo.
> A They own their home here. I never heard of their home in Killisnoo if they have one.[86]

Another witness—sympathetic to the defense—identified Killisnoo as the "headquarters" of the Littlefield family. He placed the Littlefield's residence at Killisnoo with "frequent visits to Sitka" that lasted a few months at a time.[87] The Littlefields faced a no-win situation. If they did not live full-time in Sitka, they were not residents of Sitka and thus had no claim on the school there. Alternately, if their place of residence was "indeterminate," then they could not qualify as "civilized," and so again, had no right to attend the Sitka school.

Seasonal economic mobility was one manifestation of ongoing tribal relations. The potlatch was another. To the court, potlatches were likewise displays of the persistence of uncivilized material culture. Non-Tlingit residents of Sitka were familiar with potlatches, which were a major attraction for Whites.[88] Counsel and witnesses focused on two Sitka potlatches held in 1899 and 1904. The 1904 potlatch was particularly controversial because Governor Brady sanctioned it after Sitka chiefs promised it would be the last of its kind.[89] Picturesque as tourists found it, and Brady's qualified sanction aside, Christian churches in Sitka condemned the 1904 event and threatened to expel participants from church rolls.[90] Despite this, the majority of Sitka Tlingit, both Christian and non-Christian, attended. The potlatch was an opportunity—along with events such as the Thanksgiving dinners—for cottage and Ranche residents to interact. It was, as one Skagway newspaper recognized, an educational moment when "all the ancient customs and legends [were] acted out and explained anew to the rising generations," and when elders impressed "upon the younger members of their tribe what they regard as the necessity of maintaining their old customs and traditions."[91] Such continuities of social relations and material culture between cottage and Ranche—the supposedly "modern" and "traditional" Tlingit respectively—were easy fodder for the uncivilized cannon of defense counsel.

The evidence marshaled by the defense in relation to the potlatches was some of its most forceful. Fred Davis was host of the 1904 event along with James Jackson, Augustus Bean, and "Paddy" or Mr. Pat.[92] According to Sitka's deputy marshal, Tlingit conduct during the potlatch "was anything but civilized" in that they were "painted up and following ancient customs." Moreover, he claimed that the potlatch revived "the old trouble over the [frog] totem poles" and that arrests were subsequently made.[93]

The deputy marshall's testimony was powerfully verified by the photographic eye. As with hop fields and world's fairs, tourists, anthropologists, and photographers found potlatches eminently photogenic occasions. During the Davis hearing, potlatch photographs became legal evidence. Calling the professional local photographer E. W. Merrill to the stand, the defense offered proof based not on the error-prone human eye but the supposedly objective mechanical one. Merrill had photographed the 1899 and 1904 potlatches, and he testified to Fred Davis's participation on both occasions. One of Merrill's 1899 images of Davis beating a drum next to Bean and Jackson was entered as "Exhibit H." Looking at the photograph, everyone could see how Davis was "painted up so that you could hardly recognize him."[94]

With the introduction of this photograph into evidence, the defense turned the ideology of authenticity back against Aboriginal people. For

36. Sitka Potlatch, 1899. This photograph by E. W. Merrill of a potlatch at Sitka was entered as Exhibit "H" during the hearing. The defense claimed Fred Davis's presence in the photo (front row, far right) was evidence of an uncivilized life and thus warranted excluding Davis's children from the public school. Exhibit H, Dora Davis, et al. v. W. P. Mills, and Mrs. George Stowell, as the School Board of the Sitka School District, Civil Case File 534-A, Civil Case files 1901–10, Box 38, United States District Court for the District of Alaska, First Judicial Division (Juneau, Alaska), Record Group 21, National Archives and Records Administration–Pacific Alaska Region, Anchorage.

years, photographs like Merrill's had been collected by tourists and used by ethnographers as documentation of vanishing traditions. Such photographs were material evidence of Aboriginal authenticity. They froze Aboriginal people in supposedly authentic poses in much the same way that the colonial imagination did. The images did bring Aboriginal people benefits: directly as payment for being photographed, and indirectly as advertisements that attracted curio hunters. This situation was as true for the Puget Sound hop pickers and the Kwakwa̱ka̱'wakw performers as it was for Sitka Tlingit. Introduced into the arena of legal decision making, however, the limitations of these benefits for Aboriginal people became clear. As long as the "one-drop" theory applied to civilization, the photograph provided irrefutable proof that the Tlingit were uncivilized, and thus unentitled to equal educational rights. That the photographs captured only a slice of time and that they might have been consciously staged as picturesque tourist or ethnographic attractions was beside the point. Notions of authenticity were always double-edged. The power of the photograph was especially acute in this instance, as it was used after a man's death to deny rights to his children.

In the eyes of the public, court, and church, Fred Davis's crime was magnified because he was a member of the Presbyterian congregation at the time of the 1904 potlatch.[95] For those who sympathized with the defendants, Christian potlatchers were ultimate proof that store-bought clothing, tidy households, and even church membership constituted a thin veneer of civilization. This cast the apparent civilization of all Tlingit into doubt. Even if they appeared civilized now, what would happen during the next potlatch or sealing season? The defense argued that *Christian* Tlingit were not necessarily *civilized* Tlingit. The judge agreed in his decision where he wrote, "Many natives, for whom the claim of civilization would not be made, are members of churches of the various denominations which are striving to better the conditions in this country."[96] This attempt to sever the association between Christianity and civilization dealt a serious blow to the Church's reputation and to the children's educational opportunities.

Whether Walton attended the 1904 potlatch is uncertain. Though he was close to the hosts, Walton testified that he had not participated, and Augustus Bean confirmed this.[97] Grief over his wife Daisy's recent death and the Presbyterian Church's disapproval might well have encouraged him to stay away.[98] Walton's diary makes no mention of the event. And Rudolph and Daisy Walton's signatures on a 1902 a petition requesting the enactment of an anti-potlatch law suggest that Walton was unlikely to attend.[99] Yet other evidence suggests that Walton may have participated. On a transcript of speeches given at the potlatch, Walton's signature appears next to those of Augustus Bean, James Jackson, and two white witnesses.[100] Moreover, the Alaska State Museum houses a *Kiks.'adi* frog crest dance shirt identified as the shirt worn by Rudolph Walton at the 1904 potlatch.[101] Either way, his decision must have been difficult. By attending he would have fulfilled important kinship obligations; staying away would have breached his responsibility to Tlingit kin.[102] Although Walton could not have foreseen the Davis case in 1904, he would certainly have known that either decision carried serious consequences.

Both Fred Davis and Rudolph Walton faced inner struggles when deciding whether or not to attend the 1904 potlatch. So too did other hosts of the event. In a speech at the potlatch, Chief James Jackson described the powerful sense of obligation he felt for having been hosted generously by others in the past.

> We called you herein this feast because we wanted to do you honor. We did this best we could because we did not honor as much . . . as our great uncles did. Mrs. Brady & Capt. Kilgore are my witnesses. First I was invited by a chief to Angoon or Killisnoo. Then another chief's son Geo. Shotrich Chilcat invited me to a feast again. After that the chiefs Ya Duan Dick, Kooksee invited me to their feast. There everybody learns that I have been invited to all these feasts and have been treated well. I felt thankful for it but they did so I thought I return the feast as they had feasted me.[103]

Jackson agreed to stop potlatching after the "last potlatch," but he did not agree to relinquish the value he set on reciprocal obligations. He saw participation in the "last potlatch" as necessary fulfilment of these obligations, but non-Tlingit Sitkans, particularly members of the Presbyterian Church, saw the potlatch only as a regression to savagery. This was painful for Jackson: "We have been called all kinds of names just for doing this and we feel great shame."[104]

Augustus Bean similarly felt torn between his Tlingit kin, on the one hand, who expected him to reciprocate the hospitality he had received in the past; and on the other hand, the Church that told him he should now live by a different set of rules.

> Before this chiefs when he . . . inviting the people from the . . . places he is worried, troubles he had and people speaking unkindly to him about his doings he feels very badly the way people think of his actions. So he went on and invited them and he is very thankful to them for coming but he does not want to do this kind of way anymore. . . . Sometimes he feel very shame when they said to him Mr. Bean was doing all this feasting business so all this trouble all this old fashion is done away with. Since he began to get ready for this all his feelings go against it and . . . he is done . . . I am talking I feel bad when I think I am giving this in a right way, they think I am doing wrong and take my name from the church book. I feel this way I thank you guests.[105]

These inner struggles did not amount to the capitulation that colonial notions of authenticity said they did. They did have implications for how members of the Tlingit community worked through their own ideas of culture and community. When the hosts of the "last potlatch" publicly announced that they were giving up potlatching, they simultaneously explained what they were *not* giving up. Bean emphasized the importance of honoring the memory of this occasion: "I want to make you understand that these three houses make a totem which we hang as a picture it will stand as long as the house stand we have called you to see it. After I die my nephews still keep it as a picture in his house."[106] Moreover, the speakers explained that even without "potlatches" per se, important gatherings would take place and important obligations would be fulfilled. These men cited similarities between potlatches and "American" gatherings. They believed they were relinquishing the former and accepting the latter, which they could use as vehicles for sustaining Tlingit networks of kinship and duty. The transcriber thus recorded the words of another of the hosts, Mr. Pat:

> If he goes some other place Killisnoo, Chilcat to work perhaps some of his friends will [take/have?] him with the house. If they ask a favor to do some good for them that he will not give up. Maybe there be some friends in a different place. They will do like Governor Brady when steamer come people from the East. He invites them all and have sociables. Having good times like that he don't give up.[107]

Jackson similarly promised that "hereafter that I will not feast in the old fashion but only in American fashion."[108] The Tlingit Thanksgiving dinners that brought Ranche and cottage residents together were a prime example of this.

The testimony in the Davis hearing was structured according to the dyad of colonial authenticity, but Tlingit struggles of identity and community occurred on very different terms. The courtroom environment allowed no space for these sorts of Tlingit conversations about authenticity. Nor did it allow empathy with the wrenching decisions that these men faced. There could be no public acknowledgment of how torn they—and many others—felt by the either-or proposition with which the colonial discourse of authenticity presented them.

The judge likewise offered no evidence of empathy in his decision, which appeared almost two years after the hearing.[109] This lengthy delay meant that in a practical sense the hearing itself constituted the decision. By the time the case was formally resolved, the children in question were enrolled either in the Sitka Training School or the reopened Tlingit day school.[110] The judge's written decision—which refused to grant the writ of mandamus—confirmed what had already been accomplished.

But the decision also made law in a way that the hearing alone did not. It was part of the judge's task to turn the litany of butter, seal oil, cash registers, and dinner-party guest lists into a legal rule that bore relation to the question of children's education. The connections were not always obvious. As Rudolph Walton declared in frustration while being grilled about his cash register: "I don't see what this has to do with the school."[111] In his careful interpretation of Section 7 of the Nelson Act the judge explicated these counterintuitive connections.

After carefully reviewing the civilized qualities of each family, District Court Judge Gunnison dismissed the material evidence of civilized life as inadequate. Of the Littlefields, he concluded that "the children are unrestrained, and live the life of their native associates, rather than a civilized life."[112] He similarly found against Lizzie Allard because of her Tlingit playmates and her participation in the seasonal round.[113] Peter Allard was denied civilized status because of his father's voluntary decision to live and associate with the Tlingit. Such people, in the judge's opinion, "cannot be classed with those who live a civilized life."[114] It was, however, the judge's assessment of Rudolph Walton that was the most telling. "Civilization," he concluded, meant "more than a prosperous business, a trade, a house, white man's clothes, and membership in a church."[115] According to Judge Gunnison, Walton lacked "corresponding progress in the domestic and social relations of his family."[116]

The judge stated as a general rule that "the mixed blood is presumed to partake of the character of the tribe with which he lives, whether it be civilized or otherwise."[117] Thus, "where mixed bloods live among and associate with the uncivilized, they become subject to and influenced by their environment as naturally as water seeks its level."[118] The judge granted "mixed-blood" children a chance, but it was a tenuous one as long as the one-drop theory applied. Children who had already "risen" to the civilized level should be admitted to the public school. Those, on the other hand, who retained even a thread of the uncivilized life belonged in a different classroom.

This still did not tell Alaskans exactly how they would know when a life was civilized. After allowing that this was a relative question, the judge offered his own definition:

> the test to be applied should be as to whether or not the persons in question have turned aside from old associations, former habits of life, and easier modes of existence; in other words, have exchanged the old barbaric, uncivilized environment for one changed, new and so different as to indicate an advanced and improved condition of mind, which desires and reaches out for something altogether distinct from and unlike the old life.[119]

The judge's test emerged directly from the binary assumptions that permeated non-Aboriginal understandings of Aboriginal people. These were the same assumptions held by anthropologists who came to record remnants of tragically vanishing Indians and by tourists who flocked to collect shards of Aboriginal spectacle. In other situations, Aboriginal people could manipulate these assumptions for a degree of benefit. But, in this instance, the framework of American legal opinion left no space for mediation.

Judge Gunnison's test required Aboriginal people to dissolve themselves into dominant American society. Indians were the concentrate and Americans the solution. This was a vision of civilization comprised of isolated, atomized individuals. Under this test a civilized Aboriginal existence was an oxymoron. Only once a Tlingit *community* was no longer discernible could a Tlingit *individual* qualify as civilized. But the absence of Tlingit community would erase the traits that marked individuals as Tlingit. This logic defined Aboriginal selves as part of a collective, and civilized selves as individuals. Native American naturalization statutes similarly required Indians to give up tribal associations as the price of gaining civilized designation.[120] Set into a wider context, the preoccupation with dissolving indigenous collectivity paralleled colonial concerns as far away as India.[121]

Tlingit communities did not "dissolve" into dominant society. But the rule established by the Davis case did keep Aboriginal children out of Alaskan public schools for decades. The legacy of the Davis case persisted until 1928, when Andrew Paull, on behalf of the Alaska Native Brotherhood—of which Rudolph Walton had been a founding member in 1912—took up the case of a mixed-race student in Ketchikan.[122]

The non-Aboriginal public's refusal to accept Walton as an equal did not dim the Presbyterian Church's pride in his accomplishments. The "civilized" traits that had failed to win Walton equal educational rights for his children remained benchmarks of achievement for missionaries and their sympathizers. Pro-Presbyterian publications continued to invoke Rudolph Walton's life as evidence of the mission's success.[123] Governor Brady was appalled at the treatment Rudolph Walton received, declaring "we are more truly heathen than the natives."[124] But he remained unable to see how the dichotomies of authenticity and civilization, which were his lenses into Tlingit life, had determined the hearing's outcome. Like Brady, Sheldon Jackson was both upset by the proceedings and unable to shed his either-or assumptions. When House of Representatives member Edgar D. Crumpacker asked Jackson for information about Alaska Natives, Jackson enumerated Rudolph Walton's civilized attributes and recounted the Davis case. Then, referring to the famous critic of U.S. Indian policy, Helen Hunt Jackson (who displayed a group of "civilized" Indian students at the Chicago World's Fair), Sheldon Jackson likened the Davis case to "another chapter in Mrs. Jackson's [book] 'Century of Dishonor.' " "This," Jackson concluded, "is an example of the liberality of our American civilization on the frontier."[125]

Conclusion

Authenticity's Call

During the late nineteenth century, Aboriginal people–not just on the Northwest Coast, but throughout North America–faced contradictory thickets of tourism, anthropology, and colonialism. Notions of authenticity that were closely related to the myth of the vanishing Indian simultaneously generated and delimited opportunities for Aboriginal people. Aboriginal people did not exercise much control over the terms of this discourse, but they often manipulated it to their benefit. The growth of both anthropology and tourism provided opportunities that helped Aboriginal people make a living under the difficult economic and political conditions created by late-nineteenth-century colonialism. On the Northwest Coast, the economic opportunities that arose from playing Indian augmented the income Aboriginal people derived from other sectors of the colonial economy, such as salmon canning, hop picking, and sealing. Aboriginal workers combined these sources of income with historically entrenched subsistence activities.

Aboriginal lives were complicated and hard-won blends of indigenous and colonial practices, but this fact was lost on authenticity-seeking viewers. Aboriginal people did not even have to step on stage to be cast as stars in colonial spectacles of authenticity. The Aboriginal hop pickers in Puget Sound and Tlingit residents of the Sitka mission and Ranche were "on stage" everyday. The experiences of the Kwakwa̱ka̱'wakw at the Chicago World's Fair were more typical of Aboriginal life on the Northwest Coast than they first appear. The exhibitionary opposition between the "authentic" Aboriginal encampment and the civilized residential school exhibits reproduced the late-nineteenth-century colonial landscape in microcosm. Indian-watchers in Puget Sound saw this same opposition when they went on excursions from town to see the hop pickers. Pickers were aware that even as they worked for wages within a capitalist economy, they performed versions of their authentic selves. Sightseers viewed Aboriginal pickers as features of the hop fields' "natural" rural setting that had their counterpoint in the urban growth around Puget Sound and throughout North America more generally. This opposition was similarly apparent to visitors who arrived in Sitka. Before they disembarked from the steamer, tourists saw (and heard) arrayed on the wharf before them the distinction between the "civilized" brass-band-playing children from the mission school and the "uncivilized" curio vendors from the Ranche. Once they disembarked, visitors could turn left to delve deeper into the authenticity of the "uncivilized" Ranche, or turn right for a tour of the mission. This dynamic was all too common, a fact lamented by Frederic Ward Putnam's former ethnographic assistant, Antonio Apache, when he spoke at the 1897 Carlisle Indian School graduation. Addressing an audience that included Alaska Governor John Brady, Antonio "feelingly" declared that "some people thought the Indian only good for exhibition purposes."[1]

But as Antonio implied, an abundance of indigenous meanings thrived behind the spectacle of Indian life. The Kwakwa̲ka̲'wakw who performed in Chicago knew, even though the live audience did not, that their "cannibal dance" would humiliate Hall, undermine the truth claims of the residential school exhibits, and communicate their defiance of the potlatch law to the Canadian government. The Kwakwa̲ka̲'wakw performers also knew that once they returned home, wages from Chicago would fuel the potlatch cycle that legitimated their elite status. The performers undoubtedly faced challenges in adapting sacred dances for a secular audience, but these challenges did not undermine the ability of the potlatch and winter ceremonial to inform their identities as Kwakwa̲ka̲'wakw. Despite colonial claims to the contrary, the authenticity of Aboriginal life lay not in the mindless, mechanical reproduction of age-old rituals but in the fresh generation of meaningful ways to identify as Kwakwa̲ka̲'wakw within a changing and increasingly modern age.

A similar cache of Aboriginal meanings lay secreted within the world of Aboriginal hop camps. The harvest was not only season for picking hops and selling curios to "Indian watchers." Aboriginal people who converged on Puget Sound for the hop harvest turned the camps into important sites of gatherings for extended kin from intervillage communities. These gatherings served variously to perpetuate and transform patterns of hereditary status. The hop harvest was also a season for gambling, horse racing, canoe racing, and trading. Gambling in particular had long been associated with potlatches. In the late nineteenth century, it became associated with the hop fields. Hop-field gatherings also gave rise to new interactions between people. They were places where new forms of pan-Aboriginal identity–political, cultural, and religious–evolved. These activities extended beyond the hop camps along the length of the migration. The journey to the hop fields was often as important as the destination itself.

For Rudolph Walton, the "traditional" and the "modern" were ingredients of everyday life. Walton embodied the civilizing goals of the Presbyterian mission in his dress, speech, household, and business practices. Yet, he refused to be cut loose from Tlingit ways of life. He participated in important Tlingit community events and migratory labor cycles that continued to tie him to "uncivilized" kin and friends. Walton was a master at incorporating the priorities of Tlingit culture into his life as a successful jeweler, storekeeper, and respected member of the Presbyterian Church. But during the Davis hearing, the defense cast this ability to integrate supposedly mutually exclusive values and practices not as an accomplishment but an indictment. Walton and the other families were treated as though they were opportunistically attempting to "pass" in order to receive benefits. According to the "one-drop" racial theory, which non-Aboriginal people in Sitka and elsewhere transmuted into a theory of culture, the smallest sign of the "old," "tribal" way of life was grounds for excluding the Walton, Allard, and Littlefield children from admission to public school.

Kwakwa̱ka̱'wakw potlatches, Salish intervillage gatherings, and Tlingit peace ceremonies were all part of political, as well as cultural, orders. Risking colonial censure and punishment, the Aboriginal people in these episodes and elsewhere wove such essential practices into life under colonialism. They struggled to retain the thread of Aboriginal politics that colonizers attacked by denying its existence. Aided by the discourse of authenticity, colonizers relegated ritual to the realm of culture and set it in opposition to politics. They classed Aboriginal people not only as people without history but as people without politics.

Aboriginal attempts to fashion lives that defied dichotomies–lives that were simultaneously "Aboriginal" and "modern"–were rarely easy and often painful. As Joyce Walton Shales writes about the cottage residents in Sitka, "the stresses of trying to balance their obligations to their kin, as well as the ones they assumed by becoming residents of the cottages and Presbyterians were tremendous."[2] Many participants in the frog peace settlement and in the so-called last potlatch felt torn between their clan obligations and their desire for acceptance and equality in American society. As one Tlingit man explained to the missionary George Beck about the peace ceremony, "We know it is wrong, but so much good will come of it that we shall be justified."[3] The hosts of the "last potlatch" similarly struggled to find meaningful definitions of what was right and just.

Accounts of the "last potlatch" reveal the internal struggles that accompanied Tlingit attempts to make meaning in colonial contexts. This process was hardly unique to the Tlingit. If the emotions expressed by the hosts of the "last potlatch" seem unusual, it is only because such Aboriginal expressions so rarely survive in written sources. The Kwakwa̱ka̱'wakw faced equally difficult choices when they considered whether to go to Chicago, and which dances to perform once they arrived. Similarly, the hop pickers struggled annually to combine income-generating opportunities with cultural gatherings and priorities. Nor were these processes limited to the Northwest Coast. Aboriginal people throughout North America dealt with similar decisions during this period.

The refashioning of Aboriginal identity in the late nineteenth century would have been a challenging task even apart from the shifting ambivalences of non-Aboriginal people. Dominant society's refusal to acknowledge the possibility of fusing "traditional" and "modern," "uncivilized" and "civilized," "Indian" and "White" made it all the more difficult. Uncertainties of life under American and Canadian colonialism meant that Aboriginal people could ill afford to forgo economic opportunities that derived from the growth of anthropology and tourism. Yet these opportunities hinged upon their self-representation in terms of static colonial categories. These categories revolved around the notion of an authentic core, a notion that ultimately undermined Aboriginal people's bids for political rights, economic equality, and cultural survival. This was the "devil's bargain" of authenticity.[4]

According to prevailing notions of authenticity, Aboriginal people could not be "Aboriginal" and "modern" at the same time. These were mutually exclusive categories. Writing in 1892, a visitor to British Columbia claimed that "what little there was that was picturesque about [B.C. Indians] has vanished only a few degrees faster than their own extinction as a pure race, and they are now a lot of longshoremen."[5] For this visitor, as for so many others, the life of longshoremen was diametrically opposed to the picturesque existence of Indians. The former were no longer Aboriginal but were instead members of the laboring classes. The latter were Aboriginal, though not for long; they were quickly vanishing. Appropriately, this comment appeared in an article entitled "Canada's El Dorado," a promotional piece for mining and other resource development in British Columbia. Eliza Scidmore, a noted travel writer for Alaska (who penned a remarkably similar piece about Alaska's mining regions) characterized the Tlingit in much the same terms: "It is the Thlingit's aim to dress and live as the white man, and he fills his home with beds, table, chairs, clocks, lamps, stoves, and kitchen utensils, and even buys silk gowns for his wife. He is no longer picturesque, distinctive, or aboriginal. Even his canoe has cotton sails instead of the old bark mats, and the oar works simultaneously with the paddle."[6] Here again, "White ways" contrasted with the "picturesque" and the "aboriginal." Such characterizations of Aboriginal people abounded throughout North America at the turn of the century.

The notion that all things Aboriginal were of the past was a critical element of the colonial discourse of authenticity. By this definition, all things authentic were (and are) constantly receding into the past. Their existence in the present tense is presumed fleeting. The Kwakwa̱ka̱'wakw performers, the Puget sound hop pickers, and the Sitka Tlingit were all seen as authentic spectacles, but this designation hinged, at least in part, on the assumption that these spectacles would soon vanish. The cachet attached to viewing the Kwakwa̱ka̱'wakw in Chicago or visiting Princess Thom in Sitka derived from the audience's sense that they were among the last non-Aboriginal people to have such experiences. As the number of non-Aboriginal visitors increased, the authenticity of the experience decreased proportionally. The ideology of authenticity held that for Aboriginal people, the changes that accompanied modernity took them further away from their "authentic" selves. For Aboriginal people, modernity was cast as a process of distancing from their own culture.[7]

Yet what dominant society defined as "authentic" Aboriginal culture has not disappeared. The fluorescence of so-called primitive art (despite claims that this too is endangered) is evidence of this.[8] But if authentic Indianness was already endangered in the nineteenth century, how can it have survived into the twenty-first? Herein lies yet another of authenticity's contradictions. Although rooted in assertions of stasis, definitions of authenticity shift over time. Elements that were initially seen as corruptions of "tradition" because they developed from contact with non-Aboriginal cultures—Haida argillite carvings, Navajo wool blankets, or even horses on the Plains—have become benchmarks of Aboriginal authenticity.[9]

The long-term costs of these notions of authenticity for Aboriginal people have been high. Romantic images of (always vanishing) authentic

Indians drew not only tourists but also settlers and developers. Indeed, sightseers and developers were often one and the same. The Kwakwa̱ka̱'wakw at the Chicago World's Fair were part of a "gigantic advertising campaign," designed to demonstrate that the American and Canadian Wests were safe from savage Indians and ripe for settlement and development. The hops grown in Puget Sound were part of a global industry, but local farmers struggled to develop the infrastructure necessary to get their crop to market. Picturesque Aboriginal hop pickers presented an attraction that played a role in the extension of railway lines to hop-growing regions around Puget Sound. Aboriginal people were among the "natural wonders" that garnered national and international attention for Seattle and its environs. In Alaska too, Aboriginal people and the spectacle they presented were catalysts for the establishment of regular steamer routes. For many years "Indian watching" was the industry upon which almost the entire population of Sitka relied in one respect or another. Non-Aboriginal people took the images of Indians playing authentic roles and turned them into glossy advertisements for Aboriginal dispossession.

Innumerable pieces of text and image could illustrate this phenomenon. But one postcard in particular encapsulates this process for the Northwest Coast. The hand-colored card shows an Aboriginal man pulling his canoe ashore, while an Aboriginal woman with freshly caught salmon in each hand confronts the camera without expression. A label on the back of the card claims the location is Puget Sound, but the superimposed verses place the scene in Alaska. In reality, the couple stands on the shores of neither Puget Sound nor Alaska but Neah Bay; they are Makah, ancestors perhaps of the controversial twentieth-century whalers. Such slips in accuracy were inconsequential to the card's message.[10] The Indian man and woman were gentle personifications of place, Alaska in this incarnation; they conveyed "Alaska's Call," as the poem was entitled. They did not pose a threat to new arrivals but, on the contrary, freely offered up their fish and gold and freedom to any who would come.

Strong arms and stout hearts,
List to fair Alaska's call!
"Here's welcome to the willing!
Here is room for one and all!

"Yours—come reach out and take them—
Are the fish that swim my seas!

37. "Alaska's Call." In both image and word, this postcard, with its multiple slips in accuracy, starkly portrays the trade-off that colonial notions of authenticity involved for Aboriginal people. It was collected by the Alaska governor John Brady. Folder 42, Box 17, John G. Brady Papers, Yale Collection of Western Americana, Beinecke Rare Book and Manuscript Library.

Yours my gold and tin and copper—
Come and share my wealth of these!

"Not alone on sea and mountain
Are there fortunes to be won;
I have fields that need but tilling
And their gold outshines the sun!

"There are millions of my acres
Where now but wild grass waves,
To make homes for sturdy freemen;
Will ye linger south as slaves?"

Strong arms and stout hearts,
List to fair Alaska's call!
Here a royal realm awaits you!
Here is room and wealth for all!

This was the message that tourists and developers took away after visiting an Indian spectacle, be it in Chicago, Puget Sound, or Sitka.

Some writers extended this notion by invoking the potlatch. They cast Aboriginal people as hosts of a great potlatch who offered up their land, water, timber, minerals, plants, animals, and fish to White guests whom they welcomed with open arms. The writer who characterized British Columbia as "Canada's El Dorado" was particularly explicit in this regard. Potlatches had gained a new significance since White settlement, he claimed: "It is the white man who is to enjoy a greater than all previous potlatches in that region. The treasure that has been garnered during the ages by time or nature or whatsoever you may call the host, and the province itself is offered as the feast."[11] Typically, the author identified "time" or "nature," not Aboriginal people, as the host. This same message resonated throughout innumerable manifestations of the authentic Indian spectacle. The "Alaska's Call" postcard was only one.

Today, such unabashed pride in the so-called bonanza that White immigrants found on the Northwest Coast has largely disappeared.[12] But the binary categorizations that buttressed this pride are intact. Aboriginal and non-Aboriginal people today continue to use assumptions about authenticity that their nineteenth-century predecessors wielded as tools of both colonial authority and Aboriginal self-expression. In relation to nearly all aspects of Aboriginal life–from basketry to politics–people use authenticity, as art historian Marvin Cohodas puts it, "as an abstraction of the 'past' . . . to maintain ethnic boundaries crucial to the modernization paradigm."[13] They do so even as conditions of modernity destabilize these boundaries and thereby confuse the question of who has legitimate claims on state services or Aboriginal rights.[14] Static markers of dress and food were never reliable indicators of inner identity. Global movements of people and capital have made them even less so. Heightened attention to the value of ethnic boundaries occurs at a time when these boundaries have never been less certain. The result can be a destructive spiral capable of culminating in the brutality of ethnic violence. Here is the ultimate price of the authenticity we have manufactured. Far from fading into extinction, claims to authenticity have taken on even greater emotional and political currency in recent years, at times with deadly results.[15]

Notions of authenticity have done and continue to do damage. This might lead some to argue that the concept is unsalvageable. Yet it remains far too prevalent and persuasive a force to be simply jettisoned. If, as this study has attempted to demonstrate, Aboriginal people had good reason to "play Indian" in the late nineteenth century, they have even greater reason to do so more than a century later.[16] When Aboriginal people today assert rights and identities that are at once "Aboriginal" and "modern," many non-Aboriginal people still reply with invocations of static categories of authentic Indianness. White society continues to station authenticity as the gatekeeper of Aboriginal people's rights to things like commercial fisheries, land, and casinos. Whatever the long-term cost of playing Indian, there is as yet no evidence that the immediate, and thus more pressing, cost of *not* doing so have diminished. We need look no further than the Makah whale hunt as illustration of this point.

Equally, if not more significantly, the category of authenticity has become one of the most powerful rhetorical devices in Aboriginal communities today. Many practices that may have begun by "playing Indian" in the nineteenth century have long since been assimilated as traditions in their own right.[17] This does not mean the Makah who seek to revive the whale hunt have fallen victim to false consciousness and internalized the categories of their own oppression. It does mean they have been involved in the contested and dialogical practice of producing cultural meaning, of making past and the present speak to one another, of using old things in ways that resonate with new needs. Absent such utility, tradition becomes not much more than a burden Aboriginal people must carry.[18]

To suggest that we discard authenticity because it is so intensely problematic a concept would seem the worst sort of academic hubris. Scholarly recognition that race and gender are constructed categories of analysis has not brought an end to the real work that these categories do in the world. It seems no more likely that such recognition will do so for the category of authenticity. This does not mean that identifying authenticity as a category of analysis, rather than a natural manifestation of common sense, is a futile exercise. History cannot point to the future, but it can help us get our bearings. Awareness of the assumptions that structure our everyday lives, and mindfulness of their implications, may not provide ready answers, but they can provoke important questions that we otherwise do not know to ask. If, to invoke Mary Douglas again, we want to stop hitting each other with authenticity's implications, we need to first remove our blinders.

Having glimpsed even some of these implications in this study, we might begin by asking what a more just, less destructive notion of authenticity might look like. In retrospect it seems remarkable that given the weight of contradictory evidence, so many nineteenth-century "Indian watchers" maintained the belief that the binary terms of authenticity accurately represented Aboriginal existence. While hardly ineffable, many of the self-determined elements of Aboriginal authenticity remained unexpressed in ethnographic enumerations of kinship, housing, food, and mortuary practices. Today, many pizza-eating, satellite-television-watching Indians retain a clear sense of what sets them apart from non-Aboriginal people with similar consumer habits. As an Aboriginal elder in central British Columbia explains, "I think sometimes you get fooled into thinking the only way we can be a true Indian is to live how people did 100 years ago. . . . Tradition evolves. It's ongoing every day."[19] Rather than strict insistence on purity and persistence, some indigenous writers have looked to history—itself a mechanism of change and transformation—as richer soil for modern Aboriginal identities. They lay claim to their own historical trajectories shaped by indigenous temporality and topography.[20] Others call for a "self-conscious traditionalism," a selective use of indigenous values with presentist goals in mind.[21] And still others invoke a "radical indigenism" rooted in carefully defined kinship frameworks.[22] These proposals challenge colonial notions that locate Aboriginal authenticity in the past at the same time as they forcefully affirm the existence of definable and usable indigenous rights, values, and practices. They assert their own indigenous forms of authenticity.

Surely, any just notion of authenticity must be self-determined. Yet attempts to envision such authenticity in practice invariably evoke questions about who will adjudicate difficult situations: what if Indian men oppress Indian women? What if tribal monies are not fairly distributed? What if children of mixed heritage are treated unequally? But the inequalities generated by sexism, capitalism, and racism have hardly been resolved by non-Aboriginal people. It is disingenuous to hold Aboriginal people to a standard of social justice and equity yet to be achieved by others. So doing maintains the stranglehold of colonial paternalism. And it perpetuates the romantic image of noble savages imbued with qualities that White society lacks.

Self-determined authenticity is more a necessary beginning than a final ending. Restoring definitions of Aboriginal authenticity to their rightful owners will not end conflicts over belonging and entitlement. The Makah would quite likely still not achieve unanimity over whether to revive the whale hunt. But if public discourse allowed a wider range of possibility for legitimate manifestations of Aboriginal authenticity, the stakes of these internal struggles might be a little lower and their resolution perhaps a little quicker. Adjudication of authenticity is a task for Aboriginal communities; releasing some of the steam from authenticity's pressure cooker is a problem for which everyone bears responsibility. A century ago, colonial notions of authenticity carried long-term costs for Aboriginal people. Whether these costs still shadow Aboriginal invocations of authenticity in the twenty-first century remains an open question.

List of Abbreviations

AR	Annual Report
ASA	Alaska State Archives, Juneau, Alaska
ASHL	Alaska State Historical Library, Juneau, Alaska
BAE	Bureau of American Ethnology
BCA	British Columbia Archives, Victoria, British Columbia
BIA	Bureau of Indian Affairs (U.S.)
CMS	Church Missionary Society
DIA	Department of Indian Affairs (Canada)
FATG	Files of the Alaska Territorial Governors
FWPP	Frederic Ward Putnam Papers, Harvard University Archives, Cambridge, Massachusetts
JGBP	John G. Brady Papers, Beinecke Rare Book and Manuscript Library, Yale University, New Haven, Connecticut
MOHI	Museum of History and Industry, Seattle, Washington
NAC	National Archives of Canada
RG	Record Group
SJC	Sheldon Jackson Correspondence
SJSL	Sheldon Jackson Stratton Library Archives, Sitka, Alaska
SP	Sessional Papers
SVHS	Snoqualmie Valley Historical Society, North Bend, Washington
USNA	United States National Archives
USNA-A	United States National Archives, Alaska Region, Anchorage, Alaska
UW	University of Washington, Seattle, Washington
WRVHS	White River Valley Historical Society, Auburn, Washington
WSHS	Washington State Historical Society, Tacoma, Washington

Notes

Introduction Authenticity and Colonial Cosmology

1 Douglas, *Implicit Meanings*, 61.

2 "Many Calls, Messages Oppose Hunt," *Seattle Times*, 18 May 1999, A9. For a sampling of these opinions, see the editorial pages in section B of the *Seattle Times* from 18 May 1999 through 23 May 1999, as well as Jane Batsell, "Rant and Rave," *Seattle Times*, 23 May 1999, L4. The controversy over the hunt, which had been brewing for over a year since the International Whaling Commission's decision, was framed in these terms from the beginning. As an Everett man wrote in October 1997: "I would argue that to capture the true spirit of the kill would best be achieved by absolute adherence to traditional, tribal methods. This would include no motorized vehicles (no powerboats), absence of any firearms (introduced by Europeans), traditional dress (no Nike shoes as are in the photo, metallic belt buckles, or fancy zippered tribal jackets.), handy totebags, or modern meat-processing devices for the utilization of the whale. If the Makah were able to use 'traditional methods' in harvesting the whales instead of picking and choosing tools from the modern world, then I would support them." Gary C. Watkins, Everett, letter to the editor: "Makah Whaling Decision—If Need for Capturing Whales Cultural, Then Use Traditional Makah Methods, Equipment," *Seattle Times*, 30 October 1997, B7.

3 Michael McInnis, Seattle, letter to the editor: "Makah Whaling—Giant Rifle to Hunt Whales not Makah Cultural Tradition," *Seattle Times*, 22 March 1998, B7.

4 Brad Newall, Port Ludlow, letter to the editor: "Makah Whaling—No Need to Kill Whales; Start Whale-Watching Tour Business," *Seattle Times*, 12 January 1999, B5; Dr. Robert G. Stagman, Mercer Island, letter to the editor: "Native Tribes and Treaties—Renewing Whaling to Revive Makah Culture Is a Sham," *Seattle Times*, 5 August 1998, B5.

5 Mike Millman, Woodinville, letter to the editor: "Makah Whale Hunt—Money-Making Publicity Ploy," *Seattle Times*, 23 May 1999, B8. Rumor had it that the Makah only wanted to kill the whale so that they could sell its meat to Norway and Japan for "a million dollars." In fact, the Makah had signed an agreement with the United States that the meat would not be sold. Jim Dunn, Maple Valley, letter to the editor: "Makah Whale Hunt—Only Thing Restored Is Greed," *Seattle Times*, 20 May 1999, B5; Dr. Robert G. Stagman, Mercer Island, letter to the editor: "Native Tribes and Treaties—Renewing Whaling to Revive Makah Culture Is a Sham," *Seattle Times*, 5 August 1998, B5; Eric Sorenson, "Foes Spin Web to Attack Whalers—Internet Site Mocks Indians' Makah.com," *Seattle Times*, 22 May 1999, A1.

6 Katherine LeBrane, Seattle, letter to the editor: "Makah Whale Hunt—Indeed a Lost People," *Seattle Times*, 23 May 1999, B8.

7 Sherry Greene, letter to the editor: "Makah Indians' Whale Hunt," *Los Angeles Times*, 23 May 1999, M4; Stephen D. Bennett, Shoreline, letter to the editor: *Seattle Times*, 24 May 1999, B5; Alex Tizon, "E-mails, Phone Messages, Full of Threats, Invective," *Seattle Times*, 23 May 1999, A1.

8 Brad Newall, Port Ludlow, letter to the editor: "Makah Whaling," *Seattle Times*, 12 January 1999, B5; Alex Tizon, "E-mails, Phone Messages Full of Threats, Invective," *Seattle Times*, 23 May 1999, A1; Katherine LeBrane, Seattle, letter to the editor: "Makah Whale Hunt—Indeed a Lost People," *Seattle Times*, 23 May 1999, B8; Brad Newall, Port Ludlow, letter to the editor: *Seattle Times*, 23 May 1999, B9.

9 "Many Calls, Message Oppose Hunt," *Seattle Times*, 18 May 1999, A9.

10 Stephen D. Bennett, Shoreline, letter to the editor, *Seattle Times*, 24 May 1999, B5.

11 Deur, "The Hunt for Identity," 147.

12 Ibid., 158–59. This is hardly the only instance in which the resurrection of tradition was a source of community division. For others see Riddington, "All the Old Spirits Have Come Back to Greet Him," 168–74; and Harkin, "A Tradition of Invention," 104. Bruce Miller discusses the political instrumentality of tradition in *The Problem of Justice*, 34–53.

13 My use of the word "authenticity" differs from its most frequent usage. I do not associate authenticity with purity or timeless tradition. Nor do I automatically attribute a positive valence to the term. A useful gloss in most cases would be something like "traits that colonizers assumed were authentic" or "colonially defined notions of authenticity." Because such formulations are cumbersome, I have used them sparingly, mostly to remind the reader of the meaning that is intended throughout. I have likewise not used scare quotes each time "authenticity" appears, as that too would have been a distraction.

14 Douglas, *Implicit Meanings*, 61.

15 Cohodas, *Basket Weavers for the California Curio Trade*, 4.

16 McDiarmid, "Our Neighbors, the Alaskan Women."

17 I have thus employed collective terms such as "Aboriginal people" and "Indians" judiciously and as the context warrants. I use the term "Aboriginal people" to refer to groups or individuals of indigenous descent in Canada or the United States. In Alaska, "Alaska Native" is commonly employed and in the rest of the United States "Indians" and "Native Americans" remain widely in use. I also use "Indian" on occasion to indicate the historical usage of the term. Choosing a collective label for the colonizers is more problematic still. My choice of the collective term "White" can obscure the heterogeneity within settler society. I employ it reluctantly for lack of a better one. "White" is more historically accurate than "European" or "Western," and less awkward than the compound phrase, "Euro-American and Euro-Canadian." I have capitalized "White" to indicate that I refer not so much to a static racial group as to members of an immigrant, colonizing society. Where

this was not true (when Chinese individuals were involved, for example), I make this clear. I have used negative terms such as "non-Aboriginal" and "non-Indian" where they are appropriate.

18 Boswell and Evans, eds., *Representing the Nation*, 239, 367. This thousand-mile stretch of coastline remained a maritime region for Aboriginal people who were not simply integrated into the world system but who integrated the world system into their own "system of the world." Sahlins, "Cosmologies of Capitalism," 413. Remote from the eastern centers of American and Canadian national governments, non-Aboriginal displays of regional cooperation also endured. In 1879, for example, Americans fearing a Tlingit uprising called a British warship from Victoria to Sitka, Alaska. Moreover, Canada and the United States regularly looked to each other to formulate government Indian policy. Even their most significant divergences—there was no Canadian equivalent to the Plains Indian wars, for example—did not give rise to radically different results for Aboriginal people. For a comparative survey of Canadian and American Indian policies, see Nichols, *Indians in the United States and Canada*. For a comparative study of a cross-border Plains community, see Samek, *The Blackfoot Confederacy*.

19 King, "Tradition in Native American Art," 70; Dippie, *The Vanishing American*, chap. 14; Briggs and Bauman, " 'The Foundation of All Future Researches,' " 503–5; Harkin, "(Dis)Pleasures of the Text," 94–100. On the history of anthropology, see Stocking Jr., *Race, Culture, and Evolution*; Stocking Jr., *Victorian Anthropology*; Stocking Jr., *The Ethnographer's Magic*; and Stocking Jr., *Delimiting Anthropology*; Hinsley, *Savages and Scientists*; Bieder, *Science Encounters the Indian*; Baker, *From Savage to Negro*; and Darnell, *Invisible Genealogies*. On the history of anthropology with specific reference to the Kwakwa̱ka̱'wakw, see Jacknis, *The Storage Box of Tradition*.

20 Baker, *From Savage to Negro*, 28. Links between professional anthropology and colonialism were not unique to North America. See Dirks, *Castes of Mind*. The development of natural history lent a similar scientific mantle to earlier European conquests in the eighteenth century. Pratt, *Imperial Eyes*, chaps. 2, 3.

21 Cole, *Captured Heritage*.

22 Darnell, "The Pivotal Role of the Northwest Coast," 33–52. See also Harkin, "Past Presence," 1, 11.

23 Huyssen, *After the Great Divide*, viii;. Levine, *Highbrow/Lowbrow*.

24 Lears, *No Place of Grace*, xii. On the Arts and Crafts movement in American culture, see ibid., 60–96. On Arts and Crafts and collecting on the Northwest Coast, see Lee, "Appropriating the Primitive," 6–15. On nostalgia and imperialism, see Rosaldo, "Imperialist Nostalgia," 68–87. And on the links between authenticity, tourism, and imperialism, see MacCannell, *The Tourist*; Nash, "Tourism as a Form of Imperialism," 37–52; and MacCannell, *Empty Meeting Grounds*.

25 McKay, *The Quest of the Folk*; Becker, *Selling Tradition*.

26 Becker, *Selling Tradition*, 61; Roediger, *The Wages of Whiteness*.

27 On "tensions of empire," see Cooper and Stoler, eds., *Tensions of Empire*; Thomas, *Colonialism's Culture*; Christophers, *Positioning the Missionary*; and Harris, *The Resettlement of British Columbia*. Colonialism typically tolerated such contradictions. Deloria, *Playing Indian*, 126; Dirks, *The Hollow Crown*, 397; Pratt, *Imperial Eyes*, 153. On relations between tourists and anthropologists, see Phillips, *Trading Identities*, 14, 69; Wade, "The Ethnic Art Market in the American Southwest, 1880–1980," 171; Cohodas, *Basket Weavers*, 46; Klein, *Frontiers of Historical Imagination*, 172–73.

28 Some of these dichotomies have received individual attention from various scholars. For a brief summary of some such works, see Cohodas, *Basket Weavers*, 37–38.

29 On the concept of the vanishing Indian in the United States, see Dippie, *The Vanishing American*.

30 On the fluid nature of eighteenth-century Indian-White interaction, see White, *The Middle Ground*. On the contrasting, and prescient, positions of what he calls "Indian haters," see ibid., 389. On the sympathetic espousal of static cultural authenticity, see Klein, *Frontiers of Historical Imagination*, 166–67, 287, 290–91, 293, 295, 297.

31 Stocking Jr., "The Turn-of-the-Century Concept of Race," 4–16; Cole, *Franz Boas*, 267–73. On the history of blood quantum requirements, see Meyer, "American Indian Blood Quantum Requirements," 231–49. For an excellent survey of the various markers of "real Indians," see Garroutte, *Real Indians*.

32 Phillips, "Why Not Tourist Art?" 100. See also Harkin, "A Tradition of Invention," 100; and Nurse, " 'But Now Things Have Changed.' "

33 The expression "playing Indian" has recently been used by Philip J. Deloria in *Playing Indian*, his study of non-Native Americans' inclination to appropriate Indian dress and act out Indian roles. I use it here to describe situations where Aboriginal people enacted the categories of "authentic Indianness" expected of them by colonial society. I do not mean to suggest that objects or practices produced while "playing Indian" were or are "inauthentic."

34 Boas, *The Ethnography of Franz Boas*, 21, 96, 100, 102; Cole, "Franz Boas and the Bella Coola in Berlin"; Haberland, " 'Diese Indianer Sind Falsch.' " On the physical characteristics of "authentic" Indianness, see also Nurse, " 'But Now Things Have Changed,' " 446, 452.

35 Schein, "Performing Modernity," 369, 377. Schein draws especially on the work of Judith Butler. See Butler, *Gender Trouble*; Butler, "Performative Acts and Gender Constitution"; and Butler, *Bodies That Matter*.

36 Curtis Hinsley calls this the theatrical "museum process." Hinsley, "Zunis and Brahmins," 170. On tourism and bodily display, see Desmond, *Staging Tourism*. On "spectacle" as a colonial trope, see Mitchell, *Colonising Egypt*. For other works that broaden the definition of theater and performance, see Myers, "Culture-Making," 680; Neumann, "The Commercial Canyon," 197; Weigle, "From Desert to Disney World"; and Little, "On Safari." Aboriginal people also consciously constructed

such theatrical presentations themselves. Nicks, "Indian Villages and Entertainments."

37 Ettawageshik, "My Father's Business," 28–29.

38 Friends of the Indian, *Uncommon Controversy*, 67; Klein, *Frontiers of Historical Imagination*, 198–99. In twentieth-century Canada, the Huron-Wyandot were almost victims of a similar anthropologically influenced political annihilation. Nurse, " 'But Now Things Have Changed,' " 454–62.

39 Culhane, *The Pleasure of the Crown*, 229. The subsequent decision, known as the Delgamuukw decision, became the object of much academic commentary and outcry. See for example, Miller, ed., "A Theme Issue." The decision was overturned by the Supreme Court of Canada in 1997. But as the violence and public outcry over the subsequent 1999 Marshall decision, and a 2002 referendum in British Columbia on First Nations treaties reveal, much public support in Canada remains with the B.C. judge. Legal and biological definitions of Indianness could likewise worked in unexpected ways to deny Aboriginal identity to certain individuals. Garroutte, *Real Indians*, 22, 53.

40 Mauzé, "On Concepts of Tradition," 11. On this double bind in other contexts, see Phillips, *Trading Identities*, 63; Furniss, *The Burden of History*, 151, 199; Catton, *Inhabited Wilderness*, chaps. 2, 3; Deloria, *Playing Indian*, 91, 106; Becker, *Setting the Virgin on Fire*,106–7, 115; Deutsch, *No Separate Refuge*, 5; Dirks, "Castes of Mind," 76; and Davidoff, "Class and Gender in Victorian England," 22. On the relegation of indigenous people to the past, see MacCannell, "Tradition's Next Step," 162; Clifford, *The Predicament of Culture*, 5; King, "Tradition in Native American Art," 78, 88, 92; Bennett, "The Exhibitionary Complex," 350, 351; Tennant, *Aboriginal Peoples and Politics*, 14, 15; Fabian, *Time and the Other*; and Wolf, *Europe and the People without History*.

41 Dirks, *The Hollow Crown*, 381.

42 Schein, "Performing Modernity," 373, 381, 386. See also Cohodas, *Basket Weavers*, 51; and Dominguez, "Invoking Culture," 19–42.

43 Nicholas B. Dirks's observations about India in this regard offer important insights relevant to the Northwest Coast. Dirks, "The Policing of Tradition," 75.

44 It had long been the practice to see such tourist-oriented performances and art as degraded, and, by, extension, to see their creators as victims. A growing number of scholars have critiqued these perspectives, emphasizing instead that producers of tourist art and performance were not passive victims of colonialism but active participants in their own Aboriginal destinies. See Moses, *Wild West Shows*; and Phillips, *Trading Identities*; and Phillips, "Why Not Tourist Art?"

45 Scott, *Domination and the Arts of Resistance*, 103. See also Dirks, "Castes of Mind," 74; and Dirks, *Castes of Mind*, 235.

46 See Silverblatt, "Becoming Indian," 293.

47 Phillips, *Trading Identities*, 182; Phillips, "Why Not Tourist Art?," 103; Nicks, "Indian

Villages and Entertainments," 301; and Neumann, "The Commercial Canyon," 197–99.

48 On Native American labor history, see Littlefield and Knack, eds., *Native Americans and Wage Labor*; Knight, *Indians at Work*; and Hosmer, *American Indians in the Marketplace*.

49 Myers, "Culture-Making," 694; Graburn, ed., *Ethnic and Tourist Arts*, 32.

50 Schein, "Performing Modernity," 368, 372, 387; Jacobs, *Edge of Empire*, 156; Furniss, *The Burden of History*, 26.

51 Cruikshank, "Negotiating with Narrative," 59; Cruikshank, *The Social Life of Stories*, 68, 97; Deur, "The Hunt for Identity," 152; Roy, "Making History Visible"; Furniss, *The Burden of History*, 178, 184–85; Dominguez, "Invoking Culture," 33; and Cohodas, *Basket Weavers*, 47.

52 I have borrowed this phrase from Julie Cruikshank, who makes a similar point for a current-day context. Cruikshank, "Negotiating with Narrative," 59. This will be especially apparent in chapters 1–3 below.

53 This was true in a number of colonial contexts. Thomas, "The Inversion of Tradition," 221; Comaroff and Comaroff, *Ethnography and the Historical Imagination*, 273, 276; Dirks, "The Policing of Tradition," 204; Nurse, " 'But Now Things Have Changed,' " 445.

54 On this process in India and Africa, see Dirks, *The Hollow Crown*, 382; and Comaroff and Comaroff, *Ethnography and the Historical Imagination*, 43.

55 For other examples, see Thomas, "The Inversion of Tradition," 226; Silverblatt, "Becoming Indian," 280, 291; Dirks, "From Little King to Landlord," 324; Dirks, *The Hollow Crown*, 133, 386.

56 Dirks, "The Policing of Tradition," 182–212.

57 Thomas, "The Inversion of Tradition.," 213–14, 217.

58 Mauzé, "On Concepts of Tradition," 12. For insightful investigations of how culture and ritual are implicated in local power relations, see Dirks, *The Hollow Crown*, 304–5; Dirks, "Ritual and Resistance"; Holland and Skinner, "Contested Ritual, Contested Femininities," 280, 285; Furniss, *The Burden of History*, 165, 178.

59 For critiques of this problem, see Ortner, "Resistance and the Problem of Ethnographic Refusal," 281–88; and the work of Nicholas B. Dirks.

60 Spivak, *The Post-Colonial Critic*, 51.

61 Dirks, "Ritual and Resistance," 487. See also Furniss, *The Burden of History*, 180; Cruikshank, *The Social Life of Stories*, 163.

62 Dirks, "Ritual and Resistance," 499. See also Cruikshank, *The Social Life of Stories*, 114.

63 MacCannell, "Tradition's Next Step," 176.

64 Ibid.

65 See Marker, " 'That History Is More a Part of the Present than It Ever Was in the Past' "; Furniss, *The Burden of History*; and Thomas, *Colonialism's Culture*.

One Local Politics and Colonial Relations

1 The tribes today known as the Kwakwaka'wakw have historically been referred to by non-Aboriginal people as the (Southern) Kwakiutl. Kwakiutl or Kwagiulth, in fact, more correctly refers to a confederacy of previously four, now three, Kwakwaka'wakw groups who moved to Fort Rupert at its founding, and to their dialect of the Kwak'wala language. Kwakwaka'wakw means roughly "those who speak Kwak'wala." It is the term First Nations people from Fort Rupert (Kwakiutl or Kwagiulth), Alert Bay ('Namgis), Cape Mudge (Lekwiltok), Knight Inlet (Mamalilikulla), and surrounding areas prefer to use to describe themselves, and it is the term I will use here. See Macnair, "From Kwakiutl to Kwakwaka'wakw." For the reader's convenience, a nontechnical phonetic reading of Kwakwaka'wakw is "Kwakwa-you-wok."

2 "Fair Wide Open Next Sunday," *New York Times*, 25 May 1893, 12.

3 A. J. Hall to CMS, 10 July 1895, "Precis," Reel A-121, CMS, NAC. See also A. J. Hall to Superintendent of Indian Affairs, 5 October 1889, File 57,045-1, Volume 3816, DIA, RG10, NAC.

4 Berman "Red Salmon and Red Cedar Bark," 56–59; Galois, *Kwakwaka'wakw Settlements*, 26.

5 Mauzé, *Les Fils de Wakai*, chaps. 2, 3.

6 Two Nuwitti villages were destroyed, and so the incident became known as the "Nuwitti incident." See Gough, *Gunboat Frontier*, 41–48; Fisher, *Contact and Conflict*, 50–53; and Galois, *Kwakwaka'wakw Settlements*, 423–26.

7 On mixed-race populations in the Pacific Northwest, see Barman and Watson, "Fort Colvile's Fur Trade Families"; Barman, "What a Difference"; and Nelson, " 'A Strange Revolution in the Manners of the Country.' "

8 Canada, DIA, AR 1883, SP 1884, #4, lxii, 48; Canada, DIA, AR 1891, SP 1892, #14, 119; Cole and Chaikin, *An Iron Hand upon the People*, 62; Knight, *Indians at Work*, 14; Haberland, "Nine Bella Coolas in Germany," 338; Codere, *Fighting with Property*, 37; Lutz, "After the Fur Trade." See chapter 4 below for an example of Aboriginal women who combined prostitution with work in the hop fields of western Washington.

9 Boas, *Kwakiutl Ethnography*, 44, 46; Codere, "Kwakiutl," 367; Mauzé, *Les Fils de Wakai*, 20–21; Berman, "Red Salmon and Red Cedar Bark," 83. The interconnection between spiritual and material worlds was further apparent in the rules and rituals surrounding the harvesting, processing, and consuming of fish. Ibid., 59–62.

10 Donald, *Aboriginal Slavery on the Northwest Coast of North America*; Donald, "The Slave Trade on the Northwest Coast of North America"; and Ruby and Brown, *Indian Slavery in the Pacific Northwest*.

11 Mauzé, *Les Fils de Wakai*, 70; Miller, *The Problem of Justice*, 77, 79–80. For examples

of Lekwiltoq forays to the south, see MacLachlan, ed., *The Fort Langley Journals, 1827–1830*, 32, 57, 59, 61, 63, 65, 101, 111, 152.

12 As Judith Berman notes, in late-nineteenth-century Kwak'wala, "the variety of types of social events that Boas called 'potlatches' were referred to by a corresponding variety of terms, the use of which depended on the status and role of the recipient, on the kind of property being distributed, and on the immediate function of the event." Berman, " 'The Culture As It Appears to the Indian Himself,' " 246. The effort to define the "potlatch" has itself been part of the colonial mission. On the discursive construction of the potlatch, see Bracken, *The Potlatch Papers*. For a sampling of the secondary literature on Kwakwa̱ka̱'wakw potlatch and ceremony, see Berman, "Red Salmon and Red Cedar Bark"; Codere, *Fighting with Property*; Drucker and Heizer, *To Make My Name Good*; Goldman, *The Mouth of Heaven*; Jonaitis, ed., *Chiefly Feasts*; Masco, " 'It Is a Strict Law That Bids Us Dance' "; Mauzé, "Boas, les Kwagul et le Potlatch"; Mauzé, "Le Canoë dans le Potlatch Lekwiltoq"; Mauzé, *Les Fils de Wakai*, chap. 6; Sewid-Smith, *Prosecution or Persecution*; Walens, *Feasting with Cannibals*; Webster, "Kwakiutl since 1980."

13 Mauzé, *Les Fils de Wakai*, 18. See also Codere, *Fighting with Property*, 97; Masco, "Strict Law," 62; and Walens, *Feasting with Cannibals*, 154.

14 Drucker and Heizer, *To Make My Name Good*, 88–89; Masco, "Strict Law," 63–64; Mauzé, *Les Fils de Wakai*, 108; Boas, *Kwakiutl Ethnography*, 50–51. A. J. Hall went so far as to claim that a Nuwitti chief had formerly been a slave. See A. J. Hall to CMS, 1 March 1879, "Original," Reel A-124, CMS. For an example of social climbing among the Nuu-chah-nulth, see Drucker, "The Northern and Central Nootkan Tribes," 141. See also Lutz, "Work, Sex, and Death," 88.

15 Walens, *Feasting with Cannibals*, 107.

16 Harris, *The Resettlement of British Columbia*, 149; Duff, *The Indian History of British Columbia*, 87.

17 Barman, *The West beyond the West*, 363.

18 Reginald Pidcock, "Diary," 17 August 1888, Box 1, Pidcock Family Papers, BCA; R. H. Pidcock to A. W. Vowell, 19 May 1896, Volume 1648, DIA, RG10, NAC; R. H. Pidcock to A. W. Vowell, "Agent's report," April 1896, Volume 1648, DIA, RG10, NAC; Galois, *Kwakwaka'wakw Settlements*, 32–33.

19 A. J. Hall to CMS, 11 June 1878, "Letterbooks," Reel A-76, CMS, NAC.

20 Hall was dismissed from Duncan's service after he lost control of a nativistic revival movement. See Murray, *The Devil and Mr. Duncan*, 124–26; Usher, *William Duncan of Metlakatla*, 95–97; Rettig, "A Nativistic Movement at Metlakatla Mission"; Bolt, *Thomas Crosby and the Tsimshian*, 43.

21 Boas, *The Ethnography of Franz Boas*, 44; Dawson, "Notes and Observations on the Kwakiool People and the Adjacent Coasts," 87; Hinckley and Hinckley, "Ivan Petroff's Journal of a Trip to Alaska in 1878," 44; Gough, "A Priest Versus the Potlatch," 75.

22 R. H. Pidcock to A. W. Vowell, 28 April 1894, Volume 1648, DIA, RG10, NAC.

23 A. J. Hall to CMS, 10 July 1895, "Precis," Reel A-121, CMS, NAC.
24 A. J. Hall to CMS, 12 March 1878, "Original," Reel A-106, CMS, NAC.
25 A. J. Hall to CMS, 20 March 1878, "Original," Reel A-106, CMS, NAC.
26 A. J. Hall to CMS, 16 December 1878, "Original," Reel A-106, CMS, NAC.
27 Cole and Chaikin, *An Iron Hand*, 37–38, 66.
28 Berman, "Red Salmon and Red Cedar Bark, 86–89. Addressing potential imbalances in human society was a broader purpose of the winter ceremonial. Ibid., 53–98.
29 LaViolette, *The Struggle for Survival*, 34.
30 Victoria *Weekly Colonist*, 19 March 1896, File 6244–1, Volume 3628, DIA, RG10, NAC.
31 Reginald Pidcock, "Diary," 1 June 1888, Box 1, Pidcock Family Papers, BCA. Fort Rupert residents, including Mrs. Hunt, had also traveled to Koskimo for the occasion. Ibid., 31 May 1888. Pidcock's predecessor, Blenkinsop, on the other hand, had on occasion managed to take advantage of potlatch gatherings to reduce the amount of travel required to complete his "annual visitation" to the various villages. Canada, DIA AR 1885, SP 1886, #4, 84.
32 A .J. Hall to CMS, 13 January 1879, "Original," Reel A-106, CMS, NAC.
33 A. J. Hall to CMS, 16 March 1880, "Original," Reel A-106, CMS, NAC. This problem was widespread. Mauzé, *Les Fils de Wakai*, 121.
34 A. J. Hall to CMS, 7 October 1884, "Precis," Reel A-121, CMS, NAC.
35 A. J. Hall to CMS, 11 June 1878, "Original," Reel A-106, CMS, NAC; R.H. Pidcock to A. W. Vowell, n.d., File 57,045-1, Volume 3816, DIA, RG10, NAC. On the sexualization of the potlatch, see Barman, "Taming Aboriginal Sexuality," 259–61, 263.
36 For an analysis that traces this discourse from the seventeenth century forward, see Smits, "The 'Squaw Drudge.' "
37 One scholar goes so far as to suggest that "there is no reason to assume that Hall's 'facts' correspond to the events they claim to describe." Bracken, *Potlatch Papers*, 49, 132.
38 Barman, "Taming Aboriginal Sexuality," 249.
39 R. H. Pidcock to I. W. Powell, 3 April 1889, File 57,045-1, Volume 3816, DIA, RG10, NAC.
40 Indians to R. H. Pidcock, 8 March, 1895, Volume 1648, DIA, RG10, NAC; Barman, "Taming Aboriginal Sexuality," 255–58. The requested legislation was not passed. Ibid.
41 Lutz, "Work, Sex, and Death," 88.
42 Suttles, "Streams of Property, Armor of Wealth," 92–95.
43 See for example, Berman, "Unpublished Materials of Franz Boas and George Hunt," 189.
44 Unknown to A. W. Vowell, 25 February 1895, Volume 1648, DIA, RG10, NAC.
45 R. H. Pidcock to Superintendent General of Indian Affairs, 2 October 1889, Volume 3628, DIA, RG10, NAC; Superintendent General of Indian Affairs, 31 October 1889 to [?], Volume 3628, DIA, RG10, NAC.

46 Less than $90 of the more than $1,400 cost of the church was donated by the Kwakwa̲ka̲'wakw at a time when the Kwakwa̲ka̲'wakw were potlatching great amounts of wealth (circa 1893). Duncan, " 'A Wretched Giving Away System,' " 55. See also Codere, *Fighting with Property*, 96–97.

47 Cole and Chaikin, *An Iron Hand*, 44–49, 117, 131–32, 139, 178–80; Tina Loo, "Dan Cranmer's Potlatch,"161–63.

48 Duncan, " 'A Wretched Giving Away System,' " 53–55.

49 A. J. Hall to CMS, 16 May 1885, "Precis," Reel A-121, CMS, NAC; A.J. Hall to CMS, 1 February 1889, "Original," Reel A-123, CMS, NAC; A. J. Hall to CMS, 11 July 1891,"Original," Reel A-123, CMS, NAC.

50 A. J. Hall, to CMS, 1 March 1879, "Original," Reel A-124, CMS, NAC. A Russian visitor to Fort Rupert in 1878 similarly observed that "the Indians seem eager enough to learn to read and write English." Hinckley and Hinckley, "Ivan Petroff's Journal," 44.

51 Boas, *Ethnography of Franz Boas*, 35. It is unlikely that this man actually received the flag from the "king" since Queen Victoria had been on the British throne since 1837.

52 S. A. Spencer to CMS, 8 March 1888, "Precis," Reel A-121, CMS, NAC.

53 Cole and Chaikin, *An Iron Hand*, 34. Many of the charges levied against Kwakwa̲ka̲'wakw individuals were alcohol-related.

54 Reginald Pidcock, "Diary," 21 March; 22 March; 24 March; 26 March; 27 March; 31 July; 26 August; 21 December 1888, Box 1, Pidcock Family Papers, BCA.

55 A. J. Hall to CMS, 19 December 1888, "Original," Reel A-123, CMS, NAC.

56 A. J. Hall to CMS, 1 February 1889, "Original," Reel A-123, CMS, NAC. It was not atypical for Aboriginal people to turn at times to missionaries for such assistance. Although prone to stereotypical representation, relationships between missionaries and Aboriginal people were complex. On missionaries to various Aboriginal people in British Columbia, see Neylan, *The Heavens Are Changing*; Christophers, *Positioning the Missionary*; Usher, *William Duncan*; Bolt, *Thomas Crosby*; Whitehead, ed., *They Call Me Father*; and Whitehead, *The Cariboo Mission*. On Christian missions in British Columbia more generally, see Knowles, ed., "Special issue on British Columbia."

57 Reginald Pidcock, "Diary," 31 July 1888, Box 1, Pidcock Family Papers, BCA.

58 Alert Bay Indians to CMS, 10 May 1890, "Original," Reel A-123, CMS, NAC.

59 See, for example, "Original," Reel A-123, CMS, NAC; Reginald Pidcock, "Diary, 18 May 1888, Box 1, Pidcock Family Papers, BCA.

60 Hall to CMS, 16 May 1888, "Original," Reel A-124, CMS, NAC.

61 The suspect convergence of Hall's missionary and commercial activities was not atypical of colonial endeavors. For the African context, see, for example, Comaroff and Comaroff, *Ethnography and the Historical Imagination*, 276.

62 Reginald Pidcock, "Diary," 19–20 May 1888, Box 1, Pidcock Family Papers, BCA.

63 Berman, "George Hunt and the Kwak'wala Texts," 484–88, 501–6; Berman, " 'The Culture as It Appears,' " 240.

64 A. J. Hall to CMS, 20 August 1880, "Original," Reel A-106, CMS, NAC.

65 Ibid.

66 A. J. Hall to CMS, 20 March 1878, "Original," Reel A-106, CMS, NAC.

67 The scholarship on Boas and his method is vast. See, for example, Cole, *Franz Boas*; Stocking Jr., *Race, Culture, and Evolution*; Stocking Jr., *The Ethnographer's Magic*, chap. 3; Stocking Jr., *Delimiting Anthropology*, chaps. 1–4; Stocking Jr., ed., *Volksgeist as Method*; Berman "Oolachan-Woman's Robe," 125–62;. Liss, "Patterns of Strangeness"; Briggs and Bauman, " 'The Foundation of All Future Researches' "; Darnell, "The Pivotal Role of the Northwest Coast in the History of Americanist Anthropology"; and Harkin, "(Dis)Pleasures of the Text."

68 On George Hunt, see Berman, " 'The Culture as It Appears' "; Berman, "George Hunt and the Kwak'wala Texts"; Jacknis, "George Hunt, Collector of Indian Specimens"; Cannizzo, "George Hunt and the Invention of Kwakiutl Culture"; and Briggs and Bauman, " 'The Foundation of All Future Researches.' " On one of Hunt's more controversial acquisitions, see Jonaitis, *The Yuquot Whaler's Shrine*. Local informants similarly collaborated with ethnographers in other colonial settings. See, for example, Clifford, *Person and Myth*, 142.

69 Williams, *Framing the West*, 174.

70 Berman, " 'The Culture as It Appears,' " 231. See also ibid., 252.

71 Both of these positions assume the spurious nature of putting old practices to new use. Countering this implication, Michael Harkin argues that pragmatic approaches to "new traditions" have a long, and unironic, history among Northwest Coast peoples. Harkin, "A Tradition of Invention."

Two "The March of the Aborigine"

1 Rydell, *All the World's a Fair*, 6, 8, 41; Heaman, *The Inglorious Arts of Peace*, 7; Bennett, "The Exhibitionary Complex," 332–61.

2 Heaman, *Inglorious Arts of Peace*, 7, 8, 141.

3 Cronon, *Nature's Metropolis*, 341.

4 Quoted in Rydell, *All the World's a Fair*, 45. Apropos this theme and the concern with the policies in the West, Frederick Jackson Turner chose the American Historical Association's meeting, held in conjunction with the Chicago exposition, to present his frontier thesis. Ibid., 47.

5 "Plan and Classification, Department M," 1892, p. 8, Misc. pamphlets: rules, World's Columbian Exposition, Chicago 1893, Chicago Historical Society, Chicago, Illinois.

6 Quoted in Rydell, *All the World's a Fair*, 44.

7 Bennett, "The Exhibitionary Complex," 333, 338–39; Walden, *Becoming Modern in*

Toronto, 119, 120. Where Michel Foucault writes that punishment ceased to be a spectacle, Bennett demonstrates that power itself continued to be publicly displayed, albeit in different form. Bennett, "The Exhibitionary Complex," 337. As the exhibitionary complex's way of displaying bodies succeeded the disciplinary spectacles that Foucault described, so they preceded the ethnic violence of the late twentieth century, which can be seen as the latest configuration of power, body, and public display. See Appadurai, "Dead Certainty," 233–34.

8 On the failed attempts to incorporate such exhibitions in the 1876 Centennial Exhibition in Philadelphia, see Trennert, "A Grand Failure."

9 This changed in 1898 with the United States' colonization of the Philippines. The 1904 St. Louis World's Fair featured 1,000 newly colonized Filipinos. Everett, *The Book of the Fair*, 295–316.

10 Fogelson, "The Red Man in the White City," 75.

11 *A Week at the Fair Illustrating the Exhibits and Wonders*, 111.

12 Ives, *The Dream City*, n.p. A similar polarization between "civilized" and "uncivilized" blacks occurred at the fair. Frederick Douglass protested the exhibit of Dahomians, arguing that they were there "to exhibit the Negro as a repulsive savage." Douglass renamed the White City a "whited sepulcher." Trachtenberg, *The Incorporation of America*, 220–21. See also Baker, *From Savage to Negro*, 60–62.

13 *Chicago Herald*, 17 July 1893, Scrapbook, Chicago World's Fair, 1891–1893, Volume II, FWPP.

14 Chicago *Daily Inter Ocean*, 9 July 1893, Scrapbook, Volume II, FWPP. See also "Curios of Indians," *Chicago Herald*, 20 May 1893, Scrapbook, Volume II, FWPP.

15 "The Man Columbus Found," *New York Press*, 28 May 1893, Scrapbook, Volume II, FWPP.

16 *Official Catalogue of Exhibits on the Midway Plaisance* (Chicago: W. B. Conkey Company, 1893), Box 38, FWPP.

17 [Newspaper clipping], 8 February 1893, Scrapbook, Volume II, FWPP; *Pioneer Press* (St. Paul, Minnesota), 15 March 1893, Scrapbook, Volume II, FWPP; Chicago *Daily Inter Ocean*, 9 July 1893, Scrapbook, Volume II, FWPP; Chicago *Daily Inter Ocean*, 13 July 1893, Scrapbook, Volume II, FWPP; "Department of Ethnology, Out of Doors Exhibits on the Ethnographical Grounds," [newspaper clipping, n.d.], Box 31, FWPP. On the racial narrative of the Midway, see Baker, *From Savage to Negro*, 56–58.

18 L. G. Moses looks at the way in which the images of Indians perpetuated by Buffalo Bill contrasted with those promoted by governments. See especially Moses, *Wild West Shows*, chaps. 7, 8. Frederick Ward Putnam and others involved in the anthropology exhibit at the fair objected to the presence of the Buffalo Bill show on the grounds that it "degraded" the Indians. See, for example, "Red Men at the Fair. The Indian Office will see that 'Lo' is Not Degraded" [newspaper clipping, May 1893], Scrapbook, Volume II, FWPP; "Will Have No Wild West Show," *Chicago Tribune*, 14 February 1892, Scrapbook, Volume II, FWPP.

19 "All Kinds of Indians," Chicago *Daily Inter Ocean*, 20 June 1893; Putnam referred to the exhibit as "The March of the Aborigine to Civilization." "Quackuhls are Here," *Chicago Tribune*, 12 April 1893, Scrapbook, Volume II, FWPP.

20 "James Deans and His Company of Indians," 186.

21 Johnson, ed., *A History of the World's Columbian Exposition*, 2:315.

22 "The Man Columbus Found," *New York Press*, 28 May 1893, Scrapbook, Volume II, FWPP. Emphasis added.

23 Final attendance at the fair was calculated at 27,529,400 people over the 179 days that the fair was open. Daily attendance exceeded 100,000 visitors on 92 of these days. On 9 October 1893, which was designated "Chicago Day," admission rose to an astonishing 700,000 visitors. Cameron, *The World's Fair*, 829–30.

24 *Chicago Herald*, 17 July 1893, Scrapbook, Volume II, FWPP.

25 F. W. Putnam to U.S. Indian agents, 13 May 1892, Box 31, FWPP; F. W. Putnam to Antonio, 13 May 1892, Box 31, FWPP; Antonio an Apache to F. W. Putnam, 7 June 1892, Box 31, FWPP; Antonio an Apache to F. W. Putnam, 25 July 1892, Box 31, FWPP.

26 Antonio an Apache to F. W. Putnam, 25 July 1892, Box 31, FWPP; F.W. Putnam to Antonio, 4 August 1892, Box 31, FWPP.

27 F. W. Putnam to Commissioner of Indian Affairs, 25 August 1893, Box 34, FWPP.

28 Antonio an Apache to F. W. Putnam, 25 July 1892, Box 31, FWPP; F.W. Putnam to Antonio, 4 August 1892, Box 31, FWPP.

29 *Chicago Herald*, 30 March 1893, Scrapbook, Volume II, FWPP; *New York Times*, 10 April 1893, 1; St. John's *Times and Commercial Gazette*, 29 April 1893, 2; Scott, "Village Performance," 214; "The Esquimau Village," New Orleans *Democratic Times*, 14 July 1893, Scrapbook, Volume II, FWPP.

30 "The Esquimau Village," New Orleans *Democratic Times*, 14 July 1893, Scrapbook, Volume II, FWPP.

31 Quoted in St. John's *Times and Commercial Gazette*, 29 April 1893, 2.

32 Chicago *Daily Inter Ocean*, 1 April 1893.

33 Ibid. Heaman, *Inglorious Arts of Peace*, 302. During the course of the fair, performers' clothing was frequently an issue. When the Kwakwa̲ka̲'wakw first arrived in Chicago, a reporter sarcastically derided one of the women's attire: "The idea is to give a glimpse of the peoples of the Western Hemisphere, as they were when Columbus discovered it. It would seem as if Katie's purple skirt must go." "Quackuhls are Here," *Chicago Tribune*, 12 April 1893, Scrapbook, Volume II, FWPP. A group of Samoans on the Midway who had adopted Western garb were similarly advised to return to their sarongs. Wayne, "1893 On the Midway," 17, 19. In other instances the reverse situation prevailed. Men who had been brought from Sri Lanka as construction workers struck for better wages and the right to wear "native costume" while in Chicago. Perhaps they hoped to earn some added income by mounting an "authentic" display of their own. Chicago *Daily Inter Ocean*, 17 March 1893, 7.

34 Chicago *Daily Inter Ocean*, 31 March 1893.

35 Chicago *Daily Inter Ocean*, 1 April 1893; Chicago *Daily Inter Ocean*, 23 April 1893; St. John's *Times and Commercial Gazette*, 29 April 1893, 2.

36 *Chicago Tribune*, 21 August 1893.

37 Heaman, *Inglorious Arts of Peace*, 300.

38 T. J. Morgan to Hayter Reed, 12 September 1892, File 85,529, Volume 3865, DIA, RG10, NAC. Indian children came from the schools in Albuquerque, New Mexico; Renssalaer, Indiana; Lincoln, Nebraska; Lawrence, Kansas; Genoa, Nebraska; Chilocco, Oklahoma; and Osage, Oklahoma. Monroe, "World's Educational Exhibits (XI)." See also Trennert, "Selling Indian Education at World's Fairs and Expositions, 1893–1904."

39 Cameron, *The World's Fair*, 732; Pratt, *Battlefield and Classroom*, 303–8. See also Badger, *The Great American Fair*, 105; Fogelson, "The Red Man in the White City," 85.

40 "Correspondence re: request to establish an Indian exhibit at the World's Columbian Exposition, 1893," File 85,529, Volume 3865, DIA, RG10, NAC; see also *The Canadian Indian*, 15 September 1893.

41 Heaman, *Inglorious Arts of Peace*, 230.

42 Canada, DIA, AR 1894, SP 1895, #14, xviii.

43 Sources give only the faintest glimmer of what the experience of living on display was like for the children. One commentator claimed that "the weary homesick look that crept into the dark eyes of the Indian girl who shyly answered 'yes,' made me wish I had not asked her if she should be glad to go back to the school home." "Work of Indian Children," *New York Times*, 12 November 1893, 18.

44 Canada, DIA, AR 1894, SP 1895, #14, xviii.

45 *The Canadian Indian*, 15 September 1893.

46 Ives, *The Dream City*, n.p.

47 Walden, *Becoming Modern in Toronto*, 91.

48 Friesen, *The Canadian Prairies*, 137; Barman, *The West beyond the West*, 363.

49 Heaman, *Inglorious Arts of Peace*, 192, 236.

50 Ibid., 297; Titley, *A Narrow Vision*, 172.

51 Heaman, *Inglorious Arts of Peace*, 307. See chapter 6 below for a fuller discussion of late-nineteenth-century conflations of Aboriginal people and nature.

52 Heaman, *Inglorious Arts of Peace*, 218.

53 Owram, "White Savagery," 6.

54 T. J. Morgan to Hayter Reed, 12 September 1892, File 85,529, Volume 3865, DIA, RG10, NAC.

55 *Ottawa Journal*, 4 May 1893.

56 Chicago *Inter Ocean Illustrated Supplement*, 9 August 1893, 4.

57 Victoria *Daily Colonist*, 2 August 1893.

58 *Ottawa Journal*, 22 May 1893.

59 "Visitors Register of the Northwest Territories Exhibit at Chicago World's Fair," 1893, NAC.

60 Ibid.

61 Ibid. On earlier annexation debates, see Williams, *Framing the West*, 35–37.

62 For the six winter months of 1892–93 the beef ration had been cut in half, with the bulk of the rations being given in bacon and flour, which themselves amounted to only 3.5 ounces of flour and 0.9 ounces of bacon per person per day. John Ross to Hayter Reed, 28 December 1892, Hayter Reed Correspondence, NAC. When hungry people understandably began killing cattle for food, ranchers blamed Reed: "It may be very pleasing for Mr. Hayter Reed to show at the end of the year how cheaply he has fed the Indians but I do not think the country or parliament will sanction a policy which compels the Indians to help themselves, as they can hardly be expected to refrain from doing, when cattle are in sight and they are insufficiently provided for by the Government." M. H. Cochrane to T. M. Daly, 30 December 1892, Hayter Reed Correspondence, NAC.

63 Canada, DIA AR 1894, SP 1895, #14, 151.

64 Heaman, *Inglorious Arts of Peace*, 306.

65 Canada, DIA AR 1895, SP 1896, #14, 49.

66 *Manitoba Free Press*, 21 February 1894.

67 Canada, DIA AR 1893, SP 1894, #14. This count could easily be higher, as the school also listed eighteen children who were simply "brought home by a parent," for reasons that were left unexplained. As Mary-Ellen Kelm points out, students who were not expected to live were often sent home for "visits," in order to lower the number of deaths that occurred at the school itself. Kelm, *Colonizing Bodies*, 75.

68 DIA figures show that a quarter of all residential school students died while on the school rolls or shortly thereafter. This death rate rises to 69 percent where post-schooling health is plotted. Brownlie and Kelm, "Desperately Seeking Absolution," 550. On residential schools across Canada, see Miller, *Shingwauk's Vision*. On disease and health issues relating to residential schools, see Kelm, *Colonizing Bodies*, 57–80; and Lux, *Medicine That Walks*, chap. 3.

69 A. J. Hall to L. Vankoughnet, 24 August 1893, File 85,529, Volume 3865, DIA, RG10, NAC; R. H. Pidcock to A. W. Vowell, 18 October 1893, File 85,529, Volume 3865, DIA, RG10, NAC.

70 Quoted in Curtis M. Hinsley, "The World as Marketplace," 363.

71 *Chicago Evening Post*, 8 August 1893, Scrapbook, Volume III, FWPP.

72 Darnell, "The Pivotal Role of the Northwest Coast," 43; Cole, *Franz Boas*, 261–267. Boas was similarly critical of popular museum displays. Jacknis, "Franz Boas and Exhibits," 75–111. Such conflicts characterized other exhibitions. Heaman, *Inglorious Arts of Peace*, 107, 221.

73 Circular letter by Emma C. Sickles and Frank Carson, Universal Peace Union, [ca. September 1893], Box 33, FWPP; *Philadelphia Times*, 19 November 1893, Scrapbook, Volume III, FWPP. Sickles was typical of reformers of her day who similarly protested the exhibition of Indians in the Wild West shows. See Moses, *Wild West Shows*, 5.

74 "Miss Sickles Makes Charges," *New York Times*, 8 October 1893; *Philadelphia Times*, 19 November 1893, Scrapbook, Volume III, FWPP. For Thomas J. Morgan's defense of Putnam, see *New York Times*, 8 October 1893.

75 Henry Standing Bear to T. J. Morgan, 15 January 1891, Box 33, FWPP.

76 Ibid.

77 Honoré J. Jaxon, Manuel S. Moldano, and Henry Standing Bear to F. W. Putnam, 15 January 1892, Box 32, FWPP. Jaxon, a white man who had "passed" as Métis for much of his life, was a controversial figure. Sickles vehemently condemned him as an untrustworthy outlaw from Canada. Folder "S(2) E. Sickles," Box 33, FWPP. See Smith, "Honoré J. Jaxon."

78 Petition, May 1891, Box 34, FWPP.

79 See, for example, Rydell *All the World's a Fair*; Rydell and Gwinn, eds., *Fair Representations*; Greenhalgh, *Ephemeral Vistas*; and Hinsley, "The World as Marketplace." For a scholar who *has* considered the meaning of performances for Native Americans see Moses, *Wild West Shows*.

Three Theaters of Contact

1 Scidmore, *Appleton's Guide-Book to Alaska and the Northwest Coast*, 22.

2 Quoted in Cole, *Captured Heritage*, 68.

3 Ibid., 131. See also Cole, "Franz Boas and the Bella Coola"; Haberland, "Nine Bella Coolas"; and Haberland, " 'Diese Indianer Sind Falsch.' "

4 "Agreement between F. W. Putnam and George Hunt," 29 September 1892, Box 36, FWPP.

5 F. H. Mead to Capt. E. H. Taylor, 22 April 1892, Box 35, FWPP; G. R. Davis to F. W. Putnam, 10 April 1893, Box 31, FWPP.

6 R. H. Pidcock to A. W. Vowell, 16 May 1893, Volume 1648, DIA, RG10, NAC.

7 *Chicago News*, 11 April 1893, Scrapbook, Chicago World's Fair, 1891–1893, Volume II, FWPP.

8 Victoria *Daily Colonist*, 20 April 1893, 3.

9 A. J. Hall to L. Vankoughnet, 24 August 1893, File 85,529, Volume 3865, DIA, RG10, NAC; Jacknis, *Storage Box of Tradition*, 402, n.19.

10 Jacknis, *Storage Box of Tradition*, 9.

11 Codere, "Kwakiutl: Traditional Culture," 368.

12 Where applicable, I have retained the orthography of Kwakwa̲ka̲'wakw from the original source cited. Jacknis, "Northwest Coast Indian Culture," 103; Bill Holm to Elizabeth Virolainen, 13 March 1981, photograph N751, #6339, Binder 3, "Other Museums Photographs-Peabody Museum, Harvard," Royal British Columbia Museum; Jacknis, "Northwest Coast Indian Culture," 103; Boas, *Ethnography of Franz Boas*, 152; Boas, "Ethnology of the Kwakiutl," 1113; *Chicago Tribune*, 7 May 1893; *Chicago Tribune*, 6 May 1893; Chicago *Daily Inter Ocean*, 7 May 1893; "Quackuhls are Here," *Chicago Tribune*, 12 April 1893, Scrapbook, Volume II, FWPP; *Chicago Times*,

7 May 1893; "Quackuhls are Here"; ibid; ibid; Holm to Virolainen, 13 March 1981; *Chicago Tribune*, 30 July 1893; "Quackuhls are Here"; Chicago *Daily Inter Ocean*, 12 April 1893; Jacknis, *Storage Box of Tradition*, 342; Holm to Virolainen, 13 March 1981; Barbeau, *Totem Poles*, 682; Holm to Virolainen, 13 March 1981; Boas, *Ethnography of Franz Boas*, 152; Holm to Virolainen, 13 March 1981; ibid; Gray, *The Federal Cylinder Project*, 3:145. Other Aboriginal names listed in newspapers include Amo Sellock or Himaseloq, a "Clacasequala"; Hamisila, the "official mouthpiece" of the house-opening ceremonial; Hawmissilatl; Numokevis; Thakoagyila; Klew-Ho-Gish, reportedly the group's "patriarch"; the Gwetele chief Ah-Wah-Lass Kidd Ness; Klow-Coot-Lass; and Na-Mo Tlass."Quackuhls are Here"; *Chicago Tribune*, 30 July 1893; *Chicago Tribune*, 6 May 1893; ibid; Chicago *Daily Inter Ocean*, 12 April 1893; ibid; "Quackuhls are Here"; *Chicago Record*, 14 April 1893, Scrapbook, Volume II, FWPP; ibid; ibid. Some of these names refer to the same people listed above. For example, the man newspapers identified as "Himaseloq, a Clacasequala," is Tom from the "Tlatlasikwala" tribe at Nuwitti. Indians to Pidcock, 8 March, 1895, Volume 1648, DIA, RGIO, NAC.

13 F. W. Putnam to J. F. Lee, 18 November 1893, Box 31, FWPP; J. F. Lee to F. W. Putnam, 15 May 1893, Box 31, FWPP; R. Kerr to F. W. Putnam, 15 November 1893, Box 31, FWPP.

14 D. McNicoll, General Passenger agent, CPR to F. W. Putnam, 19 June 1895, Box 31, FWPP; F. W. Putnam to D. McNicoll, 22 July 1895, Box 31, FWPP. For other correspondence dealing with this dispute, see the following letters in Box 31, FWPP: G. McL. Brown to J. F. Lee, 5 April 1893; F.W. Putnam to J. F. Lee, 21 October 1893; J. F. Lee to F. W. Putnam, 31 October 1893, 7 November 1893, 15 November 1893, 16 November 1893; F. W. Putnam to D. McNicoll, 3 January 1895; F. W. Putnam to G. R. Davis, 25 June 1895; D. McNicoll, to F. W. Putnam, 19 July 1895.

15 F. W. Putnam to G. R. Davis, 6 April 1893, Box 35, FWPP; F. W. Putnam to G. R. Davis, 11 April 1893, Box 31, FWPP; G. R. Davis, to F. W. Putnam, 12 April 1893, Box 32, FWPP.

16 *Chicago Herald*, 20 May 1893, Scrapbook, Volume II, FWPP.

17 Some Haida and Tsimshian expressed interest in joining the Chicago exhibit, but Putnam refused to pay their way. F. W. Putnam to A. W. Vowell, 24 September 1892, File 85,529, Volume 3865, DIA, RGIO, NAC; Unidentified addressee to A. W. Vowell, 9 November 1892, File 85,529, Volume 3865, DIA, RGIO, NAC.

18 "Franz Boas and the Kwakiutl," 214.

19 [Clipping], [July 1893], Scrapbook, Volume II, FWPP; Johnson, *History of the World's Columbian Exposition*, 2:355.

20 Johnson, *History of the World's Columbian Exposition*, 2:55; "Round the Totem Pole," *Chicago Times*, 7 May 1893; Chicago *Daily Inter Ocean*, 7 May 1893; *Chicago Tribune*, 7 May 1893; Chicago *Daily Inter Ocean*, 12 April 1893, 12; *Chicago Record*, 14 April 1893, Scrapbook, Volume II, FWPP; Victoria *Daily Colonist*, 20 April 1893, 3; Jacknis, *Storage Box of Tradition*, 84.

21 Walens, *Feasting with Cannibals*, 105.

22 Chicago *Daily Inter Ocean*, 7 May 1893; *Chicago Tribune*, 7 May 1893. By calling the performance a "ghost dance," the reporter likely evoked the fairgoers' familiarity with the well-known religious revival movement on the Plains and the prophet Wovoka. However, the Kwakwa̲ka̲'wakw had ghost dances of their own which were distinct from the Plains rituals of the same name. Boas, *Social Organization*, 482–83.

23 "Infanta at Chicago" Chicago *Daily Inter Ocean*, 13 June 1893, 2; *Chicago Herald*, 13 May 1893, Scrapbook, Volume II, FWPP; *New York Tribune*, 15 May 1893, Scrapbook, Volume II, FWPP.

24 Boas, *Social Organization*, 489.

25 "Folk-Music at the Fair: Cannibal Songs of the Indians," *New York Tribune*, 6 August 1893.

26 Boas, *Social Organization*, 495; Suttles, "Streams of Property," 100.

27 Jacknis, *Storage Box of Tradition*, 87; "The Man Columbus Found," *New York Press*, 28 May 1893, Scrapbook, Volume II, FWPP; *Chicago Herald*, 13 May 1893, Scrapbook, Volume II, FWPP; *New York Tribune*, 15 May 1893, Scrapbook, Volume II, FWPP; *Chicago Times*, 13 June 1893; Chicago *Daily Inter Ocean*, 13 June 1893. The sunrise dance was likely the Na'xnak·aqeml dance. Boas, *Social Organization*, 410–11, 484–85.

28 F. W. Putnam to G. R. Davis, 27 March 1893, Box 31, FWPP.

29 "Franz Boas and the Kwakiutl," 214.

30 Ford, *Smoke from their Fires*, 187–90.

31 Webster, "The Contemporary Potlatch," 242.

32 Jacknis, "Northwest Coast Indian Culture," 111.

33 *Chicago Record*, 14 April 1893, Scrapbook, Volume II, FWPP; Victoria *Daily Colonist*, 20 April 1893, 3.

34 Boas, *Ethnography of Franz Boas*, 152.

35 Chicago *Daily Inter Ocean*, 9 July 1893, Scrapbook, Volume II, FWPP; Harlan Smith to F. W. Putnam, 27 June 1893, Box 33, FWPP.

36 Boas, *Ethnography of Franz Boas*, 183.

37 *New York Times*, 25 May 1893.

38 Victoria *Daily Colonist*, 19 August 1893.

39 "A Brutal Exhibition," *New York Times*, 19 August 1893, 5; London *Sunday Times*, 20 August 1893. The incident was also reported in numerous other papers. See the clippings in Scrapbook, Volume III, FWPP, including: Lincoln, Nebraska *State Journal*, 7 October 1893; Columbus, Ohio *Dispatch*, 10 October 1893; San Francisco *Chronicle*, 7 October 1893; Pittsburgh *Chronicle*, 6 October 1893; Washington, D.C. *News*, 6 October 1893; Cincinnati *Enquirer*, 7 October 1893; [Chicago?] *Evening Post*, 18 August 1893; and *Philadelphia Times*, 19 November 1893.

40 London *Sunday Times*, 20 August 1893.

41 A. J. Hall to CMS, 30 September 1878, "Original," Reel A-106, CMS, NAC.

42 [CMS Notes], 1 February 1882, "Precis", Reel A-121, CMS, NAC.

43 A. J. Hall to L. Vankoughnet, 24 August 1893, File 85,529, Volume 3865, DIA, RG10, NAC.

44 Victoria *Daily Colonist*, 25 August 1893, 5.

45 A. W. Vowell to Deputy Superintendent General of Indian Affairs, 10 May 1894, File 113,639, Volume 3914, DIA, RG10, NAC.

46 F. W. Putnam to Commissioner of Indian Affairs, 29 September 1893, Box 33, FWPP. Putnam's position was reprinted in several newspapers. See Scapbook, Volume III, FWPP, especially: Lincoln, Nebraska *State Journal*, 7 October 1893; Columbus, Ohio *Dispatch*, 10 October 1893; San Francisco *Chronicle*, 7 October 1893; Pittsburgh *Chronicle*, 6 October 1893; Washington, D.C. *News*, 6 October 1893; Cincinnati *Enquirer*, 7 October 1893; [Chicago?] *Evening Post*, 18 August 1893; *Philadelphia Times*, 19 November 1893.

47 Heaman, *The Inglorious Arts of Peace*, 106, 218.

48 L. Vankoughnet to J. S. Larke, 6 September 1893, File 85,529, Volume 3865, DIA, RG10, NAC. For a similar cross-border performance of dances banned in Canada, see Burt, "Nowhere Left to Go," 201, 203.

49 Putnam to Commissioner of Indian Affairs, 29 September 1893, Box 33, FWPP.

50 Ibid.

51 Boas, "Ethnology of the Kwakiutl," 1114. See also Boas, *Kwakiutl Ethnography*, 191; Suttles, "Streams of Property," 117–33; Jacknis, *Storage Box of Tradition*, 87.

52 Ford, *Smoke from their Fires*, 186.

53 Newcombe offered commission but no wages. Jacknis, *Storage Box of Tradition*, 91.

54 Masco, "'It Is a Strict Law That Bids Us Dance,'" 67.

55 Bill Holm in McLuhan, dir., *The Shadow Catcher*; Codere, "Kwakiutl: Traditional Culture," 369; Drucker and Heizer, *To Make My Name Good*, 102–03.

56 Sewid, *Guests Never Leave Hungry*, 158–62; Spradley and McCurdy, *Anthropology*, 589; Jacknis, *Storage Box of Tradition*, 311–13.

57 Boas, *Kwakiutl Ethnography*, 171–298; Webster, "The Contemporary Potlatch."

58 *New York Tribune*, 6 August 1893. Helen Codere likewise assumed that more theatrical meant less religious; Codere, *Fighting with Property*, 6. For a contrasting view, see Goldman, *The Mouth of Heaven*, 102, 104.

59 Boas, *Kwakiutl Ethnography*, 224.

60 For a parallel situation in the South Pacific, see Clifford, *Person and Myth*, 136.

61 Ostrowitz, "Privileging the Past," 56. See also Cruikshank, "Negotiating with Narrative."

62 Chicago *Daily Inter Ocean*, 7 May 1893; *Chicago Tribune*, 7 May 1893; Boas *Social Organization*, 482–83; Boas, *Kwakiutl Ethnography*, 400–07.

63 Ford, *Smoke from their Fires*, 186–192; Jacobsen, *Alaskan Voyage*, 74–75; Webster, "Chiefly Feasts," 249; Jacknis, *Storage Box of Tradition*, 342; Klein, *Frontiers of Historical Imagination*, 198. On anthropology and the alignment of interests between colonial and indigenous elites in a different colonial context, see Dirks, "The Policing of Tradition," 194; and Dirks, "Colonial Histories and Native Informants," 297.

64 Jonaitis, "Chiefly Feasts," 257.

65 Boas, *Ethnography of Franz Boas*, 281.

66 Ostrowitz, "Privileging the Past," 56.

67 Suttles, "Streams of Property," 133; Berman, " 'The Culture as It Appears to the Indian Himself,' " 229–30. Similarly, the performances of a Kwakwa̱ka̱'wakw man at the St. Louis World's Fair in 1905 indicate that he was not merely playing *Hamat'sa* but, "*was* a Hamatsa." Ford, *Smoke from their Fires*, 186–90. Emphasis added.

68 Boas, *Kwakiutl Ethnography*, 191. Suttles, "Streams of Property," 132–33.

69 *Chicago Tribune*, 6 May 1893; *Chicago Tribune*, 7 May 1893; Chicago *Daily Inter Ocean* 7 May 1893; Boas, "Ethnology of the Kwakiutl," 1110–13.

70 Boas, "Ethnology of the Kwakiutl," 1114.

71 Ibid.

72 Ibid.

73 Boas, *Social Organization*, plates 15, 28, 35, 38, 7. See also Jacknis, "Franz Boas and Photography."

74 G. Hunt to F. Boas, 7 February 1894, *Professional Correspondence of Franz Boas*, Reel 2; Boas, *Ethnography of Franz Boas*, 178.

75 "Photographs," Box 37, FWPP.

76 On indigenous uses of photographs, see Williams, *Framing the West*, chap. 5.

77 G. Hunt to F. Boas, 7 February 1894, *Professional Correspondence of Franz Boas*, Reel 2.

78 Quoted in Boas, *Kwakiutl Ethnography*, 234–35. Two Kwakwa̱ka̱'wakw men similarly enjoyed shocking White audiences with their *Hamat'sa* performance in St. Louis. Ford, *Smoke from their Fires*, 186–91.

79 G. Hunt to F. Boas, 15 January 1894, *Professional Correspondence of Franz Boas*, Reel 2.

80 Canada, DIA AR 1893, SP 1894, #14, 124.

81 On 16 May 1893, Pidcock wrote to Vowell, "A party of fourteen Indians from among the tribes in this Agency left here by the St. Danube on Wednesday 29th March in charge of George Hunt on route to the world's fair Chicago." R. H. Pidcock to A. W. Vowell, 16 May 1893, Vol. 1648, DIA, RG10, NAC.

82 R.H. Pidcock to A.W. Vowell, 18 October 1893, Volume 1648, DIA, RG10, NAC.

83 Cole, "The History of the Kwakiutl Potlatch," 156.

84 R. H. Pidcock to A. W. Vowell, 21 October 1895, Volume 1648, DIA, RG10, NAC.

85 "Potlatch—attempts to curtail, 1899–1915," File 6244-2, Volume 3629, DIA, RG10, NAC; "Exhibitions—Indians traveling to—correspondence, 1904–1939," File 253, 430, Volume 4010, DIA, RG10, NAC; Titley, *A Narrow Vision*, 172, 222, n 45.

86 Loo, "Dan Cranmer's Potlatch," 142.

87 J. D. McLean to J. W. Waddy, Indian agent, Stony Agency, 4 March 1915, File 253,430, Volume 4010, DIA, RG10, NAC.

88 This phenomenon, whereby a project for the commercialization of an ethnic culture works against the group for which it is supposed to generate economic reve-

nue and greater cultural understanding, has been discussed by Sarah Deutsch in relation to Hispanics in the American Southwest and by Kay Anderson in relation to Vancouver's Chinese community. Deutsch, *No Separate Refuge*; Anderson, *Vancouver's Chinatown*.

89 Similar situations abound in colonial performance settings. See Buck, *Paradise Remade*, 4.

Four Picking, Posing, and Performing

1 Lindsay, "Kwelth-Elite." The name "Batterman Lindsay" appears to be a pseudonym for a woman named Annie Batterman.

2 Evans, *Little History of North Bend*, 2.

3 Ethnographic sources report that Puget Sound Indians killed slaves when their master died. Eells, *Indians of Puget Sound*, 350.

4 "Awards," Box 16, Washington World's Fair Commission, Archives and Manuscripts, UW.

5 "Hop Culture on the Pacific Coast," 466; *Washington Standard*, 26 August 1881, 2; Tomlan, *Tinged with Gold*, 34, 50, 66, 89. In 1877, the cost of each initial acre turned over to hops was estimated at $200 per acre. "A Puyallup Hop Farm," *Daily Pacific Tribune*, 30 August 1877, 2.

6 "Hops in Washington," *Pacific Rural Press*, 3 January 1891. Henry Emanuel Levy, "Reminiscences," 1843–1929, BCA; Hill, *A History of the Snoqualmie Valley*, 60; Muir, *Steep Trails*, 257.

7 The yield of a single acre in western Washington averaged 1,600 pounds and could reach 3,000 pounds. The farmer's cost per pound ranged between seven and eleven cents. Hawthorne, *History of Washington*, 2:470; Snowden, *History of Washington*, 4:304.

8 Tomlan, *Tinged with Gold*, 6, 11, 13.

9 Bagley, *History of King County Washington*,1:408; Snowden, *History of Washington*, 4: 304; Hawthorne, *History of Washington*, 2:469; *Washington Standard*, 19 September 1890, 1. Potatoes, by contrast, sold for only forty cents per hundred pounds. Buerge, "Brewery Bound,"13.

10 Canada, DIA AR 1886, SP 1887, #6, 92; Sapir and Swadesh, *Nootka Texts*, 151.

11 Fish, "Andy Wold's Tales of Early Issaquah," 7, 11.

12 "Annual report of W. H. Lomas to Superintendent General of Indian Affairs," 7 August 1885, Volume 1353, RGIO, DIA, NAC.

13 Using population figures from Jean Barman for 1881, 6,000 people would have been 23 percent of the total British Columbia Aboriginal population of 25,661. Barman, *The West beyond the West*, 363.

14 "Hop Pickers Wanted," *Daily Pacific Tribune*, 27 August 1877, 2.

15 Lutz, "Work, Sex, and Death," 82; "Puyallup Hops and Pickers," *Daily Pacific Tribune*, 20 August 1877, 3. Farmers grew hops in British Columbia too beginning in

the 1880s, but the size of the early B.C. industry did not compare with that south of the border. Later on, B.C. hop fields became a viable option for Aboriginal pickers. "Early History of Hop Culture in Saanich," Victoria *Colonist*, 7 October 1928, magazine section, 8. Kelm, *Colonizing Bodies*, 53; Carlson, ed., *A Stó:lō Coast Salish Historical Atlas*, plate 24.

16 "Good for 'Lo'," *Washington Standard*, 11 September 1875, 2.

17 Peter, *X̌əč̓usədə' 'əgʷəqʷul'cə'*, xii. See also McDonald, "Susie Sampson Peter," 7.

18 Kirk and Alexander, *Exploring Washington's Past*, 346. Anti-Chinese violence also occurred in California hop fields. Tomlan, *Tinged with Gold*, 127–28.

19 Quoted in Tollefson, "The Snoqualmie Indians as Hop Pickers," 43. A similar dynamic existed between Tlingit and Chinese workers in southeast Alaska. Wyatt, "Alaskan Indian Wage Earners in the Nineteenth Century," 44.

20 *Report of the Governor of Washington Territory, 1888*, 48–53.

21 Collins, "John Fornsby," 330.

22 Thomas Leadman, "Ledger," 1904, WRVHS.

23 Tomlan, *Tinged with Gold*, 143; Leadman, "Ledger," 1904, WRVHS.

24 Arthur Wellington Clah, "Journals," 31 August 1891, Reel A-1713, NAC. Clah is a fascinating figure in his own right. See Neylan, *Heavens Are Changing*, chap. 6; Brock, "Building Bridges"; and Galois, "Colonial Encounters."

25 Donald, *Aboriginal Slavery*, 83, 233–35. See also Ruby and Brown, *Indian Slavery*.

26 Elmendorf, *Twana Narratives*, 28, 74, 174.

27 "Hops in Washington," *Pacific Rural Press*, 3 January 1891.

28 Eells, *Indians of Puget Sound*, 270.

29 Clah, "Journals," 6, 7, 8, and 25 September 1899, Reel A-1707, NAC. The boys to whom Clah referred likely included his son and/or grandsons.

30 Canada, DIA AR 1892, SP 1893, #14, 257.

31 Poor sanitation and disease remained problems in hop camps along the Pacific Coast into the twentieth century, and in one instance sparked riots. Landis, "The Hop Industry," 91; Kelm, *Colonizing Bodies*, 38, 53–55, 149; Tomlan, *Tinged with Gold*, 146–56.

32 Charlie Meshel to W. H. Lomas, 31 October 1889 and [ca. November 1889], Volume 1336, DIA, RG10, NAC.

33 Moser, *Reminiscences of the West Coast of Vancouver Island*, 116; Canada, DIA AR 1888, SP 1889, #16, 100, 114.

34 Canada, DIA AR 1886, SP 1887, #6, 80; W. H. Lomas to A. W. Vowell, 17 July 1892, Volume 1355, DIA, RG10, NAC.

35 W. Lane to W. H. Lomas, 8 October 1888, Volume 1335, DIA, RG10, NAC; W. H. Lomas to A. W. Vowell, 17 July 1892, Volume 1355, DIA, RG10, NAC; W. H. Lomas to Levi Myers, U.S. Consul, Victoria, 9 August 1892, Volume 1356, DIA, RG10, NAC.

36 Kelm, *Colonizing Bodies*, 53.

37 R. J. Roberts, "Farm Diaries," 4 November 1888, BCA; Canada, DIA AR, 1891, SP 1892, #14, 115; "Hops and Hop-pickers," 252.

38 Fish, "Andy Wold's Tales," 11.

39 Collins, "John Fornsby," 329.

40 Lindsay, "Kwelth-Elite," 536.

41 For comparable labor problems among wheat farmers, see Thompson, "Bringing in the Sheaves."

42 *Washington Standard*, 25 August 1877, 4; *Washington Standard*, 15 September 1877, 4–5; *Daily Pacific Tribune*, 2 August 1877, 3; *Washington Standard*, 21 September 1883, 3; *Daily Pacific Tribune*, 27 August 1888, 2; Levy, "Reminiscences," 13, BCA.

43 "Hop Fields of Puyallup and White River," 345. See also "Sumner—Five Years Ago," *Puyallup Valley Tribune*, 16 September 1905, 2.

44 Muir, *Steep Trails*, 257.

45 C. O. Bean to W. H. Lomas, 17 July 1889, Volume 1336, DIA, RG10, NAC; C. O. Bean to W. H. Lomas, 17 August 1889, Volume 1336, DIA, RG10, NAC.

46 W. Lane to W. H. Lomas, 21 August 1888, Volume 1335, DIA, RG10, NAC.

47 W. Lane to W. H. Lomas, 26 July 1891, Volume 1337, DIA, RG10, NAC; W. Lane to W. H. Lomas, 16 August 1891, Volume 1337, DIA, RG10, NAC. See also Samuel [Sarbartotum?] to W. H. Lomas, 6 September 1889, Volume 1336, DIA, RG10, NAC; and James [illegible] to W. H. Lomas, 4 June 1887, Volume 1333, DIA, RG10, NAC.

48 W. Roberts to W. H. Lomas, 15 August 1884, Volume 1331, DIA, RG10, NAC. See also H. Beckett to W. H. Lomas, 15 August 1884, Volume 1331, DIA, RG10, NAC.

49 Clah, "Journals," 26 August 1891, Reel A-1713, NAC; Clah, "Journals," 2 September 1899, Reel A-1707, NAC.

50 Clah, "Journals," 5 September 1899, Reel A-1707, NAC; Thomas Leadman, "Ledger," 1904, WRVHS; Canada, DIA AR 1890, SP 1891, #18, 105; "Great Influx of Indians," Seattle *Post-Intelligencer*, 10 September 1899, 6; A. W. Vowell to W. H. Lomas, 13 July 1892, Volume 1338, DIA, RG10, NAC.

51 Craine, *Squak Valley (Issaquah)*, 4. Reaching the fields at Issaquah (between Seattle and the Snoqualmie Ranch) was similarly arduous. [Unidentified hop farmer] to Lomas, 4 June 1887, Volume 1333, DIA, RG10, NAC.

52 Collins, "John Fornsby," 330.

53 Ibid.

54 Levy, "Reminiscences," 13, BCA.

55 "Hop Fields of Puyallup and White River," 345.

56 *Washington Standard*, 15 September 1877, 4. See also Ker, "A Siwash Strike on the Yakima," 3.

57 "Hops Steady and Firm," *Puyallup Valley Tribune*, 26 September 1903, 1.

58 *Washington Standard*, 17 August 1878, 4.

59 "Hops Steady and Firm," *Puyallup Valley Tribune*, 26 September 1903, 1.

60 Clah, "Journals," 5 September 1891, Reel A-1713, NAC.

61 *Weekly Pacific Tribune*, 18 September 1874, 3.

62 Muir, *Steep Trails*, 256.

63 Lindsay, "Kwelth-Elite," 535.

64 "Hop Picking," *Washington Standard*, 24 September 1886, 2.

65 *Puyallup Valley Tribune*, 3 October 1903, 6.

66 Pomeroy, *In Search of the Golden West*, 123. See also Schwantes, "Tourists in Wonderland," 28.

67 "A Western Hop Center," 137–38.

68 "Meadowbrook Hotel Register," SVHS. Evans, *Little History of North Bend*, 39.

69 This represented a drastic shift from the 1860s. Hyde, *An American Vision*.

70 Muir, *Steep Trails*, 257.

71 "Picturesque Hop Pickers," *Puyallup Valley Tribune*, 10 September 1904, 1.

72 "At the Indian Village," *Puyallup Valley Tribune*, 19 September 1903, 1.

73 Lindsay, "Kwelth-Elite," 535.

74 "Flyer," Negative #1903.1.60, WSHS.

75 "At the Indian Village," *Puyallup Valley Tribune*, 19 September 1903, 1.

76 Guie, "Siwash Kloochman," 39.

77 See Marr, "Taken Pictures," 58, 61; Williams, *Framing the West*, 54, 143–146; Blackman, " 'Copying People,' " 88, 107; and Sandweiss, *Print the Legend*, 230. Elsewhere, Aboriginal people earned income posing in artists' as well as photographers' studios. Rodriguez, "Art, Tourism, and Race Relations in Taos," 148. On the demand for photographs of Indians see Marr, "Photographers and Their Subjects on the Southern Northwest Coast"; Marr, "Taken Pictures"; and Williams, *Framing the West*. On the history of photographs of Indians in the American West, see Sandweiss, *Print the Legend*.

78 Lindsay, "Kwelth-Elite," 536.

79 Davis, *Edward S. Curtis*, 21; photos NA292, NA663, NA690, NA758, NA760, NA866, Special Collections, UW; "Meadowbrook Hotel Register," SVHS.

80 See, for example, photo PO108, WRVHS; photo SHS 19,061, MOHI; Neylan, *Heavens Are Changing*, 165; and photo PO2088, WRVHS. On stereographs, see Williams, *Framing the West*, 73–74.

81 Suttles and Lane, "Southern Coast Salish," 493. Like photographers, ethnographers took advantage of hop field gatherings to ply their trade: they came to gather ethnographic information. Densmore, "Music of the Indians of British Columbia."

82 Clah, "Journals," 16 September 1891, Reel A-1713, NAC.

83 "Infanta at Chicago," Chicago *Daily Inter Ocean*, 13 June 1893, 2.

84 Lutz, "Work, Sex, and Death," 87.

85 Elmendorf, *The Structure of Twana Culture*, 298.

86 R. H. Pidcock to A. W. Vowell, n.d., File 57,045-1, Volume 3816, DIA, RG10, NAC.

87 Lutz, "Work, Sex, and Death," 88.

88 Harmon, *Indians in the Making*; Asher, *Beyond the Reservation*.

89 Photo #15,715, MOHI; photos NA1508 and NA897, Special Collections, UW.

90 *Told By the Pioneers*, 3:59.

91 "Siwashes Again Seek the Street," *Seattle Post-Intelligencer*, 31 May 1904, 9; "Great

Influx of Indians," *Seattle Post-Intelligencer*, 10 September 1899, 6; "Indians Returning from Hop Fields," *Seattle Post-Intelligencer*, 1 October 1906, 16. See also "Indian Life on Seattle Streets," *Seattle Post-Intelligencer*, 10 December 1905, 7; and Bull, "Indian Hop Pickers on Puget Sound," 46.

92 "Siwash Village on Tacoma Tide Flats," *Seattle Post-Intelligencer*, 15 April 1907, 20.

93 Bull, "Indian Hop Pickers on Puget Sound," 546.

94 Quoted in Dorpat, *Seattle*, 44. On attempts to remove Aboriginal people from the city streets of Victoria, see Perry, *On the Edge*, 110–123.

95 "Indians Returning from Hop Fields," *Seattle Post-Intelligencer*, 1 October 1906, 16.

96 Photo NA-698, Special Collections, UW.

97 Dorpat, *Seattle*, 45; photo NA-897, Special Collections, UW; photo #15,715, MOHI.

98 "Indian Life on Seattle Streets," *Seattle Post-Intelligencer*, 10 December 1905, 7.

99 "Siwash Village on Tacoma Tide Flats," *Seattle Post-Intelligencer*, 15 April 1907, 20.

100 Photos #2561 and #6123-N, MOHI; photos NA-1508, NA-1501, NA-1500, NA-698, NA-680, Special Collections, UW.

101 *Told by the Pioneers*, 3:59; Costello, *The Siwash*, 165; "Indian Life on Seattle Streets," *Seattle Post-Intelligencer*, 10 December 1905, 7; photos #83.10.PA2.1–2, #10,490; and possibly #83.10.7929, MOHI.

102 Upton, "Indian Hop-Pickers," 164; Hill, *A History of the Snoqualmie Valley*, 161.

103 "Siwashes Again Seek the Street," *Seattle Post-Intelligencer*, 31 May 1904, 9.

104 "Indian Life on Seattle Streets," *Seattle Post-Intelligencer*, 10 December 1905, 7.

105 "Siwash Village on Tacoma Tide Flats," *Seattle Post-Intelligencer*, 15 April 1907, 20; on the marketing strategies of Aboriginal curio sellers in the Northeast, see Phillips, *Trading Identities*, 31.

106 *Told by the Pioneers*, 3:59.

107 James C. Scott refers to such comments as the "hidden transcript." See Scott, *Domination and the Arts of Resistance*.

Five Harvest Gatherings

1 Meeker, *Hop Culture in the United States*, 18; "Hop fields of Puyallup and White River"; Canada, DIA AR 1886, SP 1887, #6, 91; Moser, *Reminiscences of the West Coast of Vancouver Island*, 142.

2 Snoqualmie Hop Farm, "Account Book," 16 December 1890, SVHS.

3 Lindsay, "Kwelth-Elite," 538.

4 Others have referred to this economic uncertainty as "fluidity and variety." Knight, *Indians at Work*, 183.

5 Canada, DIA AR 1886, SP 1887, #6, 91.

6 Niblack, "The Coast Indians of Southern Alaska and Northern British Columbia," 339.

7 Moser, *Reminiscences of the West Coast of Vancouver Island*, 143.

8 *Washington Standard*, 7 August 1885, 1.

9 Moser, *Reminiscences of the West Coast of Vancouver Island*, 143–45.

10 Canada, DIA AR 1886, SP 1887, #6, lxii; Canada, DIA AR 1883, SP 1884, #4, 48; Canada, DIA AR 1887, SP 1888, #15, 108; Canada, DIA AR 1906, SP 1907, #27, 255.

11 Canada, DIA AR 1906, SP 1907, #27, 255.

12 Moser, *Reminiscences of the West Coast of Vancouver Island*, 141.

13 Canada, DIA AR 1885, SP 1886, #4, lvii, 82.

14 Ibid. Sockeye runs on the Fraser were plentiful in 1885, and selling prices sunk so low that many packers could not afford to process fish at all. Lyons, *Salmon*, 179.

15 A similar crisis confronted Aboriginal people throughout the province in 1891. Canada, DIA AR 1891, SP 1892, #14, 118, 119, 169; Canada, DIA AR 1892, SP 1893, #14, 236.

16 Harris, *Making Native Space*, 87–90.

17 Canada, DIA AR 1892, SP 1893, #14, xx; Canada, DIA AR 1890, SP 1891, #18, 105. See also Canada, DIA AR 1884, SP 1885, #3, 99; Canada, DIA AR 1888, SP 1889, #16, 102; and Harris, *Making Native Space*, 275–78. These patterns did not differ much from those followed by many White farm families.

18 Canada, DIA AR 1895, SP 1896, #14, 163.

19 Canada, DIA AR 1897, SP 1898, #14, 189.

20 Canada, DIA AR 1886, SP 1887, #6, 92.

21 *Told by the Pioneers*, 3:187.

22 *Washington Standard*, 15 August 1879, 1; See also W.H. Tolmie to A. Campbell, 21 August 1883, File 11, Box 19, O'Reilly Family Papers, BCA.

23 Canada, DIA AR 1888, SP 1889 #16, lxxxv; Canada, DIA AR 1889, SP 1890, #12, 153; Moser, *Reminiscences of the West Coast of Vancouver Island*, 103; Arima, *The West Coast People*, 140; Eells, *Ten Years of Missionary Work*, 72.

24 Canada, DIA AR 1882, SP 1883, #5, 54; Collins, "John Fornsby," 304.

25 Doig, *Winter Brothers*, 165.

26 Eells, *Ten Years of Missionary Work*, 31; W. H. Lomas to I. W. Powell, 24 November 1885, Volume 1353, DIA, RG10, NAC; H.P. Nadeau to W. H. Lomas, 26 June 1895, Volume 1339, DIA, RG10, NAC; Canada, DIA AR 1890, SP 1891, #18, 106; W. H. Lomas to C. O. Bean, 19 July 1889, Volume 1354, DIA, RG10, NAC.

27 Eells, *Ten Years of Missionary Work*, 66; Collins, "John Fornsby," 324; "Court record written by Lomas," 7 February [1887], Volume 1353, DIA, RG10, NAC; W. H. Lomas to I. W. Powell, 1 March 1887, Volume 1353, DIA, RG10, NAC; Canada, DIA AR 1881, SP 1882, #6, 169; Canada, DIA AR 1883, SP 1884, #4, 48.

28 Canada, DIA AR 1886, SP 1887, #6, 92.

29 Quoted in Eells, *The Indians of Puget Sound*, 269.

30 Moser, *Reminiscences of the West Coast of Vancouver Island*, 144.

31 Canada, DIA AR 1884, SP 1885, #3, 100.

32 Ibid., 98. A case reported by the Reverend Myron Eells suggests that this escape hatch opened in both directions. Eells describes the case of a Clallam charged with

drunkenness who "escaped to British Columbia and was safe from trial." Eells, *Ten Years of Missionary Work*, 100.

33 Arthur Wellington Clah, "Journals," 22 August 1899, Reel A-1707, NAC.

34 Ibid., 9 October 1899.

35 W. H. Lomas to J. Johnson, Commissioner of Customs, Ottawa, 3 November 1886, Volume 1353, DIA RG10, NAC; B. H. Smith, Collection Customs, to W. H. Lomas, 19 November 1886, Volume 1333, DIA, RG10, NAC. International customs was similarly a problem for Aboriginal people in northeastern North America. Phillips, *Trading Identities*, 142.

36 W. H. Lomas to I. W. Powell, 24 November 1885, Volume 1353, DIA, RG10, NAC.

37 Clah, "Journals," 1 October 1891, Reel A-1713, NAC.

38 Harmon, *Indians in the Making*, 117.

39 Baker, *KhotLaCha*, 8, 9.

40 Van Olinda, "The Last Potlatch," Pamphlets—Indians of North America—Oregon and Washington, Special Collections, UW.

41 R. J. Roberts, "Farm Diaries," 10 December 1886, BCA; Wilson was related to Barlow through his mother, who was from Whidbey Island. Ibid., 1882.

42 Sapir and Swadesh, *Nootka Texts*, 230.

43 Quoted in ibid., 149.

44 Quoted in ibid., 151.

45 Quoted in ibid.

46 Clah, "Journals," 14 August and 31 October 1899, Reel A-1707, NAC.

47 Maybelle Cultee Thomas, "Taped Interview," 14 March 1981, Washington Women's Heritage Project, Archives and Manuscripts, UW. See also "Siwash Village on Tacoma Tide Flats," *Seattle Post-Intelligencer*, 15 April 1907, 20; Harmon, *Indians in the Making*, 156; Carlson, ed., *You Are Asked to Witness*, 119; and Bierwert, *Brushed by Cedar*, 235.

48 W. H. Lomas to Superintendent General of Indian Affairs, 7 August 1885, Volume 1353, DIA, RG10, NAC; Canada, DIA AR 1885, SP 1886, #4, 80; Canada, DIA AR 1886, SP 1887, #6, 92. This remained true of cross-border hop- and berry-picking trips through the 1950s. Squamish woman Liola Johnson explained, "Not much money, we go just to get away from here." Quoted in Verma, "The Squamish," 108.

49 Clah, "Journals," 24 June, 30 June, 29 July and 11 August 1899, Reel A-1707, NAC. For labor patterns among the Nuu-chah-nulth, see Canada, DIA AR 1882, SP 1883, #5, 57.

50 Clah, "Journals," 1 October 1899, Reel A-1707, NAC.

51 Suttles, *Coast Salish Essays*, 228.

52 Nugent, *Lummi Elders Speak*, 82. A potlatch at Musqueam in 1892, for example, included "forty canoe races, twelve tugs of war, and several hundred foot races." Victoria *Colonist*, 26 May 1892, 5.

53 Kendall, Mathe, and Miller, eds., *Drawing Shadows to Stone*, plates 46, 47; Eells,

Indians of Puget Sound, 109, 192, 290, 292, 315, 319, 323, 324, 325; Reginald Pidcock "Diary," 20 June and 4 August 1888, Box 1, Pidcock Family Papers, BCA; Sapir and Swadesh, *Native Accounts*, 45, 272–73; Harmon, *Indians in the Making*, 37; Jenness, *The Saanich Indians of Vancouver Island*, 74, 77; Haeberlin and Gunther, *The Indians of Puget Sound*, 62, 64, 65; and Elmendorf, *The Structure of Twana Culture*, 225.

54 Currier, "Some Aspects of Washington Hop Fields," 544; Clah, "Journals," Reel A-1713, 9 and 16 September 1891, NAC.

55 Canada, DIA AR 1883, SP 1884, #4, 45.

56 W. H. Lomas, to Rev. Father Douckele, Kuper Island Industrial School, Chemainus, 7 October 1893, Volume 1356, DIA, RG10, NAC.

57 Eells, *Indians of Puget Sound*, 205–10; Wayne Suttles, "Central Coast Salish," 469–70.

58 Elmendorf, *The Structure of Twana Culture*, 240; Elemendorf, *Twana Narratives*. The bone game has likewise been played since "prehistoric" times. Kew, "Coast Salish Ceremonial Life," 302. Nor is it entirely absent from oral histories. Densmore, "Music of the Indians of British Columbia," 67.

59 Culin, "Games of the North American Indians," 267; Densmore, "Music of the Indians of British Columbia," 64; Gabriel, *Gambler Way*, 7.

60 Eells, *Indians of Puget Sound*, 205; Maranda, *Coast Salish Gambling*, 29, 118; Sapir and Swadesh, *Native Accounts*, 272–74; Amoss, "Resurrection, Healing, and 'the Shake,' " 93.

61 Maranda, *Coast Salish Gambling*, 30.

62 Elmendorf, *The Structure of Twana Culture*, 244.

63 Gabriel, *Gambler Way*, 5.

64 Maranda, *Coast Salish Gambling*, 27–30, 44, 113; Currier, "Some Aspects of Washington Hop Fields," 544.

65 Olson, *The Quinault Indians*, 130–31; Eells, *Indians of Puget Sound*, 206.

66 Bonney, *History of Pierce County Washington*, 1:395; Hill, *A History of the Snoqualmie Valley*, 58.

67 Hill, *A History of the Snoqualmie Valley*, 58.

68 Meeker Family, "Notebooks," Notebook A, Archives and Manuscripts, UW, 80.

69 Meeker Family, "Notebooks," Notebook C, Archives and Manuscripts, UW, 41.

70 Ibid.; Collins, "John Fornsby," 304. For other examples of high stakes intercommunity gambling, see Elmendorf, *Twana Narratives*, 20–26; Bagley, *History of King County Washington*, 1:137; and Maranda, *Coast Salish Gambling*, 11, 26.

71 Suttles and Lane, "Southern Coast Salish," 495; Eells, *Indians of Puget Sound*, 213, 326.

72 Clah, "Journals," 20 September 1891, Reel A-1713, NAC.

73 "Hop Picking," *Washington Standard*, 24 September 1886, 2; Meliss, "Siwash," 502; Clah, "Journals," Reel A-1713, 20 September 1891, Reel A-1713, NAC; Eells, *Ten Years of Missionary Work*, 72–73; Bonney, *History of Pierce County*, 1:395; Hill, *A History of the Snoqualmie Valley*, 58; Kirk and Alexander, *Exploring Washington's Past*, 349; Tollefson, "The Snoqualmie Indians as Hop Pickers," 43.

74 Currier, "Some Aspects of Washington Hop Fields," 544; Costello, *The Siwash*, 164.
75 Meliss, "Siwash," 502.
76 Eells, *Ten Years of Missionary Work*, 72–73.
77 Canada, DIA AR 1883, SP 1884, #4, 45.
78 Costello, *Siwash*, 164. The cultural notion of "white trash" likewise emerged elsewhere at the same time. See Foley, *The White Scourge*, especially chap. 3.
79 *Told by the Pioneers*, 3:59. See also Rothery, "Tacoma," 249.
80 H. P. Nadeau to W. H. Lomas, 28 June 1895, Volume 1339, DIA, RG10, NAC.
81 Kew, "Coast Salish Ceremonial Life," 289; Suttles, *Coast Salish Essays*, 224, 228.
82 Elliot, *Memories of the Chemainus Valley*, 352; Reginald Pidcock, "Diary," 24 May 1888, Box 1, Pidcock Family Papers, BCA; Kew, "Coast Salish Ceremonial Life," 277.
83 "History of Suquamish," comp. E. E. Riddell, North End Improvement Council, 14 October 1932, Pamphlets–Indians of North America–Tribes Oregon, Washington, Special Collections, UW, 7.
84 Lomas to A. G. [Balliet?], 24 June 1895, Volume 1357, DIA, RG10, NAC; H. P. Nadeau to W. H. Lomas, 26 June 1895, Volume 1339, DIA, RG10, NAC; H. P. Nadeau to W. H. Lomas, 28 June 1895, Volume 1339, DIA, RG10, NAC.
85 Eells, *Indian of Puget Sound*, 204; Canada, DIA AR 1885, SP 1886, #4, 80; W. H. Lomas to Superintendent General of Indian Affairs, 15 September 1886, Volume 1353, DIA, RG10, NAC.
86 Eells, *Indians of Puget Sound*, 181, 203, 382, 386.
87 Ibid., 204.
88 Suttles, *Coast Salish Essays*, 220, 233; Elmendorf, *The Structure of Twana Culture*, 336, 403; Elmendorf, *Twana Narratives*, xli. For extended consideration of the geographically rooted nature of Coast Salish community, see Miller, *Lushootseed Culture*. The nature of political community among the Salish has been the topic of much debate. Tollefson, "The Snoqualmie"; Tollefson, "Political Organization of the Duwamish"; Miller and Boxberger, "Creating Chiefdoms"; Tollefson, "In Defense of a Snoqualmie Political Chiefdom Model"; Boxberger and Miller, "Evolution or History?"; and Miller, "Back to Basics."
89 Harmon, *Indians in the Making*, 121.
90 Quoted in Verma, "The Squamish," 109. On cross-border family ties, see Collins, "John Fornsby," 308–9, 324, 331; Denny, *Blazing the Way*, 385; Kellogg, *A History of Whidbey's Island*, 75; Nugent, *Lummi Elders Speak*, 38, 69, 71; Crease to W. H. Lomas, 29 December 1893, Volume 1356, DIA, RG10, NAC; W. H. Lomas to Ed Bristow, 8 December 1894, Volume 1357, DIA, RG10, NAC; W. H. Lomas to Indian agent Snohomish Washington, 18 December 1895, Volume 1357, DIA, RG10, NAC; Ed Bristow, subagent, Swinomish Indian Reservation, to W. H. Lomas, 7 January 1896, Volume 1339, DIA, RG10, NAC.
91 Suttles, *Coast Salish Essays*, 223.
92 Collins, "John Fornsby," 330.
93 Elmendorf, *The Structure of Twana Culture*, 245.

94 In many instances, separate Aboriginal identities survived the trip to the hop fields all too well intact. The antagonism between Tsimpshian pickers and Haida pole pullers on the Snoqualmie Hop Ranch is a prime example. Clah, "Journals," 31 August 1891, Reel A-1713, NAC. Alexandra Harmon makes this point, at the same time as she pushes fluidity in Indian identity further back in time to the fur trade era. Harmon, *Indians in the Making*, 36.

95 W. H. Lomas to Superintendent General of Indian Affairs, 7 August 1885, Volume 1353, DIA, RGIO, NAC. Potlatches in Alaska were likewise occasions for political discussion. *Annual Report of the Governor of Alaska*, 1899, 4–5; "Great Alaska Potlatch," *New York Times*, 13 October 1901, 15. Kenneth Tollefson argues for the fundamentally political nature of the Tlingit potlatch. Tollefson, "Potlatching and Political Organization among the Northwest Coast Indians." Labor migrations also gave certain individuals opportunities to press for land or other rights. Clah, "Journals," 20 August 1891 and 23 September 1891, Reel A-1713, NAC; Clah, "Journals," 12 and 16 October 1899, Reel A-1707, NAC. The preoccupation of colonial officials with public gatherings was also apparent in India. See Dirks, "The Policing of Tradition," 184.

96 W. H. Lomas to Superintendent General of Indian Affairs, 7 August 1885, Volume 1353, DIA, RGIO, NAC; Canada, DIA AR 1885, SP 1886, #4, 81.

97 W. H. Lomas to Superintendent General of Indian Affairs, 7 August 1885, Volume 1353, DIA, RGIO, NAC.

98 "Indians Dancing Again," *Seattle Post-Intelligencer*, 20 May 1898, 5.

99 Kew, "Coast Salish Ceremonial Life," 240.

100 Ober, "A New Religion among the West Coast Indians," 588.

101 For a summary of the growth of the Shaker church, see Harmon, *Indians in the Making*, 125–30; and Amoss, "The Indian Shaker Church," 633.

102 Barnett, *Indian Shakers*, 45.

103 Valory, "The Focus of Indian Shaker Healing," 97; Mooney, "The Ghost-Dance Religion," 749; Barnett, *Indian Shakers*, 186; Amoss, "The Indian Shaker Church," 634.

104 Myron Eells quoted in Mooney, "The Ghost-Dance Religion," 748.

105 Collins, "The Indian Shaker Church," 403, 405; Smith, "Towards a Classification of Cult Movements," 10–11.

106 Peter, *X̌əc̓̌usədə' 'əgʷəqʷul'cə'*, xii.

107 Harmon, *Indians in the Making*, 128; Smith, "Towards a Classification of Cult Movements," 11.

108 Amoss, "The Indian Shaker Church," 638.

109 Harmon, *Indians in the Making*, 128.

110 Barnett, *Indian Shakers*, 62. Barnett is inconsistent in his account of Enoch Abraham's activities in 1899. Barnett claims that Abraham spent five months from October to March on Puget Sound with Mud Bay Louis after learning about Shakerism from Louis. Elsewhere Barnett claims that Abraham's faith began with a case of

pneumonia he contracted on New Year's Eve 1899 and which lasted for several months. Barnett gives no indication that the bout of pneumonia occurred while Abraham was away on Puget Sound. Ibid., 179.

111 F. Devlin to W. H. Lomas, 26 August 1898, Volume 1348, DIA, RG10, NAC.

112 Comeakin Joe to W. H. Lomas, 12 August 1898, Volume 1348, DIA, RG10, NAC.

113 Ibid.

114 W. H. Lomas to F. Devlin, 11 August 1898, Volume 1359, DIA, RG10, NAC; W. H. Lomas to Comeakin Joe, 15 August 1898, Volume 1359, DIA, RG10, NAC.

115 F. Devlin to W. H. Lomas, 26 August 1898, Volume 1348, DIA, RG10, NAC.

116 Suttles identifies the Shaker church as the "minor" system along side the two more "major" ones of winter dancing and summer sports (canoe races). Suttles, *Coast Salish Essays*, 223.

117 On the increased stratification of Coast Salish post-contact, see Miller, *The Problem of Justice*, 77, 94. For another example of the dynamic between wage labor and social mobility, see Harkin, *The Heiltsuks*, 140–43.

Six Indian Watchers

1 Currier, "Some Aspects of Washington Hop Fields," 544.

2 Tomlan, *Tinged with Gold*, 6.

3 Costello, *The Siwash*, 165.

4 "History of Snohomish County," Hops Vertical File, WRVHS.

5 Bull, "Indian Hop Pickers on Puget Sound," 546.

6 Canada, DIA AR 1884, SP 1885, #3, 118.

7 Canada, DIA AR 1886, SP 1887, #6, 92.

8 Ibid.; Meliss, "Siwash," 503.

9 Upton, "Indian Hop-Pickers," 162.

10 Bull, "Indian Hop Pickers on Puget Sound," 546.

11 Reprinted in Muir, *Steep Trails*, 248–60.

12 "Hop Picking," *Washington Standard*, 24 September 1886, 2. For a contemporary example of White businesses profiting from Aboriginal spectacle, see Furniss, *The Burden of History*, 176.

13 "In the midst of hop picking," *Puyallup Valley Tribune*, 17 September 1904, 1.

14 Levi W. Myers, U.S. Consul, Victoria to W. H. Lomas, 28 August 1892, Volume 1338, DIA, RG10, NAC.

15 Quoted in "The Letter of the Law," Victoria *Daily Colonist*, 25 August 1892, 2.

16 *Report of the Governor of Washington Territory, 1888*, 51.

17 *Seattle Mail and Herald*, 31 August 1901, 5.

18 Currier, "Some Aspects of Washington Hop Fields," 543.

19 Quoted in *Report of the Governor of Washington Territory, 1888*, 52.

20 *Seattle Mail and Herald*, 31 August 1901, 5.

21 Joe Smith, "The West's Great Harvest," *Seattle Mail and Herald*, 21 October 1905, 4.

See also ibid., 31 August 1901, 5. Anglos in New Mexico similarly believed summer migrant labor was a "frolic" for Hispanic youth. Deutsch, *No Separate Refuge*, 130.

22 Costello, *The Siwash*, 163.

23 Currier, "Some Aspects of Washington Hop Fields," 543.

24 *Report of the Governor of Washington Territory, 1888*, 52.

25 Dean, "Of Going Hopping," 630. See also Eames, "In Hop-Picking Time," 27.

26 Jasen, *Wild Things*, 106; Schwantes, "Tourists in Wonderland," 23.

27 The ideology of the vanishing Indian separated Native Americans not only from Chinese but also from blacks, who were likewise seen as more threatening labor competition. Trachtenberg, *The Incorporation of America*, 27.

28 Photo NA887, Special Collections, UW; photo #2281, MOHI; photos P.O. 272 & P.O. 108, WRVHS.

29 Costello, *The Siwash*, 162.

30 *Seattle Mail and Herald*, 6 October 1906, 5. This "the fear/temptation split" framed the semiotic field of indigenous images in much Canadian, Australian, and New Zealand literature. Goldie, *Fear and Temptation*.

31 Norris, "The Frontier Gone at Last," 1728–29.

32 Harmon, *Indians in the Making*, 144.

33 Lindsay, "Kwelth-Elite," 534.

34 Harmon, *Indians in the Making*, 145. Similarly in Canada, the beginnings of tourism coincided with colonial land seizures. Jasen, *Wild Things*, 80.

35 Bonney, *History of Pierce County Washington*, 2:146; W. Lane to W. H. Lomas, 21 August 1888, Volume 1335, DIA, RGIO, NAC; W. H. Lomas to W. Lane, 31 August 1888, Volume 1354, DIA, RGIO, NAC; W. Lane to W. H. Lomas, 8 October 1888, Volume 1335, DIA, RGIO, NAC; W. Lane to W. H. Lomas, 26 July 1891, Volume 1337, DIA, RGIO, NAC; W. Lane to W. H. Lomas, 16 August 1891, Volume 1337, DIA, RGIO, NAC.

36 Lindsay, *Derelicts of Destiny*. As Susan Sontag writes, "When we are afraid, we shoot. But when we are nostalgic, we take pictures." *On Photography*,15.

37 Schwantes, "Tourists in Wonderland," 30. See also Spence, *Dispossessing the Wilderness*. Throughout the British empire, tourism itineraries combined "natural wonders with picturesque people." Phillips, *Trading Identities*, 26. Scenic wonders also gave rise to a "scenic nationalism" that distinguished the United States from Europe. Catton, *Inhabited Wilderness*, 1. On the links between nationalism, tourism, and nature in a different context, see Applegate, *A Nation of Provincials*, 63–78.

38 See Wolf, *Europe and the People without History*.

39 "Indians Returning from Hop Fields," *Seattle Post-Intelligencer*, 1 October 1906, 16.

40 *Seattle Mail and Herald*, 8 December 1906, 5.

41 *Seattle Mail and Herald*, 29 November 1902, 6.

42 Costello, *The Siwash*, 165.

43 "Siwashes Again Seek the Street," *Seattle Post-Intelligencer*, 31 May 1904, 9.

44 "Picturesque Hop Pickers," *Puyallup Valley Tribune*, 10 September 1904, 1.

45 The equation between indigenous people and nature was linked to the development of natural history as a discipline. Pratt, *Imperial Eyes*, 31. Within this naturalized framework, Aboriginal souvenirs were "doubly nostalgic," because they represented both a personal experience with nature and with a people thought of as closer to a "natural" way of life." Phillips, *Trading Identities*, 199. On nineteenth-century photographers' tendency to situate Aboriginal subjects as part of nature, see Lyman, *The Vanishing Race and Other Illusions*, 37. On totem poles as the embodied conflation of Indians and nature, see Jonaitis, "Northwest Coast Totem Poles," 120. On the "naturalizing" tendencies of colonial discourse in general, see Spurr, *The Rhetoric of Empire*, chap. 10. Aboriginal people and other "ethnics" are often still seen as closer to nature. See Jacobs, *Edge of Empire*,132–38; Phillips and Steiner, "Art, Authenticity, and the Baggage of Cultural Encounter," 17–18; and Little, "On Safari," 152–53. On this link in academic discourse, see Klein, *Frontiers of Historical Imagination*, 247.

46 *Seattle Mail and Herald*, 31 August 1901, 5.

47 Trachtenberg, *The Incorporation of America*, 112–13; Haraway, "Teddy Bear Patriarchy," 82; White, *The Organic Machine*, 32–24.

48 *Seattle Mail and Herald*, 6 October 1906, 5.

49 Fabian, *Time and the Other*, 11.

50 Patricia Jasen's argument for Canada that "a consistent feature of nineteenth-century tourism was the association of wilderness, as a place, with the past" holds true for the United States as well. Jasen, *Wild Things*, 82.

51 Schama, *Landscape and Memory*, 517, 525; Klein, *Frontiers of Historical Imagination*, 231.

52 Ballou, *The New Eldorado*, 80.

53 Muir, *Steep Trails*,183.

54 Forster encapsulates this point in the title of chapter 6 of *A Room with a View*: "The Reverend Arthur Beebe, the Reverend Cuthbert Eager, Mr. Emerson, Mr. George Emerson, Miss Eleanor Lavish, Miss Charlotte Bartlett, and Miss Lucy Honeychurch Drive Out in Carriage to See a View; Italians Drive Them." *A Room With a View*, 68.

55 "Hops in Washington," *Pacific Rural Press*, 3 January 1891.

56 Muir, *Steep Trails*, 185.

57 Pratt, *Imperial Eyes*, 135.

58 On fire ecology in the Pacific Northwest, see Boyd, ed., *Indians, Fire and the Land in the Pacific Northwest*.

59 Muir, *Steep Trails*, 183.

60 Williams, "Ideas of Nature," 79–81. Celia Applegate makes a similar point about members of Germany's forest societies. Applegate, *A Nation of Provincials*, 70.

61 Lears, *No Place of Grace*, 10.

62 Spence, *Dispossessing the Wilderness*. Whereas Spence downplays the significance

of Aboriginal people as tourist attractions in the parks, treating them almost as anachronistic exceptions to the rule of empty wilderness, I would argue that the presence of "authentic Indians" was part of, even constitutive of, the wilderness ideal.

63 "Meadowbrook Hotel Register," SVHS.

64 Hill, *A History of the Snoqualmie Valley*, 60.

65 Bagley, *History of King County*, 1:66, 68.

66 Ibid., 1:55.

67 Hill, *A History of the Snoqualmie Valley*, 60.

68 Bagley, *History of King County*, 1:70.

69 Ibid., 3:58, 64, 66.

70 "Meadowbrook Hotel Register," SVHS.

71 Bagley, *History of King County*, 3:45.

72 Ibid., 3:255.

73 Ibid., 3:260–61.

74 The railway was a major factor behind Frederick Jackson Turner's declaration that the frontier was closed, and a crucial element of settlement, colonization, and control. In Canada, too, it was the railway that brought the militia to quell the uprising of Louis Riel and it was the promise of a railway connection to the rest of Canada that finally convinced British Columbia to join Confederation in 1871. Cities, communities, and businesses were made or broken by their capacity to attract a railway line. Annie Dillard gives a vivid account of the vicissitudes a town could experience from the railway in *The Living*, her novel about pioneer life in northwest Washington. On tourism and railways in the Pacific Northwest, see Schwantes, "Tourists in Wonderland," 30. On photographs of the railroad in the American West, with specific reference to photographs of Indians, see Sandweiss, *Print the Legend*, 157–80. On tourism and transportation infrastructure in Ontario, see Jasen, *Wild Things*, 119. On the impact of railways in the Southwest, see Wade, "The Ethnic Art Market in the American Southwest, 1880–1980."

75 Ruffner, *A Report on Washington Territory*, facing page 74.

76 On the use of photographs in this ideological process, see Williams, *Framing the West*, 3–11, chap. 2.

77 Castile, "The Indian Connection," 124–25; Castile, "The 'Half-Catholic' Movement," 166.

78 Wickersham, "Nusqually Mythology." Examples of this sort of convergence between ethnology and exploitation abound in the long history of European imperialism. For example, Sir Joseph Banks, founder of the African Association (1788), the antecedent to the Royal Geographical Society, was a powerful supporter of the slave trade. He was involved in backing Captain William Bligh's attempt to increase the profitability of slave plantations in the West Indies by importing breadfruit from Tahiti. Bravo, "Ethnological Encounters," 341–42.

79 Castile, "The Indian Connection," 125.

80 Quoted in ibid., 126.

81 Castile, "The Indian Connection," 124–25; Castile, "The 'Half-Catholic' Movement," 166.

82 Sucher, ed., *The Asahel Curtis Sampler*, i–ii.

Seven The Inside Passage to Authenticity

1 Mrs. G. Stowell to Rudolph Walton, 26 January 1906, copy enclosed in letter from J. G. Brady to Hon. J. J. Boyce, 29 January 1906, John G. Brady, Letters Sent, The ninth volume, Roll 7, FATG, Microcopy T-1200, USNA.

2 *The North Star* 2, no. 2 (Jan. 1889) in *The North Star: The Complete Issues*, 56; *Annual Report of the Governor of Alaska*, 1894, 4; Case, *Alaska Natives and American Laws*, 8.

3 This was so on other frontiers too. See Perry, *On the Edge*, 36; Stoler, "Sexual Affronts and Racial Frontiers," 225.

4 Hearing transcript, Dora Davis, Tilly Davis, John Littlefield, Lottie Littlefield, Lizzie Allard, and Peter Allard, by their Guardian Rudolph Walton, Plaintiffs v. W. P. Mills and Mrs. George Stowell, as the School Board of the Sitka School District, Defendants, Civil Case File 534-A, Civil Case Files 1901–1910, Box 38, United States District Court for the District of Alaska, First Judicial Division (Juneau, Alaska), RG21, USNA-A, 9.

5 For a full and intimate treatment of Rudolph Walton's life, see Shales's forthcoming book, based on her dissertation: "Rudolph Walton."

6 Shales, "Rudolph Walton," 23.

7 On the structure of Tlingit society and culture, see de Laguna, "Tlingit"; and Dauenhauer and Dauenhauer, eds., *Haa Kusteeyí*, 3–23. On Sitka clan houses, see ibid., 797–822.

8 Scidmore, "The First District of Alaska," 52.

9 de Laguna, "Tlingit," 224; Wyatt, "Alaskan Indian Wage Earners in the Nineteenth Century."

10 *The Alaskan*, 17 May 1890, 2.

11 Ibid.

12 "Against Brady," Skagway *Daily Alaskan*, 21 December 1904, 2; "Sitka Residents Object," *The Seattle Daily Times*, 5 December 1904, Folder 4, Box 14, JGBP; *The Alaskan*, 19 August 1899, 2. For a similar example in the capital of another U.S. territory, see Wilson, *The Myth of Santa Fe*, 79, 80, 86–87, 94, 110.

13 Lee, "Tourism and Taste Cultures," 270. Lee, "Appropriating the Primitive," 6–7.

14 Pomeroy, *In Search of the Golden West*, 57.

15 Manning, "To Alaska," 246.

16 Hinckley, "The Inside Passage," 68–69; Hinckley, *Alaskan John G. Brady*, 63; de Laguna, *Under Mount Saint Elias*, 183.

17 Hinckley, "The Inside Passage," 70. For illustrations of Alaska's incorporation into transcontinental tours, see Schwatka, *Wonderland*; Hyde, *Wonderland*; Sessions, *From Yellowstone Park to Alaska*..

18 Dannenbaum, "John Muir and Alaska," 14; Grinnell, *Alaska 1899*, 1; Porter, *Report on Population and Resources of Alaska*, 250–51.

19 Muir, *Travels in Alaska*, 10.

20 Cole, *Captured Heritage*, 96. This remained so throughout the twentieth century. Jonaitis, "Northwest Coast Totem Poles," 106.

21 J. Stokes to J. Brady, 9 September 1903, Folder 39, Box 2, JGBP; Pacific Steamship Company Brochures, Folders 1 & 2, Box 1, ASHL.

22 MacDowell, *The Totem Poles of Alaska and Indian Mythology*. For similar events among the Pueblo, see Weigle and Babcock, eds., *The Great Southwest of the Fred Harvey Company and the Santa Fe Railway*; and Dilworth, *Imagining Indians in the Southwest*.

23 See my discussion of this distinction—borrowed from Carlos Schwantes—in chapter 6 above.

24 For tourist descriptions of Russian Sitka, see "Sitka and its Sights," *The Alaskan*, 9 May 1891, 1, excerpted from Hallock, *Our New Alaska*; and "Sitka from Within," *The Alaskan*, 14 February 1891, 1, 4. A similar double romance attracted tourists to Quebec. Phillips, *Trading Identities*, 108.

25 Sessions, *From Yellowstone Park to Alaska*, 88. See also Hickey, "Waiting for the Steamboat," *The Alaskan*, 14 September 1889, 1; Manning, "To Alaska," 241, 253; *The North Star* 3, no. 7 (June 1890) in *The North Star: The Complete Issues*, 124; Ballou, *The New Eldorado*, 309; Collis, *A Woman's Trip to Alaska*, 98; "Sitka from Within," *The Alaskan*, 14 February 1891, 1, 4; "Sitka and its Sights," *The Alaskan*, 9 May 1891, 1; *The Alaskan*, 9 May 1891, 3; Scidmore, "Alaska's Mining Regions," 471; Stromstadt, *Sitka, The Beautiful*, 6; and Hallock, *Our New Alaska*, 178–79.

26 A. P. Swineford to Postmaster General, 27 October 1885, A. P Swineford, Letters sent (official) 1885–1889, Roll 1, FATG, Microcopy T-1200, USNA; L. E. Knapp to John Wanamaker, Postmaster General, 15 December 1890, L. E. Knapp, Letters sent (departmental) 1889–1892, Roll 1, FATG, Microcopy T-1200, USNA; Cassia Patton, to Commissioner of Education, 8 June 1911, School Files—Sitka, General Correspondence 1908–1935, Records of the BIA, Alaska Division, RG75, Roll 23, AR-37, ASHL.

27 Hickey, "Waiting for the Steamboat," *The Alaskan*, 14 September 1889, 1.

28 Hickey, "The Tourist Season of '89," *The Alaskan*, 7 September 1889, 4.

29 Scidmore, "Alaska's Mining Regions," 465. On this period of Alaska's history, see Hinckley, *The Americanization of Alaska*. Alaska would not gain an elected legislature until 1912, and even then, the governor remained a federal appointee.

30 Porter, *Report on Population and Resources of Alaska*, 251; [Clipping from unnamed Winnipeg newspaper], 17 October 1892, George Kostrometinoff, Scrapbook, 1876–1908, ASHL.

31 *The Alaskan*, 13 January 1906, 2.

32 James, "Indian Basketry in House Decoration," 620.

33 Quoted in Hinckley, *Alaskan John G. Brady*, 63. See also Hickey, "The Tourist Season of '89," *The Alaskan*, 7 September 1889, 4; "Sitka from Within," *The Alaskan*, 14 February 1891, 1.

34 "Sitka From Within," *The Alaskan*, 14 February 1891, 1. See also *The North Star* 3, no. 5 (April 1890) in *The North Star: The Complete Issues*, 113.

35 Carr, "Alaska Journal," BCA.

36 MacDowell, *Alaska Indian Basketry*.

37 *The North Star* 3, no. 5 (April 1890) in *The North Star: The Complete Issues*, 113.

38 Jones, *A Study of the Thlingets of Alaska*, 90.

39 Photos 764, 2473, 904, 1503, Special Collections, UW; [postcard], Folder 96, Box 25, JGBP; [photographs], Folder 181, Box 28, JGBP; [photographs] Folder 357, Box 38, JGBP; Emmons, *The Tlingit Indians*, 218.

40 Lukens, *The Inland Passage*, 54.

41 *The Alaskan*, 13 July 1889, 3; *The Alaskan*, 17 July 1886, 3. Mail order of Indian curios was also significant. "Victoria and Seattle Curio shop brochures," ca. 1904, Folder 4, Volume 45, Newcombe Family Papers, BCA; and "Published notes on Indian relics. H. H. Tammen Curio Co., Denver Colorado," Folder 7, Volume 46, Newcombe Family Papers, BCA; Batkin, "Tourism Is Overrated."

42 Scidmore, "Alaska's Mining Regions," 471. See also Collis, *A Woman's Trip to Alaska*, 99–100. Like the Kwakwa̲ka̲'wakw who went to the Chicago World's Fair, Tlingit also sought out photographers for reasons of their own. Gmelch, "Elbridge Warren Merrill," 167, 169.

43 Photo NA 904, Special Collections, UW. Out of respect for the apparent wishes of these women, I have not reproduced this photograph here. On Aboriginal reluctance to be photographed, see Williams, *Framing the West*, 54.

44 Emmons, *The Tlingit Indians*, 213.

45 Jones, *A Study of the Thlingets*, 88. According to Jones, beadwork had undergone a similar transformation. Ibid., 78.

46 Ibid., 88; Mrs. J. G. Brady to S. Jackson, 1 August 1892, SJC, Reel 97-640, SJSL.

47 Keeler, "To an Indian Basket," 528. On Victorian associations between baskets and nature, see Cohodas, *Basket Weavers for the California Curio Trade*, 20, 35.

48 James, "Indian Basketry," 620.

49 Jones, *A Study of the Thlingets*, 75; Hickey, "The Tourist Season of '89," *The Alaskan*, 7 September 1889, 4; *The North Star* 5, no. 6 (May 1892) in *The North Star: The Complete Issues*, 214.

50 Pomeroy, *In Search of the Golden West*, 60.

51 "Alaska's Exhibit," *The Alaskan*, 30 September 1893, 1.

52 Jones, *A Study of the Thlingets*, 75; Shales, "Rudolph Walton," 229, 230, figs. 37, 38; *The North Star* 6, no. 4 (April 1895): 2.

53 Scidmore, *Alaska, Its Southern Coast*, 179. See also Lukens, *The Inland Passage*, 54.

54 *The North Star* 5, no. 8 (August 1892) in *The North Star: The Complete Issues*, 228.

55 Rudolph Walton, "Diary," 16 April 1900, private collection of J. W. Shales.

56 Rudolph Walton, "Diary," 1900–1904, private collection of J. W. Shales; *The Alaskan*, 30 June 1906, 1.

57 *The North Star* 5, no. 8 (August 1892) in *The North Star: The Complete Issues*, 228.

58 "Alaskan Curios," *The Alaskan*, 10 May 1890, 1. Silver art among the Tlingit dates to the early nineteenth century when Tlingits received Mexican silver dollars through trade with California. Emmons, *The Tlingit Indians*, 189.

59 On Tlingit silver-working techniques, see *The North Star* 5, no. 8 (August 1892) in *The North Star: The Complete Issues*, 228; Emmons, *The Tlingit Indians*, 189–90; "Correspondence about Emmons' book, notes," Folder 16, Volume 61, Newcombe Family Papers, BCA; Niblack, "The Coast Indians of Southern Alaska and Northern British Columbia," 262.

60 *The North Star* 6, no. 4 (April 1895): 2; *The North Star* 5, no. 8 (August 1892) in *The North Star: The Complete Issues*, 228; Shales, "Rudolph Walton," 227, fig. 35.

61 Scidmore, *Alaska, Its Southern Coast*, 177. See also Sessions, *From Yellowstone Park to Alaska*, 64; "The Indian Carvers," *The Alaskan*, 26 December 1885, 4; Lukens, *The Inland Passage*, 54; Briggs, *Letters from Alaska and the Pacific Coast*, 53; Horace Briggs, "Alaskan Natives," *The Alaskan*, 21 March 1891, 1; Bugbee, "The Thlinkets of Alaska," 191.

62 Rudolph Walton, "Diary," 28 January 1902, 15 November 1902, 15 October 1903, 24 October 1903, 8 December 1903, 28 February 1910, 30–31 January 1927, 22 March 1928, private collection of J. W. Shales.

63 Ballou, *The New Eldorado*, 226–27.

64 MacDowell, *Alaska Indian Basketry*. See also Phillips, *Trading Identities*, 31. For a similar phenomenon in Appalachia, see Becker, *Selling Tradition*, 194–95.

65 *The North Star* 6, no. 1 (January 1895): 4; *The North Star* 6, no. 4 (April 1895): 2–3; *The North Star* 6, no. 8 (August 1895): 4.

66 *The Alaskan*, 30 June 1906, 1. This advertisement ran regularly in *The Alaskan* on either the first or third page from June 1906 through March 1907. See also *The Sitka Cablegram*, 3 May 1906, 4; and *The North Star* 6, no. 4, (April 1895): 2.

67 *The North Star* 6, no. 1 (January 1895): 4; *The North Star* 6, no. 4 (April 1895): 2–3; *The North Star* 6, no. 8 (August 1895): 4.

68 Scidmore, *Alaska, Its Southern Coast*, 50.

69 "The Indian Carvers," *The Alaskan*, 26 December 1885, 4; Hallock, *Our New Alaska*, 89. See also Porter, *Report on Population and Resources of Alaska*, 250; and *The Alaskan*, 20 August 1887, 4.

70 Mrs. J. G. Brady to S. Jackson, 1 August 1892, SJC, Reel 97-640, SJSL. John Brady estimated in 1901 that in the previous four years the prices of baskets had increased three or four times. *Annual Report of the Governor of Alaska*, 1901, 29.

71 "Chilcats and Sitkas," *New York Times*, 30 June 1888, 4. A Cowichan from British

Columbia forcefully challenged the assumption implicit in Canadian Indian policy that Indians, by definition, eked out a meager subsistence and that those who accumulated surplus lost their traditional Aboriginal rights to fish and other resources. The author of a letter to the editor pointed to the double standard whereby White businessmen would never be asked to relinquish their profits simply because they provided more than basic necessities. "The Cowichan Indians Complaint," *Victoria Daily Times*, 29 June 1895, 7.

72 Porter, *Report on Population and Resources of Alaska*, 250. See also Scidmore, "Attractions of Alaska," 7; Stromstadt, *Sitka, The Beautiful*, 6.

73 Higginson, *Alaska*, 100.

74 "Alaskan curios at the Fair," *The Alaskan*, 21 October 1893, 1, 4.

75 Cole, *Captured Heritage*, 45, 93. Franz Boas was a particularly virulent critic of "amateur ethnographers." See also Darnell, "The Pivotal Role of the Northwest Coast," 35, 37.

76 Horace W. Briggs, "Alaskan Natives," *The Alaskan*, 21 March 1891, 1; Briggs, *Letters from Alaska*, 48–49; Trump, " 'The Idea of Help,' " 165. See also Huyssen, *After the Great Divide*, 44–62.

77 Karr, *Shores and Alps of Alaska*, 59; Cole, *Captured Heritage*, 87; Hinckley, *The Canoe Rocks*, 299.

78 Cole, *Captured Heritage*, 87, 159, 290–91; Smith, *Decolonizing Methodologies*, 3, 90.

79 Jones, *A Study of the Thlingets*, 85–86. On Tlingit spruce root basketry techniques, see Emmons, *The Tlingit Indians*, 213–22; and Emmons, *The Basketry of the Tlingit*.

80 *The Alaskan*, 20 June 1891, 3.

81 "Sitka and its Sights," *The Alaskan*, 7 December 1889, 1.

82 "Sitka from Within," *The Alaskan*, 14 February 1891, 1.

83 *The Alaskan*, 5 June 1897, 1.

84 Ibid. Accounts indicate that as far back as 1870 White visitors took the liberty of entering Tlingit houses. Cracroft, *Lady Franklin Visits Sitka, Alaska 1870*, 24.

85 Carr, *The Emily Carr Omnibus*, 427.

86 "The Alaska Indian Mythology," n.d., The Alaska Steamship Company, Folder 17, Box 16, JGBP.

87 Scidmore, *Alaska, Its Southern Coast*, 176.

88 Collis, *A Woman's Trip to Alaska*, 104–08; Shepard, *The Cruise of the U.S. Steamer "Rush" in the Behring Sea*, 216.

89 Collis, *A Woman's Trip to Alaska*, 105; Knapp and Childe, *The Thlinkets of Southeastern Alaska*, 103.

90 Knapp and Childe, *The Thlinkets of Southeastern Alaska*, 103; Scidmore, *Alaska, Its Southern Coast*,176.

91 Lukens, *The Inland Passage*, 54. Vendors like Mrs. Thom were likely aware that White buyers found items more authentic if they had been made for and used by Aboriginal people.

Eight "The Trend Is Upward"

1 "The Orthodox Indian Temperance," *The Alaskan*, 10 July 1897, 1.
2 *The Thlinget* 3, no. 3 (October 1910): 1.
3 Ibid. On missionary uses of photographs, see Williams, *Framing the West*, 12–13, chap. 3.
4 For a similar situation in British Columbia, see Christophers, *Positioning the Missionary*, 19, 34, 40.
5 *The North Star* 1, no. 2 (January 1888) in *The North Star: The Complete Issues*, 6.
6 Scidmore, "Attractions of Alaska," 6; Scidmore, *Appleton's Guide-Book to Alaska and the Northwest Coast*, 119; *The North Star* 1, no. 1 (December 1887) in *The North Star: The Complete Issues*, 3; *The North Star* 1, no. 10 (September 1888) in *The North Star: The Complete Issues*, 38; *The North Star* 3, no. 7 (June 1890) in *The North Star: The Complete Issues*, 124; *The North Star* 5, no. 6 (May 1892) in *The North Star: The Complete Issues*, 215.
7 *The North Star* 3, no. 7 (June 1890) in *The North Star: The Complete Issues*, 124. The students' first public performance took place in 1886. "The Mission School Entertainment," *The Alaskan*, 3 April 1886, 3. See also *The North Star* 3, no. 7 (June 1890) in *The North Star: The Complete Issues*, 124; and *The North Star* 3, no. 8 (July 1890) in *The North Star: The Complete Issues*, 127.
8 *The North Star* 3, no. 8 (July 1890) in *The North Star: The Complete Issues*, 127.
9 "Alaskan Curios," *The Alaskan*, 10 May 1890, 1. On this phenomenon elsewhere, see Phillips, *Trading Identities*, 175; and Trump, " 'The Idea of Help,' " 168–69.
10 Cole, *Captured Heritage*, 76, 93.
11 Quoted in ibid., 94.
12 Ibid.
13 C. Baldwin to S. Jackson, 18 July 1887, SJC, Reel 97-638, SJSL.
14 A. E. Austin to S. Jackson, 20 November 1891, SJC, Reel 97-640, SJSL.
15 A. E. Austin to S. Jackson, 8 January 1895, SJC, Reel 97-641, SJSL. On Saxman, see Hinckley, *The Canoe Rocks*, 287–88.
16 *The North Star* 1, no. 3 (February 1888) in *The North Star: The Complete Issues*, 12. Missionaries in British Columbia were similarly dependent on contributions. Neylan, *The Heavens Are Changing*, 81.
17 "Indian Girls," *Presbyterian Home Missionary* (August 1883): 189.
18 *The North Star* 5, no. 8 (August 1892) in *The North Star: The Complete Issues*, 228.
19 A. Docking, Supt, Sitka Training School to Sheldon Jackson, 24 February 1892, SJC, Reel 97-640, SJSL.
20 *The Alaskan*, 23 January 1891, 4.
21 *The North Star* 1, no. 1 (December 1887) in *The North Star: The Complete Issues*, 2–3.
22 Ibid.
23 Ibid.
24 Kan, *Memory Eternal*, 214–15.

25 *The North Star* 3, no. 8 (July 1890) in *The North Star: The Complete Issues*, 127. At many boarding schools for Aboriginal children academics was not the central concern of school staff. See Coleman, *American Indian Children at School*; and Miller, *Shingwauk's Vision*.

26 S. Jackson to W. H. Miller, 30 August 1888, SJC, Reel 97-638, SJSL; B. K. Wilbur, "The Model Cottages," *The Alaskan*, 3 August 1895, 1; Wyatt, "Ethnic Identity and Active Choice," 278.

27 W. H. Miller to S. Jackson, 16 July 1887, SJC, Reel 97-638, SJSL.

28 S. Jackson to W. H. Miller, 30 August 1888, SJC, Reel 97-638, SJSL.

29 S. Jackson to A. E. Austin, 21 November 1892, SJC, Reel 97-660, SJSL. On disputes over cottage payments, see S. Jackson to W. H. Miller, 30 August 1888, SJC, Reel 97-638, SJSL; A. E. Austin to S. Jackson, 19 December 1892, SJC, Reel 97-640, SJSL.

30 W. H. Miller to S. Jackson, 16 July 1887, SJC, Reel 97-638, SJSL; W. H. Miller to S. Jackson, 9 August 1887, SJC, Reel 97-638, SJSL.

31 J. Converse to W. H. Miller, 25 July 1888, SJC, Reel 97-638, SJSL; W. H. Miller to S. Jackson, 27 July 1888, SJC, Reel 97-638, SJSL.

32 S. Jackson to W. H. Miller, 30 August 1888, SJC, Reel 97-638, SJSL.

33 See *The North Star* 5, no. 8 (August 1892) in *The North Star: The Complete Issues*, 228; B. K. Wilbur, "The Model Cottages," *The Alaskan*, 3 August 1895, 1.

34 Stromstadt, *Sitka, The Beautiful*, 9. See also *The North Star* 5, no. 8 (August 1892) in *The North Star: The Complete Issues*, 228. Colonizers elsewhere drew similar connections between Christianity, civilization, and domestic goods. See Comaroff and Comaroff, *Ethnography and the Historical Imagination*, 265–95; Viswanathan, "Coping with (Civil) Death," 205; and Deutsch, *No Separate Refuge*, 77. Keith Walden sees the preoccupation with the relationship between people and material goods as broadly emblematic of modernity. Walden, *Becoming Modern in Toronto*, 119–66.

35 B. K. Wilbur, "The Model Cottages," *The Alaskan*, 3 August 1895, 1.

36 *The North Star* 1, no. 2 (January 1888) in *The North Star: The Complete Issues*, 6.

37 *The North Star* 4, no. 5 (April 1891) in *The North Star: The Complete Issues*, 161; S. Jackson to W. H. Miller, 30 August 1888, SJC, Reel 97-638, SJSL.

38 Bugbee, "The Thlinkets of Alaska," 194; B. K. Wilbur, "The Model Cottages," *The Alaskan*, 3 August 1895, 1; *The North Star* 1, no. 2 (January 1888) in *The North Star: The Complete Issues*, 6.

39 *The North Star* 4, no. 5 (April 1891) in *The North Star: The Complete Issues*, 161.

40 *The North Star* 5, no 8 (August 1892) in *The North Star: The Complete Issues*, 225; Briggs, *Letters from Alaska and the Pacific Coast*, 59.

41 "Sitka Residents Object," *The Seattle Daily Times*, 5 December, 1904, Folder 4, Box 14, JGBP; *The Seattle Daily Times*, ca. March 1899, Folder 4, Box 14, JGBP; "Against Brady," Skagway *Daily Alaskan*, 21 December 1904, 2.

42 *The North Star* 5, no. 8 (August 1892) in *The North Star: The Complete Issues*, 228.

43 *The North Star* 5, no. 8 (August 1892) in *The North Star: The Complete Issues*, 228; *The*

Alaskan, 23 February 1889, 2. For a parallel Mexican example, see Becker, *Setting the Virgin on Fire*, 70, 71–72, 111, 112.

44 Barman, "Separate and Unequal," 120; and Hoxie, *A Final Promise*, chap. 6.

45 *The Alaskan*, 23 January 1891, 4.

46 B. K. Wilbur, "The Model Cottages," *The Alaskan*, 3 August 1895, 1.

47 Shales, "Rudolph Walton," 99–100.

48 de Laguna, *Under Mount Saint Elias*, 294.

49 *The North Star* 6, no. 1 (January 1895): 1.

50 "Annual Report of the Work of the Department of Education in the Native Village at Sitka, 1914," School Files–Sitka, General Correspondence 1908–1935, Records of the BIA, Alaska Division, RG75, Roll 23, AR-37, ASHL.

51 *The North Star* 5, no. 8 (August 1892) in *The North Star: The Complete Issues*, 228.

52 *The Thlinget* 3, no. 9 (April 1911): 2. Participation by mission graduates in this annual migratory cycle went largely unrecorded by *The North Star* but received more attention in *The Thlinget*, which began publication in 1908. As Victoria Wyatt points out, when the school newspaper changed names it became more geared toward an Aboriginal audience, in part because Aboriginal school staff had greater influence in the publication of *The Thlinget*. The more numerous examples of the ongoing relationship between Ranche and cottage residents in *The Thlinget*, as opposed to *The North Star*, does not mean that these connections suddenly sprang up after 1908. Rather, it makes sense to assume that they remained intact even through the period for which we have less evidence. Wyatt, "Ethnic Identity and Active Choice," 293.

53 See for example, Rudolph Walton, "Diary," April 1900, April 1901, private collection of J. W. Shales.

54 On this Tlingit pattern more generally, see Niblack, "The Coast Indians of Southern Alaska and Northern British Columbia," 311.

55 *The Thlinget* 3, no. 9 (April 1911): 2.

56 Rudolph Walton, "Diary," 6–26 February 1900, private collection of J. W. Shales. For a parallel example among the Anishinaabe, see Meyer, *The White Earth Tragedy*, 128.

57 Rudolph Walton, "Diary," 28 November 1902, private collection of J. W. Shales.

58 *The Thlinget* 1, no. 4 (November 1908): 2.

59 Kan, *Memory Eternal*, 281; Kan, "Russian Orthodox Brotherhoods," 215; Kan, "Recording Native Culture and Christianizing the Natives," 306.

60 Examples abound of Christian converts imbuing colonial events with indigenous meanings. See Harkin, *The Heiltsuks*, 112–14; and Silverblatt, "Becoming Indian," 288.

61 Dauenhauer and Dauenhauer, eds., *Haa Kusteeyí*, 648.

62 Rudolph Walton, "Diary," 10 and 22 September 1900, 20 October 1900, private collection of J. W. Shales.

63 I. Austin to S. Jackson, 2 December 1891, SJC, Reel 97-640, SJSL.

64 Quoted in de Laguna, *Under Mount Saint Elias*, 291.

65 W. A. Kelly to J. G. Brady, 1 February 1889, SJC, Reel 97-642, SJSL.

66 O. Hilton to S. Jackson, 4 February 1899, SJC, Reel 97-642, SJSL.

67 Ibid.

68 "Will Bury the Hatchet," *The Alaskan*, 22 December 1900, 3.

69 Ibid.

70 Rudolph Walton, "Diary," 5 February 1901, private collection of J. W. Shales.

71 de Laguna, *Under Mount St. Elias*, 291.

72 *The Alaskan*, 9 November 1901, 3.

73 Rudolph Walton, "Diary," 16 January 1903, private collection of J. W. Shales. The *New York Times* report on a meeting between Brady and Tlingit leaders may be a reference to this meeting of Walton's. "Indians Quarrel over Frog Problem," *New York Times*, 23 March 1903, 34.

74 *The North Star* 2, no. 5 (April 1889) in *The North Star: The Complete Issues*, 67. On Tlingit use of American courts, see Hinckley, *The Canoe Rocks*, 252.

75 Beck, "A Clan Excitement," 179–80.

76 Rudolph Walton, "Diary," 3 and 8 February 1903, private collection of J. W. Shales.

77 Dauenhauer and Dauenhauer, eds., *Haa Kusteeyí*, 15–23.

78 Ibid., 244.

79 For a similar parallel, see Harkin, *The Heiltsuks*, 90–91.

80 For a description of this ceremony in Sitka in the 1890s, see *The Alaskan*, 16 January 1892, 3.

81 Dauenhauer and Dauenhauer, eds., *Haa Kusteeyí*, 358.

82 de Laguna, *Under Mount Saint Elias*, 598.

83 Rudolph Walton, "Diary," 17 January–2 February 1903, private collection of J. W. Shales; de Laguna, *Under Mount Saint Elias*, 592–603; Swanton, *Social Condition, Beliefs and Linguistic Relationships of the Tlingit Indians*, 451, note b; Shales, "Rudolph Walton," 172.

84 Kan, "Russian Orthodox Brotherhoods," 204; Kan, *Memory Eternal*, 318–22.

85 Emmons, *The Tlingit Indians*, 352.

86 Shales, "Rudolph Walton," 172–74.

87 For comparable circumstances in Canada, see Nurse, " 'But Now Things Have Changed,' " 448–50.

88 Shales, "Rudolph Walton," 112, 151–53. Walton was active again in the Church by 1912. Ibid., 156.

89 Ibid., 112–13.

90 Ibid., 112.

91 Ibid., 113–14.

92 See chapter 9 below. This is especially clear in Shales's biography. Ibid., 216–18.

93 Kan, *Symbolic Immortality*, 208.

Nine Civilization on Trial

1 *Davis et al. v. Sitka School Board*, 1908, WL343 (D. Alaska), 3 Alaska, 491.

2 Hearing transcript, Dora Davis, Tilly Davis, John Littlefield, Lottie Littlefield, Lizzie Allard, and Peter Allard, by their Guardian, Rudolph Walton, Plaintiffs v. W. P. Mills, and Mrs. George Stowell, as the School Board of the Sitka School District, Defendants, Civil Case File 534-A, Civil Case Files 1901–1910, Box 38, United States District Court for the District of Alaska, First Judicial Division (Juneau, AK), RG21, USNA-A, 14–15. [This document is hereinafter cited as "Transcript."]

3 "Changes!" *The Sitka Cablegram*, 9 February 1905, 1–2. School funding was cut in favor of funding for roads. This early manifestation of road fever was especially absurd in the context of southeast Alaska, a region that even today remains inaccessible by road due to the mountainous terrain.

4 Ibid.

5 J. G. Brady to Secretary of the Treasury, 19 May 1905, Box 2624, Series 448, RG101, ASA.

6 Case, *Alaska Natives and American Laws*,198–99.

7 Ibid., 199.

8 *Annual Statement of the Commissioner of Education, 1906*, 26–27; *Annual Report of the Governor of Alaska, 1901*, 57; Sheldon Jackson to J. G. Brady, 2 May 1905, Box 2604, Series 445, RG101, ASA.

9 "Question of Race in Sitka Schools," *Seattle Post-Intelligencer*, 8 February 1906.

10 *Annual Statement of the Commissioner of Education, 1906*, 40.

11 Mrs. George Stowell to Rudolph Walton, 26 January 1906, R. Walton to J. G. Brady, 26 January 1906, and J. G. Brady to Sitka School Board, 27 January 1906, Copies enclosed in letter from J. G. Brady, Governor of Alaska to Hon. J. J. Boyce, 29 January 1906, John G. Brady, Letters Sent, The ninth volume, Roll 7, FATG, Microcopy T-1200, USNA.

12 J. G. Brady to S. Jackson, 31 January 1906, SJC, Reel 97-63, SJSL.

13 Sitka School Board to John G. Brady, 29 January 1906, Copy enclosed in letter from J. G. Brady to Hon. J. J. Boyce, 29 January 1906, John G. Brady, Letters Sent, The ninth volume, Roll 7, FATG, Microcopy T-1200, USNA.

14 On the debate over the status of mixed-race students in western Alaska, see S. Jackson to J. G. Brady, 1 April, 1905, Box 2604, Series 445, RG101, ASA; S. Jackson to J. G. Brady, 2 May 1905, Box 2604, Series 445, RG101, ASA; J. G. Brady to Sheldon Jackson, 19 April 1905, Folder 84, Box 5, JGBP.

15 This fear was related to confusion over whether the twenty-student quorum required of school districts could include those of "mixed blood who lead a civilized life." See J. G. Brady to Secretary of the Interior, 21 July 1905, Folder 87, Box 5, JGBP; Secretary to the Governor to Ed. H. Lakin, Clerk, U.S. District Court, 12 July 1912, File 14 (1–5), Box 104–4, Series 130, RG101, ASA; E. H. Lakin, Clerk, U.S. District Court, Valdes, to W. E. Clark, Governor, 25 July 1912, File 14 (1–5), Box 104–4, Series

130, RG101, ASA; Secretary to the Governor to Governor W. E. Clark, 17 August 1912, File 14 (1–5), Box 104–4, Series 130, RG101, ASA; W. E. Clark to J. W. Chapman, Anvik, 16 December 1912, File 14 (1–5), Box 104–4, Series 130, RG101, ASA.

16 "Question of Race in Sitka Schools," *Seattle Post-Intelligencer*, 8 February 1906.

17 Transcript, 2, 7, 9, 25, 40. Schools were a similar focus of concern in Texas, where Mexicans similarly constituted an "in-between" race. Foley, *The White Scourge*, chap. 2.

18 For examples, see, Hinckley, *Alaskan John G. Brady*, 96; F. Moore to S. Jackson, 7 April 1892, SJC, Reel 97-640, SJSL; Stepan M. Ushin, "Diary," 10 March 1885, 22 March 1885, 6 March 1887, BCA; and "In an Old Russian Fort," *New York Times*, 14 October 1888, 10. In the Alaskan context, "Creole" refers to a person of mixed Russian and Alaska Native background. Most Creoles in Sitka were of Russian-Aleut or Russian-Koniag descent. Kan, "Russian Orthodox Brotherhoods," 216, n. 8.

19 Kan, *Memory Eternal*, 179, 180, 235, 242, 249, 275, 291, 313–17; Kan, "Russian Orthodox Brotherhoods," 200, 203, 217 n.19.

20 "Order," 7 March 1906, Dora Davis, Tilly Davis, John Littlefield, Lottie Littlefield, Lizzie Allard, and Peter Allard, by their Guardian Rudolph Walton, Plaintiffs v. W. P. Mills and Mrs. George Stowell, as the School Board of the Sitka School District, Defendants, Civil Case File 534-A, Civil Case Files 1901–1910, Box 38, United States District Court for the District of Alaska, First Judicial Division (Juneau, Alaska), RG21, USNA-A. Transcript, 5, 6–7, 21, 22 47. The children ranged in age from six to fourteen. Tillie and Dora were seven and eight respectively, Peter Allard was seven, his cousin Lizzie Allard was fourteen, John Littlefield was twelve, and his sister, Lottie, was eight.

21 "Sitka Residents Object," *The Seattle Daily Times*, 5 December 1904, Folder 4, Box 14, JGBP.

22 *The Seattle Daily Times*, ca. March 1899, Folder 4, Box 14, JGBP.

23 "Against Brady," Skagway *Daily Alaskan*, 21 December 1904, 2.

24 *The Alaskan*, 31 August 1901, 2.

25 *The Alaskan*, 27 August 1898, 3; J. G. Brady to S. Jackson, 31 January 1906, SJC, Reel 97-644, SJSL.

26 See *The Alaskan*, 23 September 1899, 3; *The Alaskan*, 15 September 1900; *The Alaskan*, 6 March 1904, 3.

27 *The Alaskan*, 12 May 1900, 3; Mrs. George Stowell, "Native Foods," *The Alaskan*, 26 May 1900, 1; Mrs. George Stowell, "Chilcat Blanket and Its Origin," *The Alaskan*, 11 October 1902, 2 and 25 October 1902, 2.

28 J. G. Brady to M. K. P. Tamaree, Wrangell, 30 January 1906, Folder 93, Box 5, JGBP.

29 J. G. Brady to Captain A. R. Couden, 17 January 1902, Folder 94, Box 5, JGBP.

30 J. G. Brady to H. D. Reynolds, 23 February 1906, Folder 100, Box 5, JGBP.

31 *The Alaskan*, 20 May 1899, 2; *The Alaskan*, 11 May 1901, 3.

32 Rudolph Walton, "Diary," 4 January 1902, private collection of J. W. Shales.

33 "Question of Race in Sitka Schools," *Seattle Post-Intelligencer*, 8 February 1906.

34 "Sitka Residents Object," *The Seattle Daily Times*, 5 December 1904, Folder 4, Box 14, JGBP.

35 J. G. Brady to H. D. Reynolds, 23 February 1906, Folder 100, Box 5, JGBP. On the controversy over Brady's involvement with H. D. Reynolds and this company, see Hinckley, *Alaskan John G. Brady*, 330–35, 342, 361.

36 J. G. Brady to H. D. Reynolds, 23 February 1906, Folder 100, Box 5, JGBP.

37 "Question of Race in Sitka Schools," *Seattle Post-Intelligencer*, 8 February 1906.

38 "The School Board is Vindicated," *The Sitka Cablegram*, 3 May 1906, 1; "What was Kelly's Real Motive?" *The Sitka Cablegram*, 17 May 1906, 2.

39 *The Alaskan*, 1 June 1895, 1.

40 *The Alaskan*, 2 December 1890, 2; DeArmond, *A Sitka Chronology*, 202.

41 Transcript, 26. See also ibid., 1, 32, 33.

42 Shales, "Rudolph Walton," 199.

43 According to *The Alaskan* in 1901, eight out of every ten jurors asserted that "I will not believe Indian testimony under any circumstances." And in 1910, *The Thlinget* complained that southeastern Alaskan newspapers branded Alaska Native testimony entirely unreliable. "Indian Evidence," *The Alaskan*, 7 September 1901, 2; "Why Discriminate," *The Thlinget* 2, no. 8 (March 1910): 2. See also Kan, *Memory Eternal*, 301.

44 Transcript, 17, 19, 20.

45 "Report of United States Naval Officers," 1 February 1881, U.S. Navy Census; Census of the United States, Thirteenth Census, 1910, Alaska; Transcript, 3–4, 6, 31.

46 Transcript, 30.

47 *Davis et al. v. Sitka School Board*, 1908, WL343 (D. Alaska), 3 Alaska, 493.

48 On the symmetry of discourses of race and class, see Slotkin, *The Fatal Environment*, especially chaps. 14, 18, and 19; and Stoler, *Race and the Education of Desire*, 123–30. In many colonial situations, social reforms in the metropole and colonies were "complementary sides of one process." Comaroff and Comaroff, *Ethnography and the Historical Imagination*, 42; see also ibid., 267–68, 292–93. Susan Thorne, for example, notes how the language of race traveled home to Britain from the empire in the early nineteenth century, where it was transformed into a domestic language of class. White fathers in the Davis case faced a similarly racialized rhetoric of class, although the setting was colony, not metropole. Adele Perry shows similar forces at work in the backwoods of British Columbia where working-class settler men faced the efforts of reformers. Thorne, " 'The Conversion of Englishmen and the Conversion of the World Inseparable,' " 238–62; and Perry, *On the Edge*, chap. 3. See also Bravo, "Ethnological Encounters," 345, 350; and Walden, *Becoming Modern in Toronto*, 22.

49 For similar sentiments in British Columbia, see Perry, *On the Edge*, 69–74; and Fisher, *Contact and Conflict*, 93. Elsewhere, this period saw significant changes in

notions of "Whiteness" with the spread of eugenics and the elaboration of the notion of "white trash." Foley, *The White Scourge*, especially chap. 3.

50 J. G. Brady to Hon. J. J. Boyce, 29 January 1906, John G. Brady, Letters Sent, The ninth volume, Reel 7, FATG, Microcopy # T-1200, USNA.

51 Ibid.; J. G. Brady to Knute Nelson, U.S. Senate, 29 January 1906, Folder 100, Box 5, JGBP.

52 *The Alaskan*, 28 April 1906, 3.

53 Arjun Appadurai sees this anxiety about the reliability of people's past and present identities as one of the many uncertainties that characterize modernity. Appadurai, "Dead Certainty," 229, 242.

54 This occurred, for example, in White Earth, Minnesota, where mixed-bloods were automatically assumed to be competent and their property deemed alienable by non-Indian buyers. Meyer, *The White Earth Tragedy*, chap. 3.

55 Kan, "Russian Orthodox Brotherhoods," 199–200.

56 Transcript, 5. Attempts to determine ethnicity among the Anishinaabe elicited similarly absurd results. Meyer, *The White Earth Tragedy*, 119.

57 Transcript, 24, 51.

58 Ibid., 45, 47, 48; Census of the United States, Thirteenth Census, 1910, Alaska.

59 Transcript, 11, 19; Census of the United States, Thirteenth Census, 1910, Alaska.

60 Transcript., 9.

61 Ibid., 16, 24, 27.

62 Ibid., 9–13.

63 Ibid., 14, 15.

64 On Sitka, see Scidmore, *Alaska, Its Southern Coast*, 176–178; *The Alaskan*, 19 November 1887, 1; Briggs, *Letters from Alaska and the Pacific Coast*, 52, 58; Bugbee, "The Thlinkets of Alaska," 191. On Puget Sound, see Bull, "Indian Hop Pickers on Puget Sound," 545–46; Meliss, "Siwash," 503; Hawthorne, *History of Washington*, 2:228; Costello, *The Siwash*, 66; "Siwash Village on Tacoma Tide Flats," 15 April 1907, *Seattle Post-Intelligencer*, 20; Comancho, "The Story of the Hop Vine," 3–4. On this phenomenon in British Columbia, see Perry, *On the Edge*, 56. On Anglo critiques of Hispanic consumer choices, see Deutsch, *No Separate Refuge*, 189.

65 Transcript, 49. On these posts, see Shales, "Rudolph Walton," 105.

66 Ibid., 12.

67 Ibid., 37.

68 Ibid., 52–53.

69 Ibid., 52.

70 Ibid., 17, 52, 53.

71 Ibid., 20, 22.

72 Ibid., 18.

73 *The Alaskan*, 5 August 1893, 2. Commonly applied on what became the American sides of the border on the Pacific Coast, this term was rarely used in British

Columbia. Barman, "What a Difference a Border Makes," 18. Colonial elites elsewhere likewise worried about the offspring of colonial men who "went native." Cooper and Stoler, eds., *Tensions of Empire*, 5.

74 Transcript, 18, 51.

75 *Davis et al. v. Sitka School Board*, 1908, WL343 (D. Alaska), 3 Alaska, 494.

76 Transcript, 22, 50.

77 Ibid, 6. On the colonial trope of sexualized Aboriginal women, see Barman, "Taming Aboriginal Sexuality," 237–66.

78 Transcript, 9.

79 Ibid., 10, 24, 26.

80 *Davis et al v. Sitka School Board*, 1908, WL343 (D. Alaska), 3 Alaska, 494.

81 Migrant lifestyles were not, of course, limited to Aboriginal people. For just one example from the Canadian west, see Thompson, "Bringing in the Sheaves."

82 Transcript, 47.

83 Ibid., 27.

84 Ibid.

85 Ibid., 7.

86 Ibid., 11.

87 Ibid., 36.

88 Scidmore, *Alaska, Its Southern Coast*, 175; *The Alaska Indian Mythology* (Seattle: Pacific Coast Steamship Company, n.d.), 5, 10, Folder 17, Box 16, JGBP; *The Alaskan*, 5 February 1897, 1; "The Orthodox Indian Temperance," *The Alaskan*, 10 July 1897, 1; Hinckley, *The Canoe Rocks*, 244–45. Potlatches were similarly public attractions for the White community in Puget Sound. Harmon, *Indians in the Making*, 150. In the American Southwest, the Hopi Snake Dance was a similar tourist draw. Dilworth, *Imagining Indians in the Southwest*, 21.

89 This so-called last potlatch was, of course, nothing of the kind. Potlatching continued among the Sitka Tlingit, although often in hidden or disguised forms. Kan, *Memory Eternal*, 348.

90 "Sitka Potlatch Great Success," Skagway *Daily Alaskan*, 29 December 1904, 2; Transcript, 45.

91 "Sitka Potlatch Great Success," Skagway *Daily Alaskan*, 29 December 1904, 2.

92 Ibid.; transcript, 26, 45, 53.

93 Transcript, 53.

94 Ibid., 42.

95 The church session censured Davis for his involvement, and according to church records, he and Mary "on their own accord appeared before the session to express their contrition for having taken part in the recent potlatch, also to vow before the Session that they are done with 'old customs' forever." Quoted in Shales, "Rudolph Walton," 149. Their apology was never mentioned during the hearing.

96 *Davis et al v. Sitka School Board*, 1908, WL343 (D. Alaska), 3 Alaska, 490.

97 Transcript, 45, 49.

98 Shales, "Rudolph Walton," 148–49.

99 The letter was appended to Brady's annual report. *Annual Report of the Governor of Alaska*, 1902, 21.

100 Anonymous manuscript, Folder 58, Box 11, JGBP.

101 Shales, "Rudolph Walton," 148.

102 Ibid.

103 Anonymous manuscript, Folder 58, Box 11, JGBP.

104 Ibid.

105 Ibid.

106 Ibid.

107 Ibid.

108 Ibid.

109 There is no explanation for this delay other than a notation in the decision that the briefs "were but recently filed." *Davis et al. v. Sitka School Board*, 1908, WL343 (D. Alaska), 3 Alaska, 482.

110 The 1910 census shows Lizzie Allard and Dora and Tillie Davis as "at school," probably the school for Tlingit children in the Sitka Ranche. Census of the United States, Thirteenth Census, 1910, Alaska. John Littlefield and Dora and Tillie Davis Walton went on to attend Sheldon Jackson School, as the Sitka Training School was renamed, where they became model students. On John Littlefield, see *The Thlinget* 4, no. 3 (October 1911): 3. On Dora and Tillie Davis Walton, see numerous issues of *The Verstovian* between 1915 and 1921. Other Littlefield and Walton children later attended the Tlingit public school in Sitka. "Detailed report of School Work," 1918, School Files—Sitka, General Correspondence 1908–1935, Records of the BIA, Alaska Division, RG75, Roll 23, AR-37, ASHL.

111 Transcript, 14–15.

112 *Davis et al. v. Sitka School Board*, 1908, WL343 (D. Alaska), 3 Alaska, 492.

113 Ibid., 493.

114 Ibid., 494.

115 Ibid., 491.

116 Ibid.

117 Ibid., 487.

118 Ibid.

119 Ibid., 488.

120 Case, *Alaska Natives and American Laws*, 58–60.

121 See, for example, Dirks, "The Policing of Tradition," 183–84; and Viswanathan, "Coping with (Civil) Death," 191–92.

122 "William Lewis Paul," File 804.1 (8), SJSL; Fred Paul, "Then Fight For it," extract enclosed in letter from Frances Paul DeGermain to Steve Henrikson, 24 August 1997, copy in possession of author; Case, *Alaska Natives and American Laws*, 200.

123 Stewart, *Sheldon Jackson*, 324.

124 J. G. Brady to S. Jackson, 31 January 1906, SJC, Reel 97-644, SJSL.

125 S. Jackson to E. D. Crumpacker, House of Representatives, 13 March 1906, SJC, Reel 97-669, SJSL.

Conclusion Authenticity's Call

1 "The Eighteenth Anniversary and Ninth Graduating Exercises," 1.
2 Shales, "Rudolph Walton," 150.
3 Beck, "A Clan Excitement," 179–80.
4 Hal Rothman uses this phrase to describe tourism in the American West. It is an apt characterization of the relationship that derives, not just from the growth of tourism, but from the quest for authenticity in all its myriad forms. Rothman, *Devil's Bargains*.
5 Ralph, "Canada's El Dorado," 176.
6 Scidmore, "The First District of Alaska," 44; Scidmore, "Alaska's Mining Regions," 465–67, 471–72.
7 Schein, "Performing Modernity," 367.
8 For an extended discussion of this, see Errington, *The Death of Authentic Primitive Art*.
9 Cohodas, *Basket Weavers for the California Curio Trade*, 40; Cohen, "Authenticity and Commoditization in Tourism."
10 [Postcard], Folder 43, Box 17, JGBP; photo #56758, Binder 4, "United States National Museum," Royal British Columbia Museum.
11 Ralph, "Canada's El Dorado," 188. Margaret Ormsby used this same metaphor in her history of British Columbia, entitling a chapter on development in British Columbia during the 1880s and 1890s "The Great Potlatch." Ormsby, *British Columbia*.
12 Harris, *The Resettlement of British Columbia*, 30.
13 Cohodas, *Basket Weavers for the California Curio Trade*, 40.
14 Appadurai, "Dead Certainty," 229.
15 Arif Dirlik makes this point and also provides a discussion of the implications of ideas about authenticity for current-day indigenous politics. Dirlik, "The Past as Legacy and Project."
16 Garroutte, *Real Indians*, 4–6.
17 See, for example, Meyer, "American Indian Blood Quantum Requirements," 241–44; and Garroutte, *Real Indians*.
18 Thomas, "The Inversion of Tradition," 227; Clifford, *Person and Myth*, 6.
19 Quoted in Furniss, *The Burden of History*, 183.
20 Dirlik, "The Past as Legacy and Project," 18.
21 Alfred, *Peace, Power, Righteousness*, 80–88.
22 Garroutte, *Real Indians*, chap. 6.

Bibliography

NEWSPAPERS

The Alaskan (Sitka)
Daily Colonist / Colonist (Victoria)
Daily Inter Ocean (Chicago)
Chicago Times
Chicago Tribune
Daily Alaskan (Skagway)
Daily Pacific Tribune (Seattle)
Inter Ocean Illustrated Supplement (Chicago)
Los Angeles Times
Manitoba Free Press
New York Times
New York Tribune
The North Star (Sitka)
Ottawa Journal
Pacific Rural Press (California)
Puyallup Valley Tribune
Seattle Times
Seattle Mail and Herald
Seattle Post-Intelligencer
The Sitka Cablegram
The Thlinget (Sitka)
Times and Commercial Gazette (St. John's)
The Sunday Times (London, England)
Verstovian (Sitka)
Victoria Daily Times
Washington Standard (Olympia)
Weekly Pacific Tribune (Tacoma)

UNPUBLISHED SOURCES

Alaska. RG101, Series 130, "Education," 1912, ASA.
———. RG101, Series 438, "Secretary of Alaska, Letters Sent," 1905–1906, ASA.

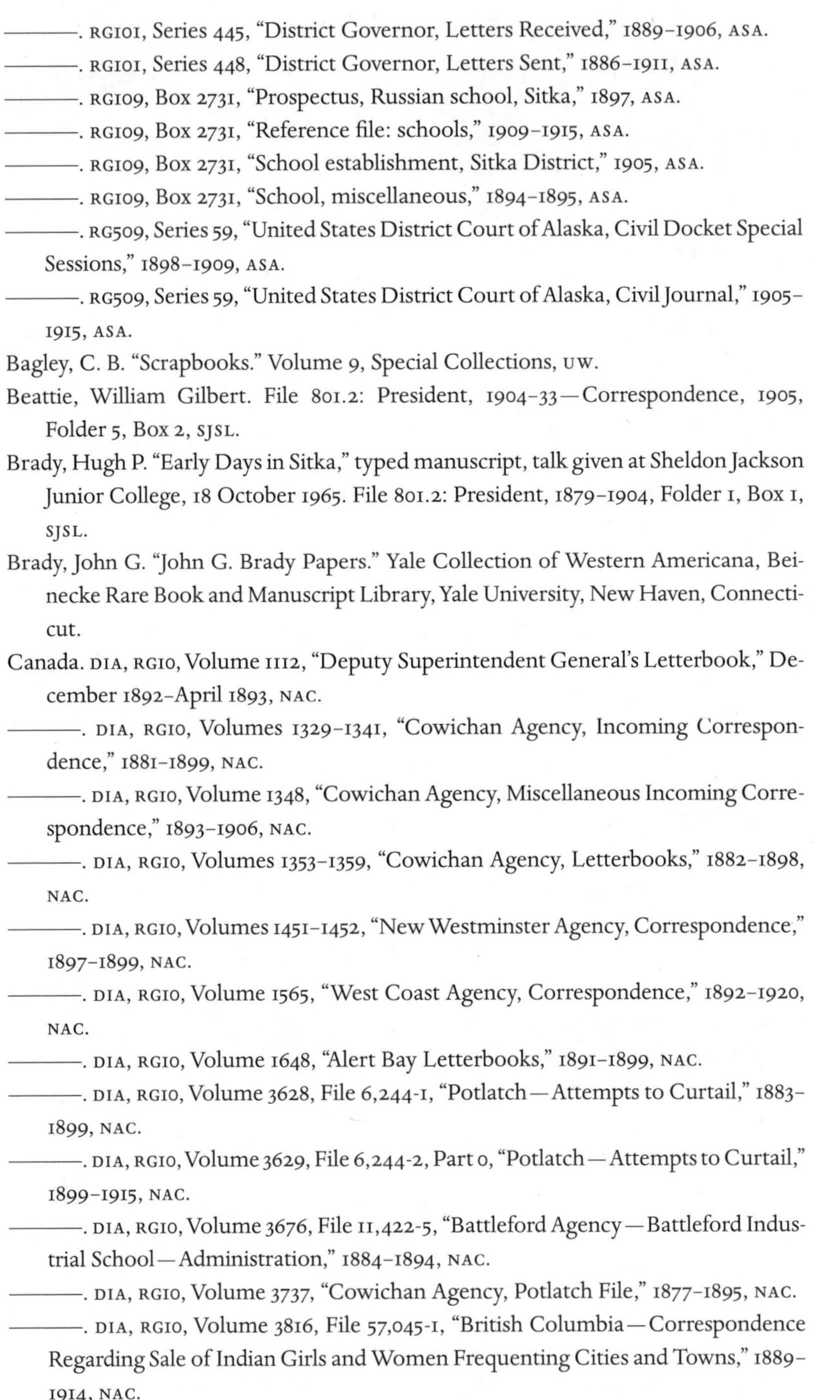

———. RG101, Series 445, "District Governor, Letters Received," 1889–1906, ASA.

———. RG101, Series 448, "District Governor, Letters Sent," 1886–1911, ASA.

———. RG109, Box 2731, "Prospectus, Russian school, Sitka," 1897, ASA.

———. RG109, Box 2731, "Reference file: schools," 1909–1915, ASA.

———. RG109, Box 2731, "School establishment, Sitka District," 1905, ASA.

———. RG109, Box 2731, "School, miscellaneous," 1894–1895, ASA.

———. RG509, Series 59, "United States District Court of Alaska, Civil Docket Special Sessions," 1898–1909, ASA.

———. RG509, Series 59, "United States District Court of Alaska, Civil Journal," 1905–1915, ASA.

Bagley, C. B. "Scrapbooks." Volume 9, Special Collections, UW.

Beattie, William Gilbert. File 801.2: President, 1904–33—Correspondence, 1905, Folder 5, Box 2, SJSL.

Brady, Hugh P. "Early Days in Sitka," typed manuscript, talk given at Sheldon Jackson Junior College, 18 October 1965. File 801.2: President, 1879–1904, Folder 1, Box 1, SJSL.

Brady, John G. "John G. Brady Papers." Yale Collection of Western Americana, Beinecke Rare Book and Manuscript Library, Yale University, New Haven, Connecticut.

Canada. DIA, RG10, Volume 1112, "Deputy Superintendent General's Letterbook," December 1892–April 1893, NAC.

———. DIA, RG10, Volumes 1329–1341, "Cowichan Agency, Incoming Correspondence," 1881–1899, NAC.

———. DIA, RG10, Volume 1348, "Cowichan Agency, Miscellaneous Incoming Correspondence," 1893–1906, NAC.

———. DIA, RG10, Volumes 1353–1359, "Cowichan Agency, Letterbooks," 1882–1898, NAC.

———. DIA, RG10, Volumes 1451–1452, "New Westminster Agency, Correspondence," 1897–1899, NAC.

———. DIA, RG10, Volume 1565, "West Coast Agency, Correspondence," 1892–1920, NAC.

———. DIA, RG10, Volume 1648, "Alert Bay Letterbooks," 1891–1899, NAC.

———. DIA, RG10, Volume 3628, File 6,244-1, "Potlatch—Attempts to Curtail," 1883–1899, NAC.

———. DIA, RG10, Volume 3629, File 6,244-2, Part 0, "Potlatch—Attempts to Curtail," 1899–1915, NAC.

———. DIA, RG10, Volume 3676, File 11,422-5, "Battleford Agency—Battleford Industrial School—Administration," 1884–1894, NAC.

———. DIA, RG10, Volume 3737, "Cowichan Agency, Potlatch File," 1877–1895, NAC.

———. DIA, RG10, Volume 3816, File 57,045-1, "British Columbia—Correspondence Regarding Sale of Indian Girls and Women Frequenting Cities and Towns," 1889–1914, NAC.

———. DIA, RG10, Volume 3831, File 63,210, "Cowichan Agency, Correspondence Regarding the Potlatch," 1889–1890, NAC.

———. DIA, RG10, Volume 3842, File 72,217, Part 0, "Cannibalism, British Columbia," NAC.

———. DIA, RG10, Volume 3865, File 85,529, "Correspondence re: Request to Establish an Indian Exhibit at the World's Columbian Exposition, 1893," NAC.

———. DIA, RG10, Volume 3914, File 113,639, "Correspondence re: Newspaper Clipping on 'Weird' Indian Customs in Fort Rupert," 1894, NAC.

———. DIA, RG10, Volume 4010, File 253,430, "Exhibitions—Indians Traveling to—Correspondence," 1904–1939, NAC.

———. DIA, RG10, Volume 6327, File 660-1, Pt. 1, "Qu'Appelle Agency—Qu'Apelle Residential School—General Administration," 1894–1950, NAC.

———. RG72, "Canadian Government Exhibition Commission, Columbian—General Correspondence," NAC.

———. RG72, Volume 105, "Report of J. S. Larke, Canadian Commissioner for the World's Columbian Exposition," NAC.

Carr, Emily. "Alaska Journal." BCA.

Church Missionary Society. "Letterbooks, Despatches," 1878–1905. NAC.

———. "Original Letters, Correspondence, etc., Incoming 1882–1900." NAC.

———. "Precis Books, North Pacific Mission," 1882–1907. NAC.

Clah, Arthur Wellington. "Journals," 1877–1909, Reels A-1706–1709, and A-1712–1714, NAC.

"Correspondence about Emmons' book, notes." Folder 16, Volume 61, Newcombe Family Papers, BCA.

Davis et al. v. Sitka School Board. Civil Case File 534-A, Civil Case Files 1901–1910, Box 38, United States District Court for the District of Alaska, First Judicial Division (Juneau, Alaska), RG21, USNA-A.

Davis et al. v. Sitka School Board, 1908. WL343 (D. Alaska), 3 Alaska, 481–95.

"Files of the Alaskan Territorial Governors," 1884–1909. Microcopy T-1200, Rolls 1–11, USNA.

"Flyer." Negative #1903.1.60, WSHS.

Grainger, John. "John Grainger Collection," 1897–1940. Volume 109: Sitka, ASHL.

Guillod, Harry. "Diaries." Anonymous manuscripts, 1881–1897, BCA.

Holm, Bill, to Elizabeth Virolainen, Royal British Columbia Museum, Ethnology Division, 13 March 1981, photograph N751, #6339, Binder 3, "Other Museums Photographs—Peabody Museum, Harvard," Royal British Columbia Museum, Victoria, British Columbia.

"History of Snohomish County," Hops Vertical File. WRVHS.

"History of Suquamish." Compiled by E. E. Riddell, North End Improvement Council, 14 October 1932. Pamphlets—Indians of North America—Tribes Oregon, Washington, Special Collections, UW.

Hop Growers Association of Snoqualmie, Washington. "Ledger," 1885–89. Archives and Manuscripts Division, UW.

"Hop Picking in Puyallup." *Harper's Weekly* 32 (20 October 1888): 795, 801.

"Hops." Photograph Archives, MOHI.

Hoskin, Arthur A. "A Trip to Alaska," 1886. BCA.

Indian Shaker Church of Washington. "History." Folder 12, Box 5, WSHS.

———. "Indians Add Tribal Customs to Traditional Religious Rites." Folder 5, Box 1, WSHS.

———. "Records of the Indian Shaker Church of Washington and the Northwest," 1892–1945. Microfilm, UW.

Jackson, Sheldon. "Correspondence," 1891–1907. Reel 97-640–97-670, SJSL.

"Journal of a Woman Visitor to Southeast Alaska." Anonymous manuscripts, ca. 1890, ASHL.

Ker Family. "Scrapbook." BCA.

Kostrometinoff, George. "Scrapbook," 1876–1908. ASHL.

Leadman, Thomas. "Farm Ledger," 1904. WRVHS.

Levy, Henry Emanuel. "Reminiscences," 1843–1929. BCA.

"Meadowbrook Hotel Register," 1888–1904. SVHS.

Meany, Edmund S. "Washington World's Fair Commission," 1891–94. Special Collections, UW.

Meeker, Ezra. "Case of Jerry Meeker." Envelope 1, Box 10, Meeker Collection, WSHS.

———. Rose Brothers, Viewmount, Kelowna, to Ezra Meeker, Puyallup, 1893. Folder 1A, Box 3, Meeker Collection, WSHS.

Meeker Family. "Notebooks," 1882–1900. Archives and Manuscripts, UW.

Olinda, Van. "The Last Potlatch," n.d. Pamphlets—Indians of North America—Oregon and Washington, Special Collections, UW.

"Pacific Steamship Company Brochures." Folders 1 and 2, Box 1, ASHL.

Paul, Fred. "Then Fight for It." Extract enclosed in letter from F. P. DeGermain to Steve Henrikson, 24 August 1997. Copy in possession of author.

Paul, William Lewis. File 804.1 (8), SJSL.

Photographs. WRVHS.

Pidcock, Reginald Heber. "Diary," 1888. Box 1, Pidcock Family Papers, BCA.

"Published Notes on Indian Relics. H. H. Tammen Curio Co., Denver Colorado," n.d. Folder 7, Volume 46, Newcombe Family Papers, BCA.

Putnam, Frederic Ward. "Frederic Ward Putnam Papers." Scrapbooks, Chicago World's Fair, 1891–93. Harvard University Archives, Cambridge, Massachusetts.

———. World's Columbian Exposition, Correspondence. Harvard University Archives, Cambridge, Massachusetts.

———. World's Columbian Exposition, Miscellaneous Papers. Harvard University Archives, Cambridge, Massachusetts.

———. World's Columbian Exposition, Miscellaneous Publications. Harvard University Archives, Cambridge, Massachusetts.

Reed, Hayter. "Correspondence," 1889–94. NAC.

Roberts, R. J. "Farm Diaries," 1878–90. BCA.

Smith, Marian Wesley. "Charlie Ashue: Notes on the Shaker Cult," 3 April 1930. Box 8, Marian Wesley Smith Collection, BCA.

Snoqualmie Hop Farm. "Account Books," 1883, 1890. SVHS.

Thomas, Maybelle Cultee. "Taped Interview," 14 March 1981. Washington Women's Heritage Project, Archives and Manuscripts, UW.

Tolmie, W. H. to A. Campbell, 21 August 1883, File 11, Box 19, O'Reilly Family Papers, BCA.

Towner, William. "Diary," 1890–1906. BCA.

United States. Census of the United States, Fourteenth Census, 1920, Alaska.

———. Census of the United States, Thirteenth Census, 1910, Alaska.

———. Census of the United States, Twelfth Census, 1900, Alaska.

———. Census of the United States, Twelfth Census, 1900, Washington.

———. RG36, Office of Collector of Customs & Deputy Collector of Customs, Sitka, Box 31, "Miscellaneous Letters Received, Sitka," 1901 March–1902 May, USNA-A.

———. RG75, Records of the Bureau of Indian Affairs, Alaska Division, Roll 8, "School Files, Haines, General Correspondence," 1908–1935, ASHL.

———. RG75, Records of the Bureau of Indian Affairs, Alaska Division, Roll 23, "School Files—Sitka, General Correspondence," 1908–1935, ASHL.

———. RG75, Records of the Bureau of Indian Affairs, Alaska Division, Roll 41, "General Correspondence, Southern District," 1908, ASHL.

———. RG75, Records of the Bureau of Indian Affairs, Alaska Division, Roll 42, "General Correspondence, Southeast," 1909–1911, ASHL.

———. U.S. Navy Census, "Report of United States Naval Officers," 1 February 1881.

Ushin, Stepan M. "Diary," [extracts] 1874–95. BCA.

"Victoria and Seattle Curio Shop Brochures," ca. 1904. Folder 4, Volume 45, Newcombe Family Papers, BCA.

"Visitors Register of the Northwest Territories Exhibit at Chicago World's Fair," 1893. NAC.

Walton, Rudolph. "Diaries," 1900–1904, 1910–14, 1919, 1927–31, 1937–41. Private collection of J. W. Shales.

Washington. World's Fair Commission. "General Correspondence," 1892–94. Archives and Manuscripts, UW.

Wilbur, Bertand K. "Just about Me." Typed manuscript, ASHL.

World's Columbian Exposition. "Plan and Classification, Department M," 1892. Miscellaneous pamphlets, Chicago Historical Society, Chicago, Illinois.

———. Exhibits and miscellaneous pamphlets, Chicago Historical Society, Chicago Illinois.

PRINTED SOURCES

"Alaska Indians Not Degenerating." *Alaska-Yukon Magazine* 4, no. 2 (1907): 188–89.

Alfred, Taiaiake. *Peace, Power, Righteousness: An Indigenous Manifesto*. Don Mills, Ontario: Oxford University Press, 1999.

Amoss, Pamela T. "The Indian Shaker Church." In *The Northwest Coast*, edited by Wayne Suttles, 633–39. Volume 7 of *The Handbook of North American Indians*, edited by William C. Sturtevant. Washington: Smithsonian Institution, 1990.

———. "Resurrection, Healing, and 'the Shake': The Story of John and Mary Slocum." *Journal of the American Acadamy of Religion—Thematic Studies* 48, no. 3–4 (1982): 87–109.

Anderson, Benedict. *Imagined Communities: Reflections on the Origin and Spread of Nationalism*. 1983. Rev. ed. New York: Verso, 1991.

Anderson, Kay. *Vancouver's Chinatown: Racial Discourse in Canada, 1875–1980*. Montreal-Kingston: McGill-Queen's University Press, 1991.

Annual Report of the Commissioner of Education and Biennial Survey of Education, 1875–1930, Washington: GPO.

Annual Report of the Governor of the District of Alaska to the Secretary of the Interior, 1885–1902. Washington: GPO.

Appadurai, Arjun. "Dead Certainty: Ethnic Violence in the Era of Globalization." *Public Culture* 10, no. 2 (1998): 225–47.

Applegate, Celia. *A Nation of Provincials: The German Idea of Heimat*. Berkeley: University of California Press, 1990.

Arima, E. Y. *The West Coast People: The Nootka of Vancouver Island and Cape Flattery*. Victoria: British Columbia Provincial Museum, 1983.

Asher, Brad. *Beyond the Reservation: Indians, Settlers, and the Law in Washington Territory, 1853–1889*. Norman: University of Oklahoma Press, 1999.

"At the World's Fair: Washington Building and Exhibits." *The Northwest Magazine* (1893): 24–25.

Badger, Reid. *The Great American Fair: The World's Columbian Exposition and American Culture*. Chicago: Nelson Hall, 1979.

Badlam, Alexander. *The Wonders of Alaska*. San Francisco: Alexander Badlam, 1890.

Bagley, Clarence B. *History of King County Washington*. Chicago: S.J. Clarke, 1929.

Baird, Donald. "Tlingit Treasures: How an Important Collection Came to Princeton." *Princeton Alumni Quarterly* 16 (1965): 6–17.

Baker, Lee. *From Savage to Negro: Anthropology and the Construction of Race, 1896–1954*. Berkeley: University of California Press, 1998.

Baker, Simon. *KhotLaCha: The Autobiography of Chief Simon Baker*. Compiled and edited by Verna J. Kirkness. Vancouver: Douglas and McIntyre, 1994.

Ballou, Maturin M. *The New Eldorado: A Summer Journey to Alaska*. Boston and New York: Houghton, Mifflin and Company, 1889.

Bancroft, Hubert Howe. *The Book of the Fair an Historical and Descriptive Presentation of the World's Science, Art, and Industry, as Viewed Through the Columbian Exposition at Chicago in 1893*. San Francisco: Bancroft Company, 1893.

Barbeau, Marius C. *Totem Poles*. Ottawa: E. Cloutier, King's Printer, 1950.

Barman, Jean. "Separate and Unequal: Indian and White Girls at All Hallows School, 1884–1920." In *Indian Education in Canada, Volume 1: The Legacy*, edited by Jean Barman, Yvonne Hébert, and Don McCaskill, 110–31. Vancouver: University of British Columbia Press, 1986.

———. "Taming Aboriginal Sexuality: Gender, Power, and Race in British Columbia, 1850–1900." *BC Studies*, no. 115–16 (1997): 237–66.

———. *The West beyond the West: A History of British Columbia*. Toronto: University of Toronto Press, 1991.

———. "What a Difference a Border Makes: Aboriginal Racial Intermixture in the Pacific Northwest." *Journal of the West* 38 (1999): 14–20.

Barman, Jean, and Bruce M. Watson. "Fort Colvile's Fur Trade Families and the Dynamics of Race in the Pacific Northwest." *Pacific Northwest Quarterly* 90 (1999): 140–53.

Barnett, H. G. *Indian Shakers: A Messianic Cult of the Pacific Northwest*. Carbondale: Southern Illinois University Press, 1957.

Batkin, Jonathan. "Tourism Is Overrated: Pueblo Pottery and the Early Curio Trade, 1880–1910." In *Unpacking Culture: Art and Commodity in Colonial and Postcolonial Worlds*, edited by Ruth B. Phillips and Christopher B. Steiner, 282–97. Berkeley: University of California Press, 1999.

Beardslee, L. A. *Reports of Captain L.A. Beardslee, U.S. Navy, Relative to Affairs in Alaska and the Operations of the U.S.S. Jamestown*. Washington: GPO, 1882.

Beck, George J. "A Clan Excitement." *Home Mission Monthly* 1903: 179–80.

Becker, Jane S. *Selling Tradition: Appalachia and the Construction of an American Folk*. Chapel Hill: University of North Carolina Press, 1998.

Becker, Marjorie. *Setting the Virgin on Fire: Lázaro Cárdenas, Michoacán Peasants, and the Redemption of the Mexican Revolution*. Berkeley: University of California Press, 1995.

Bennett, Tony. "The Exhibitionary Complex." In *Representing the Nation: A Reader*, edited by David Boswell and Jessica Evans, 332–61. London: Routledge, 1999.

Berlo, Janet, ed. *Early Years of Native American Art History*. Seattle: University of Washington Press, 1992.

Berman, Judith. " 'The Culture as It Appears to the Indian Himself': Boas, George Hunt, and the Methods of Ethnography." In *Volksgeist as Method and Ethic: Essays on Boasian Ethnography and the German Anthropological Tradition*, edited by George W. Stocking Jr., 215–56. Madison: University of Wisconsin Press, 1996.

———. "George Hunt and the Kwak'wala Texts." *Anthropological Linguistics* 36 (1994): 483–514.

———. "Oolachan-Woman's Robe: Fish, Blankets, Masks, and Meaning in Boas's Kwakw'ala Texts." In *On the Translation of Native American Literatures*, edited by Brian Swann, 125–62. Washington: Smithsonian Institution Press, 1992.

———. "Red Salmon and Red Cedar Bark: Another Look at the Nineteenth-Century Kwakwaka'wakw Winter Ceremonial." *BC Studies* 125 and 126 (2000): 53–98.

———. "Unpublished Materials of Franz Boas and George Hunt: A Record of 45 Years of Collaboration." In *Gateways: Exploring the Legacy of the Jesup North Pacific Expedition, 1897–1902*, edited by Igor Krupnik and William W. Fitzhugh, 181–213. Washington: Arctic Studies Center, National Museum of History, Smithsonian Institution, 2001.

Bieder, Robert. *Science Encounters the Indian, 1880–1920: The Early Years of American Ethnology*. Norman: University of Oklahoma Press, 1986.

Bierwert, Crisca. *Brushed by Cedar, Living by the River: Coast Salish Figures of Power*. Tucson: University of Arizona Press, 1999.

Blackman, Margaret. " 'Copying People': Northwest Coast Native Response to Early Photography." *BC Studies*, no. 52 (1981–82): 86–112.

Boas, Franz. *The Ethnography of Franz Boas: Letters and Diaries of Franz Boas Written on the Northwest Coast from 1886–1931*. Edited by Ronald P. Rohner and Evelyn C. Rohner. Translated by Hedy Parker. Chicago: University of Chicago Press, 1969.

———. "Ethnology of the Kwakiutl." In *Thirty-Fifth Annual Report of the Bureau of American Ethnology, 1913–1914*, 41–1481. Washington: GPO, 1921.

———. *Kwakiutl Ethnography*. Edited by Helen Codere. Chicago: University of Chicago Press, 1966.

———. *The Professional Correspondence of Franz Boas*. Wilmington, Del.: Scholarly Resources, 1972.

———. *The Shaping of American Anthropology, 1883–1911: A Franz Boas Reader*. Edited by George W. Stocking Jr. New York: Basic Books, 1974.

———. *The Social Organization and the Secret Societies of the Kwakiutl Indians*. In *Annual Report of the National Museum*, 313–738. Washington: GPO, 1895; reprint, New York: Johnson Reprint Corporation, 1970.

Bolt, Clarence. *Thomas Crosby and the Tsimshian: Small Shoes for Feet Too Large*. Vancouver: University of British Columbia Press, 1992.

Bonney, W. P. *History of Pierce County Washington*. Chicago: Pioneer Historical Publishing, 1927.

Boswell, David, and Jessica Evans, eds. *Representing the Nation: A Reader*. London: Routledge, 1999.

Boxberger, Daniel L., and Bruce G. Miller. "Evolution or History?: A Response to Tollefson." *Ethnohistory* 44 (1997): 135–37.

Boyd, Robert, ed. *Indians, Fire and the Land in the Pacific Northwest*. Corvallis: Oregon State University Press, 1999.

Bracken, Christopher. *The Potlatch Papers: A Colonial Case History*. Chicago: University of Chicago Press, 1997.

Bravo, Michael T. "Ethnological Encounters." In *Cultures of Natural History*, edited by N. Jardine, J. A. Secord, and E. C. Spary, 338–56. Cambridge: Cambridge University Press, 1996.

Briggs, Charles, and Richard Bauman. " 'The Foundation of All Future Researches: Franz Boas, George Hunt, Native American Texts, and the Construction of Modernity." *American Quarterly* 51 (1999): 479–528.

Briggs, Horace. *Letters from Alaska and the Pacific Coast*. Buffalo: n.p., 1889.

Brock, Peggy. "Building Bridges: Politics and Religion in a First Nations Community." *Canadian Historical Review* 81 (2000): 67–96.

Brownlie, Robin, and Mary-Ellen Kelm. "Desperately Seeking Absolution: Native Agency as Colonialist Alibi." *Canadian Historical Review* 75, no. 4 (1994): 543–56.

Buchanan, Charles Milton. "Indian Basket Work about Puget Sound." *Overland Monthly*, 2d series, 31 (1898): 406–11.

Buck, Elizabeth. *Paradise Remade: The Politics of Culture and History in Hawai'i*. Philadelphia: Temple University Press, 1993.

Buerge, David. "Brewery Bound." *Eastsideweek* (1994): 12–16.

Bugbee, Anna M. "The Thlinkets of Alaska." *Overland Monthly*, 2d series, 22 (1892): 185–96.

Bull, W. H. "Indian Hop Pickers on Puget Sound." *Harper's Weekly* 36 (1892): 545–46.

Burt, Larry. "Nowhere Left to Go: Montana's Crees, Metis, and Chippewas, and the Creation of Rocky Boy's Reservation." *Great Plains Quarterly* 7 (1987): 195–209.

Butler, Judith. *Bodies That Matter: On the Discursive Limits of "Sex"*. New York: Routledge, 1993.

———. *Gender Trouble: Feminism and the Subversion of Identity*. New York: Routledge, 1990.

———. "Performative Acts and Gender Constitution: An Essay in Phenomenology and Feminist Theory." In *Performing Feminisms: Feminist Critical Theory and Theatre*, edited by Sue-Ellen Case, 270–82. Baltimore: Johns Hopkins University Press, 1990.

Caldwell, Francis E. "Trading and Princess Tom." *Southeastern Log* 11, no. 4 (1981): 27–28.

Cameron, William E. *The World's Fair Being a Pictorial History of the Columbian Exposition*. Philadelphia: Home Library Publishing Co., 1893.

Campbell, J. B. *Campbell's Illustrated History of the World's Columbian Exposition*. Chicago: J. B. Campbell, 1894.

Canada. DIA, Annual Reports, 1881–1910. *Sessional Papers* 1882–1911.

The Canadian Indian. 15 September 1893, NAC.

Cannizzo, Jeanne. "George Hunt and the Invention of Kwakiutl Culture." *Canadian Review of Sociology and Anthropology* 20, no. 1 (1983): 44–58.

Carlson, Keith Thor, ed. *A Stó:lō Coast Salish Historical Atlas*. Vancouver: Douglas and MacIntyre, 2001.

———, ed. *You Are Asked to Witness: The Stó:lō in Canada's Pacific Coast History*. Chilliwack, B.C.: Stó:lō Heritage Trust, 1997.

Carr, Emily. *The Emily Carr Omnibus*. With an introduction by Doris Shadbolt. Vancouver: Douglas and McIntyre, 1993.

Case, David. *Alaska Natives and American Laws*. Fairbanks: University of Alaska Press, 1984.

Castile, George Pierre. "The Commodification of Indian Identity." *American Anthropologist* 98 (1996): 743–49.

———. "The 'Half-Catholic' Movement: Edwin and Myron Eells and the Rise of the Indian Shaker Church." *Pacific Northwest Quarterly* 73 (1982): 165–74.

———. "The Indian Connection: Judge James Wickersham and the Indian Shakers." *Pacific Northwest Quarterly* 81 (1990): 122–29.

Catton, Theodore. *Inhabited Wilderness: Indians, Eskimos, and National Parks in Alaska*. Albuquerque: University of New Mexico Press, 1997.

Christophers, Brett. *Positioning the Missionary: John Booth Good and the Confluence of Cultures in Nineteenth-Century British Columbia*. Vancouver: University of British Columbia Press, 1998.

Clifford, James. *Person and Myth: Maurice Leenhardt in the Melanesian World*. Berkeley: University of California Press, 1982.

———. *The Predicament of Culture: Twentieth-Century Ethnography, Literature, and Art*. Cambridge: Harvard University Press, 1988.

———. *Routes: Travel and Translation in the Late Twentieth Century*. Cambridge: Harvard University Press, 1997.

Codere, Helen. *Fighting with Property: A Study of Kwakiutl Potlatching and Warfare 1792–1930*. New York: J. J. Augustin, 1950.

———. "Kwakiutl: Traditional Culture." In *The Northwest Coast*, edited by Wayne Suttles, 359–77. Volume 7 of *The Handbook of North American Indians*, edited by William C. Sturtevant. Washington: Smithsonian Institution, 1990.

Cohen, Erik. "Authenticity and Commoditization in Tourism." *Annals of Tourism Research* 15, no. 3 (1988): 371–86.

Cohodas, Marvin. *Basket Weavers for the California Curio Trade: Elizabeth and Louise Hickox*. Tucson: University of Arizona Press, 1997.

Cole, Douglas. *Captured Heritage: The Scramble for Northwest Coast Artifacts*. Norman: University of Oklahoma Press, 1995.

———. "Franz Boas and the Bella Coola in Berlin." *Northwest Anthropological Research Notes* 16, no. 2 (1982): 115–24.

———. *Franz Boas: The Early Years, 1858–1906*. Vancouver: Douglas and McIntyre, 1999.

———. "The History of the Kwakiutl Potlatch." In *Chiefly Feasts: The Enduring Kwakiutl Potlatch*, edited by Aldona Jonaitis, 135–68. New York: American Museum of Natural History, 1992.

Cole, Douglas, and Ira Chaikin. *An Iron Hand upon the People: The Law against the Potlatch on the Northwest Coast*. Vancouver: Douglas and McIntyre, 1990.

Coleman, Michael C. *American Indian Children at School, 1850–1930*. Jackson: University Press of Mississippi, 1993.

Collins, Cary C. "Subsistence and Survival: The Makah Indian Reservation, 1855–1933." *Pacific Northwest Quarterly* 87 (1996): 180–93.

Collins, June M. "The Indian Shaker Church: A Study of Continuity and Change in Religion." *Southwestern Journal of Anthropology* 6 (1950): 399–411.

———. "John Fornsby: The Personal Document of a Coast Salish Indian." In *Indians of the Urban Northwest*, edited by Marian W. Smith, 287–341. New York: AMS Press, 1949.

Collis, Septima M. *A Woman's Trip to Alaska*. New York: Cassell Publishing Company, 1890.

Comancho, El. "The Story of the Hop Vine." *The Westerner* 16, no. 1 (1914): 3–4.

Comaroff, John, and Jean Comaroff. *Ethnography and the Historical Imagination*. Boulder: Westview Press, 1992.

Commissioner of Education for the United States. *Annual Statement of the Commissioner of Education to the Secretary of the Interior, 1905*. Washington: GPO, 1905.

———. *Annual Statement of the Commissioner of Education to the Secretary of the Interior, 1906*. Washington: GPO, 1906.

Cooper, Frederick, and Ann Laura Stoler, eds. *Tensions of Empire: Colonial Cultures in a Bourgeois World*. Berkeley: University of California Press, 1997.

Costello, J. A. *The Siwash: Their Life, Legends and Tales, Puget Sound and Pacific Northwest*. Seattle: Calvert Company, 1895.

"The Cowichan Indians Complaint." *Victoria Daily Times*, 29 June 1895, 7.

Cracroft, Sophia. *Lady Franklin Visits Sitka, Alaska 1870: The Journal of Sophia Cracroft, Sir John Franklin's Niece*. Edited by R. N. DeArmond. Anchorage: Alaska Historical Society, 1981.

Craine, Bessie Wilson. *Squak Valley (Issaquah)*. N.p.: King County Library System, 1963.

Cronon, William. *Nature's Metropolis: Chicago and the Great West*. New York: Norton, 1991.

Cruikshank, Julie. "Negotiating with Narrative: Establishing Cultural Identity at the Yukon International Storytelling Festival." *American Anthropologist* 99 (1997): 56–69.

———. *The Social Life of Stories: Narrative and Knowledge in the Yukon Territory*. Vancouver: University of British Columbia Press, 1998.

Culhane, Dara. *The Pleasure of the Crown: Anthropology, Law and First Nations*. Burnaby, B.C.: Talonbooks, 1997.

Culin, Stewart. "Games of the North American Indians." In *Twenty-Fourth Annual Report of the Bureau of American Ethnology, 1902–1903*, 1–811. Washington: GPO, 1907.

Currier, Susan Lord. "Some Aspects of Washington Hop Fields." *Overland Monthly*, 2d series, 32 (1898): 540–44.

Dall, William. "Alaska as It Was and Is, 1865–1895." *Philosophical Society of Washington Bulletin* 8 (1895).

Dannenbaum, Jed. "John Muir and Alaska." *Alaska Journal* 2, no. 4 (1972): 14–20.

Darnell, Regna. *Invisible Genealogies: A History of Americanist Anthropology*. Lincoln: University of Nebraska Press, 2001.

———. "The Pivotal Role of the Northwest Coast in the History of Americanist Anthropology." *BC Studies* 125 and 126 (2000): 33–52.

Darrah, William C. *The World of Stereographs*. Gettysburg, Penn: W. C. Darrah, 1977.

Dauenhauer, Nora Marks, and Richard Dauenhauer, eds. *Haa Kusteeyí, Our Culture: Tlingit Life Stories*. Seattle: University of Washington Press, 1994.

Davidoff, Leonore. "Class and Gender in Victorian England." In *Sex and Class in Women's History*, edited by Judith L. Newton, Mary P. Ryan, and Judith R. Walkowitz, 16–69. Boston: Routledge and Keegan Paul, 1983.

Davis, Barbara A. *Edward S. Curtis: The Life and Times of a Shadow Catcher*. San Francisco: Chronicle Books, 1985.

Dawson, George M. "Notes and Observations on the Kwakiool People and the Adjacent Coasts." In *Transactions of the Royal Society of Canada, Section 2, 1887*, 63–98. Montreal: Dawson Brothers, 1888.

de Laguna, Frederica. "Tlingit." In *The Northwest Coast*, edited by Wayne Suttles, 203–28. Volume 7 of *The Handbook of North American Indians*, edited by William C. Sturtevant. Washington: Smithsonian Institution, 1990.

———. *Under Mount Saint Elias: The History and Culture of the Yakutat Tlingit* . Washington: Smithsonian Institution Press, 1972.

Dean, Mary. "Of Going Hopping." *Lippincott's Monthly* 16 (1875): 630–34.

DeArmond, R. N. *A Sitka Chronology: 1867–1987*. Sitka: Sitka Historical Press, 1993.

Deloria, Philip J. *Playing Indian*. New Haven: Yale University Press, 1998.

Deloria, Vine, ed. *Of Utmost Good Faith*. New York: Bantam Books, 1972.

Denny, Emily Inez. *Blazing the Way*. Seattle: Rainier Printing Co., 1909.

Densmore, Frances. "Music of the Indians of British Columbia." In *Bureau of American Ethnology Bulletin 136*, 1–99. Washington: GPO, 1943.

Desmond, Jane. *Staging Tourism: Bodies on Display from Waikiki to Sea World*. Chicago: University of Chicago Press, 1999.

Deur, Douglas. "The Hunt for Identity: On the Contested Targets of Makah Whaling." In *Worldview Flux: Perplexed Values among Postmodern Peoples*, edited by Jim and Jonathan M. Smith Norwine, 145–75. Lanham: Lexington Books, 2000.

Deutsch, Sarah. *No Separate Refuge: Culture, Class, and Gender on an Anglo-Hispanic Frontier in the American Southwest, 1880–1940*. New York: Oxford University Press, 1987.

Dexter, Ralph W. "Putnam's Problems Popularizing Anthropology." *American Scientist* 54 (1966): 315–32.

Dillard, Annie. *The Living: A Novel*. New York: Harper Perennial, 1993.

Dilworth, Leah. *Imagining Indians in the Southwest: Persistent Visions of a Primitive Past*. Washington: Smithsonian Institution Press, 1996.

Dippie, Brian W. *The Vanishing American: White Attitudes and U.S. Indian Policy*. Middletown, Conn.: Wesleyan University Press, 1982.

Dirks, Nicholas B. "Castes of Mind." *Representations* 37 (1992): 56–78.

———. *Castes of Mind: Colonialism and the Making of Modern India*. Princeton: Princeton University Press, 2001.

———. "Colonial Histories and Native Informants: Biography of an Archive." In *Orientalism and the Postcolonial Predicament: Perspectives on Southeast Asia*, edited by Carol Breckenridge and Peter van der Veer, 279–313. Philadelphia: University of Pennsylvania Press, 1993.

———. "From Little King to Landlord: Property, Law and the Gift Under the Madras Permanent Settlement." *Comparative Studies in Society and History* (1986): 307–33.

———. *The Hollow Crown: Ethnohistory of an Indian Kingdom*. New York: Cambridge University Press, 1987.

———. "The Policing of Tradition: Colonialism and Anthropology in Southern India." *Comparative Studies in Society and History* (1997): 182–212.

———. "Ritual and Resistance: Subversion as a Social Fact." In *Culture/Power/History: A Reader in Contemporary Social Theory*, edited by Nicholas B. Dirks, Geoff Eley, and Sherry B. Ortner, 483–503. Princeton: Princeton University Press, 1994.

Dirlik, Arif. "The Past as Legacy and Project: Postcolonial Criticism in the Perspective of Indigenous Historicism." *American Indian Culture and Research Journal* 20, no. 2 (1996): 1–31.

Doig, Ivan. *Winter Brothers: A Season at the Edge of America*. New York: Harcourt Brace Jovanovich, 1980.

Dominguez, Virginia R. "Invoking Culture: The Messy Side of 'Cultural Politics.'" *South Atlantic Quarterly* 91, no. 1 (1992): 19–42.

———. "The Marketing of Heritage." *American Ethnologist* 13: 546–55.

Donald, Leland. *Aboriginal Slavery on the Northwest Coast of North America*. Berkeley: University of California Press, 1997.

———. "The Slave Trade on the Northwest Coast of North America." *Research in Economic Anthropology* 6 (1984): 121–58.

Dorpat, Paul. *Seattle: Now and Then*. Seattle: Tartu Publications, 1984.

Douglas, Mary. *Implicit Meanings: Essays in Anthropology*. Boston: Routledge and Kegan Paul, 1975.

Drucker, Philip. "The Northern and Central Nootkan Tribes." In *Smithsonian Institution Bureau of American Ethnology Bulletin 144*. Washington: GPO, 1951.

Drucker, Philip, and Robert F. Heizer. *To Make My Name Good: A Reexamination of the Southern Kwakiutl Potlatch*. Berkeley: University of California Press, 1967.

Duff, Wilson. *The Indian History of British Columbia: Volume 1, The Impact of the White Man*. Victoria: Provincial Museum of British Columbia, 1964.

Duncan, Emmet. "'A Wretched Giving Away System' or 'A Strict Law Bids Us Dance': Interaction, Conflict, and Re-Invention, a New Perspective on the Southern Kwakwa̱ka̱'wakw Potlatch." B.A. honors thesis, University of British Columbia, 1994.

Eames, Ninetta. "In Hop-Picking Time." *Cosmopolitan* 16 (1893): 27–36.

Earle, Edward W. *Points of View: The Stereograph in America—A Cultural History*. Rochester, N.Y.: Visual Studies Workshop Press, 1979.

"Early History of Hop Culture in Saanich." *Victoria Colonist*, 7 October 1928, Magazine section, 8.

Eells, Myron. *The Indians of Puget Sound: The Notebooks of Myron Eells*. Edited by George Pierre Castile. Seattle: University of Washington Press, 1985.

———. *Ten Years of Missionary Work among the Indians at Skokomish, Washington Territory, 1874–1884*. Boston: Congregational Sunday-School and Publishing Society, 1886.

"The Eighteenth Anniversary and Ninth Graduating Exercises." *The Red Man* 14, no. 4 (1897): 1.

Elliot, Gordon. *Memories of the Chemainus Valley*. Victoria: Chemainus Valley Historical Society, 1978.

Elmendorf, W. W. *The Structure of Twana Culture*. Pullman: Washington State University Press, 1960.

———. *Twana Narratives: Native Historical Accounts of a Coast Salish Culture*. Seattle: University of Washington Press, 1993.

Emmons, George Thornton. *The Basketry of the Tlingit*. New York: American Museum of Natural History, 1903; reprint, Sitka: Friends of the Sheldon Jackson Museum, 1993.

———. *The Tlingit Indians*. Edited by Frederica de Laguna. Seattle: University of Washington Press, 1991.

Errington, Shelly. *The Death of Authentic Primitive Art and Other Tales of Progress*. Berkeley: University of California Press, 1998.

Ettawageshik, Frank. "My Father's Business." In *Unpacking Culture: Art and Commodity in Colonial and Postcolonial Worlds*, edited by Ruth B. Phillips and Christopher B. Steiner, 20–29. Berkeley: University of California Press, 1999.

Evans, Elwood, ed. *The State of Washington*. N.p.: World's Fair Commission of the State of Washington, [1892].

Evans, Jack R. *Little History of North Bend—Snoqualmie Washington*. Seattle: SCW Publications, 1990.

Everett, Marshall. *The Book of the Fair*. N.p.: Henry Neil, 1904.

The Exhibition of the District of Alaska at the Lewis and Clark Centennial Exposition. Portland: Irwin-Hudson, 1905.

Fabian, Johannes. *Time and the Other: How Anthropology Makes Its Object*. New York: Columbia University Press, 1983.

Fagin, Nancy L. "Closed Collections and Open Appeals: The Two Anthropology Exhibits at the Chicago World's Columbian Exposition of 1893." *Curator* 27 (1984): 249–64.

Feest, Christian. "Europe's Indians." In *The Invented Indian: Cultural Fictions and Government Policies*, edited by James A. Clifton. New Brunswick, N.J.: Transaction Publishers, 1990.

Fish, Edwards R. *The Past at Present in Issaquah, Washington*. Kingsport, Tenn.: Kingsport Press, 1967.

Fish, Harriet U. "Andy Wold's Tales of Early Issaquah." *Puget Soundings* (1983): 6–11.

Fisher, Robin. *Contact and Conflict: Indian-European Relations in British Columbia, 1774–1890*. 2d ed. rev. Vancouver: University of British Columbia Press, 1992.

———. "Indian Warfare on Two Frontiers: A Comparison of B.C. and Washington Territory during the Early Years of Settlement." *Pacific Historical Review* 50, no. 1 (1980): 31–51.

Fogelson, Raymond D. "The Red Man in the White City." In *Columbian Consequences: Volume 3, The Spanish Borderlands in Pan-American Perspective*, edited by David Hurst Thomas, 73–90. Washington: Smithsonian Institution Press, 1991.

Foley, Neil. *The White Scourge: Mexicans, Blacks, and Poor Whites in Texas Cotton Culture*. Berkeley: University of California Press, 1997.

Forbush, William Byron. *Pomiuk: A Waif of Labrador*. Boston: Pilgrim Press, 1903.

Ford, Clellan S. *Smoke from Their Fires: The Life of Kwakiutl Chief*. New Haven: Yale University Press, 1941.

Forster, E. M. *A Room with a View*. New York: Alfred A. Knopf, 1923; reprint, New York: Vintage Books, 1986.

"Franz Boas and the Kwakiutl: Interview with Mrs. Tom Johnson." In *Pioneers of American Anthropology: The Uses of Biography*, edited by June Helm, 213–22. Seattle: University of Washington Press, 1966.

Frather, Julia F. A. "Fourth of July at Klamath Reservation." *Overland Monthly*, 2d series, 42 (1903): 116–23.

Freeman, Otis W. "Hop Industry of the Pacific Coast States." *Economic Geography* 12, no. 2 (1936): 155–63.

Friends of the Indian. *Uncommon Controversy: Fishing Rights of the Muckleshoot, Puyallup, and Nisqually Indians*. Seattle: University of Washington Press, 1970.

Friesen, Gerald A. *The Canadian Prairies: A History*. Lincoln: University of Nebraska Press, 1984.

"From the Past." *The Daily Sitka Sentinel*, 12 January 1988.

Furniss, Elizabeth. *The Burden of History: Colonialism and the Frontier Myth in a Rural Canadian Community*. Vancouver: University of British Columbia Press, 1999.

Gabriel, Kathryn. *Gambler Way: Indian Gaming in Mythology, History and Archaeology in North America*. Boulder: Johnson Books, 1996.

Galois, Robert. "Colonial Encounters: The Worlds of Arthur Wellington Clah, 1855–1881." *BC Studies*, no. 1115–166 (1997): 135–46.

———. *Kwakwaka'wakw Settlements 1775–1920: A Geographical Analysis and Gazetteer*. Vancouver: University of British Columbia Press, 1994.

Garroutte, Eva Marie. *Real Indians: Identity and Survival of Native America*. Berkeley: University of California Press, 2003.

General Agent of Education for Alaska. *Report on Education in Alaska, Annual Report of the Commissioner of Education and Biennial Survey of Education, 1875–1930*. Washington: GPO.

Gmelch, Sharon Bohn. "Elbridge Warren Merrill of Sitka, Alaska." *History of Photography* 19, no. 2 (1995): 159–72.

Goldie, Terry. *Fear and Temptation: The Image of the Indigene in Canadian, Australian, and New Zealand Literatures*. Kingston and Montreal: McGill-Queen's University Press, 1989.

Goldman, Irving. *The Mouth of Heaven: An Introduction to Kwakiutl Religious Thought*. New York: John Wiley, 1975.

Gordon, Beverly. "The Souvenir: Messenger of the Extraordinary." *Journal of Popular Culture* 20, no. 3 (1986): 135–46.

Gordon, Beverly, and Melanie Herzog, eds. *American Indian Art: The Collecting Experience*. Madison: Elvehjem Museum of Art, University of Wisconsin, 1988.

Gough, Barry M. *Gunboat Frontier: British Maritime Authority and Northwest Coast Indians, 1846–1890*. Vancouver: University of British Columbia Press, 1984.

———. "A Priest Versus the Potlatch: The Reverend Alfred James Hall and the Fort Rupert Kwakiutl, 1878–1880." *Journal of the Canadian Church Historical Society* 24, no. 2 (1982): 75–89.

Graburn, Nelson H. H. "The Anthropology of Tourism." *Annals of Tourism Research* 10 (1983): 9–33.

———. "Evolution of Tourist Arts." *Annals of Tourism Research* 11 (1984): 393–419.

———. "Tourism: The Sacred Journey." In *Hosts and Guests: The Anthropology of Tourism*, edited by Valene L. Smith, 22–36. Philadelphia: University of Pennsylvania Press, 1989.

———, ed. *Ethnic and Tourist Arts: Cultural Expressions from the Fourth World*. Berkeley: University of California Press, 1976.

Gray, Judith A. *The Federal Cylinder Project: A Guide to Field Cylinder Collections in Federal Agencies*. Washington: American Folklife Center, 1988.

Greenhalgh, Paul. *Ephemeral Vistas: The Expositions Universelles, Great Exhibitions, and World's Fairs, 1851–1939*. Manchester: Manchester University Press, 1988.

Grinnell, George Bird. *Alaska 1899: Essays from the Harriman Expedition*. Seattle: University of Washington Press, 1995.

Guie, H. Dean. "Siwash Kloochman." *Argus* 1943: 39, 46.

Gunther, Erna. "The Shaker Religion of the Northwest." In *Indians of the Urban Northwest*, edited by Marian W. Smith, 37–76. New York: AMS Press, 1949.

Haberland, Wolfgang. " 'Diese Indianer Sind Falsch': Neun Bella Coola Im Deutschen Reich, 1885/86." *Archiv Fur Volkerkunde* 42 (1988): 2–67.

———. "Nine Bella Coolas in Germany." In *Indians and Europe: An Interdisciplinary Collection of Essays*, edited by Christian F. Feest. Aachen: Edition Herodot, Rader Verlag, 1987.

Haeberlin, Hermann, and Erna Gunther. *The Indians of Puget Sound*. Seattle: University of Washington Press, 1930.

Hallock, Charles. *Our New Alaska; or, the Seward Purchase Vindicated*. New York: Forest and Stream Publishing Co., 1886.

Haraway, Donna. "Teddy Bear Patriarchy: Taxidermy in the Garden of Eden, New York City, 1908–1936." In *Culture/Power/History: A Reader in Contemporary Social*

Theory, edited by Nicholas B. Dirks, Geoff Eley, and Sherry B. Ortner, 50–95. Princeton: Princeton University Press, 1994.

Harkin, Michael. "(Dis)Pleasures of the Text: Boasian Ethnography on the Central Northwest Coast." In *Gateways: Exploring the Legacy of the Jesup North Pacific Expedition, 1897–1902*, edited by Igor Krupnik and William W. Fitzhugh, 93–105. Washington: Arctic Studies Center, National Museum of History, Smithsonian Institution, 2001.

———. *The Heiltsuks: Dialogues of Culture and History on the Northwest Coast*. Lincoln: University of Nebraska Press, 1997.

———. "Past Presence: Conceptions of History in Northwest Coast Studies." *Arctic Anthropology* 33 (1996): 1–15.

———. "A Tradition of Invention: Modern Ceremonialism on the Northwest Coast." In *Past Is Present: Some Uses of Tradition in Native Societies*, edited by Marie Mauzé, 97–111. Lanham: University Press of America, 1997.

Harmon, Alexandra. *Indians in the Making: Ethnic Relations and Indian Identities Around Puget Sound*. Berkeley: University of California Press, 1998.

———. "Lines in Sand: Shifting Boundaries between Indians and Non-Indians in the Puget Sound Region." *Western Historical Quarterly* 26 (1995): 429–53.

Harris, Cole. *Making Native Space: Colonialism, Resistance, and Reserves in British Columbia*. Vancouver: University of British Columbia Press, 2002.

———. *The Resettlement of British Columbia: Essays on Colonialism and Geographical Change*. Vancouver: University of British Columbia Press, 1997.

Harrison, Carter H. *A Summer's Outing*. Chicago: Donohue, Henneberry and Co., 1891.

Hawthorne, Julian. *History of Washington: The Evergreen State, from Early Dawn to Daylight; with Portraits and Biographies*. N.p.: American Historical Publishing, 1893.

Haycox, Stephen. "Sheldon Jackson in Historical Perspective: Alaska Native Schools and Mission Contracts, 1885–1894." *The Pacific Historian* 28 (1984): 18–28.

Heaman, E. A. *The Inglorious Arts of Peace: Exhibitions in Canadian Society During the Nineteenth Century*. Toronto: University of Toronto Press, 1999.

Hestwood, J. O. *The Evergreen State Souvenir*. Chicago: W. B. Conkey Co.,1893.

Higginson, Ella. *Alaska: The Great Country*. New York: MacMillan., 1908.

Hill, Ada S. *A History of the Snoqualmie Valley*. N.p., 1970.

Hinckley, Ted C. *Alaskan John G. Brady: Missionary, Businessman, Judge, and Governor, 1878–1918*. Miami: Miami University, 1982.

———. *The Americanization of Alaska, 1867–1897*. Palo Alto: Pacific Books Publishers, 1972.

———. *The Canoe Rocks: Alaska's Tlingit and the Euroamerican Frontier, 1800–1912*. Lanham: University Press of America, 1996.

———. "The Inside Passage: A Popular Gilded Age Tour." *Pacific Northwest Quarterly* 56 (1965): 67–74.

———. "Sheldon Jackson as Preserver of Alaska's Native Culture." *Pacific Historical Review* 33 (1964): 411–24.

———. "The United States Frontier at Sitka, 1867–1873." *Pacific Northwest Quarterly* 60, no. 2 (1969): 57–65.

———. " 'We Are More Truly Heathen than the Natives': John G. Brady and the Assimilation of Alaska's Tlingit Indians." *Western Historical Quarterly* 11, no. 1 (1980): 37–55.

Hinckley, Theodore C., and Caryl Hinckley. "Ivan Petroff's Journal of a Trip to Alaska in 1878." *Journal of the West* 5, no. 1 (1966): 25–70.

Hine, C. C. *A Trip to Alaska: Being a Report of a Lecture Given with Stereopticon Illustrations*. Milwaukee: King, Fowle and Co., 1889.

Hinsley, Curtis M. *Savages and Scientists: The Smithsonian Institution and the Development of American Anthropology, 1846–1910*. Washington: Smithsonian Institution Press, 1981.

———. "The World as Marketplace: Commodification of the Exotic at the World's Columbian Exposition, Chicago, 1893." In *Exhibiting Cultures: The Poetics and Politics of Museum Display*, edited by Ivan Karp and Steven Lavine, 344–65. Washington: Smithsonian Institution Press, 1991.

———. "Zunis and Brahmins: Cultural Ambivalence in the Gilded Age." In *Romantic Motives: Essays on Anthropological Sensibility*, edited by George W. Stocking Jr., 169–207. Madison: University of Wisconsin Press, 1989.

Hinsley, Curtis M., and Bill Holm. "A Cannibal in the National Museum: The Early Career of Franz Boas in America." *American Anthropologist* 78 (1976): 306–16.

Holland, Dorothy C., and Debra G. Skinner. "Contested Ritual, Contested Femininities: (Re)Forming Self and Society in a Nepali Women's Festival." *American Ethnologist* 22, no. 2 (1995): 279–305.

Holm, Bill. "Kwakiutl: Winter Ceremonies." In *The Northwest Coast*, edited by Wayne Suttles, 378–86. Volume 7 of *The Handbook of North American Indians*, edited by William C. Sturtevant. Washington: Smithsonian Institution, 1990.

"Hop Culture on the Pacific Coast." *The West Shore* 14 (1888): 466–71.

"Hop Fields of Puyallup and White River." *The West Shore* 10 (1884): 345–50.

"Hops and Hop-pickers." *The Living Age* 199 (28 October 1893): 249–55.

Hosmer, Brian C. *American Indians in the Marketplace: Persistence and Innovation among the Menominees and Metlakatlans, 1870–1920*. Lawrence: University of Kansas Press, 1999.

Howard, O. O. "Famous Indian Chiefs." *St. Nicholas Magazine* 35 (1908): 622–24.

Hoxie, Frederick E. *A Final Promise: The Campaign to Assimilate the Indians, 1880–1920*. Lincoln: University of Nebraska Press, 1984.

Hughes, George. "Authenticity in Tourism." *Annals of Tourism Research* 22 (1995): 781–803.

Huyssen, Andreas. *After the Great Divide: Modernism, Mass Culture, Postmodernism*. Bloomington: Indiana University Press, 1986.

Hyde, Anne Farrar. *An American Vision: Far Western Landscape and National Culture, 1820–1920*. New York: New York University Press, 1990.

Hyde, John. *Wonderland; or the Pacific Northwest and Alaska, with a Description of the Country Traversed by the Northern Pacific Railroad*. St. Paul: Northern Pacific Railroad, 1888.

An Illustrated History of Skagit and Snohomish Counties. N.p.: Interstate Publishing Company, 1906.

"Indian Girls." *Presbyterian Home Missionary* (1883): 189.

"Indian Shakers." *South Bend Journal* (1895): 1.

"Indians of the Far Northwest." *Overland Monthly* 4 (1884): 405–11.

Ives, Halsey Cooley. *The Dream City*. St. Louis: Thompson Publishing Co., 1893.

Jacknis, Ira. "Franz Boas and Exhibits: On the Limitations of the Museum Method of Anthropology." In *Objects and Others: Essays on Museums and Material Culture*, edited by George Stocking Jr., 75–111. Madison: University of Wisconsin Press, 1985.

———. "Franz Boas and Photography." *Studies in Visual Communication* 10, no. 1 (1984): 2–60.

———. "George Hunt, Collector of Indian Specimens." In *Chiefly Feasts: The Enduring Kwakiutl Potlatch*, edited by Aldona Jonaitis, 177–226. New York: American Museum of Natural History, 1992.

———. "Northwest Coast Indian Culture and the World's Columbian Exposition." In *Columbian Consequences: Volume 3, The Spanish Borderlands in Pan-American Perspective*, edited by David Hurst Thomas, 91–118. Washington: Smithsonian Institution Press, 1991.

———. *The Storage Box of Tradition: Kwakiutl Art, Anthropologists, and Museums, 1881–1981*. Washington: Smithsonian Institution Press, 2002.

———. "The Storage Box of Tradition: Museums, Anthropologists, and Kwakiutl Art, 1881–1981." Ph.D. dissertation, University of Chicago, 1989.

Jackson, Sheldon. *Alaska, and Missions of the North Pacific Coast*. New York: Dodd, Mead and Co., 1880.

———. *The Presbyterian Church in Alaska*. Washington: Press of Thomas McGill, 1886.

Jacobs, Jane M. *Edge of Empire: Post Colonialism and the City*. New York: Routledge, 1996.

Jacobsen, Johan Adrian. *Alaskan Voyage, 1881–1883: An Expedition to the Northwest Coast of America*. Translated by Erna Gunther. Chicago: University of Chicago Press, 1977.

James, George Wharton. "Indian Basketry in House Decoration." *Chautauquan* (1901): 619–24.

"James Deans and His Company of Indians." *American Antiquarian and Oriental Journal* 15 (1893): 185.

Jasen, Patricia. *Wild Things: Nature, Culture, and Tourism in Ontario, 1790–1914*. Toronto: University of Toronto Press, 1995.

Jenness, Diamond. *The Saanich Indians of Vancouver Island*. [Victoria]: Haunted Bookshop, [1974?].

Johnson, Rossiter. *A History of the World's Columbian Exposition Held in Chicago in 1893*. New York: D. Appleton and Co, 1897.

Jonaitis, Aldona. "Chiefly Feasts: The Enduring Kwakiutl Potlatch from Salvage Anthropology to a Big Apple Button Blanket." *Curator* 35 (1992): 255–67.

———. "Northwest Coast Totem Poles." In *Unpacking Culture: Art and Commodity in Colonial and Postcolonial Worlds*, edited by Ruth B. Phillips and Christopher B. Steiner, 104–21. Berkeley: University of California Press, 1999.

———. *The Yuquot Whaler's Shrine*. Seattle: University of Washington Press, 1999.

———, ed. *Chiefly Feasts: The Enduring Kwakiutl Potlatch*. New York: American Museum of Natural History, 1991.

———, ed. *A Wealth of Thought: Franz Boas on Native American Art*. Seattle: University of Washington Press, 1995.

Jones, Livingston F. *A Study of the Thlingets of Alaska*. New York: Fleming H. Revell Co., 1914.

Kamenskii, Anatolii. *Tlingit Indians of Alaska* . Translated by Sergei Kan. Fairbanks: University of Alaska Press, 1985.

Kan, Sergei. *Memory Eternal: Tlingit Culture and Russian Orthodox Christianity through Two Centuries*. Seattle: University of Washington Press, 1999.

———. "Recording Native Culture and Christianizing the Natives—Russian Orthodox Missionaries in Southeastern Alaska." In *Russia in North America: Proceedings of the Second International Conference on Russian America*, edited by Richard A. Pierce, 298–313. Kingston, Alaska: Limestone Press, 1990.

———. "Russian Orthodox Brotherhoods among the Tlingit: Missionary Goals and Native Response." *Ethnohistory* 32 (1985): 196–223.

———. "Shamanism and Christianity." *Ethnohistory* 38 (1991): 363–87.

———. *Symbolic Immortality: The Tlingit Potlatch of the Nineteenth Century*. Washington: Smithsonian Institution Press, 1989.

Karr, H. W. Seton. *Shores and Alps of Alaska*. London: Sampson, Low, Marston, Searle and Rivington, 1887.

Keeler, Charles A. "To an Indian Basket." *Overland Monthly* 24 (1894): 528.

Kellogg, George Albert. *A History of Whidbey's Island*. Oak Harbor, Washington: George B. Astel, 1934.

Kelm, Mary-Ellen. *Colonizing Bodies: Aboriginal Health and Healing in British Columbia, 1900–1950*. Vancouver: University of British Columbia Press, 1998.

Kendall, Laurel, Barbara Mathe, and Thomas Ross Miller, eds. *Drawing Shadows to Stone: The Photography of the Jesup North Pacific Expedition, 1897–1902*. New York: American Museum of Natural History, 1997.

Ker, William. "A Siwash Strike on the Yakima." *The Northwest Magazine* 12 (1894): 3–4.

Kew, J. E. Michael. "Central and Southern Coast Salish Ceremonies Since 1900." In *The Northwest Coast*, edited by Wayne Suttles, 476–80. Volume 7 of *The Handbook of North American Indians*, edited by William C. Sturtevant. Washington: Smithsonian Institution, 1990.

———. "Coast Salish Ceremonial Life: Status and Identity in a Modern Village." Ph.D. dissertation, University of Washington, 1970.

———. "History of Coastal British Columbia Since 1849." In *The Northwest Coast*, edited by Wayne Suttles, 159–168. Volume 7 of *The Handbook of North American Indians*, edited by William C. Sturtevant. Washington: The Smithsonian Institution, 1990.

King, J. C. H. "Tradition in Native American Art." In *The Arts of the North American Indian: Traditions in Evolution*, edited by Edwin L. Wade, 65–92. New York: Hudson Hills Press, 1986.

Kirk, Ruth, and Carmela Alexander. *Exploring Washington's Past: A Road Guide to History*. Seattle: University of Washington Press, 1990.

Klein, Kerwin Lee. *Frontiers of Historical Imagination: Narrating the European Conquest of Native America, 1890–1990*. Berkeley: University of California Press, 1999.

Klotz, Otto J. "Alaska." *Ottawa Naturalist* 1894.

Knapp, Frances, and Rheta Louise Childe. *The Thlinkets of Southeastern Alaska*. Chicago: Stone and Kimball, 1896.

Knight, Rolf. *Indians at Work: An Informal History of Native Labour in BC, 1858–1930*. Rev. ed. Vancouver: New Star Books, 1996.

Knowles, Norman, ed. "Special Issue on British Columbia." *Journal of the Canadian Church Historical Society* 38, no.1 (April 1996).

Krause, Aurel. *The Tlingit Indians: Results of a Trip to the Northwest Coast of America and the Bering Straits*. Translated by Erna Gunther. Seattle: University of Washington Press, 1972.

Krupat, Arnold. "Irony in Anthropology: The Work of Franz Boas." In *Modernist Anthropology: From Fieldwork to Text*, edited by Marc Manganaro, 133–45. Princeton: Princeton University Press, 1990.

Landis, Paul H. "The Hop Industry, a Social and Economic Problem." *Economic Geography* 15, no. 1 (1939): 85–94.

LaViolette, Forrest E. *The Struggle for Survival: Indian Cultures and the Protestant Ethic in British Columbia*, rev. ed. Toronto: University of Toronto Press, 1978.

Lazell, J. Arthur. *Alaskan Apostle: The Life Story of Sheldon Jackson*. New York: Harper and Brothers, 1960.

Lears, T. J. Jackson. *No Place of Grace: Antimodernism and the Transformation of American Culture, 1880–1920*. New York: Pantheon Books, 1981.

Lee, Molly. "Appropriating the Primitive: Turn-of-the-Century Collection and Display of Native Alaskan Art." *Arctic Anthropology* 28, no. 1 (1991): 6–15.

———. "Tourism and Taste Cultures: Collecting Native Art in Alaska at the Turn of the Century." In *Unpacking Culture: Art and Commodity in Colonial and Postcolonial Worlds*, edited by Ruth B. Phillips and Christopher B. Steiner, 267–81. Berkeley: University of California Press, 1999.

Levine, Lawrence W. *Highbrow/Lowbrow: The Emergence of Cultural Hierarchy in America*. Cambridge: Harvard University Press, 1988.

Lindsay, Batterman. *Derelicts of Destiny*. New York: Neely Co., 1900.

———. "Kwelth-Elite, The Proud Slave." *Overland Monthly*, 2d series, 33 (1899): 534–39.

Liss, Julia E. "Patterns of Strangeness: Franz Boas, Modernism and the Origins of Anthropology." In *Prehistories of the Future: The Primitivist Project and the Culture of Modernism*, edited by Elazar Barkan and Ronald Bush, 114–30. Stanford: Stanford University Press, 1995.

Little, Kenneth. "On Safari: The Visual Politics of a Tourist Representation." In *The Varieties of Sensory Experience: A Sourcebook in the Anthropology of the Senses*, edited by David Howes, 148–63. Toronto: University of Toronto Press, 1991.

Littlefield, Alice, and Martha C. Knack, eds. *Native Americans and Wage Labor: Ethnohistorical Perspectives*. Norman: University of Oklahoma Press, 1996.

Loo, Tina. "Dan Cranmer's Potlatch: Law as Coercion, Symbol, and Rhetoric in British Columbia, 1884–1951." *Canadian Historical Review* 73 (1992): 125–65.

Lukens, Matilda Barns. *The Inland Passage; a Journal of a Trip to Alaska*. [San Francisco]: n.p., 1889.

Lutz, John. "After the Fur Trade: The Aboriginal Labouring Classes of BC, 1849–1890." *Journal of the Canadian Historical Association New Series*, New Series, 3 (1992): 69–93.

———. "Work, Sex, and Death on the Great Thoroughfare: Annual Migrations of 'Canadian Indians' to the American Pacific Northwest." In *Parallel Destinies: Canadian-American Relations West of the Rockies*, edited by John M. Findlay and Ken S. Coates, 80–103. Seattle: University of Washington Press, 2002.

Lux, Maureen K. *Medicine That Walks: Disease, Medicine and Canadian Plains Native People, 1880–1940*. Toronto: University of Toronto Press, 2001.

Lyman, Christopher M. *The Vanishing Race and Other Illusions: Photographs of Indians by Edward S. Curtis*. Washington: Smithsonian Institution Press, 1982.

Lyons, Cicely. *Salmon: Our Heritage, The Story of a Province and Industry*. Vancouver: Mitchell Press, 1969.

MacCannell, Dean. *Empty Meeting Grounds: The Tourist Papers*. New York: Routledge, 1992.

———. *The Tourist: A New Theory of the Leisure Class*. New York: Schocken Books, 1976.

———. "Tradition's Next Step." In *Discovered Country: Tourism and Survival in the American West*, edited by Scott Norris, 161–79. Albuquerque: Stone Ladder Press, 1994.

MacDowell, Lloyd W. *Alaska Indian Basketry*. Seattle: Alaska Steamship Company, 1906.

———. *The Totem Poles of Alaska and Indian Mythology*. Seattle: Alaska Steamship Company, 1905.

MacLachlan, Morag, ed. *The Fort Langley Journals, 1827–1830*. Vancouver: University of British Columbia Press, 1998.

Macnair, Peter. "From Kwakiutl to Kwakwa̱ka̱'wakw." In *Native Peoples: The Canadian Experience*, 2d ed., edited by R. Bruce Morrison and C. Roderick Wilson, 586–605. Toronto: McClelland and Stewart Inc., 1995.

Manning, Agnes M. "To Alaska." *Overland Monthly* 3 (1884): 241–55.

Maranda, Lynn. *Coast Salish Gambling Games*. Ottawa: National Museums of Canada, 1984.

Marino, Cesare. "History of Western Washington since 1846." In *The Northwest Coast*, edited by Wayne Suttles, 169–79. Volume 7 of *The Handbook of North American Indians*, edited by William C. Sturtevant. Washington: Smithsonian Institution, 1990.

Marker, Michael. " 'That History Is More a Part of the Present Than It Ever Was in the Past': Toward an Ethnohistory of Native Education." *History of Education Review* 28, no. 1 (1999): 17–29.

Marr, Carolyn J. "Photographers and Their Subjects on the Southern Northwest Coast: Motivations and Responses." *Arctic Anthropology* 27, no. 2 (1990): 13–26.

———. "Taken Pictures: On Interpreting Native American Photographs of the Southern Northwest Coast." *Pacific Northwest Quarterly* 80 (1989): 52–61.

Masco, Joseph. "Competitive Displays: Negotiating Genealogical Rights to the Potlatch at the American Museum of Natural History." *American Anthropologist* 98 (1996): 837–52.

———. " 'It Is a Strict Law That Bids Us Dance': Cosmologies, Colonialism, Death, and Ritual Authority in the Kwakwa̲ka̲'wakw Potlatch, 1849–1922." *Comparative Studies in Society and History* 37, no. 1 (1995): 41–75.

Mauzé, Marie. "Boas, Les Kwagul et le Potlatch: Élements pour une réévaluation." *L'Homme* 26 (1986): 21–63.

———. "Le Canoë dans le Potlatch Lekwiltoq." *L'Homme* 29, no. 1 (1989): 117–28.

———. *Les Fils de Wakai: Une Histoire des Indiens Lekwiltoq*. Paris: Éditions Recherche sur les Civilisations, 1992.

———. "On Concepts of Tradition: An Introduction." In *Past Is Present: Some Uses of Tradition in Native Societies*, edited by Marie Mauzé, 1–15. Lanham: University Press of America, 1997.

McDiarmid, Clara A. "Our Neighbors, the Alaskan Women." In *The Congress of Women Held in the Woman's Building, World's Columbian Exposition, Chicago, USA 1893*, edited by Mary Kavanaugh Oldham Eagle, 723–25. Chicago: American Publishing House, 1894; reprint, New York: Arno Press, 1974.

McDonald, Eleanor W. "Here and There in Alaska." *Pacific Monthly* 15 (1906): 683–90.

McDonald, Lucile. "Susie Sampson Peter, Oldest of the Kikiallis." *Seattle Times*, 2 November 1958, 7 (Magazine).

McKay, Ian. *The Quest of the Folk: Antimodernism and Cultural Selection in Twentieth-Century Nova Scotia*. Montreal: McGill-Queen's University Press, 1994.

McLuhan, T., dir. *The Shadow Catcher: Edward S. Curtis and the North American Indian*. Mystic Fire Video Inc., 1982.

Meeker, Ezra. *The Busy Life of Eighty-Five Years of Ezra Meeker* . Seattle: Ezra Meeker, 1916.

———. *Hop Culture in the United States*. Puyallup, Washington Territory: E. Meeker and Co., 1883.

———. *Pioneer Reminiscences of Puget Sound*. Seattle: Lowman and Hanford, 1905.

Meliss, E. "Siwash." *Overland Monthly*, 2d series, 20 (1892): 501–6.

Meyer, Melissa. "American Indian Blood Quantum Requirements: Blood Is Thicker than Family." In *Over the Edge: Remapping the American West*, edited by Valerie J. Matsumoto and Blake Allmendinger, 231–49. Berkeley: University of California Press, 1999.

———. *The White Earth Tragedy: Ethnicity and Dispossession at a Minnesota Anishinaabe Reservation, 1889–1920*. Lincoln: University of Nebraska Press, 1994.

Miller, Bruce G. *The Problem of Justice: Tradition and Law in the Coast Salish World*. Lincoln: University of Nebraska Press, 2000.

———, ed. "A Theme Issue: Anthropology and History in the Courts." *BC Studies* 95 (1992).

Miller, Bruce G., and Daniel L. Boxberger. "Creating Chiefdoms: The Puget Sound Case." *Ethnohistory* 41 (1994): 267–93.

Miller, J. R. *Shingwauk's Vision: A History of Native Residential Schools*. Toronto: University of Toronto Press, 1996.

Miller, Jay. "Back to Basics: Chiefdoms in Puget Sound." *Ethnohistory* 44 (1997): 375–87.

———. *Lushootseed Culture and the Shamanic Odyssey: An Anchored Radiance*. Lincoln: University of Nebraska Press, 1999.

Mitchell, Donald Craig. *Sold American: The Story of Alaska Natives and Their Land, 1867–1959: The Army to Statehood*. Hanover, N.H.: University Press of New England, 1997.

Mitchell, Timothy. *Colonising Egypt*. Cambridge: Cambridge University Press, 1988.

Monroe, Will S. "World's Educational Exhibits (XI)." *Journal of Education* 38 (1893): 285.

Mooney, James. "The Ghost-Dance Religion and the Sioux Outbreak of 1890." In *Fourteenth Annual Report of the Bureau of American Ethnology, 1892–93*, 641–1110. Washington: GPO, 1896.

Morris, Rosalind C. *New Worlds from Fragments: Film, Ethnography, and the Representation of Northwest Coast Cultures*. Boulder: Westview Press, 1994.

Moser, Charles. *Reminiscences of the West Coast of Vancouver Island*. Victoria: Acme Press, 1926.

Moses, L. G. *Wild West Shows and the Images of American Indians, 1883–1933*. Albuquerque: University of New Mexico Press, 1996.

Muir, John. *Steep Trails*. Edited by William Frederic Badé. Boston: Houghton Mifflin, 1918.

———. *Travels in Alaska*. Boston: Houghton Mifflin, 1915; reprint, New York: Penguin Books, 1997.

Murray, Peter. *The Devil and Mr. Duncan*. Victoria: Sono Nis Press, 1985.

Myers, Fred R. "Culture-Making: Performing Aboriginality at the Asia Society Gallery." *American Ethnologist* 21 (1994): 679–99.

Nash, Dennison. "Tourism as a Form of Imperialism." In *Hosts and Guests: The Anthropology of Tourism*, edited by Valene L. Smith, 37–52. Philadelphia: University of Pennsylvania Press, 1989.

Nelson, Jay. "'A Strange Revolution in the Manners of the Country': Aboriginal-Settler Intermarriage in Nineteenth-Century British Columbia." In *Regulating Lives: Historical Essays on the State, Society, the Individual, and the Law*, edited by John McLaren, Robert Menzies, and Dorothy E. Chunn, 23–62. Vancouver: University of British Columbia Press, 2002.

Neumann, Mark. "The Commercial Canyon: Culturally Constructing the 'Other' in the Theater of the West." In *Discovered Country: Tourism and Survival in the American West*, edited by Scott Norris, 196–209. Albuquerque: Stone Ladder Press, 1994.

Neylan, Susan. *The Heavens Are Changing: Nineteenth-Century Protestant Missions and Tsimshian Christianity*. Montreal: McGill-Queen's University Press, 2003.

Niblack, A. P. "The Coast Indians of Southern Alaska and Northern British Columbia." In *U.S. National Museum Annual Report, 1888*, Board of Regents of the Smithsonian Institution, 225–386. Washington: GPO, 1890.

Nichols, Roger L. *Indians in the United States and Canada: A Comparative History*. Lincoln: University of Nebraska Press, 1998.

Nicks, Trudy. "Indian Villages and Entertainments: Setting the Stage for Tourist Souvenir Sales." In *Unpacking Culture: Art and Commodity in Colonial and Postcolonial Worlds*, edited by Ruth B. Phillips and Christopher B. Steiner, 301–15. Berkeley: University of California Press, 1999.

Norris, Frank. "The Frontier Gone at Last." *The World's Work* (1902): 1728–31.

The North Star: The Complete Issues from December 1887–December 1892. Seattle: Shorey Book Store, 1973.

Nugent, Ann. *Lummi Elders Speak*. Lynden, Washington: Lynden Tribune, 1982.

Nurse, Andrew. "'But Now Things Have Changed': Marius Barbeau and the Politics of Amerindian Identity." *Ethnohistory* 48 (2001): 433–72.

Ober, Sarah Endicott. "A New Religion among the West Coast Indians." *Overland Monthly*, 2d series, 56 (1910): 583–94.

Olson, Carmen. "Hop Growing Industry." *Issaquah Press*, 11 November 1954, 5.

Olson, Ronald L. *The Quinault Indians*. Seattle: University of Washington Press, 1936.

Ormsby, Margaret A. *British Columbia: A History*. [Toronto]: Macmillan, 1958.

Ortner, Sherry B. "Resistance and the Problem of Ethnographic Refusal." In *The Historic Turn in the Human Sciences*, edited by Terrence J. McDonald, 281–304. Ann Arbor: University of Michigan Press, 1996.

Orvell, Miles. *The Real Thing: Imitation and Authenticity in American Culture, 1880–1949*. Chapel Hill: University of North Carolina Press, 1989.

Ostrowitz, Judith. "Privileging the Past: A Case Study in Contemporary Kwakwaka'wakw Performance Art." *American Indian Art Magazine* 20, no. 1 (1994): 54–61.

———. *Privileging the Past: Reconstructing History in Northwest Coast Art*. Vancouver: University of British Columbia Press, 1999.

Owram, Douglas Robb. "White Savagery: Some Canadian Reactions to American Indian Policy, 1867–1885." M.A. thesis, Queen's University, 1971.

Pascoe, Peggy. "Miscengenation Law, Court Cases, and Ideologies of 'Race' in Twentieth-Century America." *Journal of American History* 82, no. 1 (1996): 44–69.

Perry, Adele. *On the Edge of Empire: Gender, Race and the Making of British Columbia, 1849–1871*. Toronto: University of Toronto Press, 2001.

Peter, Susie Sampson. *X̌əčusədə' 'əgʷəqʷul'cə': The Wisdom of a Skagit Elder.* Seattle: Lushootseed Press, 1995.

Phillips, James W. *Washington State Place Names*. Seattle: University of Washington Press, 1997.

Phillips, Ruth B. *Trading Identities: The Souvenir in Native North American Art from the Northeast, 1700–1900*. Seattle: University of Washington Press; Montreal: McGill-Queen's University Press, 1998.

———. "Why Not Tourist Art? Significant Silences in Native American Museum Representations." In *After Colonialism: Imperial Histories and Postcolonial Displacements*, edited by Gyan Prakash, 98–125. Princeton: Princeton University Press, 1995.

Phillips, Ruth B., and Christopher B. Steiner. "Art, Authenticity, and the Baggage of Cultural Encounter." In *Unpacking Culture: Art and Commodity in Colonial and Postcolonial Worlds*, edited by Ruth B. Phillips and Christopher B. Steiner, 3–19. Berkeley: University of California Press, 1999.

"Pioneer Resident, Merchant, Passes Here Friday." *Daily Sitka Sentinel*, 21 May 1951, 1.

Pomeroy, Earle. *In Search of the Golden West: The Tourist in Western America*. New York: Alfred A. Knopf, 1957.

Porter, Robert P. *Report on Population and Resources of Alaska at the Eleventh Census, 1890*. Washington: GPO, 1893.

Pratt, Mary Louise. *Imperial Eyes: Travel Writing and Transculturation*. London: Routledge, 1997.

Pratt, Richard Henry. *Battlefield and Classroom: Four Decades with the American Indian, 1867–1904*. Edited by Robert M. Utley. New Haven: Yale University Press, 1964.

"Progress in Alaska." *The Northwest Magazine* (1899): 35.

Ralph, Julian. "Canada's El Dorado." *Harper's New Monthly Magazine* 84 (January 1892): 171–88.

Replogle, Charles. *Among the Indians of Alaska*. London: Headly Brothers, 1904.

Report of the Governor of Washington Territory, 1888. Washington: GPO, 1888.

Rettig, Andrew. "A Nativistic Movement at Metlakatla Mission." *BC Studies*, no. 46 (1980): 28–39.

Riddington, Robin. "All the Old Spirits Have Come Back to Greet Him: Realizing the Sacred Pole of the Omaha Tribe." In *Past Is Present: Some Uses of Tradition in Native Societies*, edited by Marie Mauzé, 159–74. Lanham: University Press of America, 1997.

Rodriguez, Sylvia. "Art, Tourism, and Race Relations in Taos: Toward a Sociology of the Art Colony." In *Discovered Country: Tourism and Survival in the American West*, edited by Scott Norris, 143–60. Albuquerque: Stone Ladder Press, 1994.

Roediger, David R. *The Wages of Whiteness: Race and the Making of the American Working Class*. 1991. Rev. ed. New York: Verso, 1999.

Rohner, Ronald P. "Franz Boas: Ethnographer on the Northwest Coast." In *Pioneers of American Anthropology: The Uses of Biography*, edited by June Helm, 149–212. Seattle: University of Washington Press, 1966.

Rony, Fatimah Tobing. *The Third Eye: Race, Cimena and Ethnographic Spectacle*. Durham: Duke University Press, 1996.

Roppel, Patricia. "Loring." *Alaska Journal* 5, no. 3 (1975): 168–78.

Rosaldo, Renato. "Imperialist Nostalgia." In *Culture and Truth: The Remaking of Social Analysis*. Boston: Beacon Press, 1989.

Rothery, S. E. "Tacoma: Past, Present, and Future." *Overland Monthly*, 2d series, 31 (1898): 245–54.

Rothman, Hal K. *Devil's Bargains: Tourism in the Twentieth-Century West*. Lawrence: University of Kansas Press, 1998.

Roy, Susan. "Making History Visible: Culture and Politics in the Presentation of Musqueam History." M.A. thesis, Simon Fraser University, 1999.

Ruby, Robert H., and John A. Brown. *Indian Slavery in the Pacific Northwest*. Spokane, Washington: Arthur H. Clark Co., 1993.

Ruffner, W. H. *A Report on Washington Territory*. New York: Seattle, Lake Shore and Eastern Railway, 1889.

Ryan, Maureen. "Picturing Canada's Native Landscape: Colonial Expansion, National Identity, and the Image of a 'Dying Race.'" *Canadian Art Review* 17, no. 2 (1990): 138–49.

Rydell, Robert W. *All the World's a Fair: Visions of Empire at American International Expositions, 1876–1916*. Chicago: University of Chicago Press, 1984.

Rydell, Robert W., and Nancy Gwinn, eds. *Fair Representations: World's Fairs and the Modern World*. Amsterdam: VU University Press, 1994.

Sahlins, Marshall. "Cosmologies of Capitalism: The Trans-Pacific Sector of 'The World System.'" In *Culture/Power/History: A Reader in Contemporary Social Theory*, edited by Nicholas B. Dirks, Geoff Eley, and Sherry B. Ortner, 412–55. Princeton: Princeton University Press, 1994.

Samek, Hana. *The Blackfoot Confederacy, 1880–1920: A Comparative Study of Canadian and U.S. Indian Policy*. Albuquerque: University of New Mexico Press, 1987.

Sandweiss, Martha A. *Photography in Nineteenth-Century America*. Fort Worth: Amon Carter Museum, 1991.

———. *Print the Legend: Photography and the American West*. New Haven: Yale University Press, 2002.

Sapir, Edward, and Morris Swadesh. *Native Accounts of Nootka Ethnography*. Bloomington: Indiana University Research Center in Anthropology, Folklore, and Linguistics, 1955; reprint, New York: AMS Press, 1978.

———. *Nootka Texts: Tales and Ethnological Narratives*. Philadelphia: Linguistic Society of America, University of Pennsylvania, 1939; reprint, New York: AMS Press, 1978.

Schama, Simon. *Landscape and Memory*. New York: Alfred A. Knopf, 1996.

Schein, Louisa. "Performing Modernity." *Cultural Anthropology* 14 (1999): 361–95.

Schuknecht, Mary E. "A Familiar Glance." *Home Mission Monthly* 1903: 178.

Schwantes, Carlos A. "Tourists in Wonderland: Early Railroad Tourism in the Pacific Northwest." *Columbia* 7, no. 4 (1993–1994): 22–30.

Schwatka, Frederick. *Wonderland; or Alaska and the Inland Passage, with a Description of the Country Traversed by the Northern Pacific Railroad*. St. Paul: Northern Pacific Railroad, 1886.

Scidmore, E. Ruhamah. *Alaska, Its Southern Coast and the Sitkan Archipelago*. Boston: D. Lothrop and Co., 1885.

———. "Alaska's Mining Regions." *Harper's Weekly* 36 (1892): 465–67, 471–72.

———. *Appleton's Guide-Book to Alaska and the Northwest Coast*. New York: D. Appleton and Co., 1893.

———. "Attractions of Alaska: Its Scenery, Settlements, Citizens and Siwashes." *The Northwest Magazine* 9 (1891): 3–8.

———. "The First District of Alaska from Prince Frederick Sound to Yakutat Bay." In *Report on Population and Resources of Alaska at the Eleventh Census, 1890*, Robert P. Porter, 42–53. Washington: GPO, 1893.

———. "The Northwest Passages to the Yukon." *National Geographic Magazine* 9 (1898): 105–08.

Scott, Gertrude M. "Village Performance: Villages at the Chicago World's Columbian Exposition, 1893." Ph.D. dissertation, New York University, 1991.

Scott, James C. *Domination and the Arts of Resistance: Hidden Transcripts*. New Haven: Yale University Press, 1990.

Sears, John A. *Sacred Places: American Tourist Attractions in the Nineteenth Century*. New York: Oxford University Press, 1989.

Sessions, Francis C. *From Yellowstone Park to Alaska*. New York: Welch, Fracker Company, 1890.

Sewid, James. *Guests Never Leave Hungry: The Autobiography of James Sewid, a Kwakiutl Indian*. Edited by James P. Spradley. Montreal-Kingston: McGill-Queen's University Press, 1969.

Sewid-Smith, Daisy. *Prosecution or Persecution*. Cape Mudge, B.C.: Nu-Yum-Baleess Society, 1979.

Shales, Joyce Walton. "Rudolph Walton: One Tlingit Man's Journey through Stormy Seas, Sitka, Alaska, 1867–1951." Ph.D. dissertation, University of British Columbia, 1998.

Shepard, Isabel S. *The Cruise of the U.S. Steamer "Rush" in Behring Sea*. San Francisco: Bancroft Company, 1889.

Shepp, James W., and Daniel B. Shepp. *Shepp's World's Fair Photographed*. Chicago: Globe Bible Publishing, 1893.

Shiner, Larry. " 'Primitive Fakes,' 'Tourist Art,' and the Ideology of Authenticity." *Journal of Aesthetics and Art Criticism* 52 (1994): 225–34.

Sicade, Henry. "The Indians' Side of the Story." In *Building a State, Washington 1889–1939*, edited by Charles Miles and O. B. Sperlin, 490–503. Tacoma: Washington State Historical Society, 1940.

Silverblatt, Irene. "Becoming Indian in the Central Andes of Seventeenth-Century Peru." In *After Colonialism: Imperial Histories and Postcolonial Displacements*, edited by Gyan Prakash, 279–98. Princeton: Princeton University Press, 1995.

Simmons, Rose. "Old Angeline, The Princess of Seattle." *Overland Monthly*, 2d series, 20 (1892): 506–12.

Slotkin, Richard. *The Fatal Environment: The Myth of the Frontier in the Age of Industrialization, 1800–1890*. Middletown, Conn.: Wesleyan University Press, 1985.

Smith, Donald B. "Honoré J. Jaxon: A Man Who Lived for Others." *Saskatchewan History* 34 (1981): 81–101.

Smith, Linda Tuhiwai. *Decolonizing Methodologies: Research and Indigenous Peoples*. London: Zed Books, 1999.

Smith, Marian W. *The Puyallup-Nisqually*. New York: Columbia University Press, 1940; reprint, New York: AMS Press, 1969.

———. "Towards a Classification of Cult Movements." *Man* 59, no. 1–2 (1959): 8–12.

Smits, David D. "The 'Squaw Drudge': A Prime Index of Savagism." *Ethnohistory* 29 (1982): 281–306.

Snowden, Clinton A. *History of Washington; The Rise and Progress of an American State*. N.p.: Century History Company, 1909.

Sontag, Susan. *On Photography*. New York: Farrar, Straus and Giroux, 1977.

The Soul of Alaska. New York: Gorham Company, 1905.

Spence, Mark David. *Dispossessing the Wilderness: Indian Removal and the Making of the National Parks*. New York: Oxford University Press, 1999.

Spivak, Gayatri Chakravorty. *The Post-Colonial Critic: Interviews, Strategies, Dialogues*. Edited by Sarah Harasym. New York: Routledge, 1990.

Spradley, James P., and David W. McCurdy. *Anthropology: The Cultural Perspective*. New York: John Wiley, 1975.

Spurr, David. *The Rhetoric of Empire: Colonial Discourse in Journalism, Travel Writing, and Imperial Administration*. Durham: Duke University Press, 1993.

State of Washington. *Biennial Report of the Washington World's Fair Commission, 1891 and 1892*. Olympia, Washington: O. C. White, State Printer, 1893.

———. *Final Report of the Washington World's Fair Commission, 1894*. Olympia, Washington: O. C. White, State Printer, 1894.

Stewart, Robert Laird. *Sheldon Jackson, Pathfinder and Prospector of the Missionary Vanguard in the Rocky Mountains and Alaska*. New York: F. H. Revell, 1908.

Stocking, George W., Jr. *Delimiting Anthropology: Occasional Essays and Reflections*. Madison: University of Wisconsin Press, 2001.

———. *The Ethnographer's Magic and Other Essays in the History of Anthropology*. Madison: University of Wisconsin Press, 1992.

———. *Race, Culture, and Evolution: Essays in the History of Anthropology*. New York: Macmillan, 1968; reprint, Chicago: University of Chicago Press, 1982.

———. "The Turn-of-the-Century Concept of Race." *Modernism/Modernity* 1 (1993): 4–16.

———. *Victorian Anthropology*. New York: Free Press, 1987.

———, ed. *Volksgeist as Method and Ethic: Essays on Boasian Ethnography and the German Anthropological Tradition*. Madison: University of Wisconsin Press, 1996.

Stoler, Ann Laura. *Race and the Education of Desire: Foucault's History of Sexuality and the Colonial Order of Things*. Durham: Duke University Press, 1995.

———. "Sexual Affronts and Racial Frontiers: European Identities and the Cultural Politics of Exclusion in Colonial Southeast Asia." In *Tensions of Empire: Colonial Cultures in a Bourgeois World*, edited by Frederick Cooper and Ann Laura Stoler, 198–237. Berkeley: University of California Press, 1997.

Stromstadt, Dazie M. Brown. *Sitka, The Beautiful*. Seattle: Homer M. Hill Publishing Co., 1906.

Sucher, David, ed. *The Asahel Curtis Sampler: Photographs of Puget Sound Past*. Seattle: Puget Sound Access, 1973.

Suttles, Wayne. "Central Coast Salish." In *The Northwest Coast*, edited by Wayne Suttles, 453–75. Volume 7 of *The Handbook of North American Indians*, edited by William C. Sturtevant. Washington: Smithsonian Institution, 1990.

———. *Coast Salish Essays*. Vancouver: Talonbooks, 1987.

———. "Streams of Property, Armor of Wealth: The Traditional Kwakiutl Potlatch." In *Chiefly Feasts: The Enduring Kwakiutl Potlatch*, edited by Aldona Jonaitis, 71–133. New York: American Museum of Natural History, 1992.

Suttles, Wayne, and Barbara Lane. "Southern Coast Salish." In *The Northwest Coast*, edited by Wayne Suttles, 485–502. Volume 7 of *The Handbook of North American Indians*, edited by William C. Sturtevant. Washington: Smithsonian Institution, 1990.

Swanton, John R. *Social Condition, Beliefs and Linguistic Relationships of the Tlingit Indians*. Washington: GPO, 1908.

Sweet, Jill. "Burlesquing 'the Other' in Pueblo Performance." *Annals of Tourism Research* 16 (1989): 62–75.

Tennant, Paul. *Aboriginal Peoples and Politics: The Indian Land Question in British Columbia, 1849–1989*. Vancouver: University of British Columbia Press, 1990.

Thomas, Nicholas. *Colonialism's Culture: Anthropology, Travel and Government*. Cambridge: Polity Press, 1994.

———. "The Inversion of Tradition." *American Ethnologist* 19, no. 2 (1992): 213–32.

Thompson, John Herd. "Bringing in the Sheaves: The Harvest Excursionists, 1890–1929." *Canadian Historical Review* 59 (1978): 467–89.

Thompson, John Herd, and Allen Seager. "Workers, Growers and Monopolists: The 'Labour Problem' in the Alberta Beet Sugar Industry During the 1930s." *Labour/Le Travailleur* 3 (1978): 153–74.

Thorne, Susan. " 'The Conversion of Englishmen and the Conversion of the World Inseparable': Missionary Imperialism and the Language of Class in Early Industrial Britain." In *Tensions of Empire: Colonial Cultures in a Bourgeois World*, edited by Frederick Cooper and Ann Laura Stoler, 238–62. Berkeley: University of California Press, 1997.

Titley, E. Brian. *A Narrow Vision: Duncan Campbell Scott and the Administration of Indian Affairs in Canada*. Vancouver: University of British Columbia Press, 1986.

Told by the Pioneers: Reminiscences of Pioneer Life in Washington, 3 Volumes. Olympia: Washington Pioneer Project, 1937.

Tollefson, Kenneth. "In Defense of a Snoqualmie Political Chiefdom Model." *Ethnohistory* 43 (1996): 145–71.

———. "Political Organization of the Duwamish." *Ethnology* 28 (1989): 135–49.

———. "Potlatching and Political Organization among the Northwest Coast Indians." *Ethnology* 34 (1995): 53–73.

———. "The Snoqualmie: A Puget Sound Chiefdom." *Ethnology* 26 (1987): 121–36.

———. "The Snoqualmie Indians as Hop Pickers." *Columbia* 8, no. 4 (1994–1995): 39–44.

Tomlan, Michael A. *Tinged with Gold: Hop Culture in the United States*. Athens: University of Georgia Press, 1992.

Trachtenberg, Alan. *The Incorporation of America: Culture and Society in the Gilded Age*. New York: Hill and Wang, 1994.

Trennert, Robert A., Jr. "A Grand Failure: The Centennial Indian Exhibition of 1876." *Prologue* (Summer 1974): 118–29.

———. "Selling Indian Education at World's Fairs and Expositions, 1893–1904." *American Indian Quarterly* 11, no. 3 (1987): 203–20.

Trump, Erik. " 'The Idea of Help': White Women Reformers and the Commercialization of Native American Women's Arts." In *Selling the Indian: Commercializing and Appropriating American Indian Cultures*, edited by Carter Jones and Diana Royer Meyer, 159–89. Tucson: University of Arizona Press, 2001.

Underhill, Ruth. *Indians of the Pacific Northwest*. Washington: Education Division of the United States Office of Indian Affairs, 1944; reprint, New York: AMS Press, 1978.

Upton, Mamie Ray. "Indian Hop-Pickers." *Overland Monthly*, 2d series, 17 (1891): 162–66.

Urry, John. *The Tourist Gaze: Leisure and Travel in Contemporary Societies*. London: Sage Publications, 1990.

Usher, Jean. *William Duncan of Metlakatla*. Ottawa: National Museums of Canada, 1974.

Vallault, F. I. "Patsy's Potlatch." *Overland Monthly*, 2d series, 19 (1892): 461–64.

Valory, Dale. "The Focus of Indian Shaker Healing." *Kroeber Anthropological Society Papers* 35 (1966): 67–111.

Verma, Behari L. "The Squamish: A Study of Changing Political Organization." M.A. thesis, University of British Columbia, 1954.

Viswanathan, Gauri. "Coping with (Civil) Death: The Christian Convert's Rights of

Passage in Colonial India." In *After Colonialism: Imperial Histories and Postcolonial Displacements*, edited by Gyan Prakash, 183–210. Princeton: Princeton University Press, 1995.

Wade, Edwin L. "The Ethnic Art Market in the American Southwest, 1880–1980." In *Objects and Others: Essays on Museums and Material Culture*, edited by George W. Stocking Jr., 167–91. Madison: University of Wisconsin Press, 1985.

Walden, Keith. *Becoming Modern in Toronto: The Industrial Exhibition and the Shaping of a Late Victorian Culture*. Toronto: University of Toronto Press, 1997.

Walens, Stanley. *Feasting with Cannibals: An Essay on Kwakiutl Cosmology*. Princeton: Princeton University Press, 1981.

Wall, Louise Herrick. "In a Washington Hop Field." *Atlantic Monthly* 74 (1894): 379–85.

Wardman, George. *Trip to Alaska: A Narrative of What Was Seen and Heard During a Summer Cruise in Alaskan Waters*. Boston: Lee and Shepard, 1884.

Waterman, T. T. "The Shake Religion of Puget Sound." In *Annual Report of the Board of Regents of the Smithsonian Institution, 1922*, 499–507. Washington: GPO: 1924.

Wayne, John J. "1893 On the Midway." *Library of Congress Information Bulletin* 51, no. 2 (1992): 16–20.

Webb, William Seward. *California and Alaska and Over the Canadian Pacific Railway*. New York: G. P. Putnam's Sons, 1891.

Webster, Gloria Cranmer. "Chiefly Feasts." *Curator* 35 (1992): 248–67.

———. "From Colonization to Repatriation." In *Indigena: Contemporary Native Perspectives in Canadian Art*, edited by Gerald McMaster and LeeAnn Martin, 25–38. New York: Craftsman House, 1992.

———. "The Contemporary Potlatch." In *Chiefly Feasts: The Enduring Kwakiutl Potlatch*, edited by Aldona Jonaitis, 227–48. New York: American Museum of Natural History, 1992.

———. "Kwakiutl since 1980." In *The Northwest Coast*, edited by Wayne Suttles, 387–90. Volume 7 of *The Handbook of North American Indians*, edited by William C. Sturtevant. Washington: Smithsonian Institution, 1990.

A Week at the Fair Illustrating the Exhibits and Wonders of the World's Columbian Exposition. Chicago: Rand, McNally and Co., 1893.

Weigle, Marta. "From Desert to Disney World: The Santa Fe Railway and the Fred Harvey Company Display the Indian Southwest." *Journal of Anthropological Research* 45 (1989): 115–37.

Weigle, Marta, and Barbara A. Babcock, eds. *The Great Southwest of the Fred Harvey Company and the Santa Fe Railway*. Phoenix: Heard Museum, 1996.

"Western Hop Center." *The West Shore* 16 (1890): 137–38.

Wettrick, Frederick J. "The Schools of Alaska." *Alaska Monthly* 1906: 66–67.

White, Richard. "Frederick Jackson Turner and Buffalo Bill." In *The Frontier in American History*, edited by James R. Grossman, 7–50. Berkeley: University of California Press, 1994.

———. *The Middle Ground: Indians, Empires, and Republics in the Great Lakes Region, 1650–1815*. New York: Cambridge University Press, 1991.

———. *The Organic Machine: The Remaking of the Columbia River*. New York: Hill and Wang, 1995.

Whitehead, Margaret. *The Cariboo Mission: A History of the Oblates*. Victoria: Sono Nis Press, 1981.

———, ed. *They Call Me Father: Memoirs of Father Nicolas Coccola*. Vancouver: University of British Columbia Press, 1988.

Wickersham, James. "Nusqually Mythology: Studies of the Washington Indians." *Overland Monthly*, 2d series, 32 (1898): 345–51.

Wickwire, Wendy. " 'We Shall Drink from the Stream and So Shall You,': James A. Teit and Native Resistance in British Columbia, 1908–22." *Canadian Historical Review* 79 (1998): 199–236.

Williams, Carol J. *Framing the West: Race, Gender and the Photographic Frontier in the Pacific Northwest*. New York: Oxford University Press, 2003.

Williams, Raymond. "Ideas of Nature." In *Problems in Materialism and Culture*. New York: Verso, 1997.

Wilson, Chris. *The Myth of Santa Fe: Creating a Modern Regional Tradition*. Albuquerque: University of New Mexico Press, 1997.

Wolf, Eric R. *Europe and the People without History*. Berkeley: University of California Press, 1982.

Worl, Rosita. "History of Southeastern Alaska since 1867." In *The Northwest Coast*, edited by Wayne Suttles, 149–58. Volume 7 of *The Handbook of North American Indians*, edited by William C. Sturtevant. Washington: Smithsonian Institution, 1990.

Wyatt, Victoria. "Alaskan Indian Wage Earners in the Nineteenth Century: Economic Choices and Ethnic Identity on Southeast Alaska's Frontier." *Pacific Northwest Quarterly* 78 (1987): 43–49.

———. "Ethnic Identity and Active Choice: Foundations of Indian Strength in Southeast Alaska, 1867–1912." Ph.D dissertation, Yale University, 1985.

———. *Shapes of Their Thoughts: Reflections of Culture Contact in Northwest Coast Indian Art*. Norman: University of Oklahoma Press, 1984.

Index

Paige Raibmon is an assistant professor of history at the University of British Columbia.

Library of Congress Cataloging-in-Publication Data
Raibmon, Paige Sylvia, 1971–
Authentic Indians : episodes of encounter from the late-nineteenth-century Northwest coast / Paige Raibmon.
p. cm.
"A John Hope Franklin Center book."
Includes bibliographical references and index.
ISBN 0-8223-3535-2 (cloth : alk. paper) —
ISBN 0-8223-3547-6 (pbk. : alk. paper)
1. Indians of North America—Northwest, Pacific—Ethnic identity. 2. Indians of North America—Northwest, Pacific—Cultural assimilation. 3. Indians, Treatment of—Northwest, Pacific—History—19th century. 4. Northwest, Pacific—Race relations. 5. Northwest, Pacific—History—19th century. I. Title.
E78.N77R25 2005
323.1197'0795'09034—dc22 2004028247